Recipes from Paradise

Life and Food on the Italian Riviera

Recipes

FRED PLOTKIN

from Paradise

Life and Food on the Italian Riviera

Little, Brown and Company   Boston New York Toronto London

First Edition

Unless otherwise indicated, all photographs are by the author.

Library of Congress Cataloging-in-Publication Data

Plotkin, Fred.
    Recipes from paradise : life and food on the Italian Riviera /
  Fred Plotkin
      p.   cm.
    Includes index.
    ISBN 0-316-71071-7
    1. Cookery, Italian.   2. Cookery — Italy — Riviera.   3. Food habits —
Italy.   4. Liguria (Italy) — Social life and customs.   I. Title.
TX723.P594   1997
641.5945918 — dc21   97-1813

10 9 8 7 6 5 4 3 2 1

RRD-OH

Book design by Julia Sedykh

Published simultaneously in Canada by Little, Brown & Company (Canada) Limited
Printed in the United States of America

for my AUNT SYLVIA and UNCLE LOU

KNOW YE THE LAND...

Where the citron and olive are fairest fruit
and the voice of the nightingale never is mute?
Where the tints of the earth and the hues of the sky,
in colour though varied, in beauty may vie,
and the purple of ocean is deepest in dye?

Fair Italy!
Thou art the garden of the world, the home
of all Art yields and Nature can decree;
even in thy desert, what is like to thee?

—Lines written near La Spezia
by Lord Byron

Acknowledgments   *ix*

Poetry, Perfume, Practicality . . . and Pesto   *3*

The Disappearance of *La Civiltà Contadina*   *37*

Equipment for a Ligurian Kitchen   *47*

Sauces, Condiments, and Spreads   *57*

Breads and Savory Pies   *115*

Antipasti (Appetizers)   *169*

Pasta, Rice, and Polenta   *197*

Soups   *269*

Vegetables and Salads   *293*

Fish and Seafood   *321*

Egg, Poultry, and Meat Dishes   *357*

Fruits and Desserts   *379*

The Wines of Liguria   *407*

A Ligurian Larder   *419*

Sources for Ligurian Ingredients and Products   *439*

Bibliography   *463*

Index   *473*

Contents

Acknowledgments

There is always the tendency, when an author sets out to acknowledge the help and support of people who were instrumental in the genesis of a book, to want to list every person who was encountered as the book was being created. If I were to do that, somehow that would diminish the contributions of those who really had great impact, and without whom this book could not be a gastronomic and social portrait of a place that I love. I have come to understand that I am a member of several families, and that each of these has nurtured me and my work.

First, there is my extended Ligurian family. Above all, Roberto, Lorenza, and Simone Volpini, of Recco and Camogli, who are my closest friends there. Roberto was helpful to me in too many ways to list, but he knows how grateful I am. Lorenza is a wonderful cook, and she was a superb resource whenever I needed to understand certain intricacies and subtleties of things Ligurian. Simone played the very important role of helping me to see Liguria through the eyes of a child, with his sense of wonderment and discovery. He has a smile as bright as the lighthouse in Genoa, and when I think of the people of Liguria, he is the first person to come to mind.

Rocco Rizzo, extraordinary baker of Camogli, and his lovely family, were the source of my daily bread, pasta, torta, and crostata as I wrote this book. He also sells the best pesto I have encountered outside of a home. The Rizzos' products are the gold standard that I use in describing these fundamental Ligurian foods.

Alfredo Ferrozzi, owner of Il Portolano bookstore in Camogli, was a font of information about Ligurian food and culture. For that matter, all of the people of Camogli, in one way or another, have made me feel welcome and loved.

In Genoa, my thanks to Dottoressa Patrizia Schiappacasse and Dr. Carlo Bitossi, who granted me access to the State Archive of Liguria in Genoa and were my guides to its splendid collection. That research formed the backbone of the cultural and historic aspects of this book. Many people were helpful at the offices of the Regione Liguria, particularly Maria Paola Profumo, Carlo Arcolao, Mauro Boccaccio, and Andrea Jelenkovich.

Paola Grieco and Andrea Marmori kindly introduced me to many of the flavors of La Spezia and its province. Pietro Pesce and Franco Boeri taught me about the stockfish and olive oil in the province of Imperia. Many food producers and chefs in the provinces of Savona and Imperia carefully instructed me about preparing the dishes of western Liguria. Thanks also to Giovanna Gelmini in Cervo

Stella, Adam, Thea, and Nicholas Baillie, of London and Camogli, are sources of infinite happiness. Thanks also to Laura Morris, Claudia Herr, and Abner Stein of the Abner Stein literary agency in London. I am also grateful to the staff at the London Library on St. James Square, where additional research for this book was conducted.

Then there is my family of colleagues in North America: Arlene Wanderman, who died as this book was being completed, was a friend to so many food writers and the world's finest advocate for olive oil. Dun Gifford, Sara Baer-Sinnott, Annie Copps, and Vita Juan at Oldways Preservation and Exchange Trust in Cambridge, Massachusetts, are ardent defenders and conservators of food traditions in many countries. Their enthusiasm for the food of Liguria, which represents the best of the Mediterranean Diet, has been a source of inspiration for me. "Hoppin' John" Taylor, of Charleston, South Carolina, is a talented man of food and of life, who knew of the glories of Liguria before most Americans, and freely shared his knowledge with me. Darrell Corti, of Corti Brothers in Sacramento, California, is a passionate defender of the region of his ancestors who plied me with provocative ideas and enticing directions to Ligurian treasures. Steven Jenkins, the master cheesemonger, helped me approach the use of cheese in Liguria. He is both passionate and talented.

My professional family in North America includes many people I count as friends. Jennifer Josephy is an author's dream as an editor. This is my second book with her, and I have enjoyed deepening our working relationship and our friendship. Many other people at Little, Brown and Company have helped make *Italy for the Gourmet Traveler* and this volume into books that I am proud of. Sarah Crichton has been an advocate of my work (and cooking) and was particularly supportive when it was needed. Abigail Wilentz has done so many kind things, most of which I am sure went unnoticed. Beth Davey, Katie Long, and Christine Stanley all are masterful at helping the world discover good books. Peggy Freudenthal is rigorous in the process of producing a book, and I am grateful to her. Thanks also to Julia Sedykh, Leslie Goldman, Michael Ian Kaye, Dana Gallagher (who did some of this book's food photography), Margarette Adams, and Michael Mattil, this book's expert copyeditor.

David Black, my beloved agent, has come to love Liguria as much as I do, thanks to regular helpings of pesto and focaccia. He makes it fun to be an author. Susan Raihofer in his office makes everything work, and she does it with sweetness and dedication. Greg Eisenberg, Gary Morris, Lev Fruchter, also of Black, Inc., have made valuable contributions as well. Katharine Pollak brought talent and sensitivity to developing the black-and-white photographs in this book.

Then there is my family of friends, whom I count as family in the classic sense of the word. All of them helped me in vital ways as this book was being written: Mark Anderson, Laura DeAngelis, and their daughter, Silvia; Nancy Bachrach and Orin Wechsberg; Fern Berman; Cara De Silva; Carol Field; Len Horovitz and Valerie Saalbach; Corby Kummer; Carol and Frank Lalli; Rosalyn and Stanley Luckman; Michael Romano; Lynne Rossetto Kasper; Andrea Alberto Visconti and Francisco Pelizzoli.

My mother, Bernice, first took me to Italy in 1973. On the train from Milan to Tuscany I caught my first sight of the coast of Liguria from Genoa to La Spezia. I decided that I had to come back and discover this place that enchanted me so. I am glad that my mother has traveled with me there since, and has stayed with me in Camogli.

My father, Edward, died as this book was being completed. It gratifies me immensely that he was able to visit and travel with me in Liguria. He said that being there was a window into paradise for him and, given that we did not know that he was ill at the time, his words resonate in me now more than I could have ever imagined. I was indeed living on the Golfo di Paradiso and I'm glad he found heaven on Earth. He said that those were the best two weeks of his life, and I know that they were.

Edward Plotkin in Liguria

Camogli 1949

This is the best description I have read about Camogli, the town where most of this book was written. Although these words are from 1949, much of what they evoke is still true today.

"From Sori I moved on down the Riviera to a little fishing village which is the gem of the whole coast from Savona to Spezia. Camogli is well off the main road, and this has preserved it from modernisation. It is a functional fishing village, not a tourist resort. It is so crushed down to the seashore by the hills that its houses have had to be built to an unusual height to contain all its inhabitants. As they rise up, one behind another, on the steep hill, the whole village looks up from the sea like a cluster of skyscrapers that glow in the sun like palaces carved from coral. In these tenements families are piled on top of families in the crowded warrens which are entered under dim arches that lead to steep stone stairs. The lanes are almost as narrow, as steep and as stepped. Down along the shingled beach, and between the beach and the tiny cluttered harbour, there are more crooked houses on every square foot of crooked space, all this way and that way, with taverns built over the water, a ruined castle to top the rocks, and a gaudy, glittering, golden church approached by a flight of noble steps. Being so crowded, Camogli has a beautiful restless vivacity. The sails, the boats and the yachts and the sparkling water are never for a moment still; sailors and their womenfolk go up and down all day long. Your eye wanders, delighted, from the harbour to the tiers of houses, from the houses out over the Mediterranean, is recalled by the tawny children, plunging into the harbour, caught by the endless come-and-go of the fishing folk, or by their arguments over the wine-flasks, the cards, or the political papers from Genoa, on trestled tables under

Camogli, viewed from the north

trellised vines. The whole place is brilliant with allure for the painter. Its war of colour is not to be described. The gaudiest blue-and-rose of a picture post card cannot do it violence. I have never seen a place with so vibrant a personality.

"... As I knelt there [in the church] in the half-light and silence I became aware that the silence was not absolute. There was a soft weeping sound, a gentle groaning sound, falling rhythmically to a whisper as of wings in the air. I looked for the altar, shaped gracefully like a boat, and I gradually realised that this gentle and regular throb came from behind the apse. It was the sea pushing eternally on the shingle below. That muttering of water pervades Camogli. Children are born to its rocking, sleep to it, live on it, age on it, and too often sink into it. Around the walls of the church are several lovely *ex voto* models of sailing ships — lost and saved — and black obituary photographs. I see again, with special vividness, the face of the jovial, fat, moustached sea-captain in the jaunty straw hat smiling down at me; while that old siren outside, beyond this shadow that is a light, the blue, placid and seemingly innocent sea, sighs like a dreaming tiger.

"The sense of the sea's power is everywhere. Here, in the sun of the quay, is a woman in black, cross-legged on the ground, sewing a feather mattress into a snowy case; a pleasant and public way for a widow to work. One of the tall houses behind her is the Casa di Riposo per la Gente di Mare, the inevitable 'Sailors' Home'. Old Ligurian seamen sit all day long in these windows, watching the ships go by."

— Sean O'Faolain,
A Summer in Italy, 1949

Recipes from Paradise

Life and Food on the Italian Riviera

Poetry, Perfume, Practicality

...and Pesto

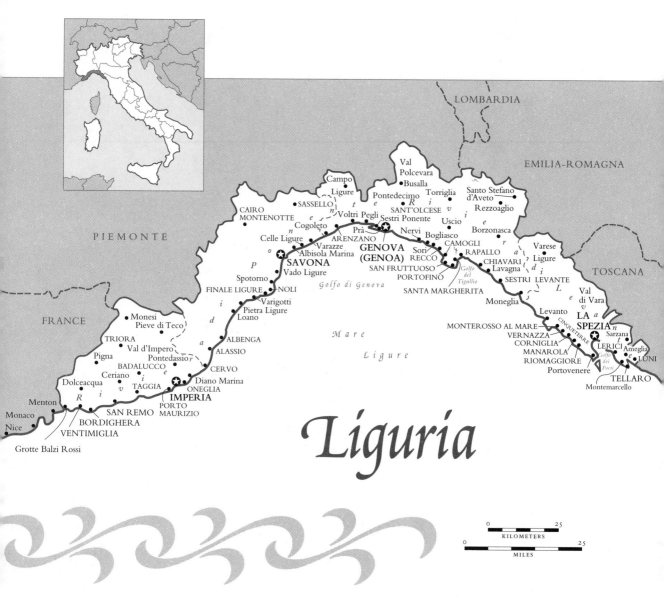

LOMBARDIA

EMILIA-ROMAGNA

PIEMONTE

FRANCE

Menton
Monaco
Nice

Grotte Balzi Rossi

Campo
Ligure
SASSELLO
CAIRO
MONTENOTTE
Cogoleto
Celle Ligure
Varazze
Albisola Marina
SAVONA
Vado Ligure
Spotorno
FINALE LIGURE
NOLI
Varigotti
Pietra Ligure
Loano
ALBENGA
ALASSIO
CERVO
Diano Marina
ONEGLIA
IMPERIA
PORTO
MAURIZIO

Monesi
Pieve di Teco
TRIORA
Val d'Impero
Pigna
BADALUCCO
Ceriano
Dolceacqua
TAGGIA
SAN REMO
BORDIGHERA
VENTIMIGLIA
Pontedassio

Val
Polcevara
Busalla
Torriglia
Pontedecimo
SANT'OLCESE
Voltri Pegli
Sestri Ponente
Prà
ARENZANO
GENOVA
(GENOA)
Nervi
Bogliasco
SAN FRUTTUOSO
RECCO
Sori
CAMOGLI
RAPALLO
PORTOFINO
CHIAVARI
Lavagna
SANTA MARGHERITA
Golfo del
Tigullio
SESTRI LEVANTE
Moneglia
Golfo di Genova

Mare
Ligure

Santo Stefano
d'Aveto
Rezzoaglio
Uscio
Borzonasca
Varese
Ligure
TOSCANA

MONTEROSSO AL MARE
VERNAZZA
CORNIGLIA
MANAROLA
RIOMAGGIORE
Portovenere
Levanto
Val
di Vara
LA
SPEZIA
LERICI
Sarzana
Ameglia
LUNI
Golfo
dei
Poeti
TELLARO
Montemarcello

Liguria

0   25
KILOMETERS
0   25
MILES

*L*IGURIA, the region on the Mediterranean Sea in northwestern Italy that foreigners call the Italian Riviera, may be as close to paradise as one can find on this earth. The gift of warm weather, sea air, and mountains that shelter the region from northern cold has created a little paradise where flowers and herbs blossom in astonishing and fragrant profusion and variety, while delicate vegetables, succulent fruits, and outstanding wild mushrooms abound.

Yes, there are wonderful places like Hawaii that have gorgeous beaches and swaying palms, but so does Liguria. So, too, are there urban places with magnificent architecture and a vibrant patchwork of cultures, but you can find this in Liguria, too. Richard Wagner was enchanted by Genoa, the region's capital, writing in 1853 that "It is something unbelievably beautiful, grandiose and characteristic. By comparison with this divine city, Paris and London appear like simple agglomerations of houses and streets without any form." In the Ligurian town of La Spezia, Wagner first heard in his head the E-flat chords that begin *Das Rheingold* and set the stage for *Der Ring des Nibelungen,* the four-opera cycle that is the most monumental musical work ever created.

Liguria has inspired outpourings of poetry and prose since ancient times. Perhaps nowhere else have writers attempted to describe the meaning of beauty as in Liguria. It is remarkable that beauty, which might be thought of as a truth and an absolute if ever there was one, can elicit so many varied evocations. To quote Ralph Waldo Emerson, "The difference between landscape and landscape is small, but there is a great difference between the beholders." Yet there is something in the Ligurian landscape that is unique. What is it? The true mystery of the world, said Oscar Wilde, is in the visible, not the invisible.

The first mistake that many people make in envisioning Liguria is to think that the Italian Riviera and the French Riviera to the west are the same thing. Although the French Riviera, especially Nice, was under Ligurian political and cultural influence at numerous times during history, there have always been major differences. The first is terrain: Liguria is denser and more inaccessible than Nice and Provence. The land is beautiful but unyielding when compared to the French side. This land made tenacious and inventive people out of the Ligurians, who had to study it, listen to it, and come to terms with what it could provide.

Provence belonged to France for centuries, and Nice and Menton definitively joined the French Republic after a referendum in 1855 that was inspired, in part, by the opinion that local lemons would find a better market in France than in Italy. Ever since, Nice has drawn closer to France in government, language, taste, custom, and tradition, and unquestionably has more in common with Paris than it does with Genoa. The Republic of Monaco, which is full of people of Genoese origin, including a family called Grimaldi, is a separate entity, but clearly one allied with France.

The French Riviera has often been about an easygoing lifestyle, about being soigné, chic, and a haven for jetsetters. There has always been more of a "scene," full of starlets, roués, Impressionist and Cubist painters on high-profile vacations, tax exiles (in Monaco), and British people who write books of quirky charm and dubious veracity about the peculiar local population. This jumble has created an anomaly, more of a playground than a paradise. What the French Riviera lacks and that Liguria has in abundance is genuineness. In Liguria, one feels the past, a legacy, a tradition. One can hear echoes of ancient voices that across the border are drowned out by the chaos. Living in paradise also means finding inner peace, and that is something that in Liguria is still possible. And then there is the food, which gives the notion of inner gratification new meaning. But more later.

Let us first understand the land that has created the Ligurian people and their divine cuisine. Liguria has been inhabited since the earliest documented days of human history. Its first known peoples were the Liguri, who were able mariners and creators of many of the picturesque ports in the region's tiny

A British Slave to Fashion

Here is a rather extreme example of one person's need to be an arbiter of taste. Not surprisingly, in describing several towns on the Italian Riviera in 1949, the writer felt the need to put them in the context of the French Riviera — with all of its attendant snob appeal — rather than finding glory in the Italian towns on their own terms, as we might do today. How tastes have changed!

"Visitors to [Liguria] may perhaps be classified into six main groups; the fashionable, the ultra-fashionable and the would-be-fashionable; the once-fashionable, the unfashionable and the anti-fashionable. For the first group San Remo on the Ponente, and Rapallo on the Levante, can offer something of the attraction of Cannes or Monte Carlo in France. For the ultra-fashionable there are possibilities at Parragi or Portofino on the Levante, and possibly at Alassio on the Ponente, comparable to the French Cap Ferrat or the Cap d'Antibes. For the once-fashionable, Bordighera and Ospedaletti on the Ponente, and Santa Margherita Ligure on the Levante, provide the same discreet respectability as Menton or Hyères in France. For the unfashionable, who in France are so admirably catered for on the coast between Hyères and St. Tropez, one may suggest Diano Ligure on the Ponente, and Sestri Levante and Levanto on the Levante. The anti-fashionable, those, for instance, who are determined to go native and catch and eat their cuttle-fish with the local fishermen, may be recommended to try Loano on the Ponente, and on the Levante some of the smaller places around the Spezia Gulf."

— Jasper More, *The Land of Italy,* 1949

coves. Then came the Greeks, Celts, and later the Romans, who introduced olive trees, vineyards, and numerous vegetables. For the next nineteen hundred years Liguria received many visitors — many of them unwelcome — including Saracens, Venetians, Gauls, Lombards, Piedmontese, and the French. In the Middle Ages, Liguria was under the domain of the Republic of Genoa, and to this day this small region feels like a city-state with Genoa as its heart and soul.

Liguria arcs along the Mediterranean from Ventimiglia on the border with France for 220 miles (343 kilometers) to Luni, which borders Tuscany and the city of Carrara, where Michelangelo quarried the marble that made the *David* and the *Pietà*. Liguria is the third smallest of the twenty Italian regions (the Valle d'Aosta and Molise are smaller). It is bordered by four important Italian regions: Piemonte (Piedmont) abuts the western half of Liguria; Lombardia (Lombardy) touches a small section near Genoa; Emilia-Romagna is inland from much of eastern Liguria; and Tuscany borders the southeastern tip.

Liguria has many high mountains that plunge dramatically to the sea at various points, creating dazzling visual juxtapositions and allowing an almost infinite .variety of the play of light on land, vegetation, and water. This light benefits agriculture, contributes to the mood of the people, and creates beautiful visual images as shadows creep across little piazzas. Throughout the day, solar illumination reveals small details in nature and architecture that were previously unnoticed. Almost all of Liguria has mountains that stand about 15 miles (23 kilometers) from the sea, offering protection from cold winds that blow from the adjoining regions of Piedmont, Lombardy, Emilia-Romagna, and Tuscany. One of the great pleasures for a winter-weary citizen of Turin or Milan is to come through one of Liguria's mountain tunnels into the sudden warmth of a mid-February day on the Italian Riviera.

The region's shape has been variously described as a boomerang, an amulet, a crescent moon, and even as a slice of watermelon. The most appropriate de-

"The sea has its morning mantle of light sky-blue, seamed with bars of white. It seems to take the prime of the sunshine hours to endow it with depth of colour. There is absolutely no emerald green, which in the afternoon will be the clasping girdle of the coast."

> — Henry Alford,
> *The Riviera: Pen and Pencil Sketches*
> *from Cannes to Genoa, 1869*

scription, however, is that Liguria is like a rainbow. This is not only because of the shape of the region. Liguria is perhaps the most polychromatic place you will ever encounter. As anyone who has read my book *Italy for the Gourmet Traveler* can tell you, I think that all of Italy is beautiful and I have happily lived in and traveled its highways and byways for nearly twenty-five years. Each region has its beauties and its virtues, and I revel in them. But I defy anyone to show me an Italian region that has more diversity in color and fragrance (only Sicily comes close in any way).

Liguria has the azure blue of the sea and the lighter blue of the sky. Its stunning beaches have golden yellow sand or gray-black rocks. The inland valleys are radiant green with herbs; the leaves on its olive trees are silver. The mountains are gray-purple year round, and in winter have snowy white hoods. In the area around Chiavari is an abundant cache of black ardesia (slate), the material used to make blackboards for classrooms but which also can be decoratively carved to adorn doorways. Such is the case in the town of Lavagna (whose name has come to mean "blackboard" in Italian). And then there is the amazing color palette of what grows in this region: Liguria is one of the major flower-growing regions of the world.

Although it is often said that Ligurian soil is unyielding (that is, the uneven terrain does not produce sufficient food to graze animals), the enterprising populace has nurtured enough vegetation to rival the Garden of Eden. In gardens, beaches, and railway stations, there are majestic palm trees that first arrived from Egypt around the fifth century A.D. (The palm fronds from the town of Bordighera are sent to the Vatican each spring for Palm Sunday observances.) Among the many other trees are cypresses, parasol pines, orange, lemon, morello cherry, peach, apricot, apple, jacaranda, Ligurian cork, fig, olive, hazelnut, walnut, chestnut, almond, and oak. Plants and flowers are everywhere, including thistle, bramble, dandelions, daisies, roses, lavender, carnations, jasmine, hydrangea, bougainvillea, bell heather, lupins, clover, chamomile, convolvulus, wild strawberries and blackberries, wistaria, and juniper.

There are incomparable herbs and greens such as basil, rosemary, marjoram, sage, mint, thyme, tarragon, oregano, sorrel, borage, wild chicory, chervil, lovage, and sometimes pimpernel and dandelion greens. Vegetables include garlic, artichokes (green and white), the sweetest peas, the most buttery lettuces, and flavorful potatoes. After each rainfall, the hills are full of hunters gathering some of the most extraordinary *funghi porcini*. The only significant flour is grown in western Liguria, but it is enough to make the region one of the principal pasta areas of Italy, along with Campania, Sicily, and Emilia-Romagna. Ligurian flour also makes focaccia, one of Italy's most divine breads.

All of this vegetation is fundamental in Ligurian cooking. The flavors and fragrances of fruit and flowers go into honeys, syrups, teas, and scented waters. Native Ligurian grapes make delicate wines that marry well with the cuisine. The olives from Liguria's trees produce an oil that many experts, and this writer, consider the world's best. Pine cones yield *pinoli* (pine nuts, or what are curiously referred to in English as pignoli). Fruit becomes jam and preserves; chestnuts become marrons glacés, are made into paste, or are dried and used for flour. Fava beans and chickpeas are also dried to make flours used for breads and soups.

Wander in this paradise and you will see bees going about their work, drawing from flowers and trees to make extraordinary honey. The skies are full of butterflies and songbirds who lend visual and aural beauty, and on a warm night there are more fireflies than stars in the sky.

Then there is the sun. Liguria is said to have more sunshine than any other Italian region and, despite its being quite northerly (its northernmost spot is on the same latitude as Toronto, its southernmost places are on the same latitude as Detroit or Boston), it almost never hits freezing at the shore and seldom does in the mountainous inland areas of the region. This is due to the nearly omnipresent sunshine as well as the warming breezes from the Mediterranean, which, after all, is an inland sea not subject to the sort of turbulence one would find on the Atlantic or Pacific oceans.

The sun also provided free energy to early Ligurian cooks, and they harnessed it to preserve food. Sun-dried tomatoes, those now ubiquitous and much misunderstood status symbols of 1980s foodies, seem to be Ligurian natives, although similar notions of sun-drying as a means of food preservation have appeared in Sicily, Sardinia, and other areas of the Mediterranean that had flourishing civilizations and resourceful peoples in ancient times. For example, Sicilians have for centuries dried tomato puree or sauce in the sun on large wooden boards as a means of making tomato paste that can flavor foods through the many months when fresh tomatoes are unavailable. The sun-dried tomato served this same function in Ligurian dishes.

You will have noticed that until this point I have spoken almost entirely about the land, even though most people who think about the Italian Riviera first think of the sea. Yes, the waters of the Mediterranean — here known as the Mar Ligure, the Ligurian Sea — are spectacularly beautiful and serve as a sort of mirror of Ligurian life on land. For Ligurians the sea represents opportunity as well as terror. Since ancient times Ligurians have been outstanding sailors and decent fishermen.

This part of the Mediterranean provides a poorer catch than, for example,

The light in Liguria is incomparable

the Adriatic or the Aegean, so that fish and seafood in Ligurian cuisine were primarily what Italians call *pesce azzuro:* fresh sardines and anchovies, plus other humble fish. In addition, there were mussels (called *cozze* in Italian, but *muscoli* in Liguria), cuttlefish, squid, octopus, and clams. An additional source of fish appeared in the form of dried cod — (*stoccafisso* or stockfish) and salt cod (*baccalà*) that appeared in the sixteenth century as trade increased between Genoa and Norway. But what magnificent things they have done with these humble foods! Tuna has been a part of the local diet because the medieval Republic of Genoa had fishing rights in a tuna-rich zone near Tunisia.

Although the land of Liguria created all of those wonderful products I described above, most of which found their way into the cuisine, only a few things — olive oil, pasta, flower products such as perfumes and oils — were made in enough quantity to be exported on Ligurian vessels. Therefore, Liguria took on another role: as a market and crossroads between the land and the sea. The Liguri (the sturdy peoples of pre-Roman times) were formidable traders in the ancient world. They traded with the Phoenicians and with the Celts, who settled there and became part of the population. It is often said that Ligurians have much in common with people from the British Isles in terms of humor, outlook, a certain coolness of demeanor, and a long seafaring tradition. By the thirteenth century, the Republic of Genoa was among the most powerful ports and markets in Europe. Products from inland (Lombardy, Piedmont, Switzerland) were shipped from the Ligurian ports of Genoa and Savona, while products from Emilia-Romagna left from La Spezia. These regions still are served by Ligurian ports.

Ligurian ships sailed throughout the Mediterranean, the Black Sea, and later on the Atlantic Ocean. Wherever they went, Ligurians brought merchandise and food back home. It is thought, for example, that the tradition of making sauces with walnuts came from the Black Sea, where the Genoese had important markets for many centuries. Ligurians were among the foremost spice traders, but, unlike the Venetians, used very little spicing in their own dishes.

I can go no further without mentioning the most famous man ever to go to sea. Cristoforo Colombo (Christopher Columbus to you; Cristobal Colòn to King Ferdinand and Queen Isabella of Spain) was born in Genoa. The house of his birth, right in the city center, can be visited today. It has been fashionable in recent years to attack Columbus and his impact on native peoples in places he visited. While there is still much to explore about him, it is indisputable that Columbus had more influence on geopolitics, geography, navigation, slavery, freedom, exploration, and the world economy than just about anyone else. Columbus (1451–1508) is among the most influential persons in world his-

The house where Christopher Columbus was born, Genoa

tory. He was a courageous man of his times who dreamed on a big scale and was persuasive enough to have the Spanish royal couple finance his dreams.

He also had a staggering effect on the way the world eats. Many of the foods Columbus brought back from the Americas were presented to Ferdinand and Isabella at a square in Barcelona, and all of this is now depicted on a mural in Barcelona's city hall. To name but a few foods that would not exist in the European diet had Columbus and other early explorers not brought them back: potatoes, tomatoes, sweet and hot peppers, beans (white, red, brown, and green, although not fava beans, which were native to Europe), corn, squash, zucchini, pumpkin, turkey, and cocoa.

Try to envision Italian cuisine without these ingredients and you will have a sense of what people ate, and didn't eat, before 1492. In fact, many ingredients, including tomatoes and potatoes, took many years to gain acceptance in the Old World. There are many scholars who believe, for example, that potatoes did not become part of the Ligurian diet until the early nineteenth century, while now they are central to many dishes. So it was Christopher Columbus, a Ligurian, who did more to revolutionize eating in Europe than anyone else.

Before Columbus, what was there to eat in Liguria? The olive and its oil, wheat to be used to make pasta and bread, grapes for wine, wild mushrooms, artichokes, greens, cultivated and spontaneous herbs, some cheese (especially Pecorino from Sardinia and Parmigiano-Reggiano from Emilia), salt, seafood, dried fish from Norway, fruit, various nuts, and chickpeas. The available meat included poultry, although fowl were meant to provide eggs, a pig that would be slaughtered in the winter to create ham and sausage to eat sparingly throughout the year, and rabbits, if you could catch them. All of these became the foundation of Ligurian cuisine, and with the extraordinary New World vegetables, are now the foundations of what is known as the Mediterranean Diet.

We often hear about how the Mediterranean Diet can help promote a healthy lifestyle. There is a great deal of truth in this, if you couple it with exercise and reduction of stress. Peoples in much of the developed world eat vast amounts of saturated fats and do not have enough fruits, vegetables, nuts, olive oil, fish, and moderate amounts of wine. They sit at desks and in their cars, or on the sofa watching television. They lead overstressed lives that are unrelieved by the solace of beauty.

It should not surprise you then that in Italy, where people have one of the longest life expectancies in the world, no one lives longer than the Ligurians. They are regularly ranked with the Japanese and certain Scandinavians in the world's championship of longevity, but they feast on a much more sophisticated cuisine than those other peoples. In 1995, La Nonnina d'Italia (Italy's Granny) died at the age of 110 in a small town north of Genoa. In an interview she gave on her last birthday, she was still quite fit, loved life, and was making plans.

If you look at Liguria and its people, you will understand. The topography of the place means there is a lot of exertion required: climbing hills and trails, walking up and down steps in cities, tilling terraces carved from hillside, working aboard ships and boats. Ligurians are solidly built people; men are broad-shouldered, women often have strong forearms. All have strong legs from the climbing, cycling, and walking they do. They excel in the sports of sailing, swimming, and particularly water polo — some of the world's top players are Ligurian. All of this physical labor and exercise, combined with the healthful aspects of the cuisine, contribute to their long life expectancy and their ruddy health.

The presence of older people is more a part of the landscape in Liguria than elsewhere. But these are not feeble old people. A lifetime of work and the Ligurian diet has produced old people who can carry six liters of water up a hundred steps (a feat I witnessed numerous times). It is also a common sight to see an eighty-year-old on a bicycle peddling steadily uphill or blithely cruising downward with no fear of falling. These and other scenes put one in mind of the film *Cocoon*.

So we have a region of contradictions. This is Northern Italy, one of the richest places in the world, but many people enjoy manual labor. There is almost no cream or butter in the food, and very little cheese. Olive oil and garlic, essential in cooking farther south in Italy, are consumed each day. Liguria is on the Mediterranean, but fish does not have the overwhelming impact you might expect on the way people eat.

What is it then that has made the food of the Italian Riviera unique, a cuisine that is considered among the most sophisticated in the world? At the heart of the evolution and development of Ligurian civilization and cuisine — and something you must always keep in mind when you think about this region — is a dialogue between land and sea that has gone on for thousands of years.

Ligurians who spent long periods at sea had an inextinguishable longing for fresh flavors. The Ligurians and the Venetians were the chief spice traders during the Middle Ages and the Renaissance, at least until the Portuguese rounded the horn of Africa in 1488. Yet the Venetians incorporated spices into their cuisine, while the Genoese avoided them and always favored herbs. It is typically theorized that the Genoese, who sailed longer distances in deeper seas than the Venetians, came to despise the smells of the spices that sat for weeks in the galleys of their ships. To the Genoese, the fragrance of herbs brought sensations of home, of Ligurian soil. So the cuisine of the Ligurians is one in which the fresh flavors from the sun, the soil, and the sea are conserved so that they can always be cherished. Ligurians believe that the soil and sea air combine to give their herbs and vegetables their outstanding flavor and color. The salt in the air is thought to keep green herbs green.

When sailors went away, they took along oil, dried pasta, sea biscuits, and jarred sauces and condiments that gave them a taste of home. Many of the sauces were created to convey terrestrial flavors to mariners and fishermen who would be away for a long period of time. It should not surprise you that festive ceremonial dishes in Liguria generally contain little fish, because when the men came home from the sea, they wanted food of the land. Ligurian food is also about dryness and freshness. Dry foods are portable and durable; fresh foods speak of flavor and life.

In terms of condiments, Liguria has few rivals anywhere. Much of Southern Italy uses a hot condiment called *diavolicchio* (there are regional variations in this spelling) that is based on peperoncino, or red chili pepper. A couple of drops of *diavolicchio* are used to spike many dishes, much as someone in Louisiana might use Tabasco. In Northern Italy one finds *mostarda,* which is fruit preserved with mustard seed that is used to accompany sliced meats or is ground and added to pasta fillings. There is a generic sauce called *salsa verde,* which is used to accompany boiled meat. The sauce is generally made with oil, vinegar, parsley, egg, capers, and other herbs and is found wherever boiled meats are served. But the most delicate and sophisticated *salsa verde* is from Liguria. Other than these three, most Italian sauces that are not destined to top pasta or rice are really just gravies and pan-drippings that are by-products of cooking.

The most famous Ligurian sauce (and Italian sauce, for that matter) is pesto. The name implies that it is a sauce made by a pestle pounding ingredients in a mortar. But pesto has very specific connotations: It is made with basil, salt, olive oil, and cheese. Additional ingredients, such as pine nuts, walnuts, and garlic, have appeared through the years. But you cannot call anything else pesto. When stored in jars topped with a little olive oil, pesto can last for several months. In most Ligurian homes you will see jars of pesto made when basil was at its peak.

The first food chapter in this book is dedicated to many of the outstanding sauces and condiments of Liguria. These, along with bread, pasta, and vegetables, are the fundamental building blocks of the cuisine. You will be impressed by the versatility of the sauces. They enliven everything they encounter, but because of their subtlety, they do not overwhelm other foods. Some sauces are made with vegetables, some with fish and seafood, some with meat, some with cheese, some with nuts, and almost all use herbs and exquisite Ligurian olive oil. It is the way some or all of these ingredients are combined that creates the amazing variety of sauces that Ligurians love. You will find more than forty in this book. Most of these require a mortar and pestle, and this is the only essential piece of kitchen equipment that you must acquire if you want to become a Ligurian cook.

I have often heard speculation by non-Italians that the Ligurian use of sauces is probably due to the region's being on the French border and France's customary use of sauces in its cuisine. Nothing in my research indicates that this is so, and I would like to take this occasion to clear up a few misapprehensions about French influence in Ligurian cooking and especially the notion that "Riviera cooking" was born on the French side of the Riviera and spilled over to Italy.

Since ancient times, most positive things have gone from Liguria toward France, while in return the French have sent occupying armies at the order of various kings and of Napoleon Bonaparte (who incidentally was of Ligurian origin — his family was from near La Spezia). Part of the reason there had been so much communication between these two countries was because of a road built by the ancient Romans.

The Via Aurelia is one of the oldest routes in Europe. It begins in Rome and goes up the coast of Lazio and Tuscany before entering Liguria near La Spezia. It threads along the entire coastline of the region (still the only road to do so) and enters France. This country was known as Gaul to the Romans. The Via Aurelia goes all the way to Paris and up to the English Channel. In England there is a Roman road that was trod upon by the Twentieth Legion as it went to its encampment at what is now Dorchester, near Oxford. It is not too much to assert that a particular Ligurian-Anglican connection existed then, if not even earlier with the arrival of the Celts on Ligurian shores.

As peoples went west along the Via Aurelia, they brought agricultural and gastronomic traditions to France. Thus did winemaking arrive. Many dishes in Nice and Provence can claim Ligurian origin. Pesto became *pistou*, *agliata* (garlic sauce) in France is *aillade* (not *aioli*, as is often stated), *farinata* (chickpea tart) becomes *socca*, and the fish stew known as *buridda* in Italy is *bourride* across the border. But this is more a question of influence rather than uniformity. By now, Niçoise cooking draws more from French traditions and products. The principal difference in the kitchens on either side of the border is that a Ligurian

Gustave Flaubert Visits Genoa

". . . I am now in a beautiful city, a truly beautiful city, this Genoa. One walks on marble, everything here is marble: stairs, balconies, palaces. . . . There was once a time when I would have reflected more than I do now (though I don't know well when that would have been) and perhaps have observed less. Now, instead, I open my eyes to everything, naively and simply, and that perhaps is better."

— from a letter to Alfred Le Poittevin,
1845

Flaubert speaks here to something very important about how we consider and experience new places (or foods or people for that matter). In a world where people feel compelled to attach definition and analysis to everything they en-counter, the simple act of experiencing, using the senses more and saving eval-uation for later, is almost revolutionary. Think of the first time you tasted a peach, or an olive, and you will understand.

cook almost always insists on fresh herbs while the Provençal uses many dried herbs.

For you to understand Liguria well, you must give further consideration to history and geography. The region has a population of about 1.7 million, about half of whom live in metropolitan Genoa. Liguria has four provinces, each named for a principal city. Moving from west to east, there is the province of Imperia, then that of Savona, then the province of Genoa, and finally the province of La Spezia.

Genoa (Genova to Italians) is an extraordinary and much misunderstood place. More than most Italian regions, Liguria is dominated by its capital (only Rome in Lazio and Naples in Campania are comparable). Genoa occupies such a physical and psychological centrality in Liguria that the two names are often interchangeable. The regional dialect is called Genovese rather than Ligurian.

Genoa, as the capital of a republic, ruled most of Liguria for so many years that there is a legacy of slight subservience and mild distrust for the capital on the part of many Ligurians. Unlike most regions, where people read different national newspapers based on their political views, Ligurians read Genoa's *Il Secolo XIX* ("The Nineteenth Century") and find it a mirror of who they are. This is an important concept: Liguria is nothing if not a large, extended society of shared values. This is distinct from most of Italy, where values, preferences and attitudes can easily shift from town to town within a region. In Liguria, there is a commonality of outlook that is rare, and actually quite positive.

Ligurians like to brag about their shared values, and their *tessuto sociale* (social fabric). Here again we find the tradition of solidarity born of the region's relationship to the sea. Sailors had to work together or ships would go off course and sink. Women ran businesses and towns in the men's absence, and created a social order of helpfulness and support. Ligurians think in terms of mutual support on a civic and regional scale. For example, they have built the Ospedale San Martino, Europe's largest hospital, in Genoa to serve all the people of the region. This behavior is very unusual in Italy, where the family is the nucleus of support and solidarity, and the state exists as a distant entity that collects taxes and creates laws that must be circumnavigated. Liguria exists as a city-state, and Genoa is its hub.

Consider this: Outsiders refer to Liguria as the Italian Riviera, but Ligurians believe that there are two Rivieras in the region: the Riviera del Levante and the Riviera del Ponente. Both names refer to the rising and the setting of the sun and, of course, from the Genoa-centric point of view, the sun only rises and sets in Liguria's capital city. So if you live in Camogli, Portofino, Chiavari, the Cinqueterre, or La Spezia, you live on the Levante (rising) side and might refer to yourself as a Levantino. If you live in Finale Ligure, Savona, Imperia, or San Remo, you live on the Ponente (setting) side and might refer to yourself as a Ponentino.

Also implied in the words "Levante" and "Ponente" is that the epicenter, the place where the sun shines brightest, is Genoa. Liguria is like an ancient city-state in which a glorious city dominates the region. The way Liguria is shaped, Genoa is the sun, the moon, the place from which all power and influence radiate.

Throughout this book you will find many references to Levante and Ponente, and these terms should become second nature to you. In addition to Levante and Ponente, there are two other key phrases to know when describing geography and terrain in Liguria: *costa* (or *costiera*) and *entroterra*. The former obviously means coast and relates to anything at or very near the shore. *En-*

troterra means inland, hinterland, or away from the shore and has mythical significance for Ligurians. This is because the coastline has been visited for centuries by everyone from conquerors and merchants in earlier times to tourists and artists in the past three hundred years. So the *entroterra* is where Ligurians retreat to rediscover themselves and their identity. The *entroterra* is the flavor, the fragrance, the poetry, and the solitude that are central to Ligurian identity.

When you visit Genoa, it is hard to believe that the quiet *entroterra* is nearby. This city vies with Palermo, Sicily, for the ranking of Italy's fifth largest (after Rome, Milan, Naples, and Turin). Here is the city with the largest medieval quarter in Europe, an endless maze of winding streets that fascinate and frighten all at once. Called the Centro Storico, this tangled web of color, intrigue, fascination, and danger lets one most palpably experience the fauna, rather than the flora, of Genoa. It is a setting that can rival any North African souk. Guy de Maupassant referred to this district as an "immense labyrinth of stone," and it is here that the most enticing sounds and smells of Genoese cooking are to be found. Eugenio Montale, a Genoese poet who won the Nobel Prize for literature in 1975, said that "Seen from a plane, Genoa must look like a snake who has swallowed a rabbit whole and is unable to digest it."

Montale's comment speaks to another Genoese characteristic. The tenacity of the people has earned the admiration and a bit of contempt from other Italians. Genoese are characteristically self-critical, doing this, in part, as a preemptive strike before anyone else will do it. Although Genoa and Venice both were fabled maritime republics in the past, one city became a touristic theme park, while the other hides its treasures and bitterness. Despite some urban problems, Genoa is an extraordinarily gorgeous place blessed with stunning architecture, wonderful weather, and a dazzling setting in an amphitheater of hills that surround the most important port in the Mediterranean.

In the city center, the Via Balbi and Via Garibaldi, with their palaces and splendor, are to Genoa what the Grand Canal is to Venice. The buildings are lovingly maintained, and much of the rest of Genoa has recovered from the devastation of World War II, in which its port and palaces were bombed repeatedly.

Foreigners have always found the city more beautiful, more mysterious, yet also more perplexing than do the Genoese themselves. Alexandre Dumas wrote in 1841 that "From six or seven leagues away, one can already glimpse [Genoa] on the horizon, lying at the end of its gulf with the unconcerned majesty of a queen." This majesty is the converse side to Genoese self-criticism. The city is universally called "La Superba," which means Genoa the Proud. And it has a lot to be proud of. Its civic traditions are enviable, and it has given generously

Genoa is full of staircases
leading from the sea to the mountains

of people and ideas in the formation of the Italian Republic in the mid-nineteenth century. While Turin, to the northwest, was the seat of the House of Savoy, which wanted to make Italy a constitutional monarchy with the Piedmontese Camillo Cavour as prime minister, the Genoese argued for the creation of a national republic. They did not get their way, but in the long run, Italy did indeed become a republic on the Genoese model.

Liguria gave Italy many of its foremost leaders. Giuseppe Mazzini (1805-1872) was a Genoese whose writings were influential in the promulgation of revolutionary ideals. His house is a museum in central Genoa that you may visit. Giuseppe Garibaldi (1807-1882), the George Washington of Italy, was the great soldier who led the battles to liberate much of the Italian peninsula from foreign domination. He was born in Nice at a time when it was very much a part of Liguria. Garibaldi and the Mille (his thousand freedom fighters) set sail for Sicily on May 5, 1860, from Quarto dei Mille, just outside of Genoa, to start the campaign that led to national unification.

Mazzini and Garibaldi are considered, along with Cavour (1810-1861) from neighboring Piedmont, the three most important political figures of the Risorgimento, the movement that led to Italian unification and independence. To this trio one must add the composer Giuseppe Verdi (1813-1901), whose early operas were often thinly veiled calls to arms in which oppressed peoples strive to gain their freedom. Although Verdi was from near Parma in neighboring Emilia-Romagna and often lived in Milan (in Lombardy), he was also in many ways a Ligurian. Parma and Liguria have historic commercial links — a trade route between Parma and La Spezia was paved through difficult Apennine mountain passes in ancient times.

As a child, Verdi certainly knew Ligurians. As an adult, he wintered for many decades in or near Genoa, and until recently one could meet elderly Genoese who had had some contact with the Maestro. For example, at the Klainguti bakery and café in the city center Verdi used to frequently enjoy coffee and cake during his afternoon walks. They created a cake called the "Falstaff" in honor of his last opera, and at Klainguti they still have a letter from Verdi informing the baker that "your Falstaff is better than mine!" In the early 1970s I used to chat with an elderly fruit seller near the Klainguti who, as a boy, used to be patted on the head by Giuseppe Verdi!

Part of the reason Verdi found Genoa so congenial, apart from the mild weather, was the city's strong republican tendencies at a time people elsewhere in Italy were talking about a government that might include the royal family in Turin or even the pope in Rome. In fact, Italy was initially unified (in 1861) as a constitutional monarchy under King Vittorio Emanuele, and it took decades until the Republic of Italy would be created in the wake of Mussolini's downfall in 1943.

But Liguria, which had known republican government since the thirteenth century, always held to its ideals no matter what the prevailing situation was on the rest of the Italian peninsula. In fact, it was Antonio Gramsci, a Ligurian, who was the most persuasive anti-Fascist agitator and was a source of great frustration for Mussolini. Gramsci was imprisoned and frequently tortured, becoming one of the more famous political prisoners of the early twentieth century. His prison diaries are powerful and wrenching, not only for what he discusses but for the high quality of his writing.

Sandro Pertini, of Savona, was an active anti-Fascist who more quietly took up Gramsci's cause. He had a very successful and productive career in postwar Italian politics, and was the president of Italy in the late 1970s and early 1980s. He is generally regarded as the most beloved of Italian presidents. Gramsci and Pertini were typically Ligurian in their tenacity and their willingness to fight for freedom.

There are adjectives that are used to describe the Genoese and other Ligurians. The one usually heard outside of Liguria is tightfisted or cheap, although Ligurians have another description of this. Within the region, people refer to themselves as *schietto*. This is a word with layered meanings. It implies pure, genuine, frank, and describes the no-nonsense attitudes of Ligurians. It also denotes the absence of pretense and false manners and courtesies one might find elsewhere. I think the Ligurians are very kind, hard-working people with little to prove to anyone else and much to love about where they live and what they have created. In other words, they are proud but unpretentious. The somewhat austere nature of Ligurians (as compared with other Italians) often invites ridicule, but once you get used to it it is actually refreshing. Their responses and gestures are sincere, and not intended to dramatize or deceive, as might occur elsewhere in Italy.

Yet they are also, shall I say, frugal. This might be a product of their centuries-old astuteness as traders. But it also is due to a significant phenomenon that I addressed earlier: the dialogue between the land and the sea. Many women in Liguria told me that the reason they scrimped and economized in the past (and even now) is that their men had gone to sea as sailors or fishermen. If their women saved money, the men could come home sooner. This puts a romantic spin on frugality, but it does strike me as logical to want a loved one back home in paradise.

I believe in a world that is ever more wasteful, one in which the notion of being disposable is considered positively, the appreciation of the intrinsic beauty and value of things — and the desire to get the most out of them — is a virtue rather than a shortcoming.

Yet occasionally Ligurian "frugality" can get excessive. If you go for a coffee with people in other Italian regions, there inevitably is a polite argument about who will pay the bill and the guest inevitably cedes the honor to the local. In Liguria I have paid for many cups of coffee and no Ligurian has ever argued with me. My favorite story about Ligurian economizing happened to me in Genoa. I had an appliance that needed fixing and brought it to a repair shop. I was told to come by in a week, and left my phone number in case there was a problem. A week later I went to the shop and was told the machine had been taken care of immediately and was ready the next morning. Why, I asked, didn't you call to let me pick it up sooner? "And who would pay for the phone call?" was the unironic response.

Ligurians are very distinct Italians in their measuredness, their relative lack of effusion, their sobriety, but they are not unemotional. The region has produced famous writers such as Montale and Italo Calvino, musicians such as Niccolò Paganini (the fabled violinist), opera star Renata Scotto, Luciano Berio (Italy's greatest living composer), and actors such as Vittorio Gassman, considered Italy's most virtuosic stage and film star, and Paolo Villaggio. The latter is little-known in North America, but is an icon in Italy every bit as much as Marcello Mastroianni, Gassman, Alberto Sordi, and Rossano Brazzi. Villaggio is not particularly the romantic lead or sex symbol, but is an Italian everyman whose cinematic alter ego, named Fantozzi, has endured all the travails of modern life. If in Fellini (who was from Emilia-Romagna) Italians tapped into their fantasy life, it is in Fantozzi that they see a mirror of themselves. The only adjectives in Italy that come from cinema are *Felliniano* and *Fantozziano*.

In addition to Genoa and its province, there are other wonderful parts of Liguria. In the westernmost part of the Ponente is the province of Imperia. While the capital city (a Fascist-era combination of the towns of Porto Maurizio and Oneglia, at the mouth of the Impero River) is not terribly interesting — although it is the main port for Ligurian agricultural exports — nearby are splendid cities such as Bordighera and San Remo on the coast, and Dolceacqua, Badalucco, Triora, Taggia, Pontedassio, and Apricale in the *entroterra*.

This zone is known as the Riviera dei Fiori, and is where most Ligurian floriculture takes place. Along with Provence, Holland, Colombia, and Thailand, this is where most of the world's flower cultivation is done. The fragrances of the Riviera dei Fiori wind up in many of the most expensive perfumes. Wandering through the hills here, where the scents of herbs, roses, and lavender compete for your attention, one can go into giddy olfactory overload. San

Remo has Italy's largest and most exciting flower market each morning, and also has one of the most wonderful fruit, vegetable, and fish markets I know. A walk through this market is a vivid lesson about why the Ligurian diet is so healthy, but one must beware of those octogenarians whizzing by on their bicycles.

Here, too, is the production of most of the region's outstanding olive oil. It is made using a single olive variety, the Taggiasca (from Taggia), much of which is grown in the Valle Argentina (the Silvery Valley, named for the color of the leaves of the olive trees). At the French border is Ventimiglia, famous for its gardens and the Balzi Rossi caves, where Cro-Magnon man is said to have dwelled 950,000 years ago.

Also in the Ponente is the province of Savona. Here, too, is the lovely beach town of Alassio. This was the residence, in 1885, of Amilcare Ponchielli, who wrote *La Gioconda*. It was also the town where Sir Edward Elgar composed his *Symphony of the South,* part of which is dedicated to Alassio. Nearby is Albenga, where the most delicious artichokes grow. There are lovely seaside towns such as Finale Ligure, Varigotti, and Noli, and some of the better wine producers in the *entroterra*.

The province of Genoa includes more than the capital. There are many small mountain and hill towns of great charm due north of the city, and the Valpolcevera is a heartland of Genoese food products such as ravioli (which were invented there) and salami. The coast on the Levante side of Genoa is a string of jewels. It is impossible to mention them all, but here are some highlights:

Nervi, just south of Genoa, has magnificent villas, parks, and a sea front, and has received visitors such as Verdi and Freud. Sori is a gem waiting to be discovered. The pesto there is the creamiest you will ever sample (page 69). The town also claims to be the ancestral home of the painter Pablo Picasso. It seems that his family had emigrated to Spain some years before his birth. This is quite possible; many people in this part of Liguria have the surname Picasso, including the proprietors of a food market I frequent.

Recco, just below Sori, may be the best food town in Liguria. There is a confluence of superb ingredients, talented cooks, willing eaters, and a love of the local gastronomic tradition. Many of the definitive recipes in this book are from Recco. Just outside town is the place where Guglielmo Marconi did his first experiments with radio transmission. The next town down, Camogli, is where I have lived in my Ligurian years, and it was my base during the years I worked on this book. Charles Dickens described it as "the saltiest, roughest, most piratical little place." In the nineteenth century this little town was a bigger shipbuilding center than Hamburg. It has retained its centuries-old seafaring tradition. Many of its men work on cruise ships as captains or staff. The captain of one cruise ship docked in Genoa passes Camogli once every two weeks. He draws the ship closer to shore at Camogli and blasts its whistle. Most of the town gathers on the shore, including his wife, and we all wave back.

Camogli is also a major fishing port. Its catch goes to Genoa and Milan, although enough is kept for local sale. On the second Sunday of May, the town holds La Sagra del Pesce, the fish festival, in which the townspeople thank their patron saint for allowing the fishermen to safely fish when the sea was mined during the Second World War. It is a sad and joyous event that underscores a major element in Ligurian life: Adversity heightens the sensation of pleasure. Joy means more if it comes in contrast to hardship. So these Ligurians pry open their famously tight fists and everyone is given free fish that are fried in an enormous pan (see page 343).

Camogli is distinct because it is one of those Ligurian towns that is really run by women. The name, Ca' Mogli (Casa delle Mogli), means "Home of Wives," and there is a sisterly solidarity that has endured for centuries. I have been through mud slides and earthquakes in Camogli, and was present when the son of one of the oldest families unexpectedly died. In each case, people pulled together and helped one another, proving that the famous and unique *tessuto sociale* of Liguria remains strong, and makes this region a paradise on a human scale, too.

Camogli becomes stunningly quiet at sunrise and sunset. At dawn I can look out my window and see elderly fishermen mending nets while the younger ones come in to the harbor from the night of fishing. They come up to the little square, deliver their fish, and buy themselves a wedge of fragrant, hot focaccia. At dusk, as the sun sets in the west, my eye follows a flock of gulls flying westward to the luminous horizon as fishermen set sail again, their boats leaving a small ripple in their wake that is illuminated by the last rays of sun. Every summer, there is the observance of the festival of the Stella Maris, the star of the sea. In Camogli, hundreds of small craft go to sea and the lights of town are turned off so that the dim lights of the small fishing boats will sparkle like jewels on the velvet darkness of the sea and sky at night.

Behind Camogli is the Portofino Peninsula, which has hiking trails up and down the mountain that separates the communities of Camogli, Ruta, San Rocco, Portofino, Paraggi, San Fruttuoso, and the larger town of Santa Margherita. Herbs grow wild and spontaneously throughout the peninsula, and it has been my custom to take a morning hike to gather what I might need for a day's meal or for a sauce I am planning to make. Part of the reason the herbs there are so outstanding is that the local stone, *la puddinda,* is so congenial to their growth. *La puddinda* is the characteristic stone, with little holes and pieces of seashell stuck in it, that one sees in Portofino's and Camogli's buildings and streets. This is ancient stone, somewhat soft and porous, that was formed at the juncture of land and sea. The herbs of the Portofino Peninsula also benefit from glorious sunshine and the moisture provided by the sea.

In San Fruttuoso, which is only accessible by foot or boat (there is no access or room for cars), there is a beautiful Benedictine monastery just above the town's rocky beach. While sun worshippers laze below, the monks tend to their duties, which include the organization of concerts in their cloister and art exhibitions in their corridors. The Benedictines have also had the primary role in maintaining the herbs of the Portofino Peninsula. They seed and replant as necessary and maintain the paths. The monks use the basil, thyme, sage, rosemary, tarragon, and other plants to make sauces for cooking, and healthful essences, salves, soaps, and liqueurs for their own well-being and for sale. Each year, around Easter, these products are sold in a market set up outside the monastery. One of the most beautiful (and fragrant) sights I have yet beheld is an enormous table piled high with newly picked basil. This was the scene at the Trattoria da Giovanni, just next to the monastery, and the chief recipient of the herbal bounty. If for no other reason, this restaurant merits a visit to understand what cooking with perfect herbs is all about.

Portofino is the most famous little harbor in the world. It is indisputably beautiful, but has become overrun with day-trippers, cruise ship passengers, and fancy boutiques housed in shops that used to be fishermen's homes. If you are nearby you will want to visit, but remember that this is now touristic Liguria, with little related to real life. Nearby is Santa Margherita, a chic resort with an immense harbor of yachts.

Just below is Rapallo, once one of the most beautiful cities in Italy. It attracted the likes of Friedrich Nietzsche (who wrote *Thus Spake Zarathustra* there), William Butler Yeats, Max Beerbohm, Jean Sibelius, and, most famously, the American poet Ezra Pound, who was an unrepentant Fascist. Pound wrote his Cantos in Rapallo, played tennis with Yeats, chess with local waiters, and liked to wander the city feeding mangy cats. Rapallo was subject to ugly overbuilding in the 1950s and 1960s, and added a new word to the Italian language: *Rapallizato.* This means ruined by modernization, and Ligurians look at Rapallo as a cautionary example.

The province of La Spezia is among the most beautiful areas in Italy. Although there are some slightly drab seaside resorts, this is also the zone of many unknown towns of immense enchantment. Montemarcello, Ameglia, Tellaro, and the other tiny towns of the Lunigiana, the land below the bay, are all breathtaking, yet this area has largely avoided tourism. Instead, day-trippers go to La Spezia's train station and journey to the Cinqueterre, the five small fishing villages that were once quiet, romantic oases, but now have been overrun almost as much as Portofino. They remain beautiful and a nice white wine is produced there, but they are hardly off the beaten track. Yet if you go inland just a bit, even in the Cinqueterre, you might see women with baskets on their heads descending from the hills carrying herbs for cooking and grapes for making wine, just as their foremothers did centuries ago. But to really discover the traditions of the province of La Spezia, my advice is to go to the Lunigiana, where paradise is not yet lost. La Spezia itself is underappreciated. The people are very friendly, and they are kind to the hundreds of young sailors who are always in residence.

La Spezia has played an important role in Italian food history. As this was a place where wonderful sea salt was produced, this ingredient was much sought-after. The people of Parma, in Emilia-Romagna, wanted the best salt possible to flavor their Parmigiano-Reggiano cheese and to cure hams and salamis. For centuries, La Spezia has provided the salt, and in return it received Parmigiano-Reggiano, prosciutto, and mortadella, which it promptly put in its dishes. Whether it is mussels stuffed with mortadella and cheese, or minced prosciutto stuffed in vegetables, La Spezia cooking has that extra touch of meat and cheese that makes it richer and more pleasing once in a great while, even if these elements are not traditional parts of the Ligurian diet.

The trade route from La Spezia to Sarzana to Parma has been a vital one, making La Spezia a major commercial port and giving the superb products of Emilia-Romagna a port of departure on the Mediterranean. There has also been a major exchange of political ideas between Parma and southern Liguria, making both areas very progressive and pro-Republic in times when much of Italy was pro-Fascist. La Spezia has always had a vibrant progressive tradition and has been a haven to certain political exiles and writers.

In reading this book and other sources about Liguria, one simple trick will make things much clearer for you: If you see the name of a city followed by two capitalized letters in parentheses, those letters indicate which Ligurian province that city is in. So San Remo (IM) means that it is in the province of Imperia; Albenga (SV) means that town is in the province of Savona; Recco (GE) indicates Genoa, and Portovenere (SP) denotes La Spezia. These abbreviations are universally recognized throughout Italy.

Liguria has received millions of foreign visitors for so long, that it inevitably has changed. Many of the most beautiful parts of the coast have now been fully exploited for tourism. In the nineteenth and early twentieth centuries, a visit to beautiful spots in Liguria such as Bordighera, San Remo, or Alassio on the Ponente and Rapallo or Portofino on the Levante was part of the Grand Tour. This tourism did not usually take place, as you might expect, in summer, but rather in winter, when the Ligurian coast was temperate while conditions in London, Berlin, or St. Petersburg would be grim. In fact, colonies of English, German, and Russian visitors were established and can still be detected today.

There are the famous Villa Hanbury gardens created by an Englishman in Ventimiglia; a look in the telephone directory for the town of Bordighera reveals many English names. The first luxury hotel to be built in San Remo, in 1860, was called the Londra (London) and was meant to appeal to well-off Englishmen. Famous English writers such as Byron, Keats, and Shelley spent a lot of time in the little coastal towns near La Spezia. This body of water is now known as the Golfo dei Poeti and it was here that Shelley drowned on July 8, 1822. Tellaro, on the other side of the gulf, is a tiny fishing village that was a beloved hideaway of D. H. Lawrence. He wrote a rather delightful and mysterious story about the Octopus of Tellaro, who liked to swim up to the town's church, which stands right at the water, and pull on the long rope to furiously ring the church bells and taunt the local priest. The story of the Octopus of Tellaro is often told (and frequently mistold in the area of La Spezia) and restaurants jokingly tell you that the boiled octopus you are eating sliced thin and served with potatoes is none other than the Octopus of Tellaro.

Another English writer who loved Liguria was Charles Dickens. He made at least two sojourns there, and was a great lover of Genoa. I have always been intrigued by the fact that most scholarship that discusses Dickens seldom notes his attachment to Liguria, since he made no secret of it himself.

If you have seen the lovely film *Enchanted April,* you will see a slice of life of Englishwomen in the early twentieth century who spend a month in a villa in the Levante. What I like about this film, aside from the fine acting, writing, and photography, is its depiction of the very distinct cultural differences between the English (who think they know how everything must be done) and the Ligurians, who smile with mild amusement and go their own way. Of course, the English characters finally relax and find the Italian Riviera perfectly marvelous.

German, Austrian, and Swiss visitors are more ubiquitous in the province of Savona, although there has always been a Germanic presence throughout much of Liguria. For example, Freud was fond of Nervi, the lovely little town just south of Genoa on the Levante side. He first went there for a conference on neurology, and liked to joke that the town, whose name means "nerves," was aptly named. Nervi has always had a particular attraction for dancers. The forerunner of ballet was an Italian art and it spread to other countries, especially Denmark, Russia, and France, where it was codified. Genoa has always had a strong ballet tradition, and the finest dance festival in Italy is in Nervi. But I digress!

It should be noted that because Switzerland is a landlocked nation that nonetheless is heavily engaged in international commerce, there is a special relationship between Switzerland and Liguria. If Genoa has always been the major seaport of Italy (exceeding Venice and Naples even in those cities' most glorious eras), Savona has always been the seaport of Switzerland and there is a quiet Swiss presence in that area.

The most intriguing foreign community in Liguria is probably Russian. The stretch from Nice (which belonged to Italy until 1855 and was known as Nizza) to San Remo has always had a well-known Russian expatriate community. In fact, you can see Russian orthodox churches with their characteristic onion domes as you drive in that area. I know a Russian orthodox priest in Imperia who likes to frequent antique shops near the port, looking for artifacts of the Russian presence in that area.

Tchaikovsky used to winter in San Remo in an effort to restore his fragile pulmonary health and is known to have observed many expatriate Russians gamble away their fortunes on the card tables of the Italian Riviera. This very likely influenced the composer's creation of the character of Ghermann in his wonderful opera *Pikovaya Dama* (*Queen of Spades*). After the Russian Revolution, much of what was left of Russian nobility moved to Monte Carlo, Nice, and San Remo. The most famous Russian resident was probably Maria Alexandrovna, consort of Tsar Alexander II. It was she who organized a glittering Russian salon in San Remo (where Tchaikovsky was a favored guest), and her patronage led to the construction of San Remo's famous Russian Orthodox cathedral. In 1874, she also donated the palm trees that line San Remo's seaside promenade.

I find it interesting that there has been relatively little impact on Ligurian cuisine by the English, German, Swiss, and Russian communities (probably a good thing too!). It is notable that in the Ponente there is more tea-drinking in the afternoon than in most of Italy, and little sandwiches do appear as an accompaniment. But this is a concession to a foreign taste that appeals to a small community, and does not really have impact on the eating habits of everyday Ligurians.

Although foreign visitors have always come to Liguria, it was not always

The Russian Orthodox cathedral, San Remo

enough to provide a living for the locals. The only answer for many was emigration. Many of them, especially from the region between Rapallo and the Cinqueterre, went to Argentina or California. Ligurian immigration to Northern California took place during the 1840s gold rush. When things didn't pan out, they remained and planted vineyards, gardens, and farms with outstanding produce. Ligurians and immigrants from neighboring Piedmont are basically responsible for the creation of the California wine industry.

They also became sailors and fishermen, introducing new ways to cook fish and seafood. One traditional Ligurian seafood stew, *ciuppin,* mutated in San Francisco to become cioppino, but don't let anyone from there try to convince you that cioppino is a California original. Ligurian sailors also wore trousers made of a tough and resistant fabric known as *blu di Genova.* It was Levi Strauss, in the late 1840s in San Francisco, who adapted *blu di Genova* and used it to make blue jeans, so every cowboy has the fishermen of Liguria to thank.

In the twentieth century, many Ligurians worked on ocean liners of the Italian, Lauro, and Costa lines. Many of these ships were built in Genoa. This work might have paid well, but it had a negative effect on Ligurian food. When the Ligurian seamen gave up the sea, they often returned home to open restaurants whose dishes reflected the notion of "Continental cuisine" of ocean liners. Not good! So cream, butter, Neapolitan spaghetti with tomato sauce, and other dishes from other Italian regions crowded out local preparations in an effort to appeal to tourists. Also, mass tourism and overbuilding of hotels and condominiums on the coast degraded Ligurian cuisine until the early 1980s, forcing lovers of traditional Ligurian food to retreat to the *entroterra* or make the acquaintance of local people who might feed them the genuine article.

Slowly, traditional dishes are returning to menus on the coast as Ligurians take more pride in their native cuisine and do not feel the need to be imitative to appeal to tourists. But, truth be told, one really must look elsewhere than most of the "typical" restaurants to discover the genuine taste of Liguria.

I would be rather suspicious of a Ligurian cookbook composed primarily of recipes drawn from the region's restaurants. Too many food writers go to Liguria and dine along the coast and in fancy restaurants in Genoa and then think they know the regional cuisine. As there are so many restaurants in touristic Liguria that gear their cooking to the perceived taste of the visitor, one has to dig much deeper to find classic Ligurian dishes. Although I have included about fifteen carefully selected recipes from restaurants, most of the dishes in this book were learned from home cooks I have met during two decades of visiting and living in Liguria. Many of the older preparations come from the handwritten family recipe books that are jealously guarded treasures in many homes. I am deeply grateful to the many Ligurian families — customarily very private people — who took me into their homes and their hearts to teach me the traditional cuisine of the Italian Riviera.

As I was completing this introduction, a book was published in England by Anna Del Conte, a native of Milan and a longtime resident of London who is one of Britain's leading authorities on Italian cuisine. Her scrupulous work, combined with her admirable lack of shyness about saying exactly what is on her mind, has gained her admirers in North America as well. Imagine my surprise and delight to read, in Anna's *The Classic Food of Northern Italy* (Pavilion, 1995), that "If I were told that I could eat dishes from only one of Italy's twenty regions, I would unhesitatingly choose Liguria. I would find in them the kind of food that appeals to me most: aromatic, delicate, with few spices but with many herbs. The dishes are complex, with many flavours that always combine well and never clash."

I took these words as great encouragement after having perhaps lived too intimately with Ligurian food and culture for a long time. I had felt that maybe this food I loved so, and this people I so admired, had blinded me to what others might experience in their contact with Liguria. But if so worthy a (non-Ligurian) expert as Anna Del Conte, whom I have since had the pleasure to meet personally, could declare the food of this Italian region her favorite, then I feel I can welcome you to the region with my own sentiments: Liguria's is the great undiscovered cuisine of Italy and ranks with that of Emilia-Romagna as the nation's finest. While the food of Emilia-Romagna is subtle, rich, sensuous, and gratifying, it is also high in saturated fat, very labor-intensive, and requires very expensive ingredients. I love that food madly — having lived in Bologna for quite a while — but it is really not relevant to how most people eat today. If the food of Emilia-Romagna is the flavor of animals (pork, beef, rich broths of meat and poultry, milk, cream, butter, cheese, egg pasta) with judicious use of spices, that of Liguria is its complete opposite. Ligurian food is the flavor of the land and of the sea: fruits, vegetables, herbs, nuts, grains, olive oil, fish and seafood, with only small amounts of meat and cheese. It is every bit as elegant and sophisticated as the cuisine of Emilia-Romagna, as gratifying in the mouth, but it is the type of food that people want to eat now.

Unlike other Italians, who customarily sit down for meals that include several courses, Ligurians have been less structured in their approach to eating. Some observers might suggest that this is parsimoniousness rearing its head, but it has more to do with the cycles of work, and the fact that great satisfaction can be had from a piece of focaccia or a slice of vegetable torte. In Liguria, where men were often at sea with food prepared for them to eat while women were running things on shore, there was not the same rigid notion of sitting down to a family meal as there once was. While the Ligurian lifestyle has come to approximate that of Italy in some ways, in terms of eating there is more flexibility.

Ligurians might be the original grazers, and their approach to constructing a meal can be free-form. If, for example, you wanted to make a meal of several different antipasti or vegetable preparations, that would be fine and no one would look askance if there were not a *primo* (soup or pasta) or *secondo* (main course). But in meals where a traditional *primo* or *secondo* is served, each of these courses should stand alone to be best appreciated.

Liguria is full of bakeries and *friggitorie* (fry shops) where for most of the day one can purchase freshly made focaccia with cheese or herbs, vegetable pies, or small pieces of fried fish. Ligurians often make two or three visits a day to such places for small bites, skipping more formal sit-down meals, especially at lunch. This is a healthful approach, but it was born not for that reason but because of a great penchant and desire to work that is common among Ligurians.

In addition to grazing (not an elegant term, but one that has achieved common usage and comprehension in food parlance), Ligurian cuisine is distinguished by interchangeability on a much greater scale than most Italian regional cuisines. The use of sauces, spreads, and pastes is meant to impart flavor not only to pasta but throughout the meal.

There is also the fact that Ligurians hold dear the foods that speak to them of their land, their history, their heritage. Many of these flavors and preparations are singular, and do not correspond to a non-Ligurian's notion of what good eating is. Above all, Ligurians prize fragrance. They refer to their cuisine as *la Cucina Profumata* (the Perfumed Kitchen) because fresh herbs and fragrant foods cast their spell.

Ligurian herbs are the building blocks of flavor in pasta sauces and in dishes made of meat, fish, or vegetables. Yet the cuisine of Liguria is made even more subtle with the judicious use of other flavors, such as pine nuts, walnuts, unusual lettuces and greens, artichokes, wild mushrooms, sweet peas, fruity olive oil, olives that range across the flavor spectrum from sweet and delicate to assertive and chewy, piquant low-fat sheep cheeses, apricots, chestnuts, figs, and a vast selection of fish and seafood. Ligurian wines are often used in local dishes, imparting a special flavor. Meat is used sparingly, usually ground and stuffed in vegetables or wrapped in lettuce and cooked in broth. Important for the American cook, most of the essential elements of Ligurian food are now available in the United States, so that reading a Ligurian cookbook will not be a vicarious experience. You will find detailed recommendations for procuring these products, starting on page 439.

Liguria is also considered one of the four ancient sources of pasta, that most famous of Italian foods (the other three are Campania, Sicily, and Emilia-Romagna, the latter being the region that makes pasta with eggs). Each of Liguria's most characteristic pastas are very distinct. From this region come ravioli, which were filled with dry cheese and sent to sea with Ligurian mariners, *corzetti* (figure-eight-shaped pasta modeled after a coin of the medieval Republic of Genoa), *pansôti* (herb-filled pillows that are always served with walnut sauce), and *trenette,* flat spaghetti that perfectly match with pesto.

Some of the most notable baking in Italy happens in Genoa and the towns nearby. Focaccia, probably the most famous Italian bread aside from pizza, is available fresh every hour. This simple bread, made of flour, herbs, olive oil, and a little water, has been the staple here for a thousand years. The social exchange that occurs as people nibble on focaccia in tiny Genoese alleyways (called *caruggi*) is one of the great pleasures to be had in Italy. But focaccia can be made in any modern kitchen, so readers of this book need not feel left out.

Genoa has other typical baked goods as well. In the mornings one eats *farinata,* a crepe made of chickpea flour. Later in the day one can accompany a glass of wine with a slice of *pissadella* or *sardeneira,* breads made with tomatoes, herbs, olives, and fish. *Torta Pasqualina,* an Easter specialty, is made of thirty-three layers of crepes, vegetables, and cheese, each layer representing a year in the life of Christ. Genoa is also thought to have some of the best pastries in Italy, most notably *genoise* (named for the city), a delicate sponge cake. One also can find *crostate,* tarts made of jam using superb local fruit.

So here is Liguria. The recipes from paradise are not only about eating, but about how to live well, how to find meaning in a confusing world where truth and beauty are compromised by cynicism and dishonesty. To eat this food is to find ancient connections to nature, to hear clearly that dialogue between the land and the sea that is obscured almost everywhere else. Attend to the distant sound of waves crashing against seaside cliffs, bite into a piece of hot, crunchy focaccia, breathe deeply of the perfume of pesto, then share this food with someone you love, and paradise lost will become paradise found.

Exploring
the Portofino Peninsula
in 1906

Eduard Strasburger, in his 1906 book, *Rambles on the Riviera* (in German, *Streifzüge an der Riviera*), describes Liguria in painstaking detail, with a particular interest in the botany and vegetation of the region. His book remains indispensable for understanding how what grows here influences the cooking, medicine, religion, and approach to life. He also makes perceptive comments about the behavior of the people he encountered.

"On a clear, sunny morning in the beginning of March we decided upon an excursion to the ridge of Portofino. Taking the train to Camogli we then proceeded to Ruta by the beautiful road which commands ever widening views over the Gulf of Genoa. At Ruta we clambered up the path leading south along the ridge of the promontory. Here the view suddenly extends to the far distance embracing both the bays which the Monte di Portofino divides. . . . A fisherman came half way up the hill and offered us his boat for the sail to Portofino. We agreed to his proposal and he walked back with us. He was a well-built youth with an intelligent expression, and may have been about twenty years old. His knowledge of plants filled me with astonishment. And Professor Penzig, who had published in 1897 a 'Flora popolare Ligure', and who has collected the popular Ligurian names of plants, had only to mention any shrub or flower of the district when the young man pointed it out. But occasionally he would merely refer to a given plant as 'mala herba' accompanying the remark with a gesture indicating aversion. These primitive men are much nearer to Nature than we are: they have lived from youth up in the open air, and their minds are stored with practical information. They have a much more lively interest in the natural objects which surround them than our educated people, whose knowledge is mainly derived from text books. Professor Penzig has invariably found among these natives a similar acquaintance with plants."

The Disappearance of
La Civiltà Contadina

*I*N MY WRITINGS about Italy, and those of colleagues such as Lynne Rossetto Kasper, Carol Field, Nancy Harmon Jenkins, and Corby Kummer, there has been an ongoing discussion about what are known either as popular traditions or peasant culture. The latter term is often discarded because there is a perceived negative connotation to the word "peasant," even if it is merely descriptive of a certain kind of country person who had different wisdom from a city person, but valuable wisdom nonetheless. The peasant (*contadino,* in Italian) understood the land, the weather, the currents, and could detect subtle changes in climate, soil, and air and know how they would affect his life and his livelihood. The peasant could recognize plants and animals that his city cousin would ignore, and would understand how to use these as sources of food or for health-giving properties.

In Liguria, there were the *contadini* who knew the land and then there were the *pescatori,* the fishermen, whom I think of as the *contadini* of the sea. They could read the weather and the waves, they knew each patch of sea, where the sandbars were, and where the treacherous sinkholes were that could cause them trouble. The *contadini* had one set of saints; the *pescatori* had another. The *contadini* could look at the sky and see the sun that nourished their crops and that served to dry fruits and vegetables for storage. The *pescatori* could look at the night sky and find the *stella maris,* the star of the sea, that would give them guidance.

What has troubled me and many of my colleagues is that there has been a relative disregard of the peasant and popular traditions in Italy, especially in the north, as the nation has moved headlong into wealth and supposed well-being. It is not that Italy is different from, say, France, Spain, Germany, England, or the United States in this regard, but merely that there is so much wisdom in the Italian peasant tradition that is irreplaceable. Just as many Americans do not endeavor to draw all of the wisdom and experience that we can from our elders, in Italy, too, these people are beloved, but looked at as colorful and folkloric rather than as custodians of the culture. I have never understood why being forward-looking must also mean having a disdain of the old.

This is especially true in Liguria. Here is a region that suffered centuries of great poverty in the hinterlands, while people lived frugally but well along the shore. There have always been pockets of wealth, such as in the banks, markets, and palaces of Genoa, or the villas of Bordighera, San Remo, Alassio, Portofino, and other towns. So there evolved over the centuries a body of knowledge about how to make do with few resources.

The result of this was that by the 1950s the people of Liguria lived longer than other Italians, and had a life expectancy that ranked among the longest in the world. Basically, this was a product of a very sound diet, using grains, nuts, fruits and vegetables, moderate amounts of wine and olive oil, protein derived largely from fish, and very little consumption of animal fats from cheese, butter, and meat. This was coupled with a fair amount of exercise from working the land. When a *contadino* had to go from one place to another, he or she would travel by foot or bicycle. Because so much of Liguria is hilly, this meant that one had to be in good shape to get about, and almost everyone was. In the province of La Spezia, women traditionally carried heavy baskets and bundles on their heads as they walked up and down hills; a few still continue this practice.

By the shore, the maintenance of fishing craft and the rigors of sailing required similar energies, and the manual labor of the men of the sea (and the women who took care of homes and cities while they were away), created a hardy people. In the past, precarious wooden boats were rowed out to sea to the areas rich with fish, particularly anchovies and sardines. When there was an abundant catch, the fish would be put in jars and preserved with salt, or converted into sauces (see pages 103). Women would put some of the fish into a basket and walk to town (baskets on their heads) to sell their wares.

Throughout Liguria, but especially in the Cinqueterre in the province of

A typical Ligurian caruggio, *Triora*

La Spezia, the principal means to transport heavier goods was by mule. Food, wine, and lumber were carried to and from the shore into distant valleys. The legacy of this are excellent paths that serve the walkers and day-trippers of today.

The advent of automobiles, powerboats, and the desire of people to earn more money in a less taxing way meant that many rural Ligurians abandoned their land and traditions, opting instead for work in the huge Ligurian tourist industry, in factories, or in service professions. When one travels in the *entroterra*, the Ligurian hinterland, there are towns that are nearly abandoned, and other places where most of the people are quite old. Many of the farmhouses have been converted to second homes for city-dwellers or people from the coast.

In that the culture of the Ligurian *contadini* continued full force only into the mid-1950s, we are now in a situation in which most of the people with strong memories of that time are dying out, and with their passings go the last witnesses of a world that likely will be lost forever. Soon this culture will be described only by historians, and not by people who lived it.

A fundamental part of my research for this book was to talk with as many *contadini* and *pescatori* as I could find, to make this an oral and social history as well as a book of recipes. Their voices and insights are woven throughout this volume, as well as in the paragraphs that follow.

In a civilization that was based on the fickleness of the land, it was customary to follow the phases of the moon as guidance for when to plant and when to reap. Seeds were planted at the new moon to insure that things would grow large: squash, celery, cabbage, melons, cauliflower, beets, eggplants, and zucchini. During a crescent moon one plants things that you want to grow quickly: herbs, lettuces, tomatoes. One harvests at the full moon. At the waning moon one harvests nuts and foods destined for jams or to be preserved. At this time one also prunes deciduous plants.

In winemaking, it was preferable to pick grapes during the crescent moon, while the decanting of wine must happen by the light of a full moon. Wine that was meant to be young and slightly fizzy was bottled at the waning moon in March. Wine meant for longer storage was bottled at the waning moon in August. Sheep were to be shorn during the waning moon.

As much as anything else, these phases of the moon were demarcations of the passage of time, and for people without clocks or calendars the moon was a reliable guide. Even when other points of reference became available, the moon was still looked to.

Another point of reference were days of the saints. In Italy, it was the custom until recently to celebrate one's saint's day in a major way, while a birthday

was a minor observance. This day is called the *onomastico*. While my birthday is in May, my *onomastico* (for San Federico) is on the 18th of July, and on that day my Italian friends call to offer good wishes. The days of the saints also offered guidance in agriculture. It was thought that medicinal herbs would be most effective if gathered on Saint John's Day (March 8). Similarly, harvesting should never take place in the week of the feast of Saint Francis of Assisi (October 4).

Before modern medicine created a whole range of pharmaceuticals, herbs, flowers, and plants were applied to resolve various complaints. They were usually brewed as teas and tisanes, and sometimes these would be used as compresses rather than for drinking. A tea made of dried figs was especially indicated for a cold. Mallow was used for inflammations of the mouth. Lavender was favored for personal hygiene. It was also rubbed on sheets and towels to keep pests away. To cure insomnia, one combined chamomile, poppy flowers, and orange flowers. Headaches were treated with marjoram, lime, verbena, and melissa. For acid stomachs it was melissa and cinnamon. To treat hypertension, one drank a tea made of mistletoe, olive leaves, and garlic. Olive oil always had to be blessed by a priest before being applied to medicinal needs. It was combined with beet greens to treat colic in babies.

Even olive harvesting has changed. Now olives are usually picked from trees at the moment they are considered ripe. In older times, nets were spread on the ground and olives were gathered as they fell. This season usually lasted from November to May; now olive harvesting usually lasts from mid-November to mid-March. Olive harvesting was typically done by women who were brought in to do the job. They were either *montanine,* from the mountains of Piedmont, or *sasselline,* women from Sassello, an inland town in the province of Savona famous for its amaretti cookies (see page 401). They would crouch for hours, selecting olives and tossing them into straw baskets. The olives were then brought to the *frantoio,* the olive press, where the *frantoiano* (the presser) would keep a portion of the oil that he would sell to make his living.

The full baskets of olives gathered by the women earned them room and board, a small allowance of oil and salt, and a nominal salary. Many of them married local men, but that did not guarantee a life of leisure. It was customary in Ligurian peasant society for the woman to raise children, chickens, livestock, and all the vegetables, fruits, and herbs in the garden. She was also responsible for making and preserving food and sauces, and forming the loaf of bread that would be baked in the communal oven (see page 119 and 121).

Perhaps the most conspicuous legacy of the peasant tradition is the use of dialect instead of regular Italian. In Liguria the dialect is usually called Genovese, which is a very telling detail. Rather than referring to the whole region, the name of the dialect suggests the real as well as psychological dominance that the capital city has exerted on the region. While dialect is first and foremost the language of *contadini* and *pescatori*, it is spoken and understood by most adults in Ligurian society. If you hear two bankers in Genoa or poets in Imperia or La Spezia using the region's dialect, it is because the peasants and fishermen saved it for them. Unfortunately, today's Ligurian children are not necessarily learning Genovese, so it too may soon be gone. Where possible, I have listed the Ligurian as well as the Italian names for the recipes in this book.

Why Are the Buildings Painted That Way?

Visitors to Liguria are inevitably struck by the remarkable paintings and frescoes that adorn so many buildings throughout the region (except for parts of the Ponente and the poorest areas of the *entroterra*). This painting is perhaps at its most developed in Camogli, although it is quite remarkable in many towns. One sees a remarkable range of colors — pinks, oranges, golds, greens, blues, reds, and yellows. Onto these surfaces are painted classical architectural details and façades, with endless trompe l'oeil to fool the eye. Why are they painted that way?

Liguria is at an interesting confluence of styles. It has always traded with the north, and Ligurians saw the extensive use of exterior decoration of houses in the Germanic and Scandinavian countries. This practice spread in Liguria in the fifteenth century. In the Mediterranean, there was contact with classical architecture of Italy, Greece, and the Levant. Then there is the use of color and the more abstract geometrics typical of art and architecture in the Islamic countries. All of these styles arrived in Liguria, where they were synthesized with two very Ligurian traits: frugality, and the love of quality and excellence.

Ligurian artists devoted themselves to creating the most faithful recreations of architecture elsewhere. So adept were they that you must often look very closely to see that what looks like a dimensional building is in fact a beautiful flat surface. This appeals, too, to homeowners who want to save money. Painting details on a building, they believed, ultimately cost less than purchasing the materials to make capitals, pillars, and ornamentation.

There is a great democratizing effect in this wall painting. Wealthy people might have their houses decorated with classical designs, but so too could working people have the effect of making their homes look like they are covered with precious marble. So the fishermen and the bakers as well as the bankers and the doctors could live in this artificial yet beguiling splendor.

Mrs. Boddington, in her *Slight Reminiscences of the Rhine, Switzerland and a Corner of Italy* (1831), attributed the practice of house painting not to parsimony but pride in a natural resource that Ligurians have more of than most Europeans: "Perhaps the simplicity of marble might be better as to taste, but I love this crowding of southern images — this affluence of proof that the bounty of the sun is not overrated. Such things become Italy; her beauty is identified with sunshine: no one ever anticipates or recollects a scene in Italy without adding a bright day to it."

Many Ligurian seafarers have told me that the reason each adjoining building in their towns is painted a different color is so they can be recognized from boats offshore. Again, Ligurian practicality has beautiful results.

Equipment for a
Ligurian Kitchen

ECAUSE LIGURIAN CUISINE is not, by its nature, fancy — although it is quite sophisticated — it evolved without requiring its practitioners to have all sorts of equipment and gadgets to make it work. There is only one indispensable item, the mortar and pestle, and for you to succeed as a Ligurian cook you must invest in one. You will probably want a pan dedicated to baking focaccia, a working surface to make doughs, a pot large enough to properly boil pasta, and knives and pasta wheels for cutting. Beyond that, your basic kitchen equipment will probably suffice. For information about acquiring equipment in Liguria and North America, see page 457.

Mortar and Pestle *(Il Mortaio)*

You will want to acquire a marble mortar large enough to move your fist about in freely, one with a bowl *at least* 5 to 6 inches/13 to 16 cm wide. If you have room for a bigger mortar in your kitchen, so much the better. This will enable you to pound herbs and nuts more evenly and to make larger portions of sauces. To truly use a mortar as the Ligurians do, the pestle you select must be made of wood. This is because a marble pestle is too heavy and can be too cold. Part of the action that happens in the pounding of herbs, nuts, and spices is a transaction of heat that releases the esters, those fragrance-bearing chemicals

*The marble mortar and wooden pestle
are the most important tools in the Ligurian kitchen*

that are part of our food. You can clean both mortar and pestle with warm water, but do not use soap (especially on the wood pestle) or the flavor will be absorbed and will wind up in your sauces.

Focaccia Pan *(Il Tegame per la Focaccia)*

An important decision to make is whether you want to use a baking stone or a pan to make focaccia. Traditionally, a stone would be used, although many bakeries now use pans because they are easier to handle and are useful for containing the bread until it is all cut and sold. For all of the focaccia recipes in this book you should use a low-sided rectangular pan with a rim. Select a pan that is 10½ x 15½ inches (27 x 39 cm) and made of dark carbon steel or heavy aluminum or a pan that is anodized nonstick coated. I prefer the first two to the latter because I like to let additional olive oil add to the crunch of the bread and prevent sticking.

Baking Stone

If you wish to produce a focaccia closer to that you might find in a traditional Ligurian bakery, you might consider buying a baking stone. You should use one large baking stone rather than two or three smaller ones. It can be kept in the oven all the time. To clean it, let it cool entirely before touching it. Wash it well in cold water, but do not use soap, whose flavor will be absorbed. Baking stones will usually produce a crunchier focaccia, although similar results can be produced in a pan.

Work Surface to Make Dough *(La Spianatoia)*

You will need ample space to roll out doughs to be used in Ligurian breads and pastas. This might be a board or surface made of plastic, wood, or marble. I favor plastic because it is lightweight, easy to clean, and does not impart flavors to doughs. However, if you use knives or other sharp tools, try not to cut deeply into the plastic. Wood surfaces are appealing to many people because they look nice. However, they too can be cut by knives, and will more easily absorb and give off flavors and eventually little splinters. Marble is probably the most attractive, but has two disadvantages. The first is that it is very heavy, so it is difficult to lift if it must be stored. The other disadvantage is that marble, in a cold to cool environment, can become quite chilled, which will inhibit certain actions in flours and doughs. Whichever surface you choose, the essential idea to recall is to keep it clean, so that bacteria and flavors will not penetrate your doughs.

Rolling Pin *(Il Matterello)*

It is necessary to use the correct rolling pin. The American type, with two handles attached, is acceptable only if you absolutely cannot get your hands on something approximating an Italian rolling pin. The main problem with the American rolling pin is that it is too thick and usually not long enough to roll out the dough. My rolling pin, which I bought very cheaply in Italy, is simply a cylinder of smoothly sanded wood. It is 1½ inches/3.8 cm in diameter and 22 inches/56 cm long. Some Italian rolling pins are longer, but mine suits me fine. I learned in Italy that when a rolling pin is new you should wash it in warm water and gentle soap, making sure to rinse it thoroughly. Wipe it with a clean towel and then let it air-dry. Rub the pin very lightly with corn oil or some other neutral vegetable oil. Wait about ten minutes and then lightly dust one hand with flour and "massage" the rolling pin gently. You should give your pin this treatment about once a month if you use it with any regularity. If you cannot buy an Italian-type rolling pin, see if you can have one made at a lumber yard.

Pasta Wheel *(Il Rotellino per la Pasta)*

These are very inexpensive and useful for cutting rows of noodles to make lasagne, *mandilli di sæa, pansôti,* ravioli, and tagliatelle. You should buy two pasta wheels. One will have a fluted edge and can be used for lasagne and other pastas where you want that ruffled look. A straight-edged wheel, sometimes called a pizza wheel, is better for *pansôti* and *mandilli di sæa.*

Knives, of course, are essential in cooking. They should be kept sharp at all times.

Pan for Torte

To make vegetable pies such as Torta Pasqualina, a 9-inch/24-cm springform pan will be suitable in most cases, although you might consider having a 10-inch/26-cm pan too.

Pan for Farinata

This is really worth the investment only if you plan to make farinata often. I bought mine at the excellent Soprano kitchenware shop in Oneglia (Imperia). The traditional farinata pan is always made of copper and must be seasoned with olive oil before each use. Mine is 12 inches/30 cm, although they can also be smaller or much bigger. If you are less of a traditionalist, or only an occasional farinata maker, a pizza pan is acceptable, the heavier the pan the better.

A Large Pot

A pot, at least 6 quarts or liters, is essential for cooking pasta. Even if you are only making a portion for one person, it is necessary to use a large pot so that the noodles can circulate freely to cook evenly.

Manual Pasta Machine

You may already have one on the top shelf of your pantry. They are not very expensive and, for the purposes of this book, not essential. I do not use manual pasta machines for flattening or stretching dough because the results obtained with a rolling pin are far superior. You should use the manual machine only for cutting noodles. But with a bit of practice this can be done by hand with a knife.

Ravioli Tray

You may already have one. They are practical gadgets, but you can certainly make ravioli without them. So only buy one if you want the option of using it.

Corzetti Stamp

This is necessary if you want to make Corzetti del Levante (see page 222) and may be acquired from sources listed on page 457. The stamps are not inexpensive, and while you may certainly serve these disks of pasta without making the imprint of the stamp, genuine *corzetti* must be stamped.

Mason Jars, which you should sterilize, are essential if you intend to store sauces that you have made in your mortar.

A hand-carved wood stamp for corzetti

Ligurians Go Food Shopping
through the Centuries

Among the most enjoyable aspects of my research for this book was that I was granted special access to the Archivio dello Stato di Genova, the State Archive of Genoa, which I frequented for six months.

One particularly intriguing detail always delighted me. Whenever a document was brought to me for my perusal, whether it had been examined by someone else the day before or two hundred years before, it was invariably closed with a string tied in one of the many sailor's knots that are used by Ligurian seafarers (rather than with a simple knot that you or I would use to tie a shoelace or a ribbon). I realized from this very subtle detail that this particular thread in the Ligurian social fabric had endured for centuries.

What impressed me in my research is that the upper classes, whether noble or mercantile, tended to buy foods that were not terribly different from what was consumed by the poor. The only difference was the greater variety found on the shopping lists of people with more money.

For example, on a typical day in the life of the family of Cammillo Pallavicino in 1668, they might acquire fish; 12 oysters (this is more unusual); 12 artichokes; milk; cabbage; cauliflower; pine nuts; raisins; *sapori e foglie* (flavors and leaves, that is, spices and herbs); lettuce; 2 eggs; salt. When the Pallavicinos made a bigger shopping trip to acquire staples for the larder, they would buy sausage; cardoons; butter; 12 eggs; sugar; cinnamon; raisins; dry biscuits for dipping; lard; *fideli* (string pasta — see page 166); milk; and a prepared meal for the servants.

By contrast, the Libro del Introito del Convento (a book of purchases by a convent in Genoa) reflects a more austere approach, but hardly deprivation. In February 1696, the nuns bought meat; fish; eggs; cheese; cod; sugar; salt; and sausage. In April of the same year, they bought much of the same, with artichokes and chestnuts added. Things must have improved by October 1698, when the nuns bought meat; fish; eggs; *prescinseua* (see page 79); salt-cured fish; mushrooms; rice; bread; *fideli;* vinegar; garlic; spelt; and four types of wine. I wondered at the almost complete absence of fruits, vegetables, and herbs from the nuns' diet. Further reading revealed that within the walls of the convent was a splendid garden that yielded all the produce they could require.

From the 1732 book of expenditures of the Spinola family, one of Genoa's most exalted clans, there is more space devoted to prepared foods than one previously encounters. This indicates that by this time Genoa had cooks in stores who created finished dishes for home consumption. So the Spinolas bought onion tart; sweet cake; cuttlefish antipasto; ravioli; cooked tomatoes, spinach, lasagne, and liver; roast beef; roast veal; meatballs; stuffed lettuce leaves; boiled cod; fried fish; stuffed mushrooms; pea sauce; sauce for *corzetti* (probably the Pine Nut–Marjoram Sauce on page 78); macaroni with mushrooms and sausage; *simma piena* (*cima ripiena,* see page 367); and "soup for the servants" (on Sunday they were served beef).

Additionally, the Spinolas kept a very rich pantry: rice; bread; chestnuts; cinnamon; onions; *bottarga* (dried tuna roe); salted fish such as anchovies; eggs; salami; pine nuts; dried chickpeas; salt cod; tuna; squash; fennel; sage; pepper; garlic; dried peas; dried mushrooms; olive oil; *fideli;* almonds; figs; and lemons.

A separate entry was made for foods that were donated to a nearby convent: capons; wine; biscuits; and chocolate.

A convent in Ventimiglia in 1802 had a rather ample shopping list, one that makes one wonder how the sisters passed their days: pasta; hazelnuts; stockfish (spelled Stockefix); rice; goat; salt; "Dutch cheese" — imported Gouda; Pecorino cheese; bread; fava beans; eggs; tuna; whitebait; chickpea flour; wine; cabbage; pork; anchovies; lard; saffron; "many, many" dried mushrooms and sardines; shoes; tobacco; needles; incense; candles; and soap.

In an 1804 listing from the same convent I found the only purchase, in all of my research, for "*una mescolanza dall'orto,*" or a mixture of vegetables and fruits from the garden. Apparently, vegetables, fruits, and herbs existed in such profusion in Liguria that they did not have to be purchased. We know this because documents of meals of the past indicate extensive consumption of vegetables, herbs, and fruit.

Sauces,
Condiments,
&
Spreads

16 PESTO RECIPES:

Classico; Antico; di Recco; di Camogli; di Sori; Vegia Zena; della Valpolcevara; del Levante; del Ponente; di Dolceacqua; Dolce; Forte; Corto; Gastronomico; al Frullatore; Bianco

Tocco de Noxe	Walnut Sauce
Crema ai Pinoli e Maggiorana	Pine Nut–Marjoram Sauce
Prescinseua (Traditional)	Prescinseua (Traditional)
Prescinseua (Less Traditional)	Prescinseua (Less Traditional)
Ricotta con le Cipolle	Onion-Scented Ricotta
Sugo di Pomodoro Fresco	Fresh Tomato Sauce
Salsa di Pomodori Secchi	Sun-Dried Tomato Sauce
Rattatuia	Tomato-Eggplant-Zucchini Sauce
Paté di Ortaggi	Garden Sauce
Salsa alla Genovese	Genoese Sauce
Sugo di Carciofi	Artichoke Sauce
Marò	Fava Bean Sauce
Tocco di Funghi	Mushroom Sauce
Pasta di Olive	Olive "Caviar"
Bagna Cauda	Hot Olive Oil–Anchovy Dip
Agliata/Aggiada	Garlic Sauce
Salsa alle Erbe Fresche	Fresh Herb Sauce
Salsa per i Pesci Fritti	Sauce for Fried Fish
Salsa Verde all'Antica	Old-Fashioned Herb Sauce for Fish
Salsa di Pinoli, Capperi, e Acciughe	Sauce of Pine Nuts, Capers, and Anchovies
Machetto	Sardine Sauce
Sugo di Muscoli	Mussel Sauce
Paté di Polpo	Octopus Sauce
Tocco	Genoese Meat Sauce
Sugo Negretto	Beef and Onion Sauce
Crema di Castagne al Profumo di Viola	Violet-Scented Chestnut Puree
Miele alle Rose	Rose Honey
Miele alle Viole	Violet Honey

$\mathcal{N}$O OTHER ITALIAN REGION uses sauces, condiments, and spreads to the extent found in Liguria. The principal reason for this is that so many fundamental Ligurian flavors are drawn from ingredients that appear only at certain times of the year, and then often in great abundance. So the frugal people of Liguria devised ingenious ways to capture and exalt these flavors and have them available throughout the year.

There are two other factors at play here. One, already discussed in the introduction, is that many Ligurians have always gone to sea for trade or for fishing. They want to take the fresh flavors of the land with them, and sauces, condiments, and spreads became a logical means to do that.

In addition, Ligurians, although they live in a splendid natural paradise that might incline them toward recreation and pleasure-seeking, have always had a remarkable propensity for work and take great pride in being industrious. So if a woman devotes some time each season to making and jarring sauces using foods that are in season, this will give her more time later to attend to other labors because the foundations of many of her meals will already be prepared.

Hardworking Ligurians can open a jar of a wonderful sauce and use it for pasta, on bread, with vegetables, fish, meat, or on sweets and will then have saved time in preparing a meal. As I am certain that you also are very busy, this application of Ligurian wisdom will work well in your life, too.

Almost every one of the oil-based sauces in this chapter, including pesto, can be stored in sterile jars as long as you fill them 90 percent with sauce and then seal it with a thin layer of olive oil before closing the jar. If, after opening the jar, you do not use all of the sauce, you should add a new layer of olive oil before closing it again. This will let the sauce last a few more days because oxygen will not penetrate it.

The cheese- and dairy-based sauces, such as *prescinseua* and *ricotta con le cipolle,* have a much shorter shelf-life, and you should refrigerate them once made and use them within a few days. The meat-based sauces should be refrigerated and used in a few days, or frozen and used within a month. Fresh tomato sauce should be used within twenty-four hours of being made. A sauce made from sun-dried tomatoes should be used immediately.

Whenever you prepare food at home, even foods that are not expressly Ligurian or even Italian, you will find yourself thinking of many of the sauces in this chapter. When you have bread, noodles, boiled potatoes, vegetables, fish, meat, cheese, biscuits, or certain fruit, you will find that one of the sauces in this chapter will turn a good ingredient into a great dish.

By keeping jars of some of your favorite sauces in the pantry, you will always have ingredients ready to serve food to unexpected guests or to make a special meal if you are unable to shop for fresh food. Above all, in every jar you will find the flavors of paradise.

Pesto

Pesto, the bewitchingly perfumed green sauce that is ubiquitous in the cooking and the hearts of every Ligurian, is now a citizen of the world. I have seen it in Tokyo, in Buenos Aires, and all throughout Europe and North America. Yet nowhere does it taste better than in Liguria, where cooks still take extraordinary care in gathering the ingredients and in making the sauce.

There is no single, definitive preparation for pesto. It varies a bit from town to town in Liguria, just like a dialect. Even within a town there will be differences in how pesto is made. Every single pesto that you will ever taste is unique, because the ingredients used will differ as will the skill and preferences of the person making the sauce. Even if you were to give two cooks equal amounts of basil, olive oil, pine nuts, garlic, and cheese from the same sources, the results

Throughout the region,
Ligurians sell homemade sauces in jars

will not be the same because of the hand and eye of the person who makes the pesto.

I must immediately address the question that I am most often asked about pesto. Yes, there is indeed a vast difference between pesto made with a mortar and pestle and that made in the blender. The flavor and perfume of the basil and the other ingredients are slowly released as they are gently pounded in the mortar. By contrast, the violent whirring of the blades and heat of the motor of a blender (*frullatore* in Italian) or food processor do not permit the release of the sensory elements of pesto's ingredients. Many people believe, as I do, that herbs and greens do not take well to metal blades, and the act of cutting robs herbs of some of their properties. You will notice throughout this book that I ask you to tear rather than cut herbs and lettuces.

A mortar and pestle mashes while the food processor or blender grinds. The flavors of herbs and nuts, their oils and essences, are released in a unique way that cannot be equaled in a machine. It is also quicker and easier to clean a mortar and pestle than a food processor. The whole process of making pesto by hand takes about twenty minutes, so do not be intimidated. Remember, the mortar must be of a certain size and weight so that it does not move about when you use it. The pestle should be made of wood — in Liguria it is traditionally made of olive wood, but you can use a wood pestle of any type.

And yes, many people in Liguria do make pesto with a blender. They acknowledge that it is not as good. But Ligurians who make pesto in a blender have a distinct advantage over most other people. Invariably, the basil they use will be much more flavorful and perfumed than that found elsewhere, so there are some compensations. However, most Ligurians will admit that handmade pesto is superior.

Many people assert, without much palpable evidence, that pesto is a relatively recent invention, probably of the nineteenth century. I am rather skeptical of this contention, because there are ancient sources that describe preparations similar to pesto, and basil has been in Liguria for more than a thousand years. Virgil describes a peasant who eats unleavened focaccia smeared with a paste made with garlic, rue, parsley, and dry cheese, all pounded in a mortar and made creamy with oil. This certainly is an antecedent of pesto.

There are sauces in the Arab world that have additions of oily nuts, including pine nuts and walnuts, and this tradition also came to Liguria through commerce. There is a centuries-old presence of Sardinian sheep's milk cheese (Pecorino) in Liguria, and a more recent presence of Parmigiano-Reggiano, made of cow's milk. There was even a period when Bra cheese, from nearby

Piedmont, was used in pesto. Ligurians have also used local products such as *prescinseua* and ricotta to flavor pesto, and there are even those cooks who add butter.

The most essential pesto ingredients are salt, basil, and olive oil. One can have a credible pesto without the pungency of garlic. Nuts and dairy products, which involved additional expenditures, came to pesto only when they became affordable. What will follow is a series of pesto recipes that I have encountered in nearly twenty-five years of visiting and living in Liguria. The first one will be the closest approximation I can offer of how pesto is eaten today in most of the region. You will then find fifteen other versions to make in a mortar and pestle, including two unusual but fully Ligurian preparations: Pesto Corto and Pesto Bianco. Finally, there will be a recipe for Pesto al Frullatore, pesto to be made in the blender. You may consult most of the other pesto recipes and adapt the ingredient combinations for use in the blender. But remember, it will not, cannot, be nearly as good as pesto you make in the mortar.

SELECTING AND USING INGREDIENTS FOR PESTO

BASIL: Ligurians have basil instinct. They believe the best basil comes in April and May, although it is cultivated through much of the year. To make pesto and for most other uses, they prefer small-leaf basil. The best basil is said to have round leaves, although these are increasingly hard to find. Small-leaf basil is more delicate and fragrant than larger-leaf basil (that usually found abroad), which has a hint of mint in fragrance and flavor. Seeds for small-leaf basil are now easy to find abroad — it is usually called Genovese basil. If you visit Liguria, buy packages of seeds and plant them when you get home or give them to your vegetable seller to have them planted.

There is another key issue: to wash or not to wash? Americans customarily wash greens and herbs for purposes of cleanliness. However, the natural oils in herbs are deadened by water and the resulting flavors are muted. Some Ligurians also wash their herbs, but most do not. Instead, they take paper toweling and rub the leaves carefully. This rubbing releases the fragrance of the herb and gets rid of any surface dirt on the leaves. Unless you feel the herbs have been treated with chemicals, you are better off rubbing rather than washing them. If you wash them, dry them gently rather than pressing them in the toweling. When you use basil for pesto, tear away the stems and remove the spine of the leaves. If you must use large-leaf basil, after removing the spine, tear the leaves in smaller pieces before adding them to the mortar. Make note of the fragrance and flavor of the basil you use, because this will influence the choice of ingredients you add to the sauce (most especially garlic and nuts).

SALT: The first ingredient to go into the mortar is a few crystals of coarse sea salt. The reason for this is that the salt protects the green color of the basil as it is mashed.

OLIVE OIL: Needless to say, pesto should be made with Ligurian olive oil. It is more delicate than most other oils and is, after all, the flavor of the region. If you cannot get Ligurian oil, select a delicate, fruity oil from Lake Garda, Tuscany, Umbria, Lazio, or Puglia.

GARLIC: Ligurian garlic is not necessarily as powerful and assertive as that found elsewhere. If you use garlic, smell how overpowering it is before determining how much of it you will use. In every case, peel the clove, split it in half and remove the green heart, which adds bitterness.

PINOLI: Pine nuts add oil and sweetness to pesto and tend to go well with Parmigiano-Reggiano.

WALNUTS: These add dryness and a slight pucker and tend to go well with Pecorino. Be sure to use unsalted walnuts.

PECORINO: Purchase a chunk of hard Pecorino from either Sardinia or Lazio (Romano) for grating. If you use pre-grated cheese or (heaven forfend!) non-Italian cheese, you will not be making real pesto.

PARMIGIANO-REGGIANO: As with Pecorino, you should buy a chunk of genuine cheese from Emilia-Romagna and grate it just before you use it in the sauce.

PARSLEY: Some chefs add a little parsley to give more color and freshness to pesto. You should use Italian (flat) parsley leaves and discard the stems.

RICOTTA: If possible, you should go to a good cheese seller and ask for ricotta romana, which is as close to traditional ricotta as you will be able to find. It should be fresh and slightly sweet. The type that is in the plastic container on the supermarket shelf is just not as good.

PRESCINSEUA: If you wish to use *prescinseua* or one of its substitutes, see page 79.

USING PESTO

A general rule about pesto is that it should not be heated. It is at its best at room temperature, when all of its ingredients can express themselves fully. The most traditional way to use pesto is as a sauce for pasta. Ligurians usually take a tablespoon of the hot water (called *aegua de vianda* in dialect) from the pot where the noodles cooked and spoon it into the pesto moments before adding the noodles to the sauce. This hot water lengthens the pesto and wakes it up a bit, causing it to release fragrance and flavor.

Because it is vividly flavored, you do not need to use as much sauce as you might be tempted to. One to two tablespoons per diner are sufficient in most cases, although you may not be able to resist adding more. Many people do, and occasionally so do I. In Genoa it is traditional to add a few thin string beans along with some pieces of boiled potato (see the recipe for Trenette alla Genovese, page 226).

Other uses for pesto include stirring it into soup (especially minestrone) just before it is served. The pesto added to minestrone usually does not contain *pinoli* or walnuts, but I have never found out why.

Try smearing some pesto on focaccia as a heavenly snack. It can also be added to poached or grilled fish, meat, or vegetables, as long as you remember not to heat the sauce first.

STORING PESTO

You may wish to make larger batches, especially if you have a lot of good fresh basil at hand. After it is made, put the basil in small sterile jars, filling them 90 percent. Then add a layer of olive oil as a buffer to protect the sauce from exposure to oxygen that would spoil it. When you open the jar, dip your spoon past the oil to reach the sauce. If you do not use all of the sauce, check how much oil remains on top, and then add a drop more to totally seal the sauce. There is debate about whether or not to refrigerate the sauce, especially if the jar has been opened. Ligurians store their jars in dark places, even after they have been opened. My inclination is to store unopened jars in the pantry, but once the jar has been opened it goes into the fridge. The cold does rob the sauce of some of its flavor, but I am concerned about spoilage, especially if there is cheese present in the sauce. Unopened jars of pesto can usually last up to six months in the pantry. There are some proponents of freezing pesto (though not in Liguria), although I feel the cold kills most of the delicate properties of the sauce. Freeze at your own risk.

Pesto Classico

Classic Pesto

1 pinch coarse sea salt
60 small or 30 large fresh basil leaves, carefully wiped, stems and spines removed
2 cloves garlic, peeled, with the green heart removed
3 tablespoons/22 g pinoli
2 tablespoons/15 g fresh, finely grated Pecorino Romano
2 tablespoons/15 g fresh, finely grated Parmigiano-Reggiano
3 to 4 tablespoons/45 to 60 ml Ligurian extravirgin olive oil

*Makes about
1 cup/225 ml*

Add the sea salt and a few of the basil leaves to your marble mortar. Using a wooden pestle, crush the leaves and salt gently but with a firm rhythm against the bottom and sides of the mortar so that the leaves gradually come apart. Keep adding leaves a few at a time until they are all used. While the leaves are still partly intact, add the garlic and then pound it too, just until it is mashed and has released its juice. Then add the *pinoli* and pound them until they are reduced to paste. Stir the pestle in the mortar so that the ingredients combine. Then add the Pecorino Romano and Parmigiano-Reggiano and stir again to combine the ingredients. Now add the olive oil a little at a time, stirring with the pestle to make a sauce of a creamy consistency. Some people like more oil, some less, so the amount I recommend is a guideline. Your goal is to have a thick creamy sauce. If you choose not to use all of the oil, that is fine. The result should be fully amalgamated and of a medium bright green color.

San Fruttuoso

"San Fruttuosa [sic], a tiny fishing village, owes its origin to a colony of monks who settled there in the tenth century. The early Gothic church contains a Roman sarcophagus and the tombs of the Doria family. Its primary charm, however, is its superb bathing. The water is so translucent that those miniature snorkel devices used for mullet-spearing are quite unnecessary. One can lie on one's face head down in the water and see everything for yards around. There is only one word of warning and that is to avoid going there on Sundays when the tiny harbour is crowded with pleasure craft and it is almost impossible to bathe owing to the complete lack of privacy. Not that the Italians mind undressing quite openly on the beach before putting on their swim suits.

"The owner of the local trattoria must make a fortune. His prices are equivalent to those in Rome. At least, however, his fish and shellfish come straight out of the sea below him, so that they are wonderfully fresh. The village consists really of this — the Unica — and an ancient monastery which has been converted into a communal block of flats. The population is 105 men, women and children who derive their living entirely from the sea. Some of their bronze fishing nets hanging up to dry are at least thirty yards long. The Unica has a specialty of basil butter, a green sauce the ingredients of which are cheese, cream, garlic and young pine kernels beaten with a pestle."

— Charles Graves, *Italy Revisited,* 1950

It is remarkable how little has changed in San Fruttuoso a half century after Graves wrote his observations. Certainly, anyone who goes there now will know that the "basil butter" is pesto and that it does not contain cream, as Graves stated. But San Fruttuoso still has a tiny beach chockablock with partially clad people just below a monastery, fully asserting the separation of Church and State. The population has not grown much, although there are more visitors arriving on pleasure craft and hourly ferries from Portofino and Camogli. And the trattoria is still there, except that it is now called da Giovanni.

Pesto Antico

Ancient Pesto

The first pesto that had added cheese only contained Pecorino from Sardinia. It also had a little more garlic and fewer nuts than the classic version.

1 pinch coarse sea salt
60 small or 30 large fresh basil leaves, carefully wiped, stems and spines removed
2 to 3 cloves garlic, peeled, with the green heart removed
1 to 2 tablespoons/7 to 15 g unsalted walnuts or pinoli
4 tablespoons/60 g fresh, finely grated Pecorino Romano
3 to 4 tablespoons/45 to 60 ml Ligurian extravirgin olive oil

*Makes about
1 cup/225 ml*
Prepare as you would the Pesto Classico (page 66), but use the amounts indicated above.

Pesto di Recco

In Recco they traditionally use *prescinseua* in their pesto, and minimize the use of garlic. This is the pesto that one traditionally serves with *trofie* pasta.

1 pinch coarse sea salt
60 small or 30 large fresh basil leaves, carefully wiped, stems and spines removed
1 small clove garlic, peeled, with the green heart removed
1 tablespoon/7 g pinoli
3 to 4 tablespoons/45 to 60 ml prescinseua (see page 79)
3 to 4 tablespoons/45 to 60 ml Ligurian extravirgin olive oil

*Makes about
1 cup/225 ml*
Prepare as you would the Pesto Classico (page 66), but use the amounts indicated above.

Pesto di Camogli

In sweet Camogli they like their pesto sweet, so there is no garlic, and ricotta is the dominant cheese.

1 pinch coarse sea salt
60 small or 30 large fresh basil leaves, carefully wiped, stems and spines removed
2 tablespoons/15 g pinoli
3 to 4 tablespoons/22 to 30 g ricotta
3 to 4 tablespoons/45 to 60 ml Ligurian extravirgin olive oil

Prepare as you would the Pesto Classico (page 66), but use the amounts indicated above. The pesto should be creamy, but if you are using basil that is not intensely fragrant and flavored, diminish the amount of ricotta you use, or the result will be pallid.

Makes about
1 cup/225 ml

Pesto di Sori

In Sori, not a mile away from Recco, the pesto is distinct. There, wild fennel becomes part of the sauce, along with ricotta.

1 pinch coarse sea salt
60 small or 30 large fresh basil leaves, carefully wiped, stems and spines removed
2 teaspoons/3 g wild fennel
1 small clove garlic, peeled, with the green heart removed
1 tablespoon/7 g pinoli
3 to 4 tablespoons/22 to 30 g ricotta
3 to 4 tablespoons/45 to 60 ml Ligurian extravirgin olive oil

Prepare as you would the Pesto Classico (page 66), but use the amounts indicated above. The wild fennel should be added with the basil.

Makes about
1 cup/225 ml

Pesto Vegia Zena
"Old Genoa" Pesto

The name means "Old Genoa," and this is a very traditional pesto that is mainly basil, with few nuts and little cheese.

1 large pinch coarse sea salt
100 small or 50 large fresh basil leaves, carefully wiped, stems and spines removed
2 cloves garlic, peeled, with the green heart removed
1 tablespoon/7 g pinoli
1 tablespoon/7 g fresh, finely grated Pecorino Romano
3 to 4 tablespoons/45 to 60 ml Ligurian extravirgin olive oil

Makes about
1 cup/225 ml
Prepare as you would the Pesto Classico (page 66), but use the amounts indicated above.

Pesto della Valpolcevara

In the *entroterra* between Genoa and Lombardy, they like their pesto with a little Parmigiano-Reggiano, and a combination of nuts.

1 pinch coarse sea salt
60 small or 30 large fresh basil leaves, carefully wiped, stems and spines removed
2 cloves garlic, peeled, with the green heart removed
2 tablespoons/15 g pinoli
2 tablespoons/15 g unsalted walnuts
2 tablespoons/15 g fresh, finely grated Parmigiano-Reggiano
3 to 4 tablespoons/45 to 60 ml Ligurian extravirgin olive oil

Makes about
1 cup/225 ml
Prepare as you would the Pesto Classico (page 66), but use the amounts indicated above.

Pesto del Levante

This is the sort of pesto you would find between Rapallo and Levanto. It combines a preference for less garlic along with a mixture of cheeses and nuts.

1 pinch coarse sea salt
60 small or 30 large fresh basil leaves, carefully wiped, stems and spines removed
1 small clove garlic, peeled, with the green heart removed (optional)
2 tablespoons/15 g pinoli
2 tablespoons/15 g unsalted walnuts
2 tablespoons/15 g fresh, finely grated Parmigiano-Reggiano
1 tablespoon/7 g fresh, finely grated Pecorino Romano
1 tablespoon/7 g or 15 ml ricotta or prescinseua
3 to 4 tablespoons/45 to 60 ml Ligurian extravirgin olive oil

Prepare as you would the Pesto Classico (page 66), but use the amounts indicated above. You should do salt and basil, then the optional garlic, then the nuts together, then the two grated cheeses, then the creamy cheese, then the oil.

Makes about
1 cup/225 ml

Pesto del Ponente

This is the sort of pesto you would find around Savona. It combines a preference for more garlic along with a mixture of cheeses.

1 pinch coarse sea salt
60 small or 30 large fresh basil leaves, carefully wiped, stems and spines removed
3 cloves garlic, peeled, with the green heart removed
2 tablespoons/15 g pinoli
2 tablespoons/15 g unsalted walnuts
2 tablespoons/15 g fresh, finely grated Parmigiano-Reggiano
2 tablespoons/15 g fresh, finely grated Pecorino Romano
3 to 4 tablespoons/45 to 60 ml Ligurian extravirgin olive oil

Prepare as you would the Pesto Classico (page 66), but use the amounts indicated above. Pound the *pinoli* and walnuts together.

Makes about
1 cup/225 ml

Upon Entering the Riviera di Ponente from France

"Starting from the French frontier at Pont St. Louis, near Menton, we may pause almost immediately to stop at Mortola, where on a picturesque promontory an English family [Hanbury] has created a world-famous garden containing some 6000 different plants. Hence, passing Ventimiglia with its population of flower merchants and customs officials, we come to the classic section of the Riviera di Ponente. This begins at Bordighera, a well-laid-out winter resort with a promenade commanding an exceptional view. Here one first becomes conscious of the luxuriance of vegetation which is the chief attraction of the Italian Riviera. The almond, the olive and the fig grow without risk upon these sheltered slopes; the lower terraces are bright with oranges and lemons; while the numerous public and private gardens display a never-ending succession of magnificent flowering plants and shrubs. Similar, though smaller, is the adjacent resort of Ospedaletti. Four miles further is San Remo, the largest, grandest and warmest of the Italian winter resorts. This is the greatest centre of the flower trade, conducting even in midwinter a vast exportation of roses, violets, hyacinths and carnations."

— Jasper More, *The Land of Italy,* 1949

Pesto di Dolceacqua

Although I have tasted this unusual pesto three times in Dolceacqua, no one has been able to confirm for me that it is the town's traditional preparation. So the name is my addition, but the recipe is as I tasted it. What makes this version unique is that there is almost no pounding. It is, instead, a suspension of pesto ingredients in olive oil. I have used it on pasta, of course, but it is also wonderful on *bruschetta* or on poached or grilled fish. Unlike other pestos, you should not add cooking water from the pasta when using this sauce. Obviously, this pesto cannot be made in a blender.

1 pinch coarse sea salt
2 cloves garlic, peeled, with the green heart removed
60 small or 30 large fresh basil leaves, carefully wiped, stems and spines removed
3 tablespoons/22 g pinoli
4 to 5 tablespoons/60 to 75 ml Ligurian extravirgin olive oil, preferably fruttato

Pound the salt and the garlic together in your mortar. Then tear all of the basil leaves into small pieces and add them to the mortar. Then add the *pinoli* (do not pound them). Now add the olive oil. You will be using a bit more than you would for other versions of pesto, and its golden color will be dominant. Stir so that all the ingredients are fully incorporated in the oil.

*Makes about
1 cup/225 ml*

Pesto Dolce
Sweet Pesto

This sweet pesto must be made with the tiny leaves typical of Liguria. It is made more sweet by the exclusive use of Parmigiano and *pinoli,* and optional butter, along with the *olio fruttato,* the fruity olive oil that is so classically Ligurian.

1 pinch coarse sea salt
60 small fresh basil leaves, carefully wiped, stems and spines removed
3 tablespoons/22 g pinoli
1 tablespoon/7 g sweet butter (optional)
3 tablespoons/22 g fresh, finely grated Parmigiano-Reggiano
3 to 4 tablespoons/45 to 60 ml Ligurian extravirgin olive oil, preferably fruttato

Prepare as you would the Pesto Classico (page 66), but use the amounts indicated above.

*Makes about
1 cup/225 ml*

Pesto Forte

Sharp Pesto

This sharp pesto is popular with people who like more piquant flavors, or those who have only large-leaf basil at hand.

1 pinch coarse sea salt
40 large fresh basil leaves, carefully wiped, stems and spines removed
4 tablespoons / 30 g unsalted walnuts
4 tablespoons / 30 g fresh, finely grated Pecorino Romano
3 to 4 tablespoons / 45 to 60 ml Ligurian extravirgin olive oil

*Makes about
1 cup / 225 ml* Prepare as you would the Pesto Classico (page 66), but use the amounts indicated above.

Pesto Corto

"Short" Pesto

In Genoa *pesto corto,* or short pesto, was first made as an economical measure since the ingredients for traditional pesto could be pricey and tomatoes are plentiful and cheap. This is a sauce that some people dote on because it can be very tasty, but other people look at it as merely second-best to classic pesto. The pasta shapes of choice for this sauce are *trenette* (linguine) or penne.

1 cup / 225 ml freshly made pesto
*½ pound / 250 g ripe plum tomatoes, washed, diced into small cubes, with many seeds
 removed*

*Makes
6 servings* After making the pesto (preferably in a mortar), stir in the pieces of tomato. After cooking your pasta al dente, you may either toss all of the sauce and noodles in a bowl and then serve, or place a portion of pasta on individual plates and then top with 2 tablespoons of *pesto corto.*

Pesto Gastronomico

Pesto for Tourists

This is a more modern pesto, one that is thought to appeal to foreign tastes. You often see it in tourist restaurants.

1 pinch coarse sea salt
50 small or 25 large fresh basil leaves, carefully wiped, stems and spines removed
2 tablespoons / 15 g fresh Italian (flat) parsley
1 clove garlic, peeled, with the green heart removed
3 tablespoons / 22 g pinoli
1 tablespoon / 7 g unsalted walnuts
4 tablespoons / 30 g fresh, finely grated Parmigiano-Reggiano
3 to 4 tablespoons / 45 to 60 ml Ligurian extravirgin olive oil, preferably fruttato

Prepare as you would the Pesto Classico (page 66), but use the amounts indicated above.

*Makes about
1 cup / 225 ml*

Pesto al Frullatore

Blender Pesto

Just in case you did not fully appreciate the intensity of my message as indicated elsewhere: Blender pesto is inferior to that made in a mortar, and there is not much extra work involved in using a mortar. The difference is because the flavors of the ingredients are released more slowly and gently in the mortar. If, however, you must use a blender (for example, there are people with arthritis or limited use of their hands who cannot use a mortar and pestle), you may use any of the above listed pesto recipes except for Pesto di Dolceacqua to make blender pesto.

BLENDER METHOD: Place all of the ingredients in a blender, except that you should add only 1 tablespoon of olive oil instead of the whole amount indicated. Blend at high speed for 1 minute. Then lift the lid carefully and scrape the sides of the blender cup using a rubber spatula. Check the consistency of the ingredients, which should be thick and somewhat creamy. Blend for a few more seconds if you think the pesto should be a bit thinner, but don't overdo it. Remove the contents to a bowl and then spoon in the rest of the olive oil a little at a time until you reach the desired consistency. A few cooks, after making blender pesto, add a touch of heavy cream to the sauce, but this is optional.

Pesto Bianco

White Pesto

Unlike the faddish but ultimately unsatisfying white chocolate, which can never replace the dark stuff, there is a validity to white pesto. It applies the same techniques as pesto and can be put to similar uses. The chief difference is that basil, the unquestioned star of pesto, has taken the night off and what remains in white pesto is most of the supporting cast, to which ricotta has been added. White pesto is significantly richer and more fattening than most Ligurian sauces, and might be considered for a special occasion. The recipe as you see it below is popular in parts of the Levante and is traditionally used with fresh noodles such as tagliatelle or with lasagne (as described in the recipe on page 244).

24 walnuts, shelled, or 48 unsalted walnut halves
1 clove garlic
4 tablespoons / 60 ml Ligurian extravirgin olive oil
2 cups / 225 g fresh ricotta
A grinding of white pepper (optional)
3 ounces / ⅜ cup / 6 tablespoons / 85 ml whole milk (optional)

Makes about 3 cups / 675 ml

Pound the walnut meats in a mortar until you have coarse grains, not unlike sand. Then pound the garlic until it is finely minced. If you prefer to do these two steps in a blender or a food processor you may do so, but the mortar is always preferable. Either keep the ingredients in the mortar or transfer them to a bowl. Add in the olive oil a little at a time, stirring gently so that the grains of walnut absorb a bit of the oil. Once the oil has been added, stir in the ricotta a little at a time (and the optional pepper), and then stir the whole combination more aggressively so that it is airy and fluffy. Do this only for less than a minute because you do not want this sauce to get too warm. If you feel that the sauce is too thick, add a little bit of milk, but not more than the amount indicated above. The sauce should be creamy — neither too dense nor too runny. This sauce should be used as soon as it is prepared.

Tocco de Noxe

Walnut Sauce

Tocco de noxe is probably of western Asian origin. It appeared in ancient Persian cuisine and still turns up in certain dishes in the Balkans and around the Black Sea. Given that the medieval Republic of Genoa traded heavily at Black Sea ports, the idea for the sauce probably originated there, although it has become a distinctly Ligurian food that marries well with many classic Riviera dishes. Traditionally this sauce is used to top *pansôti,* the herb-filled pasta that is classically Ligurian. But the walnut sauce is also very good with gnocchi, tortelloni, or even with boiled meats such as pork or veal. In its purest form, *tocco de noxe* includes *prescinseua* (see page 79). Nowadays many Ligurians use fresh whole milk or fresh ricotta that has been diluted with a little water. It is festive and delicious when spread on bread. There is a saying in Liguria — *"Pan e noxe, mangià da spoze"* ("Bread and walnuts, the food of brides").

7 ounces/200 g unsalted walnut meats
2 tablespoons/30 g unflavored bread crumbs
1 clove garlic, with the green heart removed, minced
Sea salt (optional)
2 tablespoons/30 g fresh, finely grated Parmigiano-Reggiano
1 pinch minced fresh marjoram
¾ cup/170 ml prescinseua, or 5 ounces/140 g fresh ricotta diluted with a bit of
*   tepid water*
4 tablespoons/60 ml Ligurian extravirgin olive oil

Place the walnuts, bread crumbs, garlic, and salt in a mortar and pound with a pestle to form a paste. Alternatively, place these ingredients in a blender or food processor and blend until they form a paste. Transfer to a bowl if you are not using a mortar and pestle. Add the Parmigiano-Reggiano and the marjoram. Then add the *prescinseua* or diluted ricotta to the sauce. Finally, add the olive oil to the mixture, a bit at a time, stirring to combine the ingredients.

Makes about
1 cup/225 ml

Crema ai Pinoli e Maggiorana
Pine Nut–Marjoram Sauce

This sauce is especially popular in Genoa as the ideal match for pasta that has been made with marjoram (typically *corzetti* or tagliatelle). If the pasta is made without marjoram, you should add some to this sauce. I would also recommend *crema ai pinoli* (with or without marjoram) for any stuffed vegetable recipe that calls for butter as part of the filling or to be slathered on hot farinata or plain focaccia.

6 (4 + 2) tablespoons/45 (30 + 15) g pinoli
1 small clove garlic, peeled, with the green heart removed
2 sprigs fresh marjoram, minced (only if it is not used elsewhere in the dish being prepared)
1 pinch sea salt
8 tablespoons/¼ pound/100 g sweet butter, softened
Approximately 1 tablespoon/15 ml whole or partially skimmed milk

Makes about 1½ cups/350 ml

Pound 4 tablespoons/30 grams of the *pinoli* in a mortar until they form a fine paste. Add the peeled garlic, marjoram, and salt and pound until the ingredients are amalgamated. Then add the butter and the remaining 2 tablespoons/15 grams of *pinoli* and gently fold the ingredients together without working the mixture too much. It should be slightly creamy, but you may choose to add a little milk to achieve a texture that is a bit softer. Add the milk judiciously and do not use more than 1 tablespoon. When dressing pasta with this sauce, it should be cool but not cold, or else the pasta will be unduly chilled.

STORAGE NOTE: This sauce is highly perishable and, because it is made with butter and a delicate nut, is susceptible to picking up any flavors and smells that are nearby. At most, this sauce should be stored overnight, preferably in an air-tight plastic container or a dish that is tightly covered with plastic wrap.

Prescinseua

Prescinseua is not, strictly speaking, a sauce, condiment, or spread, but rather is a fundamental ingredient in Ligurian food. It can be used in pesto, in walnut sauce, and often is stirred into other dishes in small amounts to give them a creamy tang. Some Ligurians have a bit of *prescinseua* at breakfast with fruit and a little sugar, or spooned onto thin bread and served with a glass of very light white wine as an aperitif. *Prescinseua* is a Ligurian word; in Italian it is either called *quagliata* or *latte cagliata*. The closest term in English is probably clabber, a sort of clotted sour milk. Ligurians occasionally substitute ricotta for *prescinseua*, but this will not have the same effect. You will come closer if you use half ricotta combined with half buttermilk or tangy yogurt. What follow are two recipes for *prescinseua*. The first is a more traditional preparation that takes a little more time but will have classic results. The second is a useful means of having a small amount of something that will approximate *prescinseua* without the extra effort.

Prescinseua (Traditional)

2 quarts / 2 liters whole milk
4 drops / 5 g single-strength rennet (see page 456)

Let the milk sit in a covered pot for 48 hours. Then remove 1 cup/¼ liter of the milk to another pot. Heat gently (to about 105°–120°F/40°–50°C) and then add the rennet, stirring well. Add this mixture to the larger pot of milk, cover, and let sit for 4 hours. The result should be somewhat solid. It may be sliced, or cut in smaller pieces to make it creamier. Store, tightly covered, for up to a week, in the refrigerator.

*Makes
2 quarts / liters*

Prescinseua (Less Traditional)

6 ounces / 170 ml whole milk
1 teaspoon / 5 ml lemon juice
A little light cream

*Makes
2 tablespoons*

Gently heat the milk only until it is tepid — do not let it boil. Then add the lemon juice, stir, and heat until the milk almost reaches a boil. Remove from the heat and cover. The milk will quickly coagulate. Then strain through a sieve or cheesecloth, separating the whey from the curds. Add a touch of cream to the whey, and you will have your sauce. I recommend that you place the curds in a bowl and stir or pound them with a spoon until they become creamy. Then combine with the cream/whey mixture.

Ricotta con le Cipolle
Onion-Scented Ricotta

The taste and fragrance of onion is a prominent minor chord in the symphony of flavors of the westernmost part of the Ponente. As often as not these onions are sweet rather than sharp, so that they work as a supporting character rather than a protagonist. Try to use a sweet onion such as Vidalia. If you want something slightly more assertive, use fresh chives (known in Italian as *erba cipollina*). This combination of onions, olive oil, and ricotta has two primary uses. It can be spread on toasted bread for an antipasto or, better still, can become a sauce for pasta. I would recommend penne if you are using dried pasta and tagliarini for fresh pasta. But the best way to use Ricotta con le Cipolle is as a sauce for gnocchi. You may use plain Gnocchi (page 216), Chestnut Gnocchi (page 218), or Gnocchi Variegati (page 219).

1 ounce / 4½ tablespoons / 30 g finely minced sweet onion or chive
Scant 8 ounces / scant 2 cups / 200 g fresh ricotta romana
2 tablespoons / 30 ml Ligurian extravirgin olive oil
1 pinch sea salt (optional)
Slight amount freshly ground black pepper (optional)

After mincing the onion, place it in a bowl or a mortar. Add the ricotta, olive oil, and optional salt and pepper. Stir until the ingredients have combined and the mixture takes in a bit of air and becomes fluffy. Use immediately.

Makes about 2 cups / 230 grams

VARIATION: When using this as a pasta sauce or as a spread for bread or toasts, it is possible to add a few boiled whole baby shrimp. As with most everything in Ligurian cuisine, this addition should be moderate and judicious, with the shrimp providing an additional flavor note rather than dominating the preparation. For a slice of bread or a portion of pasta, 4 or 5 baby shrimp should be sufficient.

Can be a pasta sauce for 4 servings

Sugo di Pomodoro Fresco

Fresh Tomato Sauce

The better translation of the Italian should really be tomato juice. In effect, this is the simplest of sauces, made only of tomato liquid and pulp, plus salt. Any self-respecting Ligurian cook will also add olive oil, and for Ligurian dining you should do the same.

3 pounds/1350 g ripe plum or beefsteak tomatoes*
Sea salt
2 tablespoons/30 ml Ligurian extravirgin olive oil
A few fresh basil leaves, wiped clean

> * If fresh tomatoes are not available, you may use two 28-ounce/800 g cans of excellent imported tomatoes from Italy. I recommend using any brand that indicates that the can contains San Marzano tomatoes. In preparing this recipe using canned tomatoes, you should use the liquid in the can and coarsely chop the tomatoes, which have already been peeled. Read the label to see if salt has already been added to the tomatoes. If it has, taste a bit of the liquid and adjust your addition of salt accordingly.

Makes about 1 quart/900 ml

Set a large pot of water to boil. In the meantime, wash the tomatoes. When the water reaches a full boil, drop 1 or 2 tomatoes in for about 30 seconds each. Remove with a slotted spoon. This will allow you to easily slip the skins off the tomatoes. Set the peeled tomatoes aside and repeat the process until they are all peeled. Now take a colander or strainer and set it over a large bowl or dish. Slice each tomato in half over the strainer so that the seeds will be captured but the juice will pass through to the bowl. Once this is done, pour all the juice in a saucepan, chop the tomatoes coarsely, and add them to the pan. Add a liberal pinch of sea salt and heat over moderately high heat for 1 hour. The result will be a rather condensed sauce that is concentrated in flavor and texture. Let the sauce cool slightly and then stir in 2 tablespoons of the best Ligurian extra-virgin olive oil you have. The oil will give the sauce a glistening sheen and will enhance its glorious flavor. Add the basil leaves at the moment you serve the sauce. If you plan to make pasta immediately after you have made the sauce, turn off the heat under the boiling water and then turn it on again once the sauce is done and you are ready to proceed with the cooking of the pasta.

Salsa di Pomodori Secchi

Sun-Dried Tomato Sauce

This sauce is a legacy of the time when tomatoes were dried to be used in the winter months. It is delicious on pasta or on toasted bread. It also is great as a condiment with meat, fish, vegetables, or cheese. It is also easy to make, especially if you have sun-dried tomatoes that are packed in olive oil. Note that if the tomatoes are not packed in oil, you should soak them in warm water for at least two hours to soften them and then add some olive oil to the sauce. A mortar and pestle are the preferred tools, although a blender is acceptable. I provide the ingredient list, but leave the amounts and proportions to your imagination. Some people like intense tomato flavor, while others prefer other palpable flavors — salt, garlic, lemon, nuts, and oil.

Coarse sea salt (used in moderation)
Garlic (optional)
Sun-dried tomatoes packed in olive oil
  (see page 312 to learn how to make these yourself)
Juice of fresh lemon (optional, and used in moderation)
Pinoli
Ligurian extravirgin olive oil (especially if your tomatoes are not oil-packed)

If using a mortar and pestle, separate the tomatoes from the oil. First pound the salt and optional garlic. Then add the tomatoes and pound them, taking care not to splash yourself with oil that might squirt out of the mortar. Add some optional lemon juice for flavor and then add *pinoli* (do not crush them). Finally add the oil the tomatoes were packed in (or fresh oil if you prefer), but just enough to make the sauce velvety rather than oily.

If you are using a blender, combine the salt, garlic, tomatoes, and lemon juice and blend at high speed for about 1 minute. Then remove the contents to a bowl, add the *pinoli* and enough oil to make the sauce velvety (you will probably use a little less oil in this case than if you used the mortar and pestle).

Rattatuia
Tomato-Eggplant-Zucchini Sauce

Here is a sauce that is very similar to ratatouille (in name as well as constitution). It is simple to execute if you are careful not to burn any of the ingredients, which will make many of the sweet vegetable flavors harsh and bitter. Ideally, you should use *prim-izie,* the first vegetables of the spring, which are most delicate in flavor and texture. However, this is a sauce you can make for months using more "adult" vegetables. Rat-tatuia is an ideal dressing for Gnocchi Variegati (page 219), and it goes well with all gnocchi, with tagliarini, in lasagne, or on dried pasta such as penne. It is also excellent spooned onto toasted Italian bread as an antipasto, and it is the perfect visual and gus-tatory accompaniment on a plate with poached fish. Rattatuia is good hot or tepid.

1 medium green, red, or yellow pepper, washed, cored, cut into thin strips
4 (1 + 3) tablespoons/60 (15 + 45) ml Ligurian extravirgin olive oil
2 baby eggplants, cut into thin disks or 1 medium eggplant, cut into small cubes, with
*   as many seeds removed as possible*
2 baby zucchini, cut into small pieces or 1 medium zucchini, cut into thin disks
Flour
4 ripe plum tomatoes
20 small or 12 large basil leaves, carefully wiped and then torn
1 clove garlic, green heart removed, cut into thin slivers
1 teaspoon/2 g pinoli *(optional)*

Makes 4 servings
for pasta or gnocchi

After cutting the pepper, heat 1 tablespoon of olive oil in a deep pan and then sauté the pepper slivers until they are soft. Fish out the slivers and set aside. *Lightly* flour the eggplant and zucchini pieces. Add the other 3 tablespoons of oil to the pan and swirl before heating. Once the oil is hot but not splattering, add the eggplant and zucchini and sauté for 1 minute. Then add the tomatoes, basil, garlic slivers, and the sautéed peppers. Turn down the heat, partially cover the pan, and simmer for 20 minutes. Initially the vegetables will yield their liq-uid, but then everything will concentrate and the flavors will intensify. Once it is cooked, you may stir in 1 teaspoon of *pinoli,* which will lend a slight crunch and a buttery taste.

Paté di Ortaggi

Garden Sauce

This is a versatile and delicious sauce that can be used in many ways. While there are numerous variations that can be applied in making this sauce, based on the ingredients you have at hand, this one is typical of Albenga, a town in the Ponente that is famous for its artichokes. Spoon some Paté di Ortaggi on bread as antipasto, or toss with pasta as a *primo*. I have also made risotto to which I have spooned in one tablespoon of this sauce per person a few minutes before the risotto is served. It is good as a condiment with grilled chicken breast as well as tuna steaks.

4 ounces / 1 cup / 100 g sun-dried tomatoes packed in olive oil
4 ounces / 1 cup / 100 g baby artichokes cured in olive oil (If at all possible these should
  be Ligurian. The jarred varieties from Spain, Argentina, and elsewhere are too acrid,
  and the ones from California tend to be dull.)
½ cup / 60 g fresh basil leaves, carefully wiped
¼ cup / 30 g unsalted walnut meats
1 tablespoon / 7 g minced fresh peperoncino (or 1 teaspoon dried chile pepper)
4 ounces / 1 cup / 100 g Taggia olive paste (see page 94)
Ligurian extravirgin olive oil

The ideal method for making this sauce is with a mortar and pestle. The tomatoes, artichokes, basil leaves, walnuts, and *peperoncino* would all be mashed and then the olive paste and olive oil would be added. I urge you to make it this way or, at the very least, use a knife to cut the tomatoes and artichokes into small pieces and to make a thick paste in the blender or food processor with the basil, walnuts, and *peperoncino*. In the mortar pound the ingredients (tomatoes, artichokes, basil, walnuts, and *peperoncino*) to form a paste. Then stir in the olive paste and combine thoroughly. If you feel the sauce is too dense, add olive oil, a little bit at a time. If you plan to store this sauce in a jar, use a sterile one and cover the sauce with a layer of olive oil. Once you have opened the sauce, it should be stored in the refrigerator and topped with a little more oil.

Makes about 2½ cups / 570 ml

If you must use an electric device (such as a blender or food processor) to make this sauce, make a paste of each ingredient separately and in each case only briefly use your machine. The heat of the blades and the machine will alter the flavor of the ingredient being blended. Once you have made all of these pastes, combine them in a bowl. Then proceed as indicated above, first adding the olive paste and then a judicious amount of olive oil.

Salsa alla Genovese

Genoese Sauce

If you see the term *genovese* in general Italian cookery books, two things come to mind. If it refers to a dish that connotes Liguria, then *genovese* would mean the presence of pesto. In Naples, *genovese* is a sauce of meat and onions and it has nothing to do with Liguria. But Salsa alla Genovese is something else again. This is a flavorful vegetable–red wine sauce that is considered an ideal condiment for poached fish.

6 shallots, minced
1 clove garlic, green heart removed, minced
4 large or 5 medium carrots, washed and peeled, then minced
4 tablespoons/60 ml Ligurian extravirgin olive oil
2 sprigs fresh thyme, torn into small pieces
1 tablespoon/7 g unbleached, all-purpose flour
Sea salt to taste
Freshly ground pepper to taste
1½ cups/12 ounces/350 ml light- to medium-weight red wine such as Rossese di
    Dolceacqua or Dolcetto

*Makes about
1½ cups/350 ml*

After preparing the shallots, garlic, and carrots, heat the olive oil in a heavy-bottomed pot over medium heat. Add the shallots, garlic, and carrots and sauté until the shallots become translucent and the combination gives off a beguiling fragrance. Then add the thyme, followed by the flour, stirring so that all the ingredients combine. Add salt and pepper to taste, and then the wine. Place a lid on the pot so that it is almost entirely covered, but leave a little gap for steam to escape. Cook for about an hour over very low heat. Depending on how you prefer the sauce, you may strain the liquid out or keep it as it is in the pot, which is a rather thick sauce that really seems like a condiment. Ideally, the sauce is served at room temperature, but I also like it hot, especially if the sauce is served with cold poached fish.

*This proud lion protects Genoa's
Church of San Lorenzo*

The Resilience of Genoa

"Genoa is now among the largest and most important of Mediterranean harbours. Its revival dates to some extent from the time of the opening of the Suez Canal which made it a principal entrepôt of commerce and travel between Western Europe and the Near East, but its modern prosperity is really the result of the great commercial and industrial development of Northern Italy and Switzerland. No Mediterranean city has witnessed so strangely varied fortunes, for Genoa was as long ago as the thirteenth century a leading Mediterranean power and though subsequently somewhat eclipsed by Venice remained powerful and prosperous until the general collapse of Mediterranean fortunes resulting from the discovery of the New World. Its gradual decline was sharply accentuated in the eighteenth century when the once-proud republican city was occupied and fought over by the armies of Revolutionary France; and its fortunes reached their nadir in the year 1800 when the indomitable Masséna, encircled by the Austrian armies, endured here the siege which enabled Napoleon to win the Marengo campaign but which literally starved most of the inhabitants [of Genoa] to death. That the city should have risen once more to its present eminence is the best possible tribute to the resilience of the Mediterranean spirit.

"The mountains, which as always on the Riviera crown closely down to the sea, describe here a fair-sized amphitheatre in which the city rises by successive levels almost to the skyline to make a most majestic appearance from the sea. . . . Lack of space is the perennial curse of Genoa and the central quarters are best seen to full advantage in the comparative emptiness and silence of midnight and full moon. The curious feature of the city when one is able to see it is that its character derives from precisely the period in which it was descending into an apparently irremediable decline. Huge late-Renaissance and baroque palaces dominate its central streets and give the impression that the Genoese decided, before their wealth finally vanished, to perpetuate its memory in solid, indestructible form. Some of these palaces, such as the Rosso and Bianco, now converted into museums and galleries, are on public view and invite inspection no less for their contents than for their majestic decorations and proportions of their interiors. Other princely edifices of the same period and inspiration, in less constricted situations, survive outside the town and provide the best examples on the Mediterranean seaboard of the combined Italian arts of house and garden."

— Jasper More,
The Mediterranean, 1956

Sugo di Carciofi

Artichoke Sauce

This sauce is especially popular in the province of Savona, although it is found throughout Liguria. There are two approaches to this sauce. In either case, the sauce is good with noodles or with cheese ravioli. It also makes a wonderful appetizer when spooned onto toasted bread that has been lightly doused with olive oil. The choice is whether to serve the sauce as it appears when it comes from the pan, or whether it should be turned into a cream. In that form it is often put up in jars and stored. Do what appeals to you.

4 fresh medium artichokes, tough outer leaves removed, sliced very thin
Fresh lemon juice
3 tablespoons/45 ml Ligurian extravirgin olive oil
1 tablespoon/7 g unsalted butter (optional)
1 clove garlic, green heart removed, minced
1 small onion, minced
3 ounces/⅓ cup/85 ml dry white wine, preferably Pigato
1 pinch fine sea salt
1 tablespoon/7 g minced fresh Italian (flat) parsley

After slicing the artichokes, place them in a dish and add some fresh lemon juice to keep them from discoloring. Heat the olive oil (and optional butter) gently in a small pot, then add the garlic. Sauté for a couple of minutes, then add the onion. Sauté until the onion is transparent, then add the pieces of artichoke. Add the wine and briefly raise the heat to evaporate the alcohol in the wine. Lower the flame, stir in a bit of salt, cover the pot, and simmer for 15 minutes. Add the parsley and serve immediately. If you plan to make the sauce more creamy, let it cool for a couple of minutes and then pound it in a mortar. Alternatively, you may puree the sauce gently in a blender or food processor, but remember that the sauce should be creamy rather than liquidy, so do not overprocess.

Makes
4 servings
for pasta

Marò

Fava Bean Sauce

Ligurian cooks have always appreciated the ability of singular ingredients to impart special flavor in a sauce. Famous examples include basil in pesto and garlic in *agliata,* but delicate fava beans are just as enticing when used for sauce. It is customary to serve *marò* with boiled beef (ever-economical Ligurians use inexpensive cuts of meat for boiling), but I also like to spread some on toasted focaccia or whole wheat bread, as people do in the extreme western part of the Ponente, where *marò* is thought to have originated. In the past it was the typical accompaniment for roasted goat or mutton. Nowadays, aside from beef, it is used as a sauce with firmer fleshed fish. Although it is an ancient sauce (the name probably derives from *mar-a,* the Arabic word for sauce), and in Liguria it was also called *pestun di fave* (fava bean pesto), it has been also referred to carelessly as *salsa alla marinara.* This is because it is mistakenly thought that the *mar* in *marò* refers to the sea and in that it has long occupied a place in the galleys of Ligurian ships, it is a maritime food. Its origins are from inland, but like so much in the ongoing culinary dialogue between the Ligurian land and sea, it has found a place in maritime cooking as well.

7 to 8 ounces / 200 g fresh young fava beans, peeled
1 to 2 cloves garlic, peeled
A few leaves fresh mint, carefully wiped with paper towels (but not washed) and torn
2 tablespoons / 30 g freshly grated, aged piquant Pecorino
Ligurian extravirgin olive oil

Makes about 1½ cups / 350 ml

In a mortar, use a pestle to pound the fava beans until they form a paste. Add the garlic cloves (one at a time if you are using two) and pound with the bean paste. Then add the torn mint leaves, pounding gently. Then add the grated Pecorino cheese. Remove the pestle and use a spoon to combine the ingredients while adding olive oil, a little at a time. Your objective is to form a creamy sauce, but you should determine how much or little oil you want to use. As with all oil-based Ligurian sauces, the olive oil provides a significant flavor component, so you should not think of the oil as you would in a salad dressing.

BLENDER ALTERNATIVE: The garlic should be chopped finely before adding it to the sauce. Place the fava beans and garlic together in a blender or food processor and blend quickly. Be careful not to overblend — the ingredients should form a coarse paste. Remove the paste to a bowl, then add the mint, the Pecorino, and the olive oil, as directed in the traditional recipe.

Tocco di Funghi

Mushroom Sauce

With its incomparable cache of wild mushrooms, Liguria can indulge itself in this sauce, which people in other places would consider a luxury. Therefore, many people choose to combine dried porcini with fresh ones, or with fresh cremini or cultivated ones that you buy packed in a Styrofoam container in the supermarket. If fresh porcini, cremini, or other special mushrooms are unavailable, you may make this dish using a combination of cultivated mushrooms and dried *funghi porcini* that you have soaked. After soaking the dried mushrooms, strain the liquid and then soak the sliced cultivated mushrooms in the liquid for 10 minutes so that they will absorb some of the flavor. Rossini, that exacting gourmand, always had dried Ligurian mushrooms shipped to him in Paris. This sauce is perfect on meat- or cheese-filled ravioli or over fresh noodles. Also, if you are making a plain risotto, stir this sauce into the pot 5 minutes before serving. You could serve this sauce with grated Parmigiano-Reggiano, but I think the cheese weighs down this delicate, oil-based preparation. If you do use cheese, be sparing.

1 pound / 450 grams fresh funghi porcini, *or 12 ounces / 350 g cultivated mushrooms in combination with 4 ounces / 110 g dried* funghi porcini
1 clove garlic, with the green heart removed, minced
1 small sprig fresh rosemary
2 teaspoons / 5 g pinoli *(optional)*
4 tablespoons / 60 ml Ligurian extravirgin olive oil
1 tablespoon / 7 g unsalted butter
2 tablespoons / 30 ml dry white wine
1 pinch fine sea salt
1 dash freshly ground black pepper
2 sprigs Italian (flat) parsley, minced

Gently wipe the fresh mushrooms to remove dirt and impurities. Cut into medium-slim slices, but be careful not to make them too narrow or they will fall apart. (If you are using dried mushrooms, soak them until they are soft and then squeeze out the excess liquid. Clean and slice the fresh mushrooms you are combining them with.) Once the mushrooms are ready, pound the garlic, rosemary, and optional *pinoli* in a mortar. Gently heat the oil and butter in a skillet and then add the garlic mixture. Cook for 1 minute, just until the oil-butter mixture has begun to take on the fragrance of the garlic. Then add the mushrooms

Makes
6 servings
for pasta

to the pan and sauté. About 30 seconds later, add the white wine. Season with salt and pepper. The mushrooms should cook just until they soften and the sauce should take on a little thickness. If you are serving this sauce with pasta noodles or ravioli, you might consider adding the pasta to the sauce and heating together quickly before serving. Just before serving, garnish with fresh parsley.

Along the Via Aurelia

The Romans built the Via Aurelia along the Mediterranean through Lazio, Tuscany, and all of Liguria. It would be a great engineering feat even now, but is quite miraculous for ancient times because of the numerous natural barriers that exist along the coast. It is along this road that the railway line that serves Liguria plies. You might find the following evocation of the Via Aurelia quite interesting, but I want to point out a strange phenomenon of our so-called modern times. The author writes in 1955 that finally windows can be opened in railcars, yet the newest trains of today, the great national expresses that shoot from Genoa to Rome, have windows that are sealed shut, and conditioned air replacing the real thing. Is this progress?

"Since our route into town [Alassio] ran parallel for some distance with the railway's low viaduct, we came to be familiar with and to love our part of the line and the station. The latter was a floral affair, the platforms gay with palms, scarlet canna, wistaria, clematis and purple bougainvillæa, where lamp standards were hung with baskets of flowers. It was also a place of romance, exciting the imagination whenever trains came in. The route boards on the coaches were visible from the road. They had quite an intoxicating effect on me, in whom the wanderlust has never died.

"The Riviera line is mostly a single track, operated on the block system, owing to the fact that it has been cut along terraces of rock overhanging the sea.

Frequently it runs in and out of tunnels that plunge into mountainous promontories. Journeying along this line from the Italian frontier at Ventimiglia as far as Spezia beyond Genoa, some two hundred miles, one is constantly shuttering in and out of blazing sunshine and black darkness. There are sometimes gaps in the tunnels where one has a blinding glimpse of dazzling blue sea. Someone wittily likened this coast journey to 'running down a flute'. When I first made it in 1922 the line had not been electrified, and one was blackened and suffocated by the acrid sulphurous fumes from the vile coal these trains burned. They penetrated the closed windows of the dark carriages in which one sweated at a temperature of ninety degrees. All this has changed with electrification. One can now travel with open windows.

"This line is a highway to Rome and southern Italy. It is one of the oldest routes in Europe, for along this coast the Romans built their famous Via Aurelia that carried them from Rome to their province of Gaul, and subsequently to the British Isles. It threaded its way through Liguria via Genoa . . . and eventually to Paris and the English Channel. . . . The main road threading Alassio is also [the Via Aurelia]. It pleased my fancy to think that in my cottage in the Oxfordshire Chilterns I was living on an extension of this highway, for it stood on the old Roman road along which the XXth Legion marched on its way to the camp at Dorchester, near Oxford."

— Cecil Roberts, *Portal to Paradise:*
An Italian Excursion, 1955

Pasta di Olive

Olive "Caviar"

It is now possible to buy *pasta di olive* (olive paste), which is often called *paté di olive*. These sauces are produced with great care in the Ponente and are now exported. However, many people like to make their own sauce and give it personal touches. You will see that it looks like black caviar, and is very popular on toasted bread or *crostini*. When served with pasta, the classic combination is with *farfalle* (butterflies) or with penne. Many Ligurians add a dash of cream to olive paste when serving with pasta, and the resulting sauce is called *crema di olive*. On average, I would suggest 1 teaspoon of light cream or whole milk for every tablespoon of olive paste.

2 cups / 225 g Taggia olives that have been cured in brine, pits removed
1 sprig fresh rosemary
1 pinch fresh thyme
A few juniper berries (optional)
1 tablespoon / 7 g (or less, if you wish) anchovy paste
Ligurian extravirgin olive oil
Light cream or whole milk (optional)

Makes
4 to 6 servings
on pasta or crostini

First, pit all of the olives. You need not worry about pitting them neatly, as the olives will all be pounded anyway. Set the olive pieces aside. In a mortar, pound the rosemary needles, thyme, and optional juniper berries. Then add the olive pieces and pound until they form a thick paste. Then stir in the anchovy paste. Then, according to your preferences, add some olive oil, a teaspoon at a time. You will want a sauce that is compact rather than liquidy, so beware of using too much oil. If you prefer to use a blender or food processor, add all of the ingredients except for the anchovy paste, and the oil. Process very briefly and lightly. Then remove the contents of the container to a bowl, and add the anchovy paste, olive oil, and optional cream as needed.

Liguria's exquisite Taggia olives

Bagna Cauda
Hot Olive Oil–Anchovy Dip

This is a typical dish associated with Piedmont, the region that borders western Liguria, where it is often used as an appetizer. However, its roots are Ligurian, with its use of olive oil and anchovies to form a dipping sauce for vegetables and bread. The more Piedmontese version combines butter and olive oil, although this is also done in Liguria. You may change the proportions by using less butter and more oil (see the variation indicated following the recipe). It is traditional to serve cut raw vegetables to dip into the Bagna Cauda. The most typical are cardoons, celery, radishes, and fennel. I have also used cauliflower, endive, sticks of raw zucchini, or rolled up mild-tasting leafy vegetables, such as Boston lettuce. Stronger tasting leafy vegetables conflict with the delicacy of the sauce, as do peppers, tomatoes, or eggplant. In Liguria they also use cubes of toasted bread or pieces of mildly flavored salami or sausage.

½ pound/225 g unsalted butter
6 ounces/170 ml Ligurian extravirgin olive oil
4 cloves garlic, peeled, with the green heart removed, finely minced
12 anchovy fillets
1 small piece of truffle (black or white), very finely sliced, or a pinch of truffle paste
*   (optional)*

Makes
6 servings
Heat the butter, oil, and garlic over very low heat, stirring gently so that the butter melts and combines with the oil. Make sure that the mixture does not boil or get too hot — the garlic should stay white. Remove from the heat and add the anchovy fillets. Break up the fillets with a wooden spoon, stirring gently, until they have fully integrated into the sauce. Check that the sauce is still hot. If not, return it briefly to the heat. Then, if you are using truffle, stir it in, and the sauce is ready to serve. The typical way to serve Bagna Cauda is in a small ceramic pot or chafing dish that is placed above a candle or other source of heat to keep the sauce hot. It is also possible to serve the sauce in individual dishes that have been warmed.

VARIATION: To use less butter, change the proportions to use ¼ pound/115 grams butter and 12 ounces/340 ml olive oil.

Agliata / Aggiada

Garlic Sauce
for Boiled Fish, Fried or Boiled or Grilled Meats

There is a common, and largely mistaken, assumption that you can distinguish Northern and Southern Italian cooking because the latter uses garlic and the former does not. Tell that to the Ligurians, who are unquestionably northerners and who consume more garlic than the people of Puglia at the heel of the Italian boot. In Puglia, most people favor onions over garlic, except near the city of Foggia. Conversely, the Ligurians prize garlic and use it with great sophistication. Invariably, they remove the green heart at the center of the clove, because that part gives bitterness to a dish. One classic use for *agliata* (called *aggiada* in dialect) is in tandem with Fegato alla Genovese (Genoese calf's liver; see page 369). The main difference between the two *agliata* recipes listed below is that the first one is unabashedly garlicky, while the second one has more balance among different flavors: salty, bitter, and garlicky.

Agliata — Recipe One

15 *cloves garlic, peeled and cut in half, with the green heart removed*
2 *to 3 pieces slightly stale bread, grated or crumbled*
White wine vinegar
Freshly ground black pepper and salt

Using a pestle, pound the garlic in a mortar until it forms a paste. Moisten the bread crumbs with a bit of vinegar. Add the crumbs to the garlic a bit at a time, stirring with a spoon to combine the ingredients. When the sauce is creamy, and perhaps slightly grainy, it is ready to eat. Season with a little freshly ground pepper and salt to taste.

*Makes
1 cup / 225 ml*

ALTERNATIVE PREPARATION: While the blender or food processor can never replace the hand method, if you would rather use mechanical means to make *agliata*, do as follows: First make crumbs with the bread. Remove them from the container of the blender or food processor and moisten them with a little vinegar. Then add the garlic, which will be blended to bits, absorbing the few remaining bread crumbs in the process. Pour the blended garlic into a bowl, and continue making the sauce as directed in the manual method.

Agliata — Recipe Two

6 cloves garlic, peeled
1 salted sardine fillet (from a jar or tin)
Ligurian extravirgin olive oil
Salt and pepper to taste
Heel of a loaf of bread
White wine vinegar

Makes
1 cup / 225 ml
Smash the garlic cloves and sardine fillet in a mortar. Spoon in olive oil, adding just enough to make a thick creamy sauce. Add a little salt and pepper and then the bread, which has been softened in vinegar. Stir so that the bread is incorporated into the sauce, which should remain quite thick and creamy.

Salsa alle Erbe Fresche
Fresh Herb Sauce

For a typical preparation of this sauce, see the recipe for Tagliarini alle Erbe Fresche on page 232. This sauce may be used with noodles and other shapes made from fresh or dried pastas, with sautéed vegetables, or added to sautéed chicken breasts once they have been cooked. It is also delicious spread on toasted bread as a canapé or snack.

Salsa per i Pesci Fritti

Sauce for Fried Fish

I wish there were a more place-specific or person-specific name for this sauce so that you can know more precisely what it is about. I can tell you that this particular sauce is one I have often encountered in the Levante, most especially in the province of La Spezia. Its use of Parmigiano-Reggiano cheese to go with fish is a typical La Spezia gesture that one seldom sees elsewhere. The cheese provides a sweetness that contrasts with the hot flavor of the *peperoncino* (chile pepper) and the tangy saltiness of the capers. You may increase or decrease the amounts of parsley, capers, and *peperoncino* that you use, but the amount of cheese should not be tampered with — otherwise the sauce will be too dry. Needless to say, you should use only Parmigiano-Reggiano cheese imported from Italy that you grate immediately before you make the sauce.

As a general rule, this sauce is used on small fish such as anchovies (see page 190) that have not been breaded and often not even floured. Rather, they are cooked quickly in hot oil, drained, and served with this sauce on the side. A breading would make the taste of the fish too heavy and that is, well, un-Ligurian. I have used this sauce in other contexts: with boiled beef, spread on bread or toasts as an appetizer, and especially as a condiment for hard-boiled eggs, with which it is an ideal match.

½ cup/60 g fresh Italian (flat) parsley, washed and dried
2 tablespoons/15 g fresh basil leaves, gently wiped with paper toweling
1 tablespoon/7 g capers (use less if the capers have been packed in salt instead of brine)
1 tablespoon/7 g minced fresh peperoncino
5 tablespoons/35 g freshly grated Parmigiano-Reggiano
3 tablespoons/45 ml Ligurian extravirgin olive oil

Ideally, you should use a mortar and pestle to make this sauce. First pound the parsley and basil, and then add the capers and *peperoncino,* pounding again, and then stir in the cheese. If you do not use a mortar and pestle, proceed as follows. Use a good knife or, better still, a *mezzaluna* (a two-handled, half-moon-shaped implement popular in Italy for chopping herbs and greens). Chop the parsley and basil until they are finely minced. Separately pound or mince the capers and *peperoncino* or, if you must, puree them briefly in a blender or food processor. Combine the parsley/basil mixture with the capers and *peperoncino* in a bowl. Then stir in the cheese. No matter which way you have prepared the ingredients, you have now reached an important juncture. I have given you a suggested amount of olive oil, but you must follow your own instincts and preferences. Some people like a firm sauce with little oil, others like much

Makes
1 cup/225 ml

more oil, especially if they are using delicate and delicious Ligurian, as you should. My suggestion is to stir olive oil into the ingredients until the sauce has the texture and consistency you desire. I like the sauce on the thick side — and I serve it sparingly — because the flavors are more intense and immediate.

WINE: The white wine of the Cinqueterre goes perfectly as a flavor combination with this sauce, although other Ligurian whites, as well as Vernaccia di San Gimignano, are also congenial.

Salsa Verde all'Antica

Old-Fashioned Herb Sauce for Fish

Do not confuse this sauce with Salsa alla Genovese (page 86). The chief difference is that that sauce is used with fish that has already been cooked, while this sauce may be used either while the fish is cooking (the approach I recommend) or with poached or steamed fish. Also, the flavors in this sauce are quite distinct from the Genoese sauce. Salsa Verde all'Antica is not used much in big cities, but appears more in small fishing villages in the Levante.

2 tablespoons / 30 ml Ligurian extravirgin olive oil
1 small carrot, washed, scraped, finely minced
1 clove garlic, green heart removed, finely minced
1 small onion, finely minced
1 small stalk celery, finely minced
3 tablespoons / 20 g finely minced fresh Italian (flat) parsley
1 tablespoon / 7 g tiny capers
1 tablespoon / 7 g pinoli
2 teaspoons / 3 g small raisins, preferably from white grapes (optional)
¾ cup / 6 ounces / 175 ml dry white wine, preferably Ligurian
Juice of 1 small lemon

Heat the olive oil in a saucepan over medium heat and add the carrot, garlic, onion, celery, parsley, and capers. Heat briefly until the ingredients soften and give off a heady perfume. Add the *pinoli* and optional raisins and give the pan a good shake. Add the wine and raise the heat beneath the pan. Cook until the wine evaporates but don't let the sauce become too dense. Once the sauce is cooked, stir in the lemon juice.

Makes about 1 cup / 225 ml

USING THE SAUCE: If you plan to bake or poach a fillet of fish, spread this sauce on top before cooking. If you are baking or roasting a whole fish, spread this sauce in the cavity of the fish. Once the fish is cooked (whether a fillet or a whole fish), serve with a teaspoonful of this sauce on every diner's plate.

Salsa di Pinoli, Capperi e Acciughe

Sauce of Pine Nuts, Capers, and Anchovies

This sauce is particularly suited to giving flavor to boiled or poached fish. Ideally, it should be made in a mortar, although you can also make it in a bowl using a fork and a spoon. A blender or food processor may also be used, but you must take great care not to process for too long a time. The sauce will keep for up to two days when refrigerated in a tight jar or covered dish.

2 eggs
2 tablespoons / 15 g pinoli
1 tablespoon / 7 g capers, drained (or with salt removed if the capers are salt-packed)
2 salted anchovy fillets
1 clove garlic, with the green heart removed, minced
2 sprigs fresh Italian (flat) parsley, minced
Freshly ground black pepper
White wine vinegar
8 tablespoons / 120 ml Ligurian extravirgin olive oil

Makes about 1 cup / 225 ml

Hard-boil the eggs and let cool. In the meantime, combine the *pinoli*, capers, anchovies, garlic, and parsley in a mortar. Pound with the pestle until all the ingredients are reduced to a paste. Then add the cooked yolks from the eggs and pound briefly, only until they break up and combine with the other ingredients. (If you are using a bowl and fork, you will not achieve the same delicacy as with a mortar and pestle and you will have to spend more time breaking up the ingredients. You may run all of the ingredients in a blender or food processor at a low speed for a few seconds, but be careful that the ingredients do not liquefy.) Then grind a little black pepper into the mixture, just enough to give it zip but not to unbalance the flavors. Add the vinegar and combine with the other ingredients. Then add the oil one tablespoon at a time, gently stirring it in. After 4 tablespoons of added oil you will have a thick sauce. With more oil added, the sauce will become thinner and creamier. You should use as much oil as you need to get a texture that pleases you.

Machetto

Sardine Sauce

Machetto is yet another Ligurian sauce of humble origin that winds up exalting whatever it touches because of the immediacy of its flavor. *Machetto* gives its special taste to breads and savory pies from the Ponente, including *sardenaira* and *machetusa*. Many Ligurians stir some *machetto* into fresh lemon juice before combining it with olive oil to produce a bracing salad dressing. This can nicely coat lettuce and other greens, or be used in *condiglione* (or *condiggion*), the great Ligurian summertime salad. A fine and very basic use of *machetto* is to spread it on a thick slice of good bread and wash it down with a glass of Pigato or Vermentino wine. To make *machetto* properly, it is essential to use small, fresh sardines no more than 2 to 2½ inches/5 to 6 cm long. The classic preparation for *machetto* calls for whole sardines, but I imagine that some readers might be squeamish about making a sauce with whole fish. If you are one of these, you may cut off the heads and tails and gut the fish, but you will lose a lot of the flavor. Because the sauce takes forty days to make, the taste and fragrance mellow considerably and the result is not nearly as overpowering or oppressive as you might expect.

Approximately 1 pound/½ kilo small whole fresh sardines, washed
Coarse salt (preferably sea salt)
Ligurian extravirgin olive oil

Have at hand a sterile, wide-mouthed jar that can hold 2 cups/450 ml of liquid. Carefully wash the sardines and dry them with paper toweling. Sprinkle some coarse salt on the bottom of the jar and then place a layer of sardines in the jar. Top with more coarse salt, then another layer of sardines and so on until all the sardines are tightly packed in the jar. Top with a little more coarse salt and then close the lid tightly over the mouth of the jar. Place the jar in a dark, cool place. Two days later, open the jar and give the contents a little stir with a wooden, plastic, or metal spoon. Then close the jar tightly and store for another two days. Open again and stir some more. This process should continue for forty days. You will notice that gradually the sardines will disintegrate into a paste. At this point you might want to use a sieve or a strainer to drain off extra liquid. You now have a choice: In Liguria, where this sauce is used frequently, the *machetto* is returned to the jar in which it macerated. For your purposes, I would recommend taking two or three smaller, sterile jars and filling each jar about 85 percent full with the *machetto*. Then top the sauce with a layer of oil, which will preserve its freshness and resiliency. Tightly close the jars and store in a cool, dark place. When using the *machetto,* add a little more olive oil to the jar before closing it again.

Makes approximately 2 cups/450 ml

Sugo di Muscoli

Mussel Sauce

This sauce is a particular specialty of La Spezia, whose surrounding waters have long hosted mussel farms, and whose cooks have found inspiring ways to use them. Mussel sauce works well with *trenette, corzetti del Levante,* or *maccheroni,* and is delicious when served atop ravioli filled with fish. Of course, it is also tasty when spooned over *crostini* or *bruschetta.*

2¼ pounds / 1 kilo mussels
3 ounces / 6 tablespoons / 90 ml Ligurian extravirgin olive oil
1 clove garlic, peeled, with the green heart removed, minced
2 salted anchovy fillets
4 tablespoons / 60 ml fresh tomato sauce
2 sprigs fresh Italian (flat) parsley, minced

Makes
4 servings
for pasta

Carefully wash the mussels, removing their beards. Place them in a large pot and heat so that the steam created by the water clinging to the mussels will allow them to open. Discard any shells that do not open. Remove the mussels and throw away the shells. Place the mussels in a bowl. Strain and reserve the liquid from the pot. Heat the olive oil in a saucepan and then add the garlic. Sauté until you smell the fragrance of the garlic, but make certain it does not burn. Add the anchovies and mash them. Then stir in the tomato sauce, and cook gently for 2 minutes, stirring occasionally. Then add the mussels and their liquid and cook gently for 15 minutes. When serving, toss on a little minced parsley.

Paté di Polpo

Octopus Sauce

I tasted this sauce in Tellaro, the coastal town in the province of La Spezia where D. H. Lawrence lived and wrote his story of the octopus who yanked the pullcord that sounded the church bells of the town parish. With its use of a blender, this sauce may seem a bit nouvelle, but in fact it is an older dish whose sauce used to be pounded in a mortar. While I still favor the mortar and pestle for most sauces (certainly those based on herbs and nuts), the blender or food processor is acceptable here. I had *paté di polpo* as a sauce atop *conchiglie* (pasta shells) and it was perfect. It is also very nice on toasted bread as an appetizer.

1 pound/450 g octopus, cleaned, gutted, and well washed (this can be done at
    the market)*
6 ounces/85 ml white wine vinegar
2 tablespoons/30 ml Ligurian extravirgin olive oil
3 cloves garlic, green heart removed (2 cloves minced; 1 cut in half)
1 tablespoon/7 g capers packed in vinegar (preferably balsamic)
3 tablespoons/22 g minced fresh Italian (flat) parsley
Sea salt
Freshly ground black pepper to taste
¾ pound/12 ounces/350 g pasta shells (optional)

> *Some fish markets, especially those operated by Italian, Greek, or Japanese owners, often sell octopus that has already been cleaned, cooked, and peeled. If you have this option, you may skip the steps in this recipe that involve cooking the octopus.

Set a large pot of cold water to boil. Clean the octopus by washing it thoroughly, removing the eyes and internal organs. Then wash it again, rinsing the interior and the tentacles carefully. It is customary to hit the octopus against a stone for 5 minutes to tenderize it before cooking. This can also be done with a mallet. Once these preparations are completed, place the octopus in a pot of boiling water. Cook for 2 to 3 hours, or until you can stab it through with a fork near the top of one of the tentacles. Remove the octopus from the water and peel it. (Do not turn off the heat under the pot of water.) Once the octopus is peeled, add the vinegar to the cooking water, place the octopus back in, and boil for 10 minutes over very low heat. Then drain the octopus in a colander. When it is cool enough to handle (don't let it cool too much), chop it into pieces and then process it in a blender or food processor until it forms a thick

*Makes
4 servings
for pasta or
6 to 8 for* crostini

sauce or paté. Then heat the oil in a frying pan until it is rather hot but not splattering. Add the 2 cloves of minced garlic, the capers with a bit of the vinegar they are packed in, and the parsley. Cook for 3 minutes, stirring so that all the flavors blend. Then add the octopus paté and cook for another 2 minutes, stirring to unite all of the ingredients. Add salt and pepper to taste. Pack this sauce into a large sterilized glass jar and add the other garlic clove. Top with a layer of Ligurian extravirgin olive oil and then seal tightly. This sauce tastes better after it has sat overnight, stored in the refrigerator. This is not a sauce that can be stored for a long time like most other Ligurian sauces.

NOTE: If you plan to use this sauce for pasta, it is good when lightly heated and tossed with hot pasta. Of course, do not rinse the pasta once it has been cooked — simply drain it in a colander.

Tocco

Genoese Meat Sauce

In Genoa, the dialect word *tocco* is so inextricably linked to the local meat sauce that, even though the word only means "sauce," there is universal comprehension that there is meat in it. To describe another sauce, such as walnut sauce, one must specify that it is *tocco de noxe* or, in Italian, *salsa di noci*. What there is not universal agreement about is that there are so many different ways to prepare *tocco* in Genoa that what I present to you is an approximation derived from many of the fine *tocchi* I have tasted. It is essential, though, that the sauce as made nowadays contain carrots, mushrooms, and, of course, beef or veal. In former times, *tocco* always included marrow, but this is difficult to locate if you do not have a sympathetic butcher, so mushrooms have for the most part taken the place of the marrow. Genoese *tocco* is considerably less meaty than the famous meat sauce of Bologna in Emilia-Romagna, and, given that this is Liguria, the vegetable flavors in the sauce play an important role in the flavor palette. *Tocco* is the second most popular pasta sauce in Genoa, after pesto, but it is the preferred sauce for ravioli and fresh egg noodles such as tagliatelle. Mince the meat from the *tocco* to stuff vegetables, especially zucchini, eggplant, or tomatoes.

1 ounce/30 g dried funghi porcini
2 tablespoons/30 ml Ligurian extravirgin olive oil
2 large carrots, grated
1 medium onion, minced
1 large stalk celery, minced
1 pound/450 g boneless veal, cut into 2 or 3 pieces
Flour
1 cup/225 ml dry red wine, such as Dolcetto
1 cup/225 ml crushed tomatoes
Fine sea salt

Soak the mushrooms in warm water. Change the water twice more, and set aside each soaking water. When the mushrooms are soft, combine the waters and then strain them of all impurities. Chop the mushrooms and set aside. Heat the olive oil in a heavy-bottomed pot. Add the carrots, onion, and celery and sauté for about 7 minutes, or until the ingredients are soft. Remove the vegetables from the pan, then add the pieces of meat, which have been lightly floured. Brown lightly on all sides, then add the wine. Raise the heat briefly to cook down the wine, then lower the temperature and add the mushrooms. Cook for 2 to 3 minutes, then return the cooked vegetables to the pot. Add the

*Makes about
3 cups/675 ml*

crushed tomatoes and salt to taste. Cover, and cook over low heat for 1 hour. Then check how thick the sauce has become, and add some mushroom liquid to lengthen the sauce a bit. Cook another hour, and again add some mushroom liquid. Cook another half hour, add more liquid, and cook for 30 more minutes. Remove the meat and reserve it for other purposes. The sauce is now ready.

Sugo Negretto

Beef and Onion Sauce

This sauce is the by-product of the preparation of Manzo Negretto (see page 366). It is the perfect condiment for thick tubular pasta such as rigatoni, and should be topped with freshly grated Parmigiano-Reggiano, and perhaps a few grindings of fresh black pepper.

Crema di Castagne al Profumo di Viola

Violet-Scented Chestnut Puree

Up to a certain point the procedure is not unlike that for making Castagne al Profumo di Viola (see page 390), but ultimately this will be a sauce or spread that can be stored for a while. This is a wonderful filling if you make a layer cake, or it may be spread on toast at breakfast.

Slightly more than 1 pound / ½ kilo fresh chestnuts
3 tablespoons / 20 g sea salt or coarse salt
¼ cup / 4 tablespoons / 60 ml violet honey (see page 111)

Only select fresh chestnuts in pristine shape. The most desirable are ones that were very recently harvested. Set a large pot of cold water to boil to which you have added the salt. Once it has reached a rolling boil, add the chestnuts and boil for 45 minutes, with the pot partially covered. Drain the water and, when the chestnuts are not too hot to handle, slip off their skins. Place them in a mortar and mash them into a puree. You may also use a bowl and either a potato masher or a manual food mill. As a last resort, use a blender or food processor, but make sure you only run it in brief spurts or you run the risk of making the cream too liquidy. In mashing the chestnuts you should try to create a thick paste or meal. Then stir in the honey, 1 tablespoon at a time, until you have the desired texture. You may add more or less honey, as you wish.

Makes
3½ cups / 400 g

Miele alle Rose

Rose Honey

Throughout Liguria, but especially in the Ponente, flowers are used to flavor foods and recipes. A good basic application of flowers is in honey, which you may use in baking or in any other way that you might normally eat it. This recipe uses roses, the following one uses violets.

IMPORTANT NOTE: In many parts of the world, including North America, it is customary to spray flowers with pesticides during cultivation unless they are specifically destined for eating. You must ascertain that the roses you use to make this honey are unsprayed, or else you will be concocting yourself a lethal brew. If you know the nursery where the flowers are grown, or can grow your own, this is the best solution. Store-bought roses from the neighborhood florist are too risky unless you are certain of the origin of the flowers!

1 cup/100 g rose petals
2 cups/450 ml organic honey

Makes
2 cups/450 ml

Set a small pot of cold water to boil. When it reaches a boil, add the rose petals and boil for 3 to 4 minutes. Then separate the petals from the rosewater, using a slotted spoon. Place the petals on a cheesecloth and fold in such a way that all of the petals are enclosed. Then carefully press the cloth for several minutes in such a way that a rose liquid is yielded. This process should be done over a large bowl so that all the liquid is captured. It is this liquid that should be stirred into the honey, which then should be stored in a tightly closed jar in a cool, dark place.

NOTE: Do not throw away the rosewater! Some people use it in cooking. I like to use it as the best and most natural facial cleanser and astringent. Simply moisten a cotton ball with rosewater and wipe your face.

Miele alle Viole

Violet Honey

This honey is similar in preparation to rose honey, and can be used in similar ways, but it also has a very specific application. Ligurians know that chestnuts and violets make an exquisite flavor combination. You may use this honey to coat boiled chestnuts (see page 390) or to make a violet chestnut spread to use on toast or in cakes (see page 109).

IMPORTANT NOTE: In many parts of the world, including North America, it is customary to spray flowers with pesticides during cultivation unless they are specifically destined for eating. You must ascertain that the violets you use to make this honey are unsprayed, or else you will be concocting yourself a lethal brew. If you know the nursery where the flowers are grown, or can grow your own, this is the best solution. Store-bought violets from the neighborhood florist are too risky unless you are certain of the origin of the flowers!

1 cup/100 g violet petals
2 cups/450 ml organic honey

Set a small pot of cold water to boil. When it reaches a boil, add the violet petals and boil for 3 to 4 minutes. Then separate the petals from the water, using a slotted spoon. Place the petals on a cheesecloth and fold in such a way that all of the petals are enclosed. Then carefully press the cloth for several minutes in such a way that a violet liquid is yielded. This process should be done over a large bowl so that all the liquid is captured. It is this liquid that should be stirred into the honey, which then should be stored in a tightly closed jar in a cool, dark place.

*Makes
2 cups/450 ml*

NOTE: Some people like to use a touch of violet water as a fragrance, so save the water for that special someone.

Mark Twain on the Subject of
Genoa and Its Women

"I would like to remain here. I had rather not go any further. There may be prettier women in Europe, but I doubt it. The population of Genoa is 120,000; two-thirds of these are women, I think, and at least two-thirds of the women are beautiful. They are as dressy and as tasteful and as graceful as they could possibly be without being angels. However, angels are not very dressy, I believe. At least the angels in pictures are not — they wear nothing but wings. But these Genoese women do look so charming. Most of the young demoiselles are robed in a cloud of white from head to foot, though many trick themselves out more elaborately. Nine-tenths of them wear nothing on their heads but a filmy sort of veil, which falls down their backs like a white mist. They are very fair, and many of them have blue eyes, but black and dreamy dark-brown ones are met with oftenest.

"The ladies and gentlemen of Genoa have a pleasant fashion of promenading in a large park on top of a hill in the center of the city, from six to nine in the evening, and then eating ices in a neighboring garden an hour or two longer. We went to the park on Sunday evening. Two thousand persons were present, chiefly young ladies and gentlemen. The gentlemen were dressed in the very latest Paris fashions, and the robes of the ladies glinted among the trees like so many snow flakes. The multitude moved round and round the park in a

great procession. The bands played, and so did the fountains; the moon and the gas-lamps lit up the scene, and altogether it was brilliant and an animated picture. I scanned every female face that passed, and it seemed to me that all were handsome. I never saw such a freshet of loveliness before. I do not see how a man of only ordinary decision of character could marry here, because, before he could get his mind made up he would fall in love with somebody else. . . . 'The Superb' and the 'City of Palaces' are names which Genoa had held for centuries. She is full of palaces, certainly, and the palaces are sumptuous inside, but they are very rusty without, and make no pretensions to architectural magnificence. 'Genoa, the Superb,' would be a felicitous title if it referred to the women."

— Mark Twain,
The Innocents Abroad, 1869

Twain did not remark that Genoa was a city of women in part because so many of its men had gone to sea. Also, his guides did not explain to him that "Genova, la Superba" in Italian means "Genoa, the Proud." I am glad to report that Genoese women are still as lovely as ever, that the city has begun to surmount many of the ills that beset it in the twentieth century because of war and indiscriminate industrialization. It is now superb and proud, and the palaces have regained a luster that decades of neglect had covered over.

Breads
&
Savory Pies

Fugassa all'Euio (Focaccia all'Olio)	Focaccia with Olive Oil
Fugassa co-o Formaggio (Focaccia col Formaggio)	Cheese Focaccia
Fugassa co-a Çiòula (Focaccia con la Cipolla)	Focaccia with Onions
Fugassa co-o Romanin (Focaccia col Rosmarino)	Rosemary Focaccia
Fugassa co-a Sarvia (Focaccia con la Salvia)	Sage Focaccia
Focaccia al Gorgonzola	Focaccia with Gorgonzola
Focaccia con le Olive	Focaccia with Olives
Focaccia al Tartufo	Truffle Focaccia
Fugassa co-e Patatte (Focaccia con le Patate)	Potato Focaccia
Gizzoa (Focaccia con la Salsiccia)	Sausage Focaccia
Focaccette	Cheese Puffs
Sardenaira	San Remo Pizza
Pizza all'Andrea (Piscialandrea)	Andrea Doria Pizza
La Farinata	Chickpea Tart
Paniccia	Chickpea "Bread"
Favetta	Fava Bread
Gallette del Marinaio	Sailor's Biscuits (or Sea Biscuits)
Torta	Basic Savory Pie Recipe
Torta di Verdura	Savory Pie Filled with Greens
Torta di Carciofi e Verdura	Savory Pie Filled with Artichokes and Greens
Torta di Riso e Verdura	Savory Pie Filled with Rice and Greens
Torta di Cipolle	Onion Savory Pie
Torta di Verdura, Pinoli e Uvetta	Savory Pie with Greens, Pine Nuts, and Raisins
Torta Pasqualina all'Antica	Traditional Easter Pie

BELIN CHE FUGASSA!

This is the rather off-color Ligurian exclamation to describe wonderful focaccia. It must be one of the most frequently uttered phrases in the region, but especially in the province of Genoa. And nowhere is the focaccia better than in Recco (south of the Ligurian capital), which may be the best food town on the entire Italian Riviera. Recco does not make a strong impression on the eye when compared with other nearby towns on the Riviera, especially Camogli, Portofino, Santa Margherita, and Rapallo, which are immediately to the south, and Sori, Pieve Ligure, and Bogliasco to the north.

Recco is the coastal town that leads to an inland valley. As such, it does not push dramatically against the sea as its neighboring towns do. It was an important port in the area that received goods in its harbor and sent products of the valley out to sea. It is also the place where bridges had been built to connect north and south, so that it always had key strategic importance. During World War II, Recco was the only town in the area southeast of Genoa to suffer serious bombardments because it was such a valuable linchpin of commerce and transportation. Recco today is a rebuilt town, as if after an earthquake, and is charming not because of its architecture but because of the sunniness of its people and its climate.

Perhaps it is because so much physical evidence of Recco's past has been eliminated that the people cling so tightly to its gastronomic heritage, which is, indeed, its cultural heritage. Food can be a mode of expression, a language, and in Liguria no one is more fluent and poetic than the *recchesi*. Unlike most cities, in which native specialties are prepared on certain days, the outstanding dishes of Recco — focaccia, *trofie*, pesto, *pansôti,* and excellent seafood — are lovingly prepared every day.

In Recco, on the fourth Sunday in May, there is the Festa della Focaccia. In 1995 I attended along with 15,000 other hungry people to enjoy Recco's famous specialty. In the morning plain focaccia and onion focaccia were made, while in the afternoon it was *focaccia col formaggio,* divine cheese focaccia that may be the world's most addictive food. On that feast day 500 kilos (1100 pounds) of flour were used, along with 150 kilos (330 pounds) of onions, and 120 liters (127 quarts) of Ligurian extravirgin olive oil.

There was also a new initiative called Focaccia dei Bambini in which eighty nursery school children learned to make focaccia under the supervision of Lorenzo Moltedo and Rosa Sessarego, two of Recco's foremost bakers. The idea of this feast was a reassertion of Recco's sense of identity through its food and, with the instruction of small children, an attempt to assure that the cherished knowledge is passed on.

As outstanding as the food scene is in Recco, it is merely the summit in an area where the cooking and baking are sublime. Walk down any street in Genoa, Camogli, or Santa Margherita at any hour of the day and you will see people chomping on focaccia. This is unusual because most Italians tend not to eat anything (except ice cream) as they walk down the street. Ligurians, however, know that hot focaccia must be consumed immediately because it becomes less compelling as it cools. Focaccia is a breakfast bread in Liguria, although it is also consumed throughout the day. Most Ligurians know the hours when their local baker produces hot batches of their favorite bread and they tend to find an excuse to be nearby when the focaccia is ready. The first batch comes very early in the morning. In bars along waterfronts, people cluster to eat it before starting their day. Sailors and fishermen buy it before going to sea.

This is not a new phenomenon. In centuries past, before most homes had their own ovens, each town or neighborhood had a communal oven that served as a *focal* point of the community. Look again at the word "focal" and ask yourself what it suggests. The root is from *focus,* the Latin word for hearth or fireplace. In other words, all eyes were fixed on the light and heat that came from the flames of the oven. Now look at the word *focaccia,* and you will understand that this is an ancient hearth bread. Archaeological excavations have revealed that the ancient peoples of Liguria ate a bread not unlike the focaccia of today, made simply with flour, water, olive oil, and salt.

In the little quarter of Camogli where I live, just above the ancient port, is a cluster of houses where fishermen and sailors lived until very recently, when many of them sold their flats to city-dwellers who wanted a weekend retreat. Most of these houses are 300 to 400 years old, and are huddled together around a little street just below Camogli's church. This is the nucleus of old Camogli, established before newer buildings were built along the shore in the eighteenth century. Right in the middle of this little street is the ancient *forno,* the oven that was used by all until a few decades ago. It is now covered with mold and moss, but it serves as a vivid reminder of an earlier time. This was the focal point of Camogli.

In Liguria, and much of Italy, the *forno* was used to make breads, pizzas, savory tarts, simple cakes, and biscuits. These last, by the way, are called *biscotti* in Italian, and the name implies that they are twice-baked (bis = two; cotti = cooked), which explains why they are crunchy. The task of preparing these baked goods has now reverted to bakers who have their own ovens, usually wood-burning. These bakeries are now the focal points in Ligurian towns, so little has changed.

Historically, focaccia played a role in church observances. People were allowed to nibble on it during mass, and it was eaten by bride, groom, and all in attendance at the moment of the benediction during a wedding. Apparently, around the year 1500 a custom developed of eating focaccia during funerals, but this was deemed sacrilegious. Soon thereafter, focaccia was banned from church events of all kinds.

Because there are so many talented bakers in Liguria, there is a lot of competition for clientele, and the quality remains very high. If word gets out that someone has scrimped on ingredients or has let standards slip, that can ruin a family's business. Little Camogli has about a half-dozen superb bread bakers, and most of the citizens frequent the shop they happen to be closest to.

While I patronize all of these bakers, my preferred one is Rocco Rizzo on Via della Repubblica. I was surprised to learn that Signor Rizzo is not Ligurian, but from Puglia (the heel of the Italian boot), which also has a formidable bread-baking tradition. He has applied his natural skill to Ligurian breads, and also produces a full range of Pugliese ones. He and his lovely wife and their children are scrupulous about quality and know their customers' preferences, so there are always lines at the Rizzo bakery ready to buy bread as soon as it comes out of the oven.

There are numerous variations on the basic theme of focaccia, and you will find several of these in the following pages. There are also other breads to be consumed in Liguria, including *piscialandrea* and *sardenaira,* focaccia-like breads from Imperia and San Remo that are topped with fish and vegetables. Farinata, a thin chickpea bread, is a cousin of *socca,* a classic bread of the cuisine of Nice. As you know, there are many similarities between Niçoise food and Ligurian food because that city spent a good deal of time under the influence of the Republic of Genoa until 1855.

There is also a famous local bread in the *entroterra* of the province of Imperia known as *Pane di Triora.* I have not included the recipe for two reasons. The first is that the recipe is jealously guarded and I have not been able to learn it. The second is that *Pane di Triora* is, in effect, a very well-made round of wheat bread with a crunchy crust. While it is delicious, it is not all that different from what are generally called peasant breads.

There are two other things I want you to understand about *Pane di Triora.* The first is that this bread is probably the only one in Liguria that profoundly resembles breads from other regions. Most Ligurian breads are based on local ingredients and traditions, and were created with a combination of necessity and ingenuity. What also must be said about Triora is that it sits in the one area of Liguria that has a long tradition of wheat growing in Liguria. Below the town of Triora (often called the third-oldest town in Italy, although I have not seen plausible documentation of this assertion) is the community of Molini di Triora. This is a place that used to have twenty-three mills that ground the wheat to make flour. With all of this available, it was possible to make thick, crusty wheat breads that would have been a luxury in the rest of Liguria. Nowadays, most of the wheat that is grown in this area (and there is not too much) is used to make pasta.

An additional "bread" of Liguria is the *galletta del marinaio.* This means sailor's biscuit or sea biscuit. These are also of ancient origin, and they are typically baked until they are quite hard. Sailors would take them to sea and then, when they wanted bread, would douse them with sea water and then pour on olive oil to make them more palatable. *Gallette del marinaio,* as they are known in the plural, are part of the opulent *cappon magro* (see page 340), although many people now substitute slices of bread that are made stale by heating them in an oven. It is very difficult to find *gallette del marinaio,* even in Liguria. There is one baker in San Rocco (between Camogli and Portofino) who makes them, and Rocco Rizzo in Camogli sells them as well. The recipe you will find here is his.

The ancient communal oven in Camogli

One additional note about the breads of Liguria: All of them, in one form or another, are not only for eating alone (although that may be done felicitously), but are a vessel for the flavors of the Italian Riviera. This applies most especially to the sauces and spreads found in the previous chapter. Many of these can be baked into or spread on focaccia as easily as being tossed with pasta. With the sauces of the previous chapter, the breads in this one, and the pasta in the chapter that follows, you will have learned about three of the cornerstones of Ligurian cuisine, the other being the wonderful herbs, fruits, and vegetables that flourish in the soil of the Italian Riviera.

Fugassa all'Euio (Focaccia all'Olio)
Focaccia with Olive Oil

Here is the basic recipe for focaccia as it is eaten in Genoa, where bakers put some white wine in their dough. From this recipe you will be able to make adaptations for all the other *focacce* with the exception of cheese focaccia. Although I learned focaccia-making in Genoa, Camogli, and Santa Margherita, I have drawn from a superb American source in adapting the focaccia recipes for this book. Carol Field, author of several outstanding books, including *The Italian Baker* and *Focaccia: Simple Breads from the Italian Oven,* is the leading American authority on Italian breads. When I visit top bread bakers in Italy, I often spot Carol's books, well-stained with flour and oil, on their shelves. I used techniques from Carol to make focaccia in my home oven in New York, and she has successfully figured out how to achieve the Italian taste in a home setting. Many of the additional comments in these focaccia recipes are echoes of the voices of the numerous bakers who taught me, and a few observations are the result of my own experience.

An important decision to make is whether you want to use a baking stone. It will produce a focaccia closer to that you might find in a Ligurian bakery, because it will reflect heat upward. Baking stones will usually produce a crunchier focaccia, although you can enhance the crunchiness of focaccia in a pan if you coat it with more olive oil than the light greasing described below. You should use one large baking stone rather than two or three smaller ones. To clean it, let it cool entirely before touching it. Then wash it well in cold water, but do not use soap or the flavor will be absorbed.

For all of the focaccia recipes in this book, you should use a low-sided rectangular pan with a rim. Select a pan that is 10½ x 15½ inches (27 x 39 cm) and made of dark carbon steel or heavy aluminum or one that is anodized nonstick coated. Carol Field recommends all three of these, although I am less enthusiastic about the latter, preferring to use a little more oil in the pan to prevent sticking.

The first step to making classic Genoese focaccia is to make the sponge. Then you can proceed with the rest of the recipe.

FOR THE SPONGE
⅔ cup/170 ml warm water (between 105°and 115°F/40°and 45°C)
2½ teaspoons (1 package)/6 g active dry yeast
1 cup/140 g unbleached all-purpose flour

FOR THE TOPPING
2 to 3 tablespoons/30 to 45 ml Ligurian extravirgin olive oil
1 teaspoon/3 g coarse sea salt

FOR THE DOUGH (have all of the ingredients at room temperature before you start making the dough)

½ cup/115 ml water, room temperature (68°F/20°C)

⅓ cup/85 ml dry white wine (such as Coronata, Pigato, Vermentino, Soave, or Vernaccia di San Gimignano)

⅓ cup/85 ml Ligurian extravirgin olive oil

2½ cups plus 2 teaspoons/360 g unbleached all-purpose flour, plus 1 to 2 tablespoons/7 to 15 g, as needed

2 teaspoons/5 g fine sea salt

Makes 1 focaccia

1) Make the sponge. Take a large mixing bowl and add the warm water. Sprinkle the yeast over the water, then whisk it in. Let stand until the water is creamy, about 10 minutes. Gradually stir in the flour, beating with the whisk. Beat until the mixture is smooth (that is, there are no lumps of flour). Cover tightly with plastic wrap. Set aside and let rise for about 30 minutes. The result should be puffy and bubbling.

2) Make the dough. Add the water, wine, and olive oil to the sponge. Whisk in 1 cup of flour and the sea salt, then beat in the rest of the flour gradually. The result should be soft and sticky. Turn this dough out onto a lightly floured surface, using a dough scraper if you need to guide it from the bowl. Knead for 6 to 8 minutes, gradually working in another tablespoon or two of flour, which will result in a shiny dough. The dough should be soft, but not wet.

3) Put the dough in a large bowl that has been lightly greased with olive oil. Cover tightly with plastic wrap. Let rise for about 1 hour, or until the dough has doubled in size.

4) Grease your baking pan lightly with olive oil. Stretch the dough out so that it evenly covers the pan. The dough should be soft and full of air bubbles, so it will easily conform to the shape of the pan.

5) Now comes the fun part, one that is essential to the success of your final product. Classic focaccia is famous for its many indentations. This is the way you instantly recognize what it is. I love the idea that every focaccia is made unique by the imprint of its maker. Splay your fingers as if you were going to play a chord on a piano or type a series of unrelated letters and numbers on the keyboard of your computer. Press deeply into the dough, but not so far that you push away the dough and touch the metal of the pan. The bread should look like a series of hills and valleys, not Swiss cheese. Repeat this process two or three times, until your dough has more dimples than Renata Tebaldi (that famously dimply opera star). Cover the dough with a clean towel or cloth and let rise for 45 minutes. The result should be double in height and puffy.

6) Somewhere in this process, and at least 30 minutes before you bake the dough, you should have preheated your oven to 425°F/220°C, with the baking stone inside. When you are ready to bake, revisit the dimples you have made and press more deeply, because the dough has risen in the meantime. Apply the topping by drizzling with the olive oil and then adding some coarse sea salt. Some bakers simply sprinkle the crystals on, others prefer to embed them in the dough. The choice is yours. Place the pan on your baking stone or on the middle rack of the oven. Reduce the oven temperature to 400°F/200°C.

7) You need to add cold water during the baking process to make the bread airy. Carol Field suggests spritzing the oven walls three times during the first 10 minutes of baking, using a small spritzer bottle. This works very well, and yields a good result, but a few bakers in Liguria say that opening the oven three times lowers the heat. They instead put a small ovenproof jar of cold water on the oven rack and leave the oven door shut. In my experience, the spritzing circulates the moisture better, and sometime I would love to do a taste test with an expert panel to see if they can differentiate between "spritzer" focaccia and "jar" focaccia.

8) Bake the focaccia for 25 minutes, until it is golden in color. Let cool for a few minutes, either in the pan or on a wire rack. Many bakers remove the bread from the pan immediately so that it will not stick, but in Liguria, where hot bread is quickly sold, they usually leave it in the pan and cut directly. If you plan to cut and eat the focaccia quickly, there is no need to remove it from the pan.

9) Eat it as hot as you can, and you will find yourself exclaiming, *Belin Che Fugassa!*

Fugassa co-o Formaggio (Focaccia col Formaggio)
Cheese Focaccia

Here it is: the recipe for what is probably the most addictive food on the planet. Cheese focaccia, the pride of Recco, is indescribably wonderful. The cheese has a slight tang that contrasts nicely with the silky blandness of the crêpe-like bread. This is not thick, crunchy focaccia like all the others, but is a bread of such delicacy that you cannot imagine it until you have tasted it. As you have read on page 118, the people of Recco take immense pride in their bread (and all their food), and have established a consortium to protect and defend it. I was trained in making the bread by Titta Moltedo of the Consorzio, and I feel as though I have been inducted into a society of highly privileged members. The words and information I pass along to you are largely his, although I have some observations about the cheese that you use.

In those few circumstances in which I have encountered Focaccia col Formaggio beyond a thirty-kilometer radius of Recco, it almost invariably has contained the wrong cheese. Many food writers with an inaccurate knowledge of Italian as well as Ligurian usage have perpetuated certain misconceptions. Here is the story: There is a delicious, soft, slightly sweet cow's milk cheese made in Lombardy called Stracchino. It has an edible white rind. This cheese is often eaten by Milanese children at breakfast. However, in Liguria, the word "Stracchino" is a local usage to describe Crescenza, which looks somewhat like the Lombard Stracchino, but is a different cheese. It does not have a rind, and where the Lombard cheese is sweet, Crescenza is tangy. This is the cheese that is to be used in Focaccia col Formaggio, not the sweetish Stracchino.

To further confuse things, much of the Crescenza used in Liguria is now made in Lombardy. One of the most popular brands is called Invernizzina, and that name has also entered Ligurian usage to denote the cheese (much as in North America "Kleenex" has become synonymous with "facial tissue" even though it is only a brand name).

Many brands of Crescenza are now available in North America. This is a recent development. Before that, only Stracchino was sold on this side of the ocean, and even expert cheese sellers occasionally think that Crescenza and Stracchino are the same thing. When you shop for cheese to make this bread, you want either a brand of Crescenza cheese or a cheese called Invernizzina. They are usually sold in little tubs covered with a plastic film. This is a perishable cheese and you should use it immediately. Look at the date stamped on the package for guidance; the younger the cheese, the better the result of the focaccia.

What to do if you cannot find this cheese? My suggestion is to buy either Taleggio or Stracchino. Soften this cheese in a bowl and then stir in either buttermilk or *prescinseua* (see page 79) to make the result creamy and tangy. Crescenza is not the cheese that was originally used for Focaccia col Formaggio, but it is the one that has taken over in modern times.

In the twelfth century, the Levante coast of Liguria was frequently raided by the Saracens. The people of Recco retreated to the inland hills, taking with them flour and olive oil to survive during the sieges. In the hills lived wild goats who were domesticated, and their milk was turned into cheese. The flour, oil, and water were converted into unleavened crêpe-like bread that was baked together with cheese in improvised outdoor hearths. When the people returned to Recco, they had a new specialty to feast on. At some point in history, cow's milk cheese replaced goat's milk cheese. This cow's milk cheese was called *formagetta* ("little cheese"), but there are very few people left who make it.

In the early part of the twentieth century, Emanuela Capurro of Recco served Focaccia col Formaggio, using *formagetta,* in her trattoria. Manuelina ("Little Emanuela") as she was universally called, drew diners from near and far to sample her specialty. Following World War II, when much of Recco was destroyed, her heirs expanded their restaurant on Recco's Via Roma, and were among the pioneers of the dish as it is eaten today. The restaurant, called Manuelina, is one of the best in Liguria, offering not only this bread (which most people eat as the first course of their meal), but superb pasta (especially *pansôti*) and excellent main courses.

Titta Moltedo tells me that after the war, restaurants became the primary producers of Focaccia col Formaggio, while before it was the bakers. He said that even a few miles from Recco the focaccia is not as good. I tested his assertion many times and, to my surprise, he really was not exaggerating. In Genoa, approximately 12 miles/20 km away, they use less cheese and the crust is thicker.

Titta taught me two methods for making Focaccia col Formaggio. The first is the *metodo antico,* the one that recalls the way it was made centuries ago in country hearths. This is how the traditional bakers of Recco make it. If you have a wood-burning oven, this would be the way to do it. The *metodo moderno,* or modern method, is made by bakers who are less classically oriented but it is also suitable for everyday cooks who will bake this bread in their home ovens.

5 cups/570 g unbleached all-purpose flour
1½ cups/340 ml tepid water
6 tablespoons/90 ml Ligurian extravirgin olive oil
4½ pounds/2 kilos Crescenza or Invernizzina cheese
Some cornmeal
Sea salt

METODO ANTICO

Make a dough by combining the flour, water, and oil. Do not add all of the water at first; you may find that the dough is elastic and smooth enough without it. Cover the dough with a cloth and let it sit for 1 hour in a warm, draft-free environment. Work the dough for a couple of minutes, and then let it sit for 5 more minutes. Then cut the dough into 2 pieces, one a bit larger than the

Makes
1 focaccia

other. Roll the larger piece into a giant round sheet, about ⅓ inch/1 to 1½ mm in thickness and about 20 inches/50 cm in diameter. Place the sheet on a wooden board (with a handle) on which you have sprinkled some cornmeal. Dot the dough with many scoops of cheese about the size of Ping-Pong balls. Then roll out the other piece of dough even thinner, until it is almost transparent. Place this sheet atop the bottom sheet. You will be able to see the pieces of cheese through the sheet of dough. Gently press down on the dough around the pieces of cheese, but not on top of them. In this fashion, you will see many little balls protruding from the flat surface. Be careful not to puncture the dough when you press down. Then, oil your fingers lightly and run them around the edge of the dough to crimp and seal the 2 pieces together. Add a little salt and a few drops of olive oil atop the bread. Slide the bread into the oven, which should be about 575°F/280°C. Bake for 10 minutes, or until it is golden brown on top. Remove using the wooden paddle, and slide onto a marble surface or a metal pan. Cut the bread into pieces and serve immediately, making sure not to spill too much melted cheese in the process. Focaccia col Formaggio must be eaten piping hot, perhaps with a knife and fork, and accompanied by white wine.

METODO MODERNO

Use the same ingredients as indicated above, except that you will not need the cornmeal. Have a large round pan (about 20 inches/50 cm in diameter) or a rectangular one of similar capacity. *It is very important that this pan have as thin a bottom as possible so that heat may be transferred readily to the bread.* The pan must also have a lip or rim so that the melted cheese does not run off. Make the dough and form it as indicated in the *metodo antico*. Grease the pan well with olive oil. Place the bottom sheet of dough in the pan, stretching it so that it takes the shape of the pan. Then add the cheese, top with the other, thinner sheet of dough, and press down around the balls of cheese. Then crimp and seal the 2 sheets of dough. Bake in a preheated 450°F/230°C oven for about 25 minutes, or until the top is golden brown. Cut the bread into pieces on the pan, and serve immediately.

Cheese focaccia before it is baked

Fugassa co-a Çiòula (Focaccia con la Cipolla)
Focaccia with Onions

Many people consider this the most delicious focaccia of all. I have an Italian friend who spent much of his childhood in Santa Margherita. Although he has lived in New York for more than fifteen years, he has said on many occasions, and in all seriousness, that he would cross the Atlantic simply to eat a fresh batch of onion focaccia.

The original idea of onion focaccia was to make the eater think of home. The women of Camogli have told me that in the past it was the custom for women to eat onion focaccia just before their men went to sea. As the sailors and fishermen were set to embark, their wives and girlfriends would give them a big onion-scented kiss that would supposedly make the men less desirable to women in other ports. What I have always wondered about is whether those "other women" also ate onion focaccia so that they could meet those wayward seamen on equal terms.

1 basic focaccia recipe (see page 123)
1 to 2 large onions (depending on your taste and who you are eating with), sliced thin
  or coarsely chopped, as you wish
Ligurian extravirgin olive oil

Makes
1 focaccia

After preparing the basic focaccia recipe, cut the onions according to your preference and cover the top of the dough with them. Liberally drizzle more olive oil. Bake according to the standard directions, about 25 minutes, and serve hot.

VARIATION: Steam the onions slightly before slicing them. This will take out some of the sharpness.

About Camogli

Sulla strada che porta a Camogli	On the road leading to Camogli
Andava un uomo con sette mogli	Went a man with seven wives
Ed ogni moglie aveva sette sacchi	And every wife had seven sacks
Ed in ogni sacco c'erano sette gatti.	And in every sack there were seven cats.
Tra gatti, sacchi e mogli,	Between cats, sacks and wives,
In quanti andavano a Camogli?	How many were en route to Camogli?

This tongue-twister and riddle is a popular old favorite of Italian children. While it is not as rhythmic in English as in Italian, it still makes a nice puzzle. It is also, as far as I know, the only mention of Camogli in any expression or literature that would be familiar to most Italians. (The answer, by the way, is 400 — 7 wives, 49 sacks, and 343 cats, plus the man.)

Fugassa co-o Romanin (Focaccia col Rosmarino)

Rosemary Focaccia

You are limited here only by your access to fresh rosemary. I have tasted rosemary focaccia that is only lightly flavored, yet I have also encountered focaccia that is practically covered with the herb. The choice is up to you, and depends on your own taste and that of your guests. Note: I once made Garlic Soup (page 273) and substituted rosemary focaccia for toast — it was divine!

1 basic focaccia recipe (see page 123)
Abundant fresh rosemary needles, carefully removed from stem and wiped with paper
   toweling
Ligurian extravirgin olive oil

Makes
1 focaccia

After making the dough and spreading it in the pan, top with as much rosemary as you want and bake according to the basic recipe. Brush with olive oil and serve. This focaccia is also good at room temperature.

Fugassa co-a Sarvia (Focaccia con la Salvia)

Sage Focaccia

For this recipe to work, the sage must be absolutely fresh. Dried sage will make the bread taste musty, which is unacceptable. The amount of sage indicated below is just a suggestion. You may add more or less, as you see fit.

1 basic focaccia recipe (see page 123)
20 to 24 fresh sage leaves, wiped clean, torn into very small pieces

Makes
1 focaccia

As you add the ingredients to the well in the flour while you are making your dough, add the pieces of sage leaves as well. Bake according to the basic directions for making focaccia. Serve hot, perhaps with a soft, mild cheese such as Crescenza or Stracchino smeared on top.

Focaccia al Gorgonzola

This is a relatively recent innovation, one that has become immensely popular because it is scrumptious.

1 basic focaccia recipe (see page 123)*
½ pound/225 g Gorgonzola Dolce (the yellower cheese; the whiter one, called
  Piccante, is fine too, although the result will be a bit different)

> * Rocco Rizzo in Camogli makes Gorgonzola focaccia using a dough filled with sage (see page 132). It is exquisite, but you should use less sage than you would if there were no cheese on top.

Make the focaccia dough according to the instructions. When you dimple the dough for the second time, then put little pieces of Gorgonzola in each indentation. Sprinkle on less salt than you normally would. Bake according to the instructions and serve hot or warm, so that the cheese is still soft and runny.

Makes
1 focaccia

Fugassa co-e Porpe [in the Levante] (Focaccia con le Olive)
Fugassa co-a Murcia [in the Ponente]
Focaccia with Olives

1 basic focaccia recipe (see page 123)
1¾ cups/7 ounces/200 g Taggia olives in brine, plus 20 olives, or 1¼ cups/
  5 ounces/140 g olive paste (paté di olive), plus 20 olives
Ligurian extravirgin olive oil

Drain and pit all but 20 of the olives, and chop them coarsely. Prepare the focaccia dough as indicated in the recipe. Before kneading, add the chopped olives (or the olive paste) to the well of the dough and knead thoroughly. After placing the dough in the pan, lodge the remaining 20 olives (which you may pit if you wish) in the top of the focaccia dough and bake normally, brushing with oil as usual when the bread is baked.

Makes
1 focaccia

Focaccia al Tartufo

Truffle Focaccia

Makes
1 focaccia

This is not something I have ever tasted in Liguria, where such extravagance would probably not be appreciated, but rather is a product of my own kitchen. If you purchase or are given the gift of oil that is infused with truffles, use it to brush on top of the freshly baked focaccia. Do not use truffle oil in the dough. The delicate fragrance and flavor will fade during the baking. If you have truffle paste in a tube and olive oil, you can make your own truffle oil. For every teaspoon of truffle paste, use 4 tablespoons of Ligurian extravirgin olive oil. Stir the paste into the bottom of a dish and then add the oil. Stir together so that the oil gathers and entirely incorporates the truffle paste. Then brush it on freshly baked focaccia, eliminating the added coarse salt.

1 basic focaccia recipe (see page 123)
Truffle oil

Fugassa co-e Patatte (Focaccia con le Patate)

Potato Focaccia

This focaccia is slightly softer than others and has the pleasing and unmistakable subtext of potato flavor.

1 basic focaccia recipe (see page 123), except that the dough should be made with 1¼
*   cups plus 2 teaspoons / 180 g flour instead of the customary 2½ cups*
6 ounces / 1½ cups / 175 g white mealy potatoes, peeled, boiled, cooled, and mashed

Makes
1 focaccia

Make the focaccia as indicated in the basic recipe except that when you make the dough, use less flour as described above and incorporate the mashed potatoes. Otherwise, this focaccia is made like the standard one.

Focacce with olives and herbs

Gizzoa (Focaccia con la Salsiccia)
Sausage Focaccia

This preparation is a specialty of the province of La Spezia. This should not surprise you because this area has always had access to fine pork products from nearby Emilia-Romagna. You should select a cured sausage that is already cooked, preferably one that crumbles easily when the casing is removed. In that the Italian version of such sausage is probably not available to you, consider using a good basic peppery breakfast sausage that is easily located.

1 dough recipe for Focaccia col Formaggio (see page 127)
Ligurian extravirgin olive oil
⅔ pound/300 g crumbled cooked sausage, drained
Freshly ground black pepper (optional)

Makes
1 focaccia

Preheat oven to 350°F/180°C. Make the focaccia dough as indicated. After creating two sheets of dough, stretch one on the bottom of a pan that has been lightly greased with Ligurian extravirgin olive oil. Distribute the crumbled sausage evenly around the dough. Sprinkle with pepper. Then cover with the other sheet of dough. Press down lightly so that the two sheets of dough meet in places where there is no sausage. Pierce the dough in various places with the tines of a fork so that air can escape. Seal the edges of the focaccia with a little olive oil and discard any extra dough. Bake without a water container or spraying, for 5 to 7 minutes, or until the crust begins to turn gold in color. Serve hot.

Focaccette

Cheese Puffs

This recipe, a Ligurian classic, comes from Lorenza and Roberto Volpini, dear friends from Recco. Lorenza painstakingly taught me many things about cooking in Liguria, and I am grateful to her. Simone Volpini, their son, loves his mother's cooking and devours her *focaccette* with great delight. *Focaccette* are indeed breads, sort of cheese-filled fry breads, that are popular as snacks and antipasti. They go well with a glass of light wine, either red or white.

3 cups/600 g unbleached all-purpose flour
1¾ cups/400 ml tepid whole milk
4 tablespoons/60 ml Ligurian extravirgin olive oil
¾ pound/12 ounces/350 g Crescenza or Gorgonzola, room temperature
2¼ cups/500 ml sunflower or corn oil for frying

1) Create a mound of flour on your work surface and form a well in the middle. Add the milk and then the oil to the well, a little bit at a time. As you add the liquids with one hand, use the other to incorporate the flour into the liquid. Once all the milk and oil have been added, use both hands to form a soft elastic dough. If the dough seems too firm, add more milk but not more oil. Form the dough into a ball and wrap it in a clean towel or cloth.

Makes about 36 focaccette

2) Slightly heat a large pot and place it over the cloth-wrapped dough. Leave for 15 minutes. This will warm the dough slightly and soften it.

3) Cut off a small chunk of dough about 3 inches/7.5 cm wide. Roll it out with a rolling pin or pass it through a manual pasta machine (about 5 or 6 times) until the dough is about ⅟₁₆ inch/.16 cm thick, about 15 inches/38 cm long, and almost transparent. Lift one end and fold it over so that it touches the other end. Make a crease in the fold and then open the dough again.

4) You will put portions of cheese on one side of the crease. Place 2 tablespoons of cheese about 1½ inches/3.75 cm away from the crease. Then place 2 more tablespoons of cheese 2 inches/5 cm away (toward the end of the dough) from the first mound of cheese. Create another mound of cheese 2 inches/5 cm away from the second mound and another mound 2 inches/5 cm beyond the third one.

5) Now lift the half of the dough that does not have cheese on it and fold it over the part with the mounds of cheese. Press down the dough around the mounds so that they look like little hills (see photograph on page 139). Then, using a fluted ravioli or pastry wheel, cut along the 4 outside seams of the

rectangle of dough (2 lengths and 2 widths, as in the photograph). This means that you will also be cutting the crease, which is fine.

6) Use the wheel to create 4 individual *focaccette,* each one with a mound of cheese at its center. Set aside in a draft-free place.

7) Repeat the process until you have made all of the *focaccette.*

8) Heat the sunflower or corn oil (or any odor-free vegetable oil) in a 9- to 10-inch/23- to 25-cm frying pan. The oil should not get so hot that it smokes. Put 3 or 4 *focaccette* in at a time and fry for 3 to 5 minutes, until they puff out and become slightly golden and crunchy. Let them dry briefly on paper toweling, salt lightly (if you wish), and serve immediately. *Focaccette* may be eaten by hand or with a knife and fork.

The Healthy and Unhealthy Aspects of Liguria (According to One Observer in 1879)

Of the more than forty books (mostly by Englishmen) about journeying to Liguria to restore one's health, the most distinct is probably *The Riviera: Sketches of the Health Resorts of the Northern Mediterranean Coast of France and Italy from Hyères to Spezia* by Edward I. Sparks. He deals with the salubrious aspects of the region with fastidious detail, but never feels fully comfortable with a place so many other observers rhapsodized about.

On the medical qualities of Liguria: "No doubt the Riviera possesses a remarkable combination of favorable natural conditions not to be met with in many parts of the world, and certainly not elsewhere in Europe; and this combination undoubtedly works wonders in many cases, if steady improvement from the moment of the patient's arrival on the Mediterranean coast be any criterion."

Of the many Russians who flocked to the Riviera di Ponente: "I understand . . . That they undo most of the benefits of the climate by living in hot, ill-ventilated rooms, and by frequenting theatres, and also the Casino . . . even when in an advanced state of disease."

But there are problems: "The chief objection to living close to the sea at Pegli is the near proximity of the native population *en deshabille.*"

Lorenza Volpini shapes her focaccette

Sardenaira
San Remo Pizza

It seems that for as long as there has been pizza in Naples there has been *sardenaira* in San Remo. Of course, *sardenaira* does not have cheese, and it has garlic and olives that speak in a pronounced Ligurian accent. This is a wonderful bread that makes a perfect appetizer with wine, or can accompany meals based on less flavorful preparations (poached fish, or a large green salad, are two examples). It is made with anchovies, but the name suggests that it probably was once made with sardines.

FOR THE DOUGH
⅔ cup/170 ml warm water (between 105°and 115°F/40°and 45°C)
2½ teaspoons (1 package)/6 g active dry yeast
3½ cups/400 g unbleached all-purpose flour
7 ounces/⅞ cup/200 ml Ligurian extravirgin olive oil (plus oil for greasing
    and flavoring)
1 pinch salt

FOR THE TOPPING
3½ cups/400 g peeled tomatoes (use canned San Marzano tomatoes,
    if fresh are unavailable)
1 pinch freshly ground black pepper
4 salted anchovies
2 tablespoons/15 g capers packed in vinegar
3 ounces/⅜ cup/85 ml Ligurian extravirgin olive oil
20 Taggia or Niçoise olives packed in brine or oil
10 small cloves of garlic, peeled, split, with the green heart removed
2 tablespoons/15 g minced fresh oregano or ⅔ tablespoon/5 g dried oregano
12 small or 6 large basil leaves, wiped and torn into pieces
1 pinch coarse sea salt

Makes
1 sardenaira
10½ x 15½ inches /
27 x 39 cm in size

Add the yeast to the warm water and stir lightly. Let stand until the water is creamy, about 10 minutes. Once this is ready, place your flour on a work surface and form a well in the middle. Add the olive oil, a pinch of salt, and the yeast/water combination. Work the ingredients together to form a soft and somewhat elastic dough. Add a little more water, if necessary. Spread the dough in a well-greased pan (the one you use for focaccia) so that you have a crust that is about ¼ inch/.6 cm thick. Cover with a clean cloth and place in a warm, draft-free environment. Let it rise for about 1 hour. In the meantime, prepare the topping.

Cook 2¾ cups/300 g of tomatoes with a pinch of pepper for a few minutes, just until they disintegrate. Let cool. Coarsely chop the other tomatoes and add them to the sauce. Pound the anchovies and half of the capers in a mortar to form a paste (or use 1 or 2 tablespoons of anchovy paste, although it will not taste as vibrant; you may also use a little Salsa di Pinoli, Capperi e Acciughe [see page 102], although *pinoli* are not a traditional ingredient in *sardenaira*). Add the tomato sauce to the mortar. Then add the unused capers, and stir to combine all of the elements.

Once the dough has risen, spread the tomato-anchovy mixture all over the dough. Drizzle the olive oil atop the sauce. Stud the crust with olives and half cloves of garlic. Then top with oregano and basil and a little coarse sea salt. Bake in a preheated 450°F/230°C oven for about 35 to 40 minutes, or until borders of the crust are crunchy and golden brown. Serve hot, tepid, or cool.

VARIATION: Instead of making the anchovy-caper paste, you may use *machetto*, the sardine paste described on page 103. In some areas, the resulting bread is called *machetusa*, although *machetusa* in other areas is a simpler affair, made principally with *machetto* and a few pieces of tomato (as opposed to a sauce), a few olives, and pieces of garlic. The dominant flavor becomes sardine and not tomato.

Pizza all'Andrea (Piscialandrea)
Andrea Doria Pizza

This bread is to Imperia what *sardenaira* is to San Remo. There is a small controversy (which will never be resolved) as to the origin of the name. People in Nice will say that this is a blatant appropriation of *pissaladière,* a similar bread made across the border that uses a paste of anchovies and/or sardines. In Imperia they insist that the bread is theirs, named for Andrea Doria, the renowned admiral of the Genoese Republic who was born in the port of Oneglia in the old section of Imperia. You can visit his house, directly opposite the Mercato Comunale, on the Via Andrea Doria.

FOR THE DOUGH
⅔ cup/170 ml warm water (between 105° and 115°F/40° and 45°C)
2½ teaspoons (1 package)/6 g active dry yeast
3½ cups/400 g unbleached all-purpose flour
7 ounces/⅞ cup/200 ml Ligurian extravirgin olive oil (plus oil for greasing and flavoring)
1 pinch salt

FOR THE TOPPING
¼ cup/4 tablespoons/60 ml Ligurian extravirgin olive oil (plus more oil to grease the pan and drizzle atop the bread)
1 pound/450 g fresh tomatoes, seeded, drained (whether you peel the tomatoes is your call), and coarsely chopped
12 salted anchovies, chopped into bits
2 cloves garlic, green heart removed, minced
2 large white onions, sliced fine
15 to 20 Taggia olives, packed in brine or oil
1 tablespoon/7 g fresh oregano or ⅓ tablespoon/2 g dried oregano
4 to 6 small or 2 or 3 large basil leaves, wiped, then torn

Makes 1 pizza, 10½ x 15½ inches / 27 x 39 cm in size

Add the yeast to the warm water and stir lightly. Let stand until the water is creamy, about 10 minutes. Once this is ready, place your flour on a work surface and form a well in the middle. Add the olive oil, a pinch of salt, and the yeast/water combination. Work the ingredients together to form a soft and somewhat elastic dough. Add a little more water, if necessary. Spread the dough in a well-greased pan (the one you use for focaccia) so that you have a crust that is about ¼ inch/.6 cm thick. Cover with a clean cloth and place in a warm, draft-free environment. Let it rise for about 1 hour. In the meantime, prepare the topping.

Once the dough has risen, grease it with ¼ cup/4 tablespoons/60 ml Ligurian extravirgin olive oil. Then top with pieces of tomato, anchovy, and garlic. Then carpet the entire bread with onion slices, so that you can only barely see what is underneath. Garnish with olives, oregano, and basil and bake in a preheated 450°F/230°C oven for about 35 to 40 minutes, or until borders of the crust are crunchy and golden brown. Serve hot, tepid, or cool.

The tiny port of Camogli

At work in fishing boats, Camogli

At leisure near luxury boats, Portofino

"Napoli," Camogli's oldest fisherman

A solitary fisherman prepares to go to sea

Preparing bait in Vernazza

Camogli

Ligurians dote on fresh anchovies

*The catch of the day
at the Mercato Orientale, Genoa*

*Fisherman fry fish
at Camogli's Sagra del Pesce*

Whitebait fritters are divine

*The women of Badalucco clean stockfish
for the annual feast*

Liguria's funghi *are abundant and glorious*

Bietole *(beet greens) are a Ligurian staple*

*The vegetables of the Italian Riviera
are unmatched in flavor*

Verdure Ripiene *(stuffed vegetables)*

Focaccette are perfect as an appetizer

Rocco Rizzo, Camogli's great baker

Focaccia col Formaggio, from Recco — perhaps the world's most addictive food

Focaccia,
the staff of life on the Italian Riviera

(Dana Gallagher)

La Farinata

Chickpea Tart

Farinata is a great favorite of Ligurians, although it is not well known outside of the region. The exception to this is Nice, across the border on the French Riviera, where the tart is called *socca*. On cool days in the late fall, winter, and early spring, Ligurians line up at farinata shops to get a piece of this thin crêpe-like bread as it issues from hot ovens. *Fainà,* as it is called in dialect, is always served on wax paper. While you can find farinata throughout the region, it is especially popular in Chiavari (in the Levante) and Oneglia (in the Ponente). In the past, farinata and *paniccia* (see page 147) were used as substitutes for fish on Fridays, and were served with onion and/or greens.

One can eat plain farinata, but Ligurians also like to add ingredients just before it is baked. Perhaps the most popular is fresh rosemary, although some people prefer fresh thyme. Coarsely chopped onions are a favorite in Oneglia, where the dish is then called *la frisciolata*. In the Ponente one often sees thin slices of raw baby artichoke in the batter. In the past it was popular to add whitebait to the batter, and one still occasionally encounters this delicacy. I discourage you from combining added ingredients; just use one. The added ingredient should be in a small amount. The idea is to add an interesting note, not to dominate the flavor of the tart. Warning: Farinata is delicious only when piping hot. When cool or cold it is very unappetizing. It is traditional to drink a glass of Pigato while eating a piece of hot farinata.

Good farinata is traditionally made in round copper pans that have a rim about 1⅓ inches/3 cm high. The tart should be paper-thin, the edges crunchy but not dried out, the middle somewhat moist. Before making farinata in a pan for the first time, you must prime the pan: Coat the bottom with Ligurian extravirgin olive oil, put it in a hot oven, and heat until the bottom turns gold. Then wipe with a towel. Next time, heat the pan before using it, then put in a thin coating of oil just before adding the batter. Every time the pan is used it must be hot and some oil must be added before the batter is added. This way the bread won't stick.

If you cannot find a suitable copper pan (I bought mine in Oneglia), you may substitute one made of aluminum or (preferably) stainless steel. This recipe is for a round pan that is 15 inches/38 cm in diameter.

1 quart/1 scant liter tepid water
2⅝ cups/300 g chickpea flour
1 pinch sea salt to taste
½ cup/115 ml Ligurian extravirgin olive oil
Freshly and finely ground black pepper
Olive oil to prime the pan

Place the water in a bowl and stir in the flour a little at a time, using a wooden spoon or a whisk. Stir until all the lumps are broken up. Let the mixture sit for 2 to 4 hours. In the meantime, get your oven hot (see below) and prime the pan. When you return to the batter, a slight foam may have formed on the top, and you should skim this before proceeding. Add sea salt, then the olive oil, and stir just until the oil is incorporated. If you are using fresh rosemary or other ingredients, stir them in now. Pour the batter into the pan. It is essential that the crêpe be no more than ⅓ inch/about 1 cm thick. It is better to save a little batter rather than make the crêpe too thick. Bake according to the directions that follow. The result should be golden brown. Top with freshly ground black pepper and eat immediately.

BAKING FARINATA

Every person I discussed farinata with had a different interpretation about how hot the oven should be and how long the tart should bake. There was agreement that the ideal is to have as hot an oven as possible. It is also preferable, if at all possible, to have the flame above the pan rather than below. Professional bakers usually have hotter ovens, so the results come sooner and are quite pleasing. After much trial and error, I have devised a small chart for temperatures and baking times for farinata. But the hotter the better.

TEMPERATURE	BAKING TIME
625°F/300°C (a professional oven)	5 to 7 minutes
525°F/260°C	10 to 14 minutes
425°F/220°C	20 to 25 minutes

During the course of baking, you may want to brush a little more oil on the top if the tart seems too dry.

Paniccia

Chickpea "Bread"

There has always been a healthy debate as to whether *paniccia* is a bread or should more likely be categorized among the first courses as a cousin of polenta. Because most Ligurians consider this Ponente specialty a bread, it has been placed in this chapter.

2½ cups/approximately 275 g chickpea flour
1 quart/1 scant liter tepid water dissolved with 1 pinch fine sea salt
Freshly ground black pepper (optional)
Ligurian extravirgin olive oil
Fresh lemon juice
1 pinch coarse sea salt
½ large or 1 small onion (as sweet or as sharp as you prefer), finely chopped

Take a large saucepan and add the chickpea flour and a little bit of the water. *Makes* Stir until the flour is slightly moist and then place the pan over a very low *4 to 6 servings* flame. Add more water, a few drops at a time, and keep stirring. Once the water has all been added, then put in a little black pepper, if you choose. The most important thing to do for this recipe to succeed is to never stop stirring. After about 45 minutes (it is labor-intensive, but Ligurians like that), spoon out the bread onto a dish. If you wish, form it into a loaf shape.

Eating *paniccia* hot: Cut a thin slice onto a plate and top with olive oil, lemon juice, a pinch of coarse salt, and a few pieces of chopped onion.

Eating *paniccia* cool: Cut a thin slice, top with olive oil and an abundance of chopped onion pieces.

Serve with Pigato or other Ligurian white wine.

Paul Valéry in Genoa (1910)

Valéry, ever the sensualist, paints a more vivid picture of Genoa than one usually heard from the overtly Romantic writers from Germany, Britain, or the United States. He knew Genoa well because his mother was from there, and to him the city was like one of those mysterious North African locales that was a blend of stimulation and danger. The *caruggi* he speaks of are the typical Ligurian side streets, invariably narrow and dark, often covered and tunnel-like, in which one would wander cautiously but excitedly, perhaps finding light at the other end, or perhaps not.

"Caruggi. Multitudes of children playing near poor semi-naked women who offer — not just chestnuts from nearby — but themselves, like immense golden cakes and chickpea tarts. These are like the sensations of Arab stories. . . . Concentrated smells, icy smells, drugs, cheeses, toasted coffee, delicious finely roasted cocoa. . . . Cypress trees, little churches, monks. Fragrant kitchens. There are gigantic cakes, chickpea flour [in bags], herbal mixtures, sardines in oil, hard-boiled eggs folded in pastry, spinach pies, fried fish. This is an ancient cuisine."

Gothic porticos on Genoa's busy
Via XX Settembre

Favetta

Fava Bread

Here is an ancient recipe that dates from a time, before Genoa became a major flour market in the thirteenth century, when wheat flour was a rare and precious commodity for many Ligurians. You will need to go to an Italian or Middle Eastern market or contact one of the flour sources (see pages 444–445) to locate fava flour. What surprises people nowadays is how delicate and sophisticated a food this is. This versatile bread is terrific for making canapés. I like to roll up strips of *favetta* with cooked onions or with a delicate sauce such as pine nut–marjoram or walnut or even *marò* (fava bean sauce), which is not redundant. I also like *favetta* wrapped around thin slices of Genoa salami or boiled shrimp.

1 quart / 1 scant liter cold water
1 generous pinch sea salt
2½ cups / 10 ounces / 300 g fava flour
Ligurian extravirgin olive oil
Freshly ground black pepper

Makes
4 to 6 servings

Set a large pot of water to boil to which you have added some salt. Once it reaches a boil, add the fava flour a bit at a time, stirring continuously. Lower the heat and cook for about an hour, stirring all the while so that the contents do not stick to the pot. Once this mixture is rather dense, pour it out on a broad flat plate or a marble surface so that it is quite flat. Let cool entirely. You will be able to cut this bread into finger-size strips. Top with a little olive oil and perhaps some pepper. You may also use the strips as I described above.

ALTERNATE USE: Cut this bread into strips. Take 2 sweet onions, mince well, and sauté them in olive oil along with strips of *favetta*. Eat with a fork or spoon.

Gallette del Marinaio

Sailor's Biscuits (or Sea Biscuits)

This is one of the fundamentals of the Ligurian kitchen. It is the bread that has gone to sea with sailors for many centuries. It sailed with Ligurians wherever they traveled, and represented home. These biscuits are quite hard, and may not strike you as being enticing. However, they served important functions. If someone was seasick, these were often the only things that could be digested. More usually, a sailor would add sea water to the biscuit, which would soften it and make it usable in cooking aboard ship. This is also the bread that appears in *cappon magro,* the most extravagant dish in the Ligurian kitchen, and in *capponadda.* This recipe is from Rocco Rizzo of Camogli, one of the few bakers in Liguria who still makes the *gallette del marinaio* in the traditional way.

Approximately 3 cups/700 ml warm (110°F/43°C) water
¼ cup/4 tablespoons/30 g active dry yeast
8¾ cups/1 kilo unbleached all-purpose flour
¼ cup/4 tablespoons/30 g malt powder
3 tablespoons/20 g fine sea salt

Put the yeast in a large bowl and dissolve it in about 1 cup of water. Let stand for about 10 minutes, whisking periodically so that the mixture becomes creamy. Add all but ½ cup of the flour, the malt powder, the salt, and most of the rest of the water. Your requirements for water and flour will vary slightly based on the ingredients you are using, so you should keep a little of each in reserve to make the dough wetter or drier, as need be. Whisk at first and then combine the ingredients with your hands. The dough that results should be soft, firm, and consistent, not runny or lumpy. Knead on a floured surface for 3 to 4 minutes, then cover and let the dough rest in a warm, draft-free space for 1 hour. Then take small pieces of dough and roll them out with a rolling pin until you form flat disks about 2 inches/5 cm in diameter. Lay these disks out on a work surface, cover them, and let them sit for 1 hour more. Then, using a fork, make numerous holes in each biscuit and place the biscuits on a baking stone that you have already heated for 30 minutes in a 400°F/200°C oven. Bake for 15 minutes. Let cool entirely before using. When stored in an airtight container, these biscuits can last for weeks.

Makes 30 to 35 biscuits

The Ligurian Social Fabric

The *tessuto sociale,* the social fabric of Liguria that I mention on page 19, is not a new phenomenon. Just as the Ospedale di San Martino of Genoa, Europe's largest hospital, was built for the people of Liguria, similar institutions existed in the past. Travel guides of the nineteenth century encourage people passing through Genoa to visit not only the palaces and the port, but the rest homes and social service institutions Ligurians created to care for their own. They were considered remarkable at a time when social welfare and a sense of "the common good" were rare things in Europe. Dr. Joseph Schneer, a medical doctor who was one of the many authors of books about wintering in Liguria to restore one's health, described the Ligurian social fabric in his 1887 book, *Alassio: A Pearl of the Riviera.*

"The character of the people is a kindly one. They are very neighbourly with each other, and towards strangers friendly and obliging. They are contented with their humble lot, honest and temperate, drunkenness being a rarity with them. Stealing is almost unknown here, and the houses are left, for the most part, unlocked. One sees heavily-laden donkeys standing fastened for hours at the street-corners, whilst their owners, apparently, have no fear of losing an item of their property. They are peaceful, no murder having been committed here within the memory of man, and cruelty to animals is not practised, as in the rest of Italy. . . . Owing to the frugality and contentedness of the inhabitants, there is no real poverty here. . . . An hospital, 'Ricovero di Mendicità,' is provided by the municipality for the poor who are no longer able for work. We have here the [model promoted] over all Italy by [the Ligurian] Garibaldi, the 'Società Operaia.' Each member on entering pays a contribution of two francs, besides a yearly subscription of twelve francs. This secures him, in case of illness, not only medical advice gratis, but money for maintenance during the whole time he is unfit for work."

Spreading nets out to dry, Camogli

Torta
Basic Savory Pie Recipes

While in the rest of Italy, *torta* usually means cake in the dessert sense, in Liguria a *torta* is usually a filled savory pie containing vegetables and cheese. This sort of *torta* is technically a bread, but it usually appears on the Ligurian table either as an appetizer or as a main course. It typically is eaten at room temperature so that your palate discovers flavor rather than temperature. To make things more confusing, there are certain Ligurian vegetable preparations without doughs that also go by the name *torta* (you will find some of these beginning on page 303). The following recipes are for the type of pies that Ligurians fill with ingredients between a top and bottom shell in a round pie dish. There is only one difference between Recipe 1 and Recipe 2. The first recipe is for a pie with a layer of crust above the filling and another below. The second recipe is for a pie that has layers of dough between the filling as well.

BASIC TORTA RECIPE I
5 cups/570 g unbleached flour
1 teaspoon/3 g fine sea salt
⅔ cup/170 ml water
2 tablespoons/30 ml Ligurian extravirgin olive oil

Preheat oven to 350°F/180°C. Place the flour on a flat work surface and form a well in the middle. Add the salt and then add the water, a little at a time. Amalgamate the flour, water, and olive oil to form a dough. Knead it gently, and just long enough for it to be smooth to the touch. Let the dough rest, covered, for 1 hour. Then cut the dough in two pieces. Roll out the first piece until it is slightly more than ¼ inch/½ cm thick. Do the same with the other piece of dough. Place the dough on a 12-inch/30-cm round baking pan that has been lightly greased with olive oil. (You can, if you prefer, use a springform pan instead so that you will remove the *torta* rather than cutting it in the pan.) Fill with whatever filling you are using and then cover with the other sheet of dough. Crimp around the edges so that the two pieces of dough are joined. Make a couple of slits in the top layer of dough. Drizzle a little olive oil on top of the crust. Bake in the oven for 40 minutes, or until the crust is golden.

BASIC TORTA RECIPE 2
9½ cups/1000 g unbleached flour
2 teaspoons/6 g fine sea salt
1⅓ cups/340 ml water
4 tablespoons/60 ml Ligurian extravirgin olive oil

Preheat oven to 350°F/180°C. Place the flour on a flat surface and form a well in the middle. Add the salt and then add the water, a little at a time. Amalgamate the flour, water, and olive oil to form a dough. Knead it gently and just long enough for it to be smooth to the touch. Let the dough rest, covered, for 1 hour. Then cut the dough in five pieces, two larger and three smaller. Roll out the first large piece until it is slightly more than ¼ inch/½ cm thick. Do the same with the other large piece of dough. Cover each with a cloth. Then roll the three smaller pieces until they are ¹⁄₁₆ inch/.16 cm. These will be the very thin layers that you will place in the pie between layers of filling. Cover these.

Place the large piece of dough on a 12-inch/30-cm round baking pan that has been lightly greased with olive oil. (You can, if you prefer, use a springform pan instead so that you will remove the torta rather than cutting it in the pan.) Fill with about ¼ of whatever filling you are using, then add a thin layer of dough. Add more filling, then another layer, then more filling, then another layer, then more filling.* Then cover with the other large sheet of dough. Crimp around the edges so that the two pieces of dough are joined. Make a couple of slits in the top layer of dough. Drizzle a little olive oil on top of the crust. Bake in the oven for 40 minutes, or until the crust is golden.

> * Note: This is where you can become creative. Many cooks like to create layers with different ingredients. So one might have greens, the next cheese, and the next artichokes.

"The hils and mountaines [of Italy] lying upon the South Sunne, are in generall most fertile or fruitfull of all other . . . such are the mountaines and hils of Liguria, lying upon the Tyrrhene Sea."

— Fynes Moryson,
An Itinerary, 1907-1908

Torta di Verdura

Savory Pie Filled with Greens

Your fantasy is your guide in creating this pie. Most Ligurians will put beet greens and perhaps *preboggion* in this pie, but some spinach is also nice, as is arugula and even watercress. If you plan to use assertive-tasting greens, be sure not to overdo it. Combine them with milder greens as well.

1 basic torta recipe, either #1 or #2 (see page 154)
4 cups/550 g mixed greens, well washed, with the tough stems removed
4 tablespoons/30 g unsalted butter
½ onion, minced
1¾ cups/200 g ricotta or prescinseua
1¼ cups/140 g freshly grated Parmigiano-Reggiano
2 tablespoons fresh marjoram, torn
3 large eggs, beaten
Fine sea salt
Freshly ground black pepper
1 pinch flour
Ligurian extravirgin olive oil

Rinse the greens well and then steam them, using only the water that clings to their leaves. Squeeze them dry and chop coarsely. In a small saucepan melt the butter, then sauté the onion until it is translucent. Add the chopped greens and sauté for 2 to 3 minutes. Let cool. In a large bowl combine the greens mixture (butter and all) with the ricotta or *prescinseua*, the Parmigiano-Reggiano, marjoram, eggs, salt and pepper to taste, and a pinch of flour.

Depending on which torta recipe you elect to use, you may either fill the whole pie with filling, or place layers of filling between layers of dough.

Cover everything with the upper sheet of dough. Crimp around the edges so that the upper and lower layers of dough are joined. Make a couple of slits in the top layer of dough. Drizzle a little olive oil on top of the crust. Bake in the preheated 350°F/180°C oven for 40 minutes, or until the crust is golden.

Torta di Carciofi e Verdura

Savory Pie Filled with Artichokes and Greens

This is a delicate pie in flavor, so you should use milder greens for the filling.

1 basic torta recipe, either #1 or #2 (see page 154)
2 cups/275 g mixed greens, well washed, with the tough stems removed
6 small fresh artichokes, sliced thin, then doused in lemon juice
4 tablespoons/30 g unsalted butter
½ onion, minced
1¾ cups/200 g ricotta or prescinseua
1¼ cups/140 g freshly grated Parmigiano-Reggiano
2 tablespoons torn fresh marjoram
Fine sea salt
Freshly ground black pepper
1 pinch flour
2 large hard-boiled eggs, cut into quarters
Ligurian extravirgin olive oil

Rinse the greens well and then steam them, using only the water that clings to their leaves. Squeeze them dry and chop coarsely. Prepare the artichokes. In a small saucepan melt the butter, then sauté the onion until it is translucent. Add the chopped greens and artichoke pieces. Sauté for 2 to 3 minutes. Let cool.

If you plan to make torta recipe #1, combine all of the ingredients in a large bowl (sautéed greens mixture with the ricotta or *prescinseua,* grated cheese, marjoram, salt and pepper to taste, and a pinch of flour), except for the boiled eggs. Then fill the shell with filling, placing pieces of boiled egg at various points throughout. Top with the other sheet of dough. Crimp around the edges so that the upper and lower layers of dough are joined. Make a couple of slits in the top layer of dough. Drizzle a little olive oil on top of the crust. Bake in the preheated 350°F/180°C oven for 40 minutes, or until the crust is golden.

If you plan to make torta recipe #2, separately sauté the artichokes in one pan and the onions and greens in another. Combine cheeses and mix some of that cheese with the greens, some with the artichokes, and a little with the boiled eggs. Then build the torta by placing most of the greens at the bottom, then a layer of eggs, then a layer of artichokes, and then a layer with the rest of the greens. Cover with the top layer of dough. Crimp around the edges so that the upper and lower layers of dough are joined. Make a couple of slits in the top layer of dough. Drizzle a little olive oil on top of the crust. Bake in the preheated 350°F/180°C oven for 40 minutes, or until the crust is golden.

Torta di Riso e Verdura

Savory Pie Filled with Rice and Greens

This recipe is adapted from the one made at the Salumeria Chiesa, an excellent food shop in Finale Ligure in the province of Savona.

1 basic torta recipe #1 (see page 154)
3 cups / 350 g mixed greens, well washed, with the tough stems removed
3½ cups / 800 ml whole milk
2 cups / 225 g Italian rice (preferably, or at the very least, good slow-cooking rice)
4 tablespoons / 30 g unsalted butter
1 onion, minced
1 large egg, beaten
Fine sea salt
Freshly ground black pepper
Ligurian extravirgin olive oil

Rinse the greens well and then steam them, using only the water that clings to their leaves. Squeeze them dry and chop coarsely. Now cook the rice. Heat, but do not boil, the milk in a saucepan. Add the rice and cook for 10 to 15 minutes, or until the rice is chewy and the milk is slightly thickened by the rice starch. Let cool. Melt the butter in another pan and sauté the onions until they are translucent. Then add the chopped greens. Sauté for 2 to 3 minutes. Let cool. Then combine the rice and milk mixture, the sautéed onions and greens, the beaten egg, and the salt and pepper to taste.

Place one layer of dough in the bottom of a lightly oiled baking dish. Then add the filling to the shell. Top with the second layer of dough and crimp around the edges so that the upper and lower layers of dough are joined. Make a couple of slits in the top layer of dough. Drizzle a little olive oil on top of the crust. Bake in the preheated 350°F/180°C oven for 40 minutes, or until the crust is golden.

Lining up for focaccia and torta *in Chiavari*

Torta di Cipolle

Onion Savory Pie

Try to locate sweet onions, which will give this pie a lovely flavor.

1 basic torta recipe #1 (see page 154)
3 tablespoons/45 ml Ligurian extravirgin olive oil
4 tablespoons/30 g unsalted butter
2 pounds/900 g sweet onions, chopped
2 large potatoes, peeled, cut in half, boiled, cooled, mashed
3 large eggs, beaten
1 cup/115 g freshly grated Parmigiano-Reggiano
Fine sea salt
Freshly ground black pepper

Heat the olive oil and butter together in a large pan and sauté the onions until they are translucent. Let cool slightly. Then combine the onions with the mashed potatoes, the beaten eggs, grated cheese, salt and pepper to taste. You should use more pepper than usual.

Place one layer of dough in the bottom of a lightly oiled baking dish. Then fill the shell with filling. Add the top layer of dough and crimp around the edges so that the upper and lower layers of dough are joined. Make a couple of slits in the top layer. Drizzle a little olive oil on top of the crust. Bake in the preheated 350°F/180°C oven for 40 minutes, or until the crust is golden.

Torta di Verdura, Pinoli e Uvetta

Savory Pie with Greens, Pine Nuts, and Raisins

1 basic torta recipe, either #1 or #2 (see page 154)
4 cups/550 g mixed greens, as mild or as pungent as you prefer
4 tablespoons/60 ml Ligurian extravirgin olive oil
3 large eggs, beaten
¾ cup/85 g ricotta
¾ cup/85 g freshly grated Parmigiano-Reggiano
1 tablespoon pinoli
2 tablespoons/15 g raisins, soaked in tepid water
1 tablespoon/7 g sugar
Fine sea salt
Freshly ground black pepper

Rinse the greens well and then steam them, using only the water that clings to their leaves. Squeeze them dry and chop coarsely. In a small saucepan heat the olive oil and then quickly sauté the greens. Let cool slightly. In a bowl combine the eggs, ricotta, Parmigiano-Reggiano, *pinoli,* raisins (but not their water), sugar, salt, and pepper.

If you plan to use torta recipe #1, combine all of the ingredients in a large bowl (sautéed greens mixture and the egg-cheese-nut-raisin mixture). Then fill the shell with filling. Top with the other sheet of dough. Crimp around the edges so that the upper and lower layers of dough are joined. Make a couple of slits in the top layer of dough. Drizzle a little olive oil on top of the crust. Bake in the preheated 350°F/180°C oven for 40 minutes, or until the crust is golden.

If you plan to use torta recipe #2, do not combine the greens with the egg-cheese mixture. Build the torta by placing some of the greens at the bottom, a layer of dough, then a layer of egg-cheese, a layer of dough, then a layer of greens, a layer of dough, and finally a layer with the rest of the egg-cheese. Cover with the top layer of dough. Crimp around the edges so that the upper and lower layers of dough are joined. Make a couple of slits in the top layer of dough. Drizzle a little olive oil on top of the crust and a bit of sugar. Bake in the preheated 350°F/180°C oven for 40 minutes, or until the crust is golden.

Torta Pasqualina all'Antica
Traditional Easter Pie

Torta Pasqualina is a Ligurian classic that is the centerpiece of meals throughout the Riviera on Easter Sunday. So popular is this dish, however, that it can be found throughout the year in good restaurants and home kitchens. This is a dish that was once composed of 33 layers of ingredients. Each layer represented a year in the life of Christ. It has evolved in modern times to something that may or may not be 33 layers, but it is still associated with its original inspiration.

This is basically a vegetable and cheese pie, with ingredients that vary from family to family and town to town. The recipe below is an amalgam of various preparations. The cook should note when there are alternatives in terms of which vegetables to use. Baby artichokes are available at Eastertime, and for many Ligurians are the vegetable of choice when they are in season. If you do not want to go to the trouble to make the layers of dough by hand, you may purchase 20 sheets of phyllo from a reliable source.

What follows is a traditional recipe for Torta Pasqualina, with one modern adaptation: For those who do not have *prescinseua* (see page 79), they may substitute ricotta. While *prescinseua* is considered better with beet greens and other greens, many Ligurians think that ricotta works better with artichokes. The choice is yours.

FOR THE DOUGH
5 cups / 600 g unbleached flour
6 tablespoons / 90 ml Ligurian extravirgin olive oil
Fine sea salt

FOR THE FILLING
1 pound / 450 g spinach and/or beet greens and/or borage or fresh baby artichokes
Juice of ½ lemon (if you are using artichokes)
½ onion, minced
1 tablespoon / 7 g sweet butter

12 ounces / 350 g prescinseua or fresh ricotta cheese
3½ ounces / 1 dl whole milk
2 ounces / 60 g fresh, unseasoned bread crumbs
6 eggs
2 ounces / 50 g sweet butter, cut into 4 pieces
Fine sea salt to taste
Freshly ground black pepper
4 sprigs fresh marjoram, chopped
5 to 6 ounces / 125 to 150 g freshly grated Parmigiano-Reggiano
Ligurian extravirgin olive oil

Makes 6 to 8 servings

Make the dough first. On a pastry board of marble or plastic, sift the flour and form a mound. Make a well in the middle so that the flour resembles a blown-out volcano. Add 2 tablespoons / 30 ml of olive oil and a pinch of salt. Work the ingredients together to form a dough, stintingly adding a little tepid water if necessary. Knead until smooth. Place the dough in a bowl that has been slightly warmed. Cover with a cloth and let rest for a half hour. Then cut the dough into seven equal pieces. Shape five of them by hand into balls. Combine the other two and shape it into a larger ball. Place the balls of dough on a lightly floured cloth and cover with a clean cloth. Set aside for 15 minutes.

While the dough is resting, prepare the vegetables. If you are using spinach or beet greens, wash them carefully and then steam them briefly. Squeeze out all excess water and chop the leaves. If you are using baby artichokes, remove the outer leaves and then chop vertically into several pieces. Sprinkle them with lemon juice to prevent discoloration. Mince the onion. In a large skillet, melt 1 tablespoon/7 g of sweet butter and then add the onion. Sauté until golden, then add the chopped greens or the artichokes. Cook over medium heat until the ingredients are slightly soft but not fried. Remove the vegetables from the pan to a large mixing bowl without adding any extra butter that was used for sautéeing. Let cool for 10 minutes. Then, if you wish, add the *prescinseua*/ricotta, milk, bread crumbs, and 2 eggs to the vegetables and combine thoroughly. Set aside. Or, if you prefer, place the *prescinseua*/ricotta, milk, bread crumbs, and 2 eggs in a separate bowl and set aside.

Return to the dough. Roll out the large ball until you make a circle big enough to line the bottom and sides of a 9-inch/24-cm springform pan, which has been lightly greased with olive oil. The dough should flop over the rim of the pan. After placing the circle of dough in the pan, brush it very lightly with olive oil. Roll out a second ball of dough to form a circle just large enough to place in the bottom of the pan. Then place the dough in the pan on top of the bottom layer. Brush lightly with olive oil. Make two more layers and place them on top, brushing the third but not the fourth layer with olive oil. If you have not combined the vegetables and the *prescinseua*/ricotta mixture, place the vegetables in the pan. Roll out a fifth ball of dough and place it on top of the vegetables. Then place the *prescinseua*/ricotta mixture on top of this layer in four clumps. Make an oval hollow in each cheese clump and put a piece of butter in each. Then break an egg into each hollow. Add a little salt and pepper to taste on each egg. Then sprinkle some chopped marjoram over each egg and top with freshly grated Parmigiano-Reggiano cheese.

Roll out the two remaining pieces of dough to form circles big enough to fit over the cheese. After placing the first layer on top of the cheese, brush it lightly with olive oil. Then add the second layer. Fold the dough that lines the side of the pan over the top layer of dough. This will enclose the ingredients in the torta. Brush the top layer with olive oil. Using a fork, puncture the top of the crust in various places so that air can exit from the Torta Pasqualina as it cooks. Bake in a preheated oven (375°F/190°C) for 45 minutes. Let stand for

10 minutes before removing from the pan. Serve hot or let it cool and serve at room temperature.

DOUGH VARIATION: If you are using phyllo dough, place 4 or 5 layers around the bottom and sides of the pan in such a way that most of the bottom and all of the sides are covered. Lightly brush with olive oil. Then place a layer completely on the bottom, atop the layers that partially cover the bottom. Brush it lightly with olive oil. Repeat with another 6 layers, remembering not to oil the top layer. Then proceed as above with the vegetables, two layers of phyllo, ricotta, and eggs. Then top with the remaining layers of phyllo, folding over the top layer the pieces of dough that hang outside the rim of the pan.

VEGETABLE VARIATION: You may choose to combine the vegetables and the *prescinseua* or ricotta. This will result in a flavor sensation different from, though as good as, the torta that uses these ingredients separately. If you have combined the vegetables and the *prescinseua*/ricotta, you should put half the mixture on the bottom strata of dough, creating a middle layer of dough before adding the rest of the mixture. It is into this top layer of vegetable-*prescinseua*/ricotta mixture that you should place the remaining 4 eggs. Continue layering and enclosing as directed above.

MODERN TORTA PASQUALINA: In the interest of culture and tradition, I have described above the preparation of an old-style Torta Pasqualina. This one is still prepared at Eastertime, but in much of the rest of the year, Ligurians make a simpler version of this pie by using the basic torta recipe (see page 154) and filling it with the ingredients of the traditional Torta Pasqualina. It is quite common nowadays to combine greens and artichokes, and even *prescinseua* and ricotta.

Cats and Dogs in Liguria

In Italy, for the most part, cats seem to be preferred to dogs. In Venice, for example, cats are thought to be descendants of the Lion of St. Mark, the symbol of the city's beloved patron saint. In Rome, cats wander freely in the Colosseum and love to occupy niches in arches and porticos throughout the city. Throughout the country, cats seem to have ready access to churches and palaces. Many Italians leave food and milk for stray cats who live nearby; in return, the cats keep the mouse and vermin population at bay.

It is often said that the cat first arrived in Europe aboard ships from ancient Egypt that landed in Taranto, in the heel of the Italian boot. Cats in Liguria, not surprisingly, also are seafarers. As far back as the twelfth century, it was stipulated in Genoese maritime law that a certain number of cats should reside on each boat, according to the size of the vessel. In 1719, the Genoese lawmaker Giuseppe Maria Casaregis, one of the founders of modern maritime law, said that every ship must have *u penneise,* the Ligurian term for a cat minder, who would assure the well-being of felines. Well into the twentieth century, it was a law that a cat must reside on all Genoese merchant vessels to rid the ship of mice.

There is a famous portrait of Andrea Doria and his cat painted by Sebastiano del Piombo. This tabby was nicknamed Dragut, which was the name of a wretched pirate who frequently attacked ships and property of the Republic of Genoa. Another famous Ligurian cat was Dragoncello (Tarragon), the beloved feline of Nino Bixio, a renowned sailor and adventurer.

Cats were also indicators of changes in the weather. If a cat continued to place its paw behind its ear, rain was on the way. If it leaned its back toward the fire in the hearth, snow would soon come. (Although the coast of Liguria is usually warm, even 10 miles/16 kilometers inland there is a possibility for snow on the mountains.)

In most of Italy dogs do not have the same status as cats. For the most part they have been thought of as workers more than friends, and many of them are not allowed in people's homes. While a cat can wander into a church, dogs are strictly forbidden.

In modern times, as Italians gained affluence and could afford to feed an additional mouth, some of them adopted dogs as pets and came to discover their wonderful qualities of friendship and loyalty. Ligurians, ever distinct in Italy, have always been very close to their dogs. While cats did the work, dogs provided companionship and were admired for their trustworthiness. It was thought that after dealing with crafty, calculating (more catlike) people in business, the sincerity of a dog would restore one's mood and sense of faith.

Ligurians are especially fond of a thin, strand pasta called *fedelini* (or *fideli*), which suggest faithfulness. There is much debate as to whether *fedelini* originated in Liguria or in Naples or, as the people of Catalonia would insist, whether *fedelini* are adapted from the *fideos* of eastern Iberia. I have encountered many Ligurian dogs named Fede (Faith), Fedele (Faithful), and even Fedelino (Little Faithful One). All of these names, of course, relate to Fido, that all-purpose canine name.

While in most of Liguria cats and dogs stand paw to paw in the esteem in which they are held, there is no question that in Camogli dogs rule. The *camogliesi* love to promenade up and down the Corso Garibaldi by the sea, stopping at bars, cafés, and bakeries, and always tossing a piece of focaccia to their dogs. The cats of Camogli are more mendicant, and must subsist on scraps thrown to them by the fishermen, plus anything else they can catch.

Each August, on a fine Sunday morning, there is a grand procession of the dogs of Camogli up to the Parish of San Rocco, a tiny community perched in the hills with stunning sea views. In San Rocco, the dogs are welcomed into the church and each receives a blessing and thanks for his friendship and fidelity. Hundreds of canines, tails wagging, noses sniffing, happily yelping, meet for the largest dog party you will ever see, and it is a joyful occasion that will inevitably be concluded with a bowlful of *fedelini* with pesto.

(Appetizers)

Antipasti

Pane e Olio	Bread with Olive Oil
Pane e Pomodoro	Tomato Bread
Bruschetta con Funghi Porcini	Toasts Topped with Porcini Mushrooms
Crostini con Spinasci	Spinach Toasts with Raisins and Pine Nuts
Frittelle di Foglie di Limone	Lemon Leaf Fritters
Fritelle di Fagioli	Bean Fritters
Friscoë di Borragine	Borage Fritters
Basilico Ripieno	Stuffed Basil Leaves
Insalata con Noci e Funghi Porcini	Salad with Walnuts and Porcini Mushrooms
Torta di Frittate con Funghi Porcini, Pesto e Pinoli	Frittata "Cake" with Porcini Mushrooms, Pesto, and Pine Nuts
Uova Sode con Salsa	Hard-Boiled Eggs with Special Sauce
Acciughe all'Agro	Marinated Fresh Anchovies
Acciughe in Tegame	Casserole of Fresh Anchovies
Acciughe Fritte con Salsa	Fried Anchovies with Special Sauce
Insalata di Calamaretti e Patate	Salad of Baby Calamari and Potatoes
Muscoli Ripieni	Stuffed Mussels
Fave, Salame e Pecorino Sardo	Fresh Fava Beans, Salami, and Pecorino Cheese

*T*HE USE OF APPETIZERS is relatively recent in Liguria. Most of these foods derive from other parts of the meal, or are the snacks of which Ligurians are so fond. I have not included standard Italian appetizers such as platters of cold cuts or generic seafood salads. These are found in Liguria now, too, but they are not classically Ligurian. You would seldom see, for example, a plate groaning with salami and hams at the start of a Ligurian meal. They are quite rich in flavor and hard on the wallet, too, since a Ligurian would only want the best quality. Ligurians do, however, like Sant'Olcese salami with fava beans in the springtime.

Two very popular Ligurian appetizers may be found in other chapters. The first is a slice of torta, the thin-crusted pie that is usually filled with vegetables. These may be found in the bread chapter, starting on page 154. Then there is *verdura ripiena,* the general term for stuffed vegetables. See page 304.

Another classic Ligurian antipasto is hot focaccia served with a glass of wine. The bread may be made more elaborate by topping it with whichever Ligurian sauce captures your fancy.

Pane e Olio

Bread with Olive Oil

Simple bread and oil is a standard snack that is both delicious and healthy, and is a particular favorite of children. The key to appreciating this dish comes in the exaltation of distinct individual flavors. The quality of its preparation, of course, will depend on the ingredients that you employ, so it is only worth having if you use crusty, country-style whole wheat bread and superb Ligurian olive oil, preferably oil that was recently pressed. Note that this bread is not toasted, and therefore you should not confuse this with the more famous *bruschetta*.

1 thick slice chewy whole wheat bread
Extravirgin Ligurian olive oil, as young and fresh as possible
A few drops red wine vinegar
Coarse salt, pounded with mortar and pestle, to taste

Makes
1 serving

Douse the slice of bread with abundant olive oil. Top with a few drops of vinegar and sprinkle with the salt that you have just pounded. As an option, you may use sea salt that you may or may not wish to pound.

Pane e Pomodoro

Tomato Bread

An old Ligurian expression records that when you are hungry, even bread can taste like meat. For people who were once frugal or poor, this preparation filled empty stomachs. In San Remo it is often referred to as *bisteca sanremasca* (or San Remo steak). I sampled this first near La Spezia and, as always, the flavor was outstanding because of the quality of the ingredients. There are distinctions to be understood: In the Levante (especially in the province of La Spezia near the border of Tuscany), the bread is often toasted and will usually be white. In the Ponente, and especially as one nears the French border, the bread is typically untoasted and will more often be whole wheat. Needless to say, the bread you use should be crusty and flavorful, not some pallid commercial variety.

2 slices good crusty bread or 1 roll, cut in half lengthwise
1 clove garlic, peeled and cut in half
Ligurian extravirgin olive oil
Freshly pounded coarse salt, or sea salt
1 large, firm tomato, sliced in half vertically, seeds removed if you wish

Makes 1 serving

If you wish to toast your bread, do so before preparing this dish. Rub each slice vigorously with half a clove of garlic. Then douse the slices with abundant olive oil. Sprinkle on some salt. Finally, rub a tomato half on to each slice, squeezing the tomato so that the juice and some pulp will be absorbed by the bread. This bread is tasty when served with some young red wine.

COOK'S NOTE: When I make Pane e Pomodoro, I save the garlic and tomato, and then chop them coarsely and combine them with olive oil, black pepper, and torn basil leaves, which I then toss with spaghettini or penne.

Bruschetta con Funghi Porcini

Toasts Topped with Porcini Mushrooms

Approximately 4 ounces / 100 g fresh funghi porcini
1 tablespoon / 15 ml Ligurian extravirgin olive oil
1 clove garlic, peeled
8 slices good Italian bread, about ½ inch / 1.25 cm thick
Approximately 4 ounces / 100 g olive oil–packed small mushrooms, sliced in half
1 ripe beefsteak tomato or 2 ripe plum tomatoes, cut into small cubes
24 pitted black olives, preferably Taggia or Gaeta type, cut in half
Freshly ground black pepper to taste
2 tablespoons minced fresh Italian (flat) parsley

Carefully wash the *funghi* and dry them with paper toweling. Slice them relatively thin. Heat the olive oil in a pan and add the clove of garlic. Add the *funghi* and sauté them for 2 to 3 minutes, until they are soft and fragrant. Transfer the *funghi* and pan liquid to a bowl and discard the garlic clove. Toast the bread slices in a toaster or over an open flame. While the bread is toasting, combine the sautéed *funghi,* the oil-packed mushrooms, the tomato pieces, the olive pieces, black pepper, and parsley in the bowl. When the bread is toasted, spread some mushroom mixture on each toast and, if you wish, add a few drops of the olive oil in which the jarred mushrooms were packed.

*Makes
4 servings*

Crostini con Spinasci

Spinach Toasts with Raisins and Pine Nuts

Delicious and easy.

1 recipe for Spinasci a-a Zeneize (page 297)
6 slices thin white-bread toast, cut into 4 triangles
Ligurian extravirgin olive oil (optional)
Coarse sea salt (optional)

Makes
6 servings

After preparing the spinach, toast the bread and top it with some of the spinach. You may additionally choose to drizzle a couple of drops of olive oil on the toast before adding the spinach. Similarly, a couple of crystals of coarse sea salt atop the spinach is also very good.

Hints about Better Frying
for Fritters and Other Foods

OIL: In Liguria it is the rule rather than the exception that olive oil is used for frying. This is because Ligurians are used to the flavor the oil imparts and to them this is part of the final result of the dish they are preparing. If you consider it too extravagant to use Ligurian olive oil for frying, you have two choices. One is to use a heavier oil from a region such as Tuscany, Umbria, Lazio, or Puglia. These are very good, of course, but the flavor may be more assertive. Another choice is to use a neutral-tasting vegetable oil such as canola or corn. This will save you some money, but the dish will have a somewhat different taste than it would with olive oil. How much oil? In general, to fry fritters, vegetables, or battered fish or seafood, there should be at least an inch (ca. 2.5 cm) of oil, and one and one-half inches (ca. 3.75 cm) is better still.

TEMPERATURE: The oil should be very hot, but not smoky. One way to test if the oil is ready to fry, if you are using a batter made of flour and water, is to spoon a small amount of batter into the oil. It should immediately rise to the surface. If you are deep-frying something breaded (not typical in Ligurian food), dip a corner of the breaded food into the oil. If the oil sizzles, it is the right temperature.

FRYING: When frying fritters or any other food, add enough of them so that half the pan's surface is covered. This means that the fritters will have room to move and the temperature of the oil will not be significantly lowered. Using a slotted spoon, turn them after about 30 seconds so that they will cook evenly on both sides. They will be ready when they turn a light golden color. As you remove a fritter, add batter to the pan to make a new one. Continue this process until all the batter is used.

DRAINING: The preferred way to drain fritters is on a rack set over a baking sheet or paper toweling. Failing that, drain the fritters on paper toweling, moving the fritters enough so they don't sit in their own oil.

SALT: Ligurians do not add salt to their batters because it retains liquid rather than allowing it to vaporize in the hot oil. For this reason, if you want saltier fritters, add it after they have been fried. I recommend a fine-grain sea salt, but be gentle, and consider not using salt on apple or other fruit fritters.

Frittelle di Foglie di Limone

Lemon Leaf Fritters

Here is a local specialty of Ventimiglia, an area famous for its lemon cultivation. Note that you should only use leaves from trees that you are certain have not been treated with any chemicals.

½ cup/115 ml* warm spring water
1 package (2½ teaspoons)/6 g active dry yeast
4 cups/450 g unbleached all-purpose flour
1 large egg
2 tablespoons granulated sugar
2 cups/450 ml tepid water
2 tablespoons fresh lemon juice
2 teaspoons grated fresh lemon rind, from lemons that have not been waxed or treated
　with chemicals
2 cups/225 g lemon leaves, carefully wiped with paper toweling
1 pinch salt (optional)
Ligurian extravirgin olive oil

* Note: 115 ml = 100 ml (or 1 dl) plus 1 tablespoon

*Makes
6 servings*　Place the warm water in a large mixing bowl, add the yeast, and leave for 15 minutes so that the yeast may activate. Add the flour, egg, sugar, water, lemon juice, and lemon rind. Combine the ingredients using a wooden spoon so that you make a very soft, slightly liquidy batter. Cover the bowl with a damp cloth and set aside for one hour.

When you are ready to make the fritters, take a large, heavy-bottomed pan or a wok and fill it with ½ inch/1.25 cm of olive oil. Heat the oil over medium heat. When the oil is hot (but not sputtering or smoking), you may begin. Dip a few lemon leaves into the batter until they are coated but not thick with batter. Add these to the heated oil. As the fritters begin to expand, turn them with a slotted spoon so that they cook evenly. Typically it should take about 1 minute to cook each fritter. Once they are golden in color, remove them with the slotted spoon to paper toweling to drain. Repeat the process until all the leaves have been fried. Serve immediately.

The Liguria of Eugenio Montale

Montale was often thought of as the poet laureate of Liguria, even before he won the Nobel Prize for literature in the mid-1970s. The poet, born in Genoa, was famous for his ambivalence about his region. He often found ways to be critical of it, but defended it ardently and in his writing expressed his land and its essence as few others did.

I Limoni

Ascoltami, i poeti laureati
si muovono soltanto fra le piante
dai nomi poco usati: bossi, ligustri
    o acanti.
Io, per me, amo le strade che riescono
    agli erbosi
fossi dove in pozzanghere
mezzo seccate agguantano i ragazzi
qualche sparuta anguilla:
le viuzze che seguono i ciglioni,
discendono tra i ciuffi delle canne
e mettono negli orti, tra gli alberi
    dei limoni.

The Lemon Trees

Listen to me, the poet laureates
move only among the plants
with little-used names like box,
    privet, acanthus.
For my part, I love the roads that lead
    to grassy
ditches where, in puddles
half-dried up, children grasp
the odd, slender eel:
the lanes that follow the embankments
descend among clusters of reeds
and enter vegetable gardens, amidst the
    lemon trees.

Fritelle di Fagioli
Bean Fritters

I tasted these delicacies at the Osteria del Cannon d'Oro in Badalucco. To look at this little restaurant you would not think that it produces outstanding food, but indeed it does. The area nearby provides superb ingredients, starting with fabulous olive oil but also good wheat and vegetables. The local bean is called *fagioli dell'angelo,* but they are hard to find outside Badalucco. It was suggested to me that white cannellini beans would be a suitable substitute. They were, until I decided one time to use black-eyed peas, and they came much closer to the taste and texture I remembered from Badalucco.

10 ounces/2½ cups/300 g dried black-eyed peas or cannellini or 1 pound/
    4 cups/450 g fresh or canned black-eyed peas or cannellini
1¾ cups/7 ounces/200 g unbleached all-purpose flour
Small amount of sparkling mineral water
2 small fresh onions, minced
Ligurian extravirgin olive oil
Sea salt

*Makes
6 servings*

If you are using dried beans, soak them the night before making this recipe. Once the beans are soft, drain them well, rinse, and drain again. Boil beans that were soaked for 5 to 10 minutes. If you are using fresh beans, boil them for 5 minutes in abundant water and then drain. If, as is most likely, you are using canned beans, you must drain them well before using. Place the flour in a large bowl and add enough mineral water so that you have a thick paste. Add the water a little at a time, so that you can carefully watch the thickness of the batter. Then add the beans and the chopped onions. Stir thoroughly to combine the ingredients. Cover with plastic wrap and let sit for 30 minutes. Then give it a good stir and check the consistency. The batter should cling to the tablespoon you are using rather than being runny. Adjust by adding drops of mineral water, stirring it carefully. Heat a pot of olive oil (about 3 inches/7.5 cm deep). When it becomes hot but not smoky, add a few spoonfuls of batter and cook until they expand and become a light gold color. Remove with a slotted spoon and then add a few more spoonfuls of batter. Continue the process until all the fritters are cooked. Sprinkle some sea salt on them and serve immediately.

Friscoë di Borragine

Borage Fritters

These fritters are popular in the coastal areas between Genoa and the Portofino peninsula. In little bars in Camogli *friscoë* are served with sparkling wine at cocktail hour. If it is impossible to find borage or some other fresh-tasting green such as parsley, then peel and grate fresh cucumber, carefully removing all of the seeds.

½ cup / 115 ml* warm whole milk
2½ teaspoons (1 package) / 6 g active dry yeast
4 cups / 450 g unbleached all-purpose flour
1 large egg
2 cups / 225 g borage, washed, trimmed, and finely chopped
⅓ cup / 40 g minced onion, scallion, or chive (your choice)
2 cups / 450 ml tepid water
Pinch of salt (optional)
Ligurian extravirgin olive oil

* Note: 115 ml = 100 ml (or 1 dl) plus 1 tablespoon

Place the warm milk in a large mixing bowl, add the yeast, and leave for 15 minutes so that the yeast may activate. Add the flour, egg, borage, onion, water, and salt. Combine the ingredients using a wooden spoon so that you make a very soft, slightly liquidy batter. Cover the bowl with a damp cloth and set aside for one hour.

Makes 4 to 6 servings

When you are ready to make the fritters, take a large, heavy-bottomed pan or a wok and fill it with ½ inch / 1.25 cm of olive oil. Heat the oil over medium heat. When the oil is hot (but not sputtering or smoking), dip a tablespoon into the oil and then into the batter. Start spooning tablespoonfuls of batter into the oil. As the fritters begin to take shape and expand, turn them with a slotted spoon so that they cook evenly. Typically it should take about 1 minute to cook each fritter. Once they are golden in color, remove them with the slotted spoon to paper toweling, where they will drain. Keep spooning batter into the oil until it is all used up. Serve the fritters immediately.

Basilico Ripieno

Stuffed Basil Leaves

While Ligurians favor the smallest basil leaves possible when making pesto or using the herb in cooking, they would not consider wasting larger leaves, so they cleverly found another use for them. I was introduced to this recipe for stuffed and fried basil leaves by Licia and Bruno Soprano, who own an excellent kitchenware shop in Oneglia (Imperia). It is an ancient preparation, born of the needs of poor people with few ingredients available to them, but I am certain that when this recipe becomes known to readers outside of Liguria, it will become a staple at cocktail parties.

36 large fresh basil leaves, unblemished and fragrant
2 ounces/50 g prosciutto, very finely minced
2 ounces/50 g finely grated Parmigiano-Reggiano
2 ounces/50 g (after the crusts have been removed) Italian white bread, softened in
*   milk (you may use unflavored bread crumbs in place of the softened bread, but the*
*   result will be heavier)*
Sea salt to taste
Freshly ground black pepper to taste
2 large eggs
4 tablespoons/30 g unflavored bread crumbs
Approximately 2 tablespoons/30 ml Ligurian extravirgin olive oil (per pan)

Makes
36 filled leaves

After selecting the most pristine basil leaves you can find, wipe them carefully with paper toweling and set aside (do not wash them!). In a mixing bowl combine the prosciutto, Parmigiano-Reggiano, the softened bread with the milk squeezed out, salt, and pepper along with 1 egg. The resulting mixture should be somewhat firm but also slightly wet. If it is too soft or if liquid runs off (because the egg was too big or because the milk was not effectively squeezed from the bread), you have two options. The first is to drain the excess liquid from the bowl. This is the preferable choice and will likely solve the problem. If you feel the mixture is still too wet, add a judicious amount of unflavored bread crumbs to make the mixture a bit firmer. Be careful with this — heaviness in the filling will rob the finished product of its beguiling and ethereal character and will be a waste of good ingredients. Once you have made the filling, then beat the other egg in a bowl and spread the 4 tablespoons/30 g unflavored bread crumbs on a plate. Now stuff the leaves: Place about 1 teaspoon of filling in the center of a basil leaf. Fold the leaf into a ball, dip into the beaten egg, and then roll it in the bread crumbs until it is lightly coated. Repeat the process until all the leaves are used. If you run out of bread crumbs, use more. Heat the olive oil in a large pan. There should be enough room in the pan so that all the basil balls can be easily moved about. If necessary, use two pans. There should be a very thin layer of olive oil at the bottom of each pan. Heat the oil and then add the basil balls. Using a slotted spoon, sauté them until they are a light golden color and then transfer them to absorbent paper to drain. Serve them while they are still very hot.

Bagna Cauda

This "hot bath" for vegetables is a classic appetizer in western Liguria as well as in Piedmont, the region with which it is usually associated. In the past the Piedmontese used walnut oil and butter, but the Ligurian method, favoring olive oil, has now reached Piedmont as well. See the recipe for Bagna Cauda sauce on page 96 in the sauce chapter, where you will also find suggestions for how to use this sauce.

Insalata con Noci e Funghi Porcini

Salad with Walnuts and Porcini Mushrooms

As with all good Ligurian dishes, the success of this recipe depends on the quality of the ingredients you use. Try to find an assortment of greens, such as mache, mesclun, arugula, Belgian endive, and radicchio, that are contrasting in flavor, texture, and color. Be sure that the *funghi porcini* you use are pristine and that you have washed them assiduously. The walnuts (or optional *pinoli*) should be fresh and buttery in taste.

4 ounces/1½ to 2 cups/100 g delicate greens
7 to 8 ounces/200 g fresh, perfect funghi porcini (or cremini as a substitute)
8 to 10 fresh, unsalted walnut halves, chopped or broken into small pieces
3 tablespoons/45 ml Ligurian extravirgin olive oil
½ teaspoon fresh lemon juice (optional)

Makes
4 servings

Wash and carefully dry all of the salad greens. Tear them into bite-size pieces and place them in a pretty salad bowl. After thoroughly washing the mushrooms and letting them dry for a couple of minutes, use a fine, sharp knife to make paper-thin slices of mushrooms. If you have a truffle-shaver at hand and use it with dexterity, this is a good alternative to the knife. Place the sliced *funghi* gently on top of the greens. In a small bowl, combine the walnut pieces and olive oil and then spoon atop the mushrooms. If you are using lemon juice, sprinkle it atop the nuts. Toss the ingredients thoroughly and serve.

VARIATION: Instead of walnuts, you might want to use 2 tablespoons/15 g of pine nuts. I once prepared the dish this way and added ½ teaspoon dried currants along with lemon juice, achieving delicious results.

Torta di Frittate con Funghi Porcini, Pesto e Pinoli

Frittata "Cake" with Porcini Mushrooms, Pesto, and Pine Nuts

3 (1 + 1 + 1) tablespoons / 45 (15 + 15 + 15) ml extravirgin olive oil
6 extra-large eggs
Few drops cold water (optional)
1 sprig fresh marjoram, torn into small bits (optional)
1 recipe Funghi Porcini al Pesto con Pinoli (see page 309)
3 teaspoons / 9 g pinoli
Basil leaves

Follow the instructions for making a frittata in the recipe on page 360. Make one frittata at a time, using 1 tablespoon olive oil and 2 eggs. You can make a slightly fluffier frittata by adding a little water to the egg. You may optionally add a few bits of fresh marjoram, if you wish. There are two ways to serve this dish. If you want to serve it hot, you should have the *funghi* and pesto combination at hand and hot when the frittatas have been cooked. I find the dish more interesting and flavorful when served at room temperature. In this case, you should let the three frittatas cool to room temperature and also have the *funghi* and pesto combination be tepid. No matter which temperature you serve it at, the preparation is the same.

Makes 4 servings

Place one frittata in the middle of an attractive serving dish. Spoon half of the *funghi*/pesto mixture evenly on top of the frittata, making sure the mixture does not come too close to the edge. Then sprinkle 1 teaspoon of *pinoli* on top of the mixture. Gently place the second frittata on top of this, and repeat the procedure, again making sure that the mixture does not come too close to the edge. Again, sprinkle on 1 teaspoon of *pinoli,* and then place the third frittata on top of the spread. Top it with a couple of small basil leaves. Decorate the plate with a few more basil leaves and a few more *pinoli.* Present this pretty dish before cutting. Serve by cutting the "cake" into quarters, as you would a pie.

Uova Sode con Salsa

Hard-Boiled Eggs with Special Sauce

The name of this dish almost sounds like something from a fast-food restaurant, but fear not. You need to use the Salsa per i Pesci Fritti (see page 99). Please note the various suggested preparations for eggs and special sauce, and select the ones that most appeal to you. In every case, the eggs may be served warm or chilled, as you prefer, and the sauce must be room temperature

4 extra-large hard-boiled eggs, preferably organic
4 teaspoons/20 ml Salsa per i Pesci Fritti

Makes
4 servings

PREPARATION 1: Cut the boiled eggs in half lengthwise, top each half with ½ teaspoon/2.5 ml of sauce, and serve.

PREPARATION 2: Cut the boiled eggs in half lengthwise. Remove the yolks and combine them in a bowl with the sauce. Spoon this mixture back into all the egg-white halves, and serve.

PREPARATION 3: Take *crostini* or other thin slices of good toasted bread. Spread a layer of sauce on the bread (using about 1 teaspoon/5 ml of sauce). Then slice the boiled eggs thin, arrange them neatly and artfully on the bread, and serve. Note: It will be difficult to handle warm eggs for this preparation.

PREPARATION 4: Chop the eggs coarsely and combine with the sauce. Spread this mixture on *crostini* or other thin slices of good toasted bread. Top, if you wish, with a few capers.

Acciughe all'Agro

Marinated Fresh Anchovies

Fresh anchovies are fundamental ingredients in Ligurian cooking. Think of them as fresh fish, not as the salty brown paste into which they are usually transformed. This recipe and the two that follow put fresh anchovies to good use, as does the Bagnun di Acciughe (see page 336). More fishmongers now sell fresh anchovies, and you should not hesitate to request them if you do not see them.

2 pounds / 1 kilo fresh anchovies (often available upon request from better fish markets)
2¼ cups / ½ liter dry white wine such as Vermentino
14 ounces / 4 dl white wine vinegar
4 tablespoons / 30 g coarse salt
Ligurian extravirgin olive oil
1 clove garlic, with the green heart removed, minced
3 sprigs fresh Italian (flat) parsley, minced
1 lemon

Makes 4 to 6 servings

Rinse the anchovies in cold water and set aside. Take a rectangular glass or enamel dish (large enough to hold the anchovies in a layer or two) and combine the wine, vinegar, and salt. Then, using a small, sharp paring knife, cut the head off one anchovy and then carefully cut a straight line down the fish's belly until you have almost reached the tail. Using both thumbs, open the fish as you might open a book, so that it is flat. Then lift out the skeleton from the top (that is, where the head was) all the way down to the tail. It is customary to leave the tail, primarily because it is the point where the two sides of the fillet meet. However, if you do not wish to keep the tail, carefully remove it using your knife. Place the fillet in the wine-vinegar-salt mixture. Repeat this process until you have used all the fish. You may place the fillets on top of one another if you run out of room. Cover the dish with plastic wrap and place in the refrigerator for 36 hours. Remove the fillets from the dish and drain carefully in a colander so that all the excess liquid runs off. Then transfer each fillet to a serving dish large enough to hold the fillets without stacking one atop another. As you do this, inspect each fillet to see if there are any little bones that still must be removed. Once all the fillets are on the platter, drizzle rather generously with olive oil. Combine the minced garlic and parsley and distribute evenly over the fillets. Cover with a fresh piece of plastic wrap and place in the refrigerator for another hour or two so that the flavors combine. Then serve.

Acciughe in Tegame

Casserole of Fresh Anchovies

24 fresh anchovies (often available upon request from better fish markets)
4 tablespoons / 60 ml Ligurian extravirgin olive oil
2 cloves garlic, with the green heart removed, minced
3 sprigs fresh Italian (flat) parsley, minced
12 olives, preferably Taggia or Gaeta, pitted
1 teaspoon / 3 g capers
⅜ cup / 85 ml white wine, preferably Vermentino

*Makes
4 to 6 servings*

Wash the anchovies and then remove the heads. Split down the middle and then remove the bones and the internal parts. Wash them carefully and then lay them flat and open like a book on a platter or marble surface. Heat the olive oil over low heat in a large, heavy-bottomed pan. Add the anchovies, making sure not to stack one atop another, if possible. Then add the garlic and parsley and cook gently for 2 minutes. If the anchovies have absorbed some of the oil and the bottom of the pan is rather dry, you may want to add a tablespoon of water. Cook for 2 more minutes, or until the fish turns somewhat white. Shake the pan every so often to prevent the anchovies from sticking. Then add the olives, the capers, and the white wine. Cook for another 2 minutes, shaking the pan every so often. Serve hot, accompanied by more of the white wine.

Fresh anchovies from the Ligurian Sea

Acciughe Fritte con Salsa

Fried Anchovies with Special Sauce

This recipe is for four persons, but the basic ratio is 6 ounces/150 g of fresh anchovies to 1 tablespoon/15 ml of Salsa per i Pesci Fritti.

1½ pounds/600 g fresh anchovies
  (often available upon request from better fish markets)
Unbleached all-purpose flour (optional)
Ligurian extravirgin olive oil
4 tablespoons/60 ml Salsa per i Pesci Fritti (see page 99)

*Makes
4 servings*

Wash all of the anchovies well. Cut off the heads and tails and use a small good knife to split them lengthwise down the middle and open them like a book. Remove all of the innards and gently lift the spine out of each fish so that almost all of the bones will be gone. Then rinse the anchovies again in cold water and let dry on paper toweling. Once they are dry, you have the option, if you wish, to lightly flour the fish on both sides. I have had them prepared both ways and profess no special preference. The fresh flavor of the fish is a bit more present if you do not use flour. Pour enough oil into a heavy-bottomed frying pan so that the thin fish will be completely covered. Heat the oil until it is quite hot but does not smoke. Fry these little anchovy "cutlets" until they are a light gold color and then remove to drain on paper toweling. Serve hot with sauce on the side.

FOR MARINERS: Sailors and travelers have often packed these fried anchovies in an airtight jar, topped it with the sauce, closed tightly, and set sail.

Insalata di Calamaretti e Patate
Salad of Baby Calamari and Potatoes

I sampled this dish at the Ristorante Palma in Alassio, a very chic restaurant in an unlikely setting. Alassio has a nice sandy beach and is geared more to mass tourism than to the audience that Ristorante Palma would seem to cook for. I particularly liked this dish because it exalted the flavors of the ingredients: tender, fresh baby calamari, fruity olive oil, the heavenly scent of Ligurian basil, and the sweet-saltiness of naturally ripe tomatoes. All of these flavors are tamed slightly by the soothing blandness of boiled diced potatoes.

¾ cup/170 ml Ligurian extravirgin olive oil
Juice of 1 large or 2 regular lemons
1 clove garlic, peeled, split, green heart removed, then minced
16 small very fresh basil leaves, stems removed
2 very ripe plum tomatoes, peeled, seeded, drained of liquid, then cut into little cubes
4 medium potatoes, scrubbed, peeled, cut into small cubes
1 pound/225 g very fresh baby calamari (found in better seafood shops)
1 large pot rapidly boiling water

Combine the olive oil, lemon juice, garlic, basil leaves, and cubed tomatoes in a dish. Stir gently so that all the ingredients combine to macerate. Place the diced potatoes in a colander and immerse into the boiling water. Cook for about 5 minutes, or until the cubes are cooked but still al dente. Remove the potatoes from the colander and place in the center of a large flat serving dish. Wipe the colander clean and then add the baby calamari. Place the colander in the hot water and boil for a few minutes. Very fresh calamari will cook very quickly, so be careful that they are not overdone. When properly cooked they should be delicate, not rubbery. Distribute the cooked *calamaretti* (baby calamari) over the center of the cubed potatoes. Then spoon the basil-tomato mixture around the outer parts of the cubed potatoes. Serve immediately.

Makes 4 servings

As an elegant, slightly more labor-intensive alternative, you may serve the ingredients on four individual dishes, placing portions of *calamaretti* on each bed of potatoes and then carefully spooning the basil-tomato mixture around the seafood.

Muscoli Ripieni
Stuffed Mussels

While most of Italy calls mussels *cozze,* in Liguria they are usually referred to as *muscoli.* This preparation is a specialty of the Cinqueterre; this particular recipe is from the town of Manarola. This dish is an example of how cheese and seafood, usually a difficult pairing, can go well together. You might find it a curiosity that mortadella, a typical meat of the city of Bologna in neighboring Emilia-Romagna, is in this dish. Centuries ago mortadella, prosciutto, and Parmigiano-Reggiano cheese were sent to Liguria in exchange for oil, dried fish, and salt from the coast. The salt was used in the curing of meats and the preparation of Parmigiano-Reggiano.

1 small white roll of bread
Milk
2 pounds/450 g mussels
3½ ounces/110 g mortadella, minced
2 sprigs fresh Italian (flat) parsley
1 pinch fresh thyme
1 pinch fresh marjoram
2 cloves garlic, with the green heart removed, minced
3½ ounces/110 g freshly grated Parmigiano-Reggiano
1 ounce/30 g freshly grated Pecorino
1 large egg
4 tablespoons/60 ml Ligurian extravirgin olive oil
1 medium onion, sliced
¾ pound/approximately 350 g peeled tomatoes (canned or fresh)
3 ounces/85 ml/½ glass dry white wine, preferably from the Cinqueterre
Sea salt to taste
Freshly ground black pepper, to taste

Makes
4 to 6 servings

Break the roll in half and pull out all of the bread within. Save the crust for some other cooking use, such as making crumbs. Soak the bread in enough milk so that the bread is thoroughly moistened but not overwhelmed. Scrub all the mussels thoroughly, removing the "beards" and anything else attached to the shells. Carefully using a sharp knife, slightly open about two-thirds of the mussels, making sure that you do not open the shells too wide. Place them in a colander so that any liquid will drain out. Then place enough water to cover the bottom of a flat pan that has a lid. Add the one-third of the mussels that you have not opened manually. Cover and cook over medium heat for 4 minutes, or until the mussels have opened and the meat is cooked. If any mussels do not open, discard them. Once done, remove the meat from the shells and mince finely. Place the chopped mussels in a mixing bowl, add the mortadella, moistened bread (which you have broken up by hand), parsley, thyme, marjoram, garlic, Parmigiano-Reggiano, Pecorino, egg, salt, and pepper. Gently combine all the ingredients until they are thoroughly blended. Stuff each of the uncooked mussels with some of the filling, forcing down slightly each mussel as you put filling in the shell. Then close the shell and set aside. Take a large pan with high sides (perhaps the one you used previously) and heat the olive oil over a low flame. Add the onion slices and cook them until they are translucent. Then add the tomatoes and cook over medium heat for about 5 minutes, until they begin to concentrate a bit as the excess liquid evaporates. While the tomatoes cook, you may add a little more salt and pepper, if you wish. After cooking the tomatoes, remove the pan from the heat and carefully place each stuffed mussel in so the mussels are not piled one on top of another. Add the white wine. Cover, and cook over low to medium heat for about 30 minutes. The shells will open, and the filling will be cooked through. Serve with some of the tomato sauce, which should be sopped up with some good bread once you have eaten the mussels.

Fave, Salame e Pecorino Sardo
Fresh Fava Beans, Salami, and Pecorino Cheese

In centuries past, many Italians did not eat the various types of beans that were brought from the New World during the Columbian expeditions. They did not fully trust them and were suspicious of their properties. This was not the case of the fava bean, which is native to the Mediterranean and has been consumed since ancient times. The fava has a particular association with springtime, young love, and renewal. It is customary in western Liguria to eat fresh fava beans on the first day of May to celebrate these associations. Typically one eats them with fresh, young sausage or salami and, sometimes, with shards of slightly salty Pecorino cheese from Sardinia. If this is unavailable, you may use Pecorino Romano. The much superior version of what the rest of the world calls Genoa salami is known as *salame di Sant'Olcese,* named for the town north of Genoa where this slightly fatty salami is made. It has added salt and pepper and the pork is often sweet. Sometimes the salami is made with a mixture of pork and veal. The ideal match for this *salame* is a fresh fig. This recipe does not have suggested quantities because you will find that it is something that is eaten with lusty abandon, especially when washed down with very young and fresh red wine.

Freshly picked fava beans, still in their pods
Young, somewhat sweet salami (this will vary depending what you have access to, but
   the key is that it not be too hard, aged, or salty)
Aged Pecorino, cut into shards
Crusty country bread, preferably whole wheat

Place a pile of fava bean pods in the middle of the table, not necessarily on a plate. If the salami are small (the size of a large thumb), serve one or two to each diner. Otherwise, cut chunks of salami and place them on a plate. On another plate place the shards of cheese. Serve the bread in large wedges in a pretty basket. Let each diner open his or her own pod of fava beans and chomp them with bites of salami, cheese, and bread, all the while washing it down with fruity young red wine and thinking thoughts of love.

Charles Dickens in Liguria

In 1844 Charles Dickens moved to Italy to "fade away from the public eye for a year." He chose Genoa as his place of residence and it is thought that the bells of the city gave him the idea for *The Chimes*. Dickens contributed articles to a new English newspaper, *The Daily News,* and later gathered these writings into a small volume called *Pictures from Italy*.

"[Genoa] is a place that 'grows upon you' every day. There seems to be always something to find out in it. There are the most extraordinary alleys and by-ways to walk about in. You can lose your way (what a comfort that is, when you are idle!) twenty times a day, if you like; and turn up again, under the most unexpected and surprising difficulties. It abounds in the strangest contrasts; things that are picturesque, ugly, mean, magnificent, delightful, and offensive, break upon the view at every turn.

"They who would know how beautiful the country immediately surrounding Genoa is, should climb (in clear weather) to the top of Monte Faccio, or, at least, ride round the city walls: a feat more easily performed. No prospect can be more diversified and lovely than the changing views of the harbour, and the valleys of the two rivers, the Polcevera and the Bizagno, from the heights along which the strongly fortified walls are carried, like the great wall of China in little. In not the least picturesque part of this ride, there is a fair specimen of a real Genoese tavern, where the visitor may derive good entertainment from real Genoese dishes, such as Tagliarini; Ravioli; German sausages, strong of garlic, sliced and eaten with fresh green figs; cocks' combs and sheep-kidneys, chopped up with mutton chops and liver, small pieces of some unknown part of a calf, twisted into small shreds, fried, and served up in a great dish like whitebait; and other curiosities of that kind."

What Dickens did not realize was that the garlicky "German sausages" he enjoyed were in fact the *salame di Sant'Olcese,* the most famous Ligurian pork product. It is named for Sant'Olcese, the town in the Polcevara River valley (Valpolcevara) where it originated. This salami is indeed garlicky and somewhat peppery, and its flavor pairs nicely with fruits such as figs, cantaloupes, and grapes. It is also delicious when eaten with fresh fava beans, as is often done in early May. A mundane version of the *salame di Sant'Olcese* appears in many foreign countries and is called Genoa salami.

Pasta, Rice, & Polenta

Pasta Sfoglia all'Uovo	Sheets of Egg Pasta for Noodles
Pasta Sfoglia alla Ligure	Ligurian-Style Pasta Sheets
Pasta Sfoglia al Borragine o Agli Spinaci	Green Pasta Flavored with Borage or Spinach
Pasta alla Maggiorana	Marjoram-Flavored Pasta
Tagliatelle Bastarde	Chestnut Noodles
Mandilli di Sæa	Silk Handkerchiefs
Gnocchi e Gnocchetti	Gnocchi and Tiny Gnocchi
Gnocchi di Castagna	Chestnut Gnocchi
Gnocchi Variegati	Cheese and Vegetable Gnocchi
Trofie (or Troffie)	*Trofie*
Trofie di Castagna	Chestnut *Trofie*
Corzetti del Levante	Stamped Pasta
Corzetti della Valpolcevara	Figure-Eight *Corzetti*
Trenette alla Genovese	*Trenette* with Pesto, Potatoes, and String Beans
Penne con Funghi e Timo	Penne with Mushrooms and Thyme
Tagliarini ai Porcini	Tagliarini with Porcini Mushrooms
Tagliarini alle Erbe Fresche	Tagliarini with Fresh Herb Sauce
Spaghetti "Poveri"	"Poor" Spaghetti
Spaghetti con Pomodoro e Porri	Spaghetti with a Sauce of Tomatoes and Leeks
Pasta ai Pinoli con Ricotta e Rosmarino	Pasta with Pine Nuts, Baked Ricotta, and Fresh Rosemary
Pasta al Forno con le Olive Nere e Capperi	Baked Pasta with Black Olives and Capers
Conchiglie al Paté di Polpo	Pasta Shells with Octopus Sauce
Lasagne al Pesto	Lasagne with Pesto
Lasagne Portofino	Lasagne with Pesto and Gorgonzola Cheese
Lasagne al Pesto Bianco	Lasagne with White Pesto
Rotolo Maria Pia	Mushroom–String Bean Roll
Ravioli	Ravioli
Ravioli di Pesce	Ravioli Filled with Fish
Ravioli di Carne (Ravieu)	Meat Ravioli
Ravioli di Magro	Fast-Day (Cheese) Ravioli
Ravioli di Verdura e Formaggio	Vegetable and Cheese Ravioli
Ravioli di Zucca	Pumpkin Ravioli
Barbagiuai	Fried Pumpkin Ravioli
Pansôti	Pasta Filled with Herbs and Greens
Risotto Valpolcevara	Risotto with Mushrooms, Tomatoes, and Basil
Polenta Incatenata	"Enchained" Polenta

*P*ASTA, ALONG WITH breads, sauces and spreads, and fresh vegetables, is one of the pillars of the cuisine of the Italian Riviera. Liguria is usually considered one of the four Italian regions that are the heartlands of pasta. The others are Campania (where Naples is the capital), Sicily, and Emilia-Romagna. The first two use almost exclusively dried pasta made with durum wheat. The latter is famous for its fresh egg pasta that is used to make tagliatelle, lasagne, and filled pastas such as tortellini, tortelloni, and *anolini*.

The Italian Riviera is, as always, distinct, in that it can stake equal claim to the production of dried and fresh pastas. It also uses other flours, such as chestnut and whole wheat, in combination with traditional wheat flour to make its pastas. In addition to egg pasta, Ligurians also make fresh pasta using white wine (see Pasta Sfoglia alla Ligure, page 208) and pasta with greens (see Pasta Sfoglia al Borragine, page 209). There is also *pasta sfoglia* (sheets of pasta) made with marjoram that pairs perfectly with a pine nut sauce. As a general rule, Ligurian *pasta sfoglia* is thinner and more delicate than that of other regions, which is in keeping with the local preference for lightness and subtlety in food.

The most famous native Ligurian pasta are ravioli, folded to contain either meat, cheese, fish, or vegetables. Ravioli have traveled the world in Ligurian ships, and are now one of the most renowned pastas on the planet. There are also *pansôti,* herb- or green-filled pastas that speak with a strong Ligurian accent. They are always dressed with walnut sauce. *Trenette,* flat strands of dried pasta that are the Ligurian equivalent of linguine, are the perfect pasta for pesto sauce. More exotic Ligurian pastas include *trofie,* little spirals of pasta from Recco, and *corzetti,* which are either discs of *sfoglia* stamped with a design or a small figure-eight of pasta.

An unusual Ligurian pasta are *testaroli,* thick crêpes made of chestnut or wheat flour that are sliced and boiled before being sauced. Gnocchi are highly popular in Liguria, whether made with potatoes, wheat, or chestnut flours. Rice, which comes from the neighboring regions of Piedmont and Lombardy, has gained some popularity, but most rice dishes in Liguria are adaptations from other regions, so they will not figure prominently in this chapter. Polenta, which is most popular in northeastern Italy, nonetheless appears in one Ligurian specialty, Polenta Incatenata (see page 264).

Genoa is famous for its small pasta shops. The city has always been a major flour market, and that which was not used for focaccia was employed for pasta. The only major pasta factory that makes product for export is Agnesi, an estimable old family firm based in Oneglia (Imperia) that has produced and exported pasta to Ligurians around the world since 1824. The company grew rapidly under the guidance of Vincenzo Agnesi (1893-1977), who also wrote famous histories of pasta that are often cited in pasta cookbooks.

Years ago, when I wrote *The Authentic Pasta Book,* my research took me to the town of Pontedassio, in the province of Imperia. Here was Italy's first pasta museum, yet it was so little known that even people in Imperia had not heard of it. The museum was, in fact, the private collection of the Agnesi family, and it was open only by appointment. There were amazing treasures, from ancient pasta-making machines to pasta in eighteenth-century drawings and Fascist-era propaganda to pictures of noodles being consumed by the likes of Sophia Loren and Paul Newman.

A few years ago the Agnesi family donated its collection to form the nucleus of Il Museo Nazionale delle Paste Alimentari (The National Pasta Museum) on the Piazza Scanderbeg, around the corner from the Trevi Fountain in Rome. The museum describes the history of pasta in Liguria, Campania, Sicily, and Emilia-Romagna. As you might expect, the Ligurian collection is in the first rooms and is the most detailed exhibit. Not to miss when you are in Rome.

In making dried pasta for recipes in this book, I would encourage you to use Agnesi pasta, simply because it is Liguria's own and it is what you would see in homes in San Remo, Genoa, or Chiavari. It is exported around the world. Of course, any high-quality Italian pasta, from brands such as Barilla, De Cecco, Fara di San Martino, and La Molisana, are more than acceptable substitutes. But pastas made in other countries should not be used for these recipes.

*Agnesi is Liguria's most famous
pasta producer*

When you cook pasta, your goal is to make the noodles al dente, or chewy to the taste. Soggy noodles are overcooked and have absorbed too much water. The method for cooking pasta is the same whether you are making one portion or ten. Take a very large pot (at least 6 quarts/6 liters) and fill it three-quarters full with cold water. When it reaches a boil, toss in a pinch of sea salt. After the water returns to a full boil, add the pasta. The reason for using the large pot is that the noodles will have more room to move about as they cook. This will allow them to cook more evenly and will prevent them from sticking together. Use a plastic pasta fork to stir the pasta and prevent it from sticking to the bottom. If you are cooking sheets of pasta or delicate ones such as gnocchi, use a slotted spoon to fish them out.

Fresh pasta is usually cooked in 1 to 3 minutes. You should fish out one noodle to sample it. With fresh pasta, it is better if the noodle is undercooked than overcooked.

In cooking dried pasta, consult the package for instructions on cooking times. My rule of thumb is that I start tasting the noodles 2 minutes before the recommended time. So *trenette* that might cook for 8 minutes get tested after 6. Dried pasta is ready when its interior is no longer whiter than the exterior. When you chew a mostly cooked noodle, you will see what I mean. After the pasta is cooked, empty the water and noodles into a large colander that has been placed in a clean, empty sink. Never rinse cooked pasta — if it had room to cook in, it will have not stuck together. Simply shake the colander to get rid of excess water. In Liguria, however, pasta designated for pesto or nut sauces should not be shaken so thoroughly. The extra liquid combines with, and slightly dilutes, these sauces, with good results.

Gnocchi, *trofie,* and *testaroli* are cooked when they rise to the top of the pot of boiling water. They should be fished out with a slotted spoon.

Filled pasta such as ravioli and *pansôti* have specific cooking times that are indicated in the individual recipes. In general, their contents should be cooked through and hot, but the pasta should not be overcooked or they will tear.

You should be stinting in the amount of sauce you use on pasta. Traditionally, chefs outside of Italy add too much sauce to a dish, making it very heavy and fattening. There should be just enough sauce to coat noodles. Ideally, when you are finished eating your pasta, there should be almost no sauce at the bottom of your dish. Toss noodles and sauce in a warm bowl and serve immediately.

Also, be stingy in your addition of grated Parmigiano-Reggiano or Pecorino Romano cheese. A little bit gives flavor; more would dry out the sauce and make the dish heavier. It is almost never necessary to add cheese to a dish of pesto, because the sauce already contains cheese.

Pasta Sfoglia all' Uovo
Sheets of Egg Pasta for Noodles

Here is the basic recipe for egg pasta, an essential in Italian cooking. I have adapted this recipe from the one that appears in my book *The Authentic Pasta Book* (1985). You may use this *sfoglia* to make lasagne, *corzetti,* ravioli, tagliatelle, and the thinner tagliarini, or just about any egg noodle.

To make good *sfoglia,* you need a spacious work surface, a rolling pin (preferably a simple wood cylinder without handles about 22 inches/56 cm long), a good knife, and a pasta-cutting wheel. Many people like manual pasta cutting machines, and they are indeed useful for cutting noodles. However, you should not use this machine for flattening your dough, which would make it heavy and less delicate. You might also want to buy a ravioli tray, although good ravioli can be made without one. I have never encountered an electric pasta machine that makes fresh pasta that I consider satisfactory.

When a recipe uses such simple ingredients as flour and eggs, it is important that you pay extra attention to them. In Italy, the flour used to make pasta is called "tipo 00." The wheat used to make this flour is softer (that is, it contains less gluten) than that which is used to make pasta that is to be dried, such as spaghetti and *maccheroni*. It is worth noting that much of the flour that Italians use comes from North America, especially Canada. There is a very well-regarded flour called "manitoba," named for the Canadian province that produces it. For the flour one can use outside of Italy, I recommend a good brand of unbleached flour available in most supermarkets.

As for eggs, it is important to make a distinction about size. Italian eggs are often smaller than those found in North America and northern Europe, and the yolks occupy a greater proportion of the contents. Therefore, it is not surprising that egg pasta in Italy is much yellower than its North American or European counterpart. If you are making a large amount of *sfoglia* and are using at least 4 eggs, you might consider adding 1 egg yolk and using one less egg white (in other words, have 5 eggs on hand and use 3 whole eggs and the yolks from the other 2 eggs). For the purposes of the basic recipe for *sfoglia,* you should use *large* eggs (not medium, not extra-large, not jumbo).

Through extensive trial and error I have found what I consider a successful ratio of flour and eggs. This recipe has now been used by thousands of people who have used my pasta book and I have not had one complaint. In Italy, the ratio is 100 grams of "tipo 00" flour to 1 egg. The corresponding recipe for non-metric cooks is ⅝ cup unbleached flour to 1 large egg. This will produce 5 to 6 ounces (about 150 grams) of noodles, a generous portion for one person if pasta is but one course in a larger meal, as is usually the case in Italy. Doubling the amount (200 grams of "tipo 00" flour or 1¼ cups of unbleached flour to 2 eggs) will make enough pasta for 2 persons as a main course or 3 persons as a light first course.

These proportions are not carved in marble. The flour you use and the size of the eggs you have at hand will make for small differences. Use this ratio as a point of departure as you experiment to find the ratio best suited to your ingredients. Your goal is to produce smooth, elastic dough that is neither too loose, in which case it cannot be rolled out, nor too dry, which would mean that the dough would fall apart.

The following directions for making fresh pasta assume that you are starting with 1¼ cups (200 g) of flour and 2 large eggs. If you are using more you should knead all of the ingredients at once and then, unless you are quite proficient at rolling, you should divide the dough into 2 or 3 parts, keeping covered the parts you are not rolling.

Making Pasta all'Uovo:
The Dough

1) Place your flour in the center of a working surface made either of smooth wood or Formica, at least 2 feet by 3 feet (60 cm by 90 cm). Form what looks like a cross between a volcano and a lunar crater. This mental image should yield what looks like a little hill of flour with a large hollowed center — Italians call it *la fontana* — into which you can break the eggs. Be sure you do not make the *fontana* so deep that the eggs can seep through to the working surface. Keep the sides of the "crater" high enough so that the eggs do not spill over.

2) Break the eggs into the *fontana*. If your recipe calls for salt or minced herbs (as is sometimes the case in Liguria), now is the time to add them. Beat the eggs with a fork for about 30 seconds, or until the whites and yolks are thoroughly combined. Some Italians prefer to beat the eggs in a separate bowl and then add them to the *fontana*. Do as you wish.

3) After the eggs are beaten, push a little flour from the sides of the *fontana* into the eggs. Slowly incorporate more flour into the eggs, using the tips of your fingers, until the eggs are no longer runny. Now, with your hands, bring the outskirts of the crater into its hole, working the ingredients into a soft, sticky ball. Take it into your hands, firm the ball a bit, and place to one side.

4) Scrape the extra flour to one side of the working surface, and if your hands are caked with flour, wash them in tepid water and dry them.

5) Now start to knead the dough. You should begin by forcing the heel of your hand into the ball, pressing it down against the working surface. But be careful: If the pasta is too dry, it will be useless. Knead the pasta for at least 10 minutes — more, if you are using larger amounts of flour and eggs — folding the pasta in half, pressing it hard, turning it, extending it outward with your palm, folding it again, and so on.

6) If, after 10 minutes of kneading, you poke your thumb in the ball and it comes out moist, or if the dough sticks to your hand, knead in a *little* more flour.

7) When little bubbles start to form on the surface of the dough, form it

into a ball, give it a light dusting of flour, cover it with a towel or cloth, or wrap it loosely in plastic wrap. Let it repose, as the Italians say, for 30 to 60 minutes, in an area free of drafts or extremes in temperature.

We are now ready to roll out the dough, that is, to make the *sfoglia*. There are two roads you can take to roll out the *sfoglia* and cut it into the form you desire. One is to use a rolling pin and a knife or fluted wheel; the other is to use a manual pasta machine. Doing it by hand will not yield the uniformity of the machine's product, but you will be able, with skill, to beautifully roll the dough to the very thickness you desire and then to cut the pasta precisely as you want it. The machine makes rolling much easier, and it neatly cuts the dough into tagliatelle or tagliarini that are exactly alike. Is perfection based on beauty or uniformity? The choice is yours, although the delicacy of handmade pasta leads to better flavor, so to me there is no contest. It is also possible to roll the pasta by hand and then cut tagliatelle or tagliarini noodles using the pasta machine.

Making Pasta all'Uovo:
Rolling Out the Dough by Hand

Although this is more work than using a machine, the product is superior. The essential difference is that you are making the dough thinner by extending it rather than by compressing it.

It is necessary to use the correct rolling pin. The American type, with two handles attached, is acceptable only if you absolutely cannot get your hands on something approximating an Italian rolling pin. The main problem with the American rolling pin is that it is too thick and usually not long enough to roll out the dough. My rolling pin, which I bought very cheaply in Italy, is simply a cylinder of smoothly sanded wood. It is 1½ inches (3.8 cm) in diameter and 22 inches (56 cm) long. Some Italian rolling pins are longer, but mine suits me fine. I learned in Italy that when a rolling pin is new you should wash it in warm water and gentle soap, making sure to rinse it thoroughly. Wipe it with a clean towel and then let it air-dry. Rub the pin very lightly with corn oil or some other neutral vegetable oil. Wait about 10 minutes and then lightly dust one hand with flour and "massage" the rolling pin gently. You should give your pin this treatment about once a month if you use it with any regularity. If you cannot buy an Italian-type rolling pin, see if you can have one made at a lumberyard.

1) Uncover the dough, place it on the working surface, and knead it briefly with lightly floured hands. Then give the dough a couple of good open-handed slaps to flatten it.

2) Stand so that your shoulders are parallel with the edge of the working surface. Place the flattened dough about 12 inches (30 cm) directly in front of you. Grasp the pin at each extreme, extend your arms forward, and place the pin on the dough at the point where about three-quarters of the dough is on your side and the rest is on the far side of the pin. Roll the pin away from you, using force but without leaning into the motion. The important idea here is to stretch the dough, not to compress it. Roll almost to the edge of the dough and then gently, without pressure, roll the pin backward to the point where you began. Quickly repeat this action 4 or 5 times. Without changing the position you are standing in, turn the dough 90° to the right and roll that section of the dough as you did the first. Then turn it 90° more to the right and repeat the process, then 90° more and do the procedure once again. Now you should turn the dough a little more to the right and start rolling outward with force and backward without. Stop when the circle of dough reaches about 8 inches (20 cm) in diameter.

3) Until now we have concentrated on the extremes of the dough rather than the center. To extend the center you must do the following: With one hand, place the pin parallel to you at the far edge of the dough. Grasp the middle of the pin so that the tips of your fingers get a hold on the edge of the dough. Firmly press the heel of the palm of your other hand on the edge of the dough closest to you. Roll the pin toward you, bringing the dough with it. Keep rolling until dough wraps once around the pin. Do not wrap the dough over itself. Quickly unroll the dough — always keeping your other hand tight on the near edge of the dough — by pushing the pin away from you. Remember, push away, do not press down. Repeat the process, this time rolling more dough onto the pin than you did the first time. Roll and unroll very quickly so that the dough does not stick to itself. Finally, roll the dough completely around the pin, lift the ends of the pin in each hand, then turn the pin around so that each hand now grasps the other end. Start to unfurl the dough by lodging the heel of your right hand against the exposed end of the dough and then roll the pin away from you across the working surface, stretching but being careful not to work too violently. Do this entire procedure once again, starting from the edge and gradually adding more. Remember, work quickly, and if you find that the dough is sticking, *lightly* flour your rolling pin. Working too slowly may mean that your dough will dry out.

4) Now roll the far edge of the dough once around the pin, all the while gently smoothing the dough on the pin from the center to the two extremes. Roll more dough onto the pin and repeat the same motion. Work quickly. Then do this with the side of the dough closest to you.

5) Open the dough up again on the working surface and roll the pin a couple of times across the expanse of the dough. If you have done your job well, the dough should be about ⅟₁₆ to ⅟₁₂ inch (1.5 to 2 mm) thick. Some pasta cooks think it is necessary to see your hand through the pasta. Ligurians in particular like very thin pasta. If you are just beginning to make fresh pasta, do not worry about transparency. If the pasta is as thin as you want, smooth and elastic, then you have done good work. Let the *sfoglia* dry for about 5 to 10 minutes on a clean towel or cloth and take a little rest before cutting your pasta.

Making Pasta all'Uovo:
Rolling Out the Dough in a Manual Pasta Machine

Divide the dough into 3 or 4 separate pieces. Remember to keep covered the pieces you are not working with. Set the machine on its widest setting and run the piece of dough quickly through the rollers a few times. Make the setting one notch smaller and run the dough through again. Keep narrowing the setting and running the dough until it is as thin as you want it. Let the sheet dry on a clean towel and roll out the other pieces of dough. Machine-rolled pasta *dries out* within 10 minutes, so you must work fast.

See page 212 to learn about cutting *sfoglia* into different shapes.

Pasta Sfoglia alla Ligure

Ligurian-Style Pasta Sheets

Although Ligurians enjoy egg pasta (*pasta all'uovo*) as much as any Italians would, they also have a version that puts their own spin on it. The thinking behind the Ligurian version is fully in keeping with many of the attitudes one finds in the region: the love of frugality, delicacy, and flavor. So in Ligurian pasta fewer eggs are used but olive oil takes up the slack in terms of liquid and flavor. This pasta should not be used for narrow cut noodles such as tagliatelle and tagliarini, but they work very well for lasagne, *mandilli di sœa, corzetti del Levante,* and ravioli.

4½ cups/500 g unbleached, all-purpose or "tipo 00" flour
3 large eggs
1 tablespoon/15 ml Ligurian extravirgin olive oil

Makes
4 to 6 servings
or one pan of
lasagne

Make the dough exactly as you would pasta *sfoglia all'uovo,* except that when you add the eggs you should add the olive oil at the same time and beat them together. If you think your eggs are too small or that the dough seems a little too dry, you may add a little more olive oil or, as some Ligurians do, add about a teaspoon of a white wine such as Vermentino or Pigato. This gives the pasta a distinct and delicious flavor. Since you are using a lot of flour, you will need to separate the kneaded dough into two or three balls and roll them out individually. Your goal is to roll out the dough as thin as possible, aspiring to achieve the mythical transparency in which you can see your hand through the sheet of pasta.

Pasta Sfoglia al Borragine o Agli Spinaci

Green Pasta Flavored with Borage or Spinach

While most Italians like their green pasta flavored with spinach, Ligurians favor the distinct flavor of borage, which they find goes better with some of the sauces they use. I would encourage you to follow their lead and make *sfoglia* with borage if it is available to you, but spinach pasta is also very good, and will pair well with certain sauces: pesto *bianco,* other nut sauces, vegetable sauces, meat sauces, and mushroom sauces. It does not, in my experience, marry well with pesto or with seafood. You may use this *sfoglia* for lasagne, ravioli, tagliatelle, and tagliarini.

1 pound / 450 g fresh borage or spinach
5 cups / 570 g unbleached, all-purpose flour
4 large eggs, beaten

Wash the borage or spinach well, making sure that it is clean. Gently cook it in a pan, using only the water remaining on the leaves. The borage or spinach should be cooked just until it begins to turn soft. Remove the leaves from the pan and squeeze them dry. You might want to reserve the very nutritious liquid for soup or other uses. When the borage or spinach is as dry as possible (if wet, you will need more flour in the pasta preparation — you don't want floury pasta), chop it, and force it through a sieve. You might prefer to puree the leaves in a blender or food processor.

Makes about 2 pounds / 1 kilo

Put the flour on your working surface and form a well (*la fontana*) as described in the recipe for Pasta Sfoglia all'Uovo on page 204. Place the borage/spinach and eggs in the well and then work the ingredients into the flour using the fingertips of one hand or a fork, making sure that the borage/spinach and the eggs do not slip through the well to the working surface. Continue to work the ingredients together. If all of the flour is not incorporated, add a few drops of Ligurian extravirgin olive oil or water. Add a bit more flour if the dough is too soft.

Flour your hands and the working surface frequently as you make the dough. Knead it vigorously as you would in making Pasta Sfoglia all'Uovo, using the palm of your hand as described in that recipe. This process usually takes 10 to 20 minutes. Little air bubbles should begin to appear on the surface of the dough. Cut the dough into two or three pieces and roll them out one at a time (keeping the other balls of dough covered until you use them).

Roll the dough out to the thickness you require and let rest for about 30 minutes before cutting. Do not be surprised if this green pasta does not roll out quite as neatly as Pasta Sfoglia all'Uovo. It still makes wonderful pasta.

Pasta alla Maggiorana
Marjoram-Flavored Pasta

There are very few flavored pastas (that is, where they get their flavors and colors from added ingredients rather than from sauces) that I consider valid, and most Italians concur with my view, although some pasta manufacturers have given in to nouvelle tendencies and market pressures from abroad. The simple reason that most flavored pastas do not succeed is that the taste and fragrance of the added ingredients are blunted by the flour in the pasta-making process. Ligurians certainly would frown on this approach because it is a waste of good and expensive ingredients. There are a few exceptions to this general rule, however. The intensity of spinach flavor stands up in pasta (as does borage in its Ligurian equivalent — see page 209), and tomatoes are somewhat successful, too. Of the many herbs available in Liguria, it seems that only marjoram has been deemed acceptable for use in pasta as well as on it. Marjoram is especially delicious in Corzetti del Levante (page 222), but it also gives special flavor to tagliatelle, lasagne, and ravioli. Among the most appropriate sauces for marjoram-flavored pasta are *marò,* pine nut sauce, walnut sauce, mushroom sauce, *ricotta con le cipolle,* or any sauce made with game.

Making Pasta alla Maggiorana: If you are using the Pasta Sfoglia all'Uovo recipe (page 204), you will need 2 sprigs of fresh marjoram for every egg used. If you are using the Pasta Sfoglia alla Ligure recipe (page 208), you will need 8 sprigs of fresh marjoram (you should not add wine to this dough).

There are two ways to use marjoram in pasta. The preferable way is to pound the herb in a mortar and then beat it in with the eggs that go into the dough. This will infuse the herb flavor throughout the pasta. A second choice is to tear the sprigs into tiny bits (do not cut with a knife) and beat into the eggs. Proceed to make the dough according to the instructions in the individual recipe you select.

Tagliatelle Bastarde
Chestnut Noodles

The "bastardization" of these noodles occurs in the combination of chestnut and wheat flours. It is a product of the time when wheat flour was an expensive and precious commodity, so the chestnut flour (which nowadays is the more costly item) was used to supplement the regular flour. These noodles are delicious with pesto, with pine nut–marjoram sauce, and various vegetable sauces. It is also delicious with mushroom sauce, and pairs well with meat sauce, too.

⅝ *cup / 100 g unbleached wheat flour*
⅝ *cup / 100 g chestnut flour*
2 large eggs

Combine the flours on a work surface, make a well in the center, and add the eggs. Proceed to make a *pasta sfoglia* according to the directions on page 203. Once the *sfoglia* is ready, cut it into tagliatelle as described on page 212.

Makes
¾ pound / 300 g

Cutting *Sfoglia* to Make Various Pastas

Hand-rolled pasta does not dry quite as quickly as machine-rolled pasta, which is another advantage of that procedure. Pasta should be dry — but not dried out — before you cut it so that the noodles do not stick together. Remember that if you plan to stuff the *sfoglia* to make ravioli or *pansôti,* you should not let the pasta dry because you need to fold it. You should have the filling ready before you make the *sfoglia.*

Tagliatelle

The root of the words *tagliatelle* and *tagliarini* comes from the Italian verb *tagliare,* to cut. Tagliatelle are wider and are more suited to meat sauces; they also go well with cheese sauces, nut sauces, tomato sauces, and even pesto, although this last sauce is probably more suited to a thinner pasta. Tagliatelle are easy to produce, and probably should be the first pasta you make by hand if you are new at this.

To cut tagliatelle by hand, make a *flat,* tight roll of the *sfoglia* about 2½ inches (6.5 cm) wide. Take a sharp knife and cut across the length of the roll, making cuts every ¼ inch (65 mm). Lift each strip to let the noodles unfold. Let them dry for a few minutes before tossing them into boiling water. If you are using a manual pasta machine, slide each sheet of dough through the wide cutters, cranking the noodles out with the other hand. Separate them and let them briefly dry before cooking.

Tagliarini

These are also called taglierini, tagliolini, or tagliatelline and they are narrower than tagliatelle and, therefore, more delicate in the mouth. Follow the same procedure as cutting the tagliatelle, except that the tagliarini should be about 1/16 inch (17 mm) wide. If you are using a manual pasta machine, slide the dough through the narrow cutters, cranking out the noodles with your other hand.

Lasagne

Do not let the *sfoglia* get too dry before cutting it. Use a knife or a pasta wheel with either a straight or a fluted edge. Your lasagne should be 3 to 4 inches (7.5 to 10 cm) in width and as long as you would like them to be. The average length is probably 4 to 8 inches (10 to 20 cm). Cut the sheet of *sfoglia* into widths first and then cut in the other direction to produce the desired lengths.

Mandilli di Sæa

This name is Ligurian dialect for silk handkerchiefs. You will want to make your *sfoglia* using the recipe for Pasta Sfoglia alla Ligure (page 208). The *sfoglia* should be rolled as thin as possible. Then, using a knife or a straight-edged pasta wheel, cut the handkerchiefs into squares that are about 5 inches (12.5 cm) per side. A more detailed recipe for *mandilli di sæa* may be found on page 214.

Mandilli di Sæa
Silk Handkerchiefs

Here is a classically Ligurian pasta. It requires work and patience to make, and one finds it on Ligurian tables only for certain special occasions. Because it is so labor-intensive (although not difficult), Ligurians insist that the pesto served with these noodles also be handmade.

The word *mandilli* (handkerchiefs) derives from Arabic, while *sæa* is the Ligurian word for silk. The former word connotes the shape of this pasta while the latter describes its texture. You will want to make your *sfoglia* using the recipe for Pasta Sfoglia alla Ligure (page 208). The *sfoglia* should be rolled as thin as possible. Then, using a knife or a straight-edged pasta wheel, cut the handkerchiefs into squares that are about 5 inches (12.5 cm) per side. Let them dry for about 30 minutes before boiling.

Ligurians are very precise about how these noodles are cooked. First, set a large pot of cold water to boil. Once it reaches a boil, toss in a pinch of salt. When the water returns to a boil, add a tablespoon of Ligurian extravirgin olive oil to the water and then give it a good stir. Then cook 2 or 3 noodles at a time (boil for 30 to 45 seconds and then gently fish them out of the water using a slotted spoon) and serve immediately in the following manner: Smear a little pesto on the bottom of a plate. Place one handkerchief on top and then smear on a little more pesto. Add another handkerchief, a little more pesto, another handkerchief, a bit more pesto, and a pinch of freshly grated Parmigiano-Reggiano. Using a large spoon, push the sides of the noodles a bit so that they make the center rise and look like handkerchiefs that have been casually tossed. The purpose of this act is to allow the pesto to drizzle down the surface of the noodles. Serve immediately, and insist that the lucky recipient eat right away rather than wait for you to prepare the other portions. The classic wine accompaniment is Pigato.

Potatoes arrived in Liguria from the Americas
thanks, in part, to Christopher Columbus

Gnocchi and Gnocchetti

Gnocchi are Italy's version of dumplings, but they are much more delicate than the type one finds in central Europe, where one giant dumpling may sit on a plate of meat and gravy to serve as a catch-all. Gnocchi at their best are delicate, airy little pillows that should melt in your mouth. People often think that gnocchi are heavy, but this is often the result of poor execution and oversaucing. In Liguria, delicacy is stressed and gnocchi are only lightly coated with sauce. While the classic combination is with pesto, it is also possible to serve gnocchi with nut sauces, cheese sauces, meat sauces, mushroom sauce, tomato sauce, and vegetable sauces. I also tossed gnocchi with fava bean sauce (Marò, page 90), with great results. Gnocchetti are simply small gnocchi, and they marry well with pesto and other delicate sauces.

Gnocchi in some form probably date back to ancient times, when they were made with wheat flour, but they changed after Columbus brought potatoes back from the New World. They are among the easiest handmade pastas to produce, so if you are new to this, gnocchi will give you good practice in making and shaping dough.

1¼ pounds / 570 g mealy potatoes
2½ cups / 285 g unbleached all-purpose flour
1 pinch sea salt
1 extra-large egg

Making Gnocchi

Makes
4 servings

Wash the potatoes with their skins and boil them until you can easily poke a fork through them. When they are cooked, peel and mash them. Form a mound of potatoes on a work surface (smooth wood, Formica, or marble). Let cool for 5 minutes. Then combine the potatoes with the flour and salt and gently work the mixture together. Do not work the mixture more than necessary. Form a well in the center of this mixture and break the egg into it. Work this mixture together until you have formed a dough. Now let's make the gnocchi.

1) Once the dough is made, separate it into several pieces.

2) Take one piece and roll it out with your hands until you form a cord-like cylinder the thickness of your index finger.

3) Take a sharp knife and cut pieces of the "cord" ½ to ¾ inch/1.25 to 2 cm long. To make gnocchetti (smaller, even more delicate gnocchi), cut the "cord" ¼ inch/65 mm long.

4) Take each gnocco and press it with your thumb against the back side of a cheese grater or the tines of a fork. These indentations will become recep-

tacles for sauce when you dress your gnocchi. Do not make indentations on gnocchetti, which are too small.

5) Repeat this process until you have used all the dough. Let the gnocchi rest in a draft-free, cool place. Cover with a little more flour and do not pile them one on top of another.

Cooking Gnocchi

This is an easy process. Bring a large pot of cold water to a boil. Then toss in a pinch of sea salt. As soon as the water returns to a rapid boil, add the gnocchi. Unlike most foods, the gnocchi will tell you when they are ready. Properly cooked gnocchi rise to the surface of the boiling water. You must fish them out using a slotted ladle or spoon. I usually cut the first one in half to see if it is done to my liking, and then I taste it. If the doneness is right, I proceed as described. If it is a bit grainy, I let them cook a bit longer. If it is mushy, try to retrieve them a bit sooner. Once you have removed the gnocchi from the cooking water, transfer them to a warmed bowl to which you have added a drop of pesto or whatever sauce you are using. Once the gnocchi are all cooked, add the rest of the sauce, but make sure that the gnocchi are only lightly coated and not swimming, or the final result will be too heavy.

Gnocchi di Castagna

Chestnut Gnocchi

This is a typical preparation in the province of La Spezia, where chestnut flour used to be the only type that was affordable. Now it provides flavor, color, and a sense of connection to old ways. Serve with pesto, with pine nut–marjoram sauce, or simply tossed with excellent Ligurian olive oil and a pinch of freshly grated cheese.

1¾ pounds / 800 g mealy potatoes
4½ cups / 500 g unbleached all-purpose flour
1¾ cups / 200 g chestnut flour
4 tablespoons / ¼ cup / 30 g freshly grated Parmigiano-Reggiano
2 egg yolks
1 pinch sea salt

Makes
6 servings

Make the gnocchi according to the instructions on page 216, with the following differences: Combine the potatoes (which you have let cool) and flours with the grated cheese. Form the well, add the egg yolks and salt, and then make the dough before preparing the gnocchi as directed.

Gnocchi Variegati

Cheese and Vegetable Gnocchi

These delicious gnocchi from Genoa go well with many sauces, including Agliata (page 97), Paté di Ortaggi (page 85), Rattatuia (page 84), Crema ai Pinoli e Maggiorana (page 78), Pesto Bianco (page 76), Tocco de Noxe (page 77), or Tocco di Funghi (page 91). Ideally, you will make these gnocchi with borage and *prescinseua,* but spinach and ricotta are acceptable substitutes.

12 ounces / 350 g mealy potatoes, washed
4 ounces / 115 g borage or spinach, washed and trimmed
2 ounces / 50 g prescinseua or fresh ricotta
1⅜ cups / 150 g unbleached, all-purpose flour
2 tablespoons / 15 g freshly grated Parmigiano-Reggiano
2 large eggs

Use the instructions for making gnocchi (page 216) as guidelines for making this recipe. Cook and then peel the potatoes, mash them, and let cool. Boil the borage or spinach just until soft. Drain well, squeezing out all excess liquid. Mince the borage or spinach and let cool. Combine the potatoes, borage (or spinach), *prescinseua* (or ricotta), flour, and Parmigiano-Reggiano to make a dough. Form a well, break in the eggs, and then knead as directed to make a dough before forming the gnocchi or gnocchetti.

Makes
4 servings

Trofie (or Troffie)

❧

These little bits of fresh pasta, which to me look like nerve endings, are yet another food specialty associated with the town of Recco (see page 117). However, they originated in the tiny town of Testana, about 5 miles/8 kilometers inland. The people there, I have been told, are famously tightfisted, and no food ever goes to waste. According to local legend, a few centuries ago a local woman made some pasta and the dough was a little too moist. She rubbed her palms together to clean them of the dough that was clinging, and in the act of rubbing created these skinny curls of pasta now called *trofie* (sometimes spelled with two *f*'s). As it turns out, *trofie* taste divine when tossed with pesto, and it is one of the most famous dishes in Recco. Nowadays, *trofie* can be made by machine, but they come out too regular. It is still better to produce them by hand.

Nobody I have spoken to in Liguria agrees about how much water should be used to make *trofie*. In truth, it is very little indeed — Ligurians always say *"quanto basta,"* or "as much as is necessary." For the amount of flour in this recipe, I start with 1¾ cups/400 ml of water and usually wind up adding more, a little at a time.

3 cups/350 g unbleached flour
1 pinch fine sea salt
Water, as needed
½ cup/60 g additional flour

Makes 4 to 6 servings

Create a mound of flour on your work surface, and make a well in the middle. Sprinkle in the salt. Add some water, and then fold in the sides of the mound to incorporate some of the water into the flour. Then push open to make a new well and add some more water. Start making a ball. The dough should be slightly crumbly, but should have moisture. Keep adding more water until you have a dough that is rather pliant. Wrap it in a clean cloth and let rest for 30 minutes. When you are ready to make the *trofie,* flour your work surface well. Then flour your hands. Grab a little piece of dough, about the size of a small olive, and roll it in your palms. You should produce a little worm-shaped noodle about 1½ inches/4 cm long and slightly fatter in the middle than at the extremes. You may also make *trofie* by rolling them between a well-floured thumb and index or middle finger. Keep making these until you have used up all of the dough. They are not supposed to be perfect or identical, but in fact should resemble a pasta shape that came from a blissful accident of creation. Keep enough flour around so that your hands will always be slightly coated and the *trofie* will absorb a bit of it and dry slightly before they are cooked.

COOKING TROFIE: When fresh *trofie* are added to boiling water, they rise very quickly (within a few seconds). When they do this, add a drop of olive oil to the water, stir the pot once, and then drain immediately and toss with pesto.

Trofie di Castagna

Chestnut *Trofie*

These are made just like regular *trofie*, except that there is a presence of chestnut flour. They go well with pesto, but their ideal sauce is Marò (page 90), made with fresh fava beans.

1 cup/120 g unbleached wheat flour
2 cups/240 g chestnut flour
1 pinch fine sea salt
Water, as needed
½ cup/60 g additional flour, either wheat or chestnut

Combine the two flours before making the dough. Proceed as indicated in the directions for *trofie,* page 220.

*Makes
4 to 6 servings*

Corzetti del Levante
Stamped Pasta

To my amazement, most Ligurians I spoke to, especially in the Ponente, had no idea what *corzetti* are. There is a vague recognition among some Genoese, and they are well known in the culinary citadel of Recco. The other chief town for *corzetti* is Chiavari, farther down the Levante coast. This is due in part to the artistry of Franco Casoni, who is one of the last remaining craftsmen who make *corzetti* stamps. When I asked around in other towns where I could buy *corzetti* stamps, nobody knew the stores I found in Genoa (see page 457 for sources), but many restaurateurs would squint their eyes and say, "*Già, ma c'é un artigiano giù a Chiavari, ma non so dove sta e non so come si chiama.*" ("Oh, yeah, well there's an artisan down in Chiavari, but I don't know where he is and I don't know what his name is.") I was further surprised that the tourist office and most food sellers in Chiavari had no idea who Signor Casoni is, but I finally found him simply by wandering the streets of the old quarter of town. I am glad to report that he is alive and well, still hard at work, and producing the most beautiful *corzetti* stamps I have seen. I expect that with the publication of this book he will discover more customers, as will the Buteghina Magica and the Granone & Monchieri stores in Genoa. What I love about *corzetti* is that they are handmade and they require both the artistry of the pasta maker and the person who makes the stamp. Typically the stamp will be a representation of something relating to the days of glory of the Republic of Genoa. The original design might have been a cross used by Genoese crusaders of the late thirteenth century because *corzetti* in dialect means "little crosses." Another popular early design was the seal of the Doria family, the most powerful in the Genoese Republic. On newer *corzetti* stamps there are also flowers, crests, sailing vessels, fish, or even cameo-type portraits. As you would expect, handmade *corzetti* stamps are not inexpensive, but they are treasurable and will give you a powerful link to the glory of the Liguria of old.

There are several sauces that marry well with *corzetti*. The best is probably Crema ai Pinoli e Maggiorana (page 78), but you may also use pesto, *pesto bianco, tocco* (meat sauce), *tocco de noxe, tocco di funghi,* or *ricotta con le cipolle.* A more unusual sauce is Sugo di Muscoli (page 104), but it does work well. I like to pair it with *corzetti* stamped with sailing vessels). As *corzetti* are delicate pasta, the saucing should be done with an equally light hand.

5¼ cups / 630 g unbleached all-purpose flour
2 teaspoons / 5 g fine sea salt
5 egg yolks
¾ cup / 6 ounces / 1 glass / 85 ml warm white wine such as Vermentino or Pigato
2 teaspoons / 5 g minced fresh marjoram (optional)

Corzetti *stamps are made in many designs*

Make a mound of flour with added salt as described for making *pasta sfoglia* (page 203). Add the egg yolks and the wine (and optional marjoram) and form a dough. Roll the dough out thin, as you might for lasagne. Use a knife, a pizza cutter, or a roller to make squares of pasta just a little larger than the circumference of your *corzetti* stamp. Gently insert the square in your *corzetti* stamp. Press the stamp down on each square to imprint its design on your *corzetti*. Do not press too hard or you will break the pasta. Do not discard the scraps of pasta — do as a Ligurian might and add them to broth or bean soup so that nothing will have gone to waste. Let the *corzetti* dry for about an hour before cooking them in rapidly boiling water that has been very lightly salted. As this is fresh pasta, they will cook within minutes, so do not ignore them. Fish them out of the pot delicately with a slotted spoon or gently empty the contents of the pot into a colander. Dress the *corzetti* immediately so that the sauce will be heated by the pasta, and then serve at once.

Since this is delicate pasta with a delicate sauce, a similarly delicate white wine (preferably from Liguria) would be ideal.

Corzetti della Valpolcevara

Figure-Eight *Corzetti*

These *corzetti,* like their better-known disk-shaped cousins (page 222), are also based on the idea of imitating a coin from the Republic of Genoa. The Val Polcevara is the agricultural *entroterra* of the city of Genoa, and it has never been as affluent as some of the coastal areas. So while the coins of the city were the bigger pieces, those found in the valley were smaller and more humble. They are shaped like the number 8, and are easy to make once you get the hang of it.

2½ cups / 300 g unbleached all-purpose flour
2 or 3 large eggs
1 tablespoon / 15 ml lukewarm water

Make the *fontana* of flour: Form a mound of flour on a lightly floured working surface. Move the flour in the center to form a shell; the sloping flour will resemble a volcano in shape. Break the eggs into the center, starting with two and reserving the third, if you think it is needed. Add the water and beat with a fork. Start working the flour in your hands until you form a smooth and firm dough. If you find that there is not enough moisture, add another beaten egg before the dough starts to take shape.

Makes 4 servings

Let the dough rest, covered, for 30 minutes before proceeding. Flour your hands lightly before making the *corzetti.* When you are ready, take the dough and pull off a piece the size of a cherry. Using both index fingers, flatten and stretch the dough lengthwise on your work surface and then press down on either side to form a *corzetto* shaped like the number 8. Be sure that you don't pull the piece of dough too much or you will snap it in half in the middle. Another way to form these *corzetti* is to take the cherry-sized piece of dough and press it between both thumbs and index fingers. Pull apart slightly and press down with the two fingers of each hand. This will flatten and hollow the dough, making a figure 8.

Set the *corzetti* aside for several hours to dry before cooking. When stored in a cool, dry place, they can last for several days before being used.

These *corzetti* pair well with meat sauce, mushroom sauce, or pesto.

Trenette alla Genovese

Trenette with Pesto, Potatoes, and String Beans

This is the classic pasta dish of Genoa. *Trenette* are dried flat strands of pasta that you can purchase from one of the better pasta brands of Italy that are available now in most countries. Of course Agnesi, Liguria's most famous pasta producer, makes *trenette,* as do producers from other Italian regions, including Barilla and DeCecco. If you cannot locate *trenette,* linguine (that is, "little tongues") are an acceptable substitute. While pasta with pesto is famous throughout Liguria and beyond, the addition of potatoes and string beans is classically Genoese, although the practice is thought to have originated in the smaller towns of the Levante.

4 ounces / 110 g fresh thin string beans, washed, cut in half, tips cut off
2 medium potatoes, washed, peeled, cut into bite-size cubes
12 ounces / 350 g trenette
4 tablespoons / 60 ml pesto
1 tablespoon cooking water from the pasta pot
Freshly grated Parmigiano-Reggiano (optional)

Makes
4 servings

Bring a large pot of cold water to boil. When it reaches a boil, toss in a pinch of sea salt. When the water returns to a boil, add the string beans and potato cubes. Cook for 5 to 7 minutes, or until you can poke a fork easily into one of the potato cubes. Then add the *trenette* and cook until al dente, following the instructions on the package. While the pasta is cooking, place the pesto in a large serving bowl and stir in 1 tablespoon of hot water from the pasta pot. When the pasta are al dente, drain them along with the string beans and potatoes in a colander. Immediately transfer to the serving bowl, toss well, and then serve in individual bowls. You may add a pinch of Parmigiano-Reggiano to each dish, but do not overdo it or the dish will dry out (remember, there is already cheese in the pesto).

Penne con Funghi e Timo

Penne with Mushrooms and Thyme

If fresh *funghi porcini* are at hand, they will enhance this dish significantly, but you may also make it with cremini or with cultivated store-bought mushrooms.

14 ounces/400 g penne (or other medium-size maccheroni *from Italy)*
1 tablespoon/7 g unsalted butter
1 tablespoon/15 ml extravirgin olive oil
1 shallot, peeled and sliced thin
12 ounces/350 g mushrooms, cleaned and sliced thin
3 sprigs fresh thyme
1 or 2 tablespoons/7 to 15 g freshly grated Parmigiano-Reggiano (optional)

Set a large pot of cold water to boil. Once the water reaches a boil, toss in a pinch of coarse or sea salt if you wish. If you have added salt, let the water return to a rolling boil. Cook the penne until al dente and then drain them in a colander. Do not rinse. While the water is heating up, you should begin the preparation of the sauce. In a large skillet, melt the butter with the olive oil and then add the shallot slices. Sauté until the shallot slices are translucent and have released their perfume. Then add the sliced mushrooms and one sprig of thyme, which you have torn in small bits. Cook until the mushrooms yield their liquid, making sure not to exceed this moment or the pan juices will dry up. Add the drained pasta and the other two sprigs of thyme, also torn in small bits. Combine thoroughly, quickly shut off the heat, and serve. If you find that the pan juices have dried, you will need to add ½ tablespoon more of unsalted butter along with the pasta. Before adding grated cheese you should taste this dish unadorned. Remember that while the cheese is delicious, adding too much of it to this preparation will overpower the delicate flavors in the sauce.

Makes 4 servings

The Countess Blessington
Reviews the Food of Genoa

The Countess Blessington, who is described on page 266, cast her eye intriguingly on the food of Genoa. While most nineteenth-century British travelers found Ligurian food unsavory, Countess Blessington, as was her wont, was more open-minded and receptive to things that were unfamiliar to her. What she initially describes are the *friggitorie*, the fry shops that are part of the Genoese food scene and provide a very high quality "fast food." Then, as now, the Genoese were eager to consume freshly fried fish, a piece of hot focaccia, or a wedge of vegetable pie that was purchased on the street so that they could return to work as quickly as possible.

"In passing through the streets at Genoa, it is amusing to look at the culinary occupations going on in each; with the exception of the three principal ones. Nor is there aught disgusting in the process, or in the odours exhaled; for the oil used in the *friturás* is of the pure olive, and the cooks are not only scrupulously clean in their dress, but the utensils they employ look equally so. Here the polenta, polpetta, and ravioli, the three favourite dishes of Genoa, are prepared; and great is the demand for them, and the avidity with which they are devoured. But not only are the national dishes thus cooked in the streets, but shops are in each, and ranged on the quays, in which edibles of a more costly nature are to be procured; and where cutlets and capons, smoking hot, tempt by their savoury odours the appetites of the passers by. In the back of these shops are stoves, round which are placed all the necessary apparatus for cooking; and the proprietor, with one or two assistants, white-capped and aproned, with knife in belt, stand ready to boil, stew, fry, or broil, according to the wish of their visitors. A portion of the shop is devoted to undressed dainties, which are seen peeping forth from green leaves; and snowy napkins, waiting to be selected by some pedestrian epicure, who may see his dinner cooked, and eat it on the spot, in a very short space of time. These *restaurants* are chiefly frequented by artisans, and persons of that class; and much time is saved to them by the facility of finding their repasts prepared at a few minutes' notice. Men and women roll barrows through the streets, piled with trays, on which various kinds of *comestibles* are disposed, and thus serve the inmates of the different artisans' houses, who are saved the trouble of cooking, and the expense of heat and fires. The cleanliness of these people, as well as that of the articles on which the food is placed, precludes the disgust one might experience at beholding such a constant succession of eatables passing and repassing; and it is amusing to witness the eagerness with which their approach is hailed."

Tagliarini ai Porcini

Tagliarini with Porcini Mushrooms

Here is a typical dish of the *entroterra*, although it is also wildly popular on the coast. When it rains in Liguria, the following day is invariably characterized by mushroom hunters prowling the *sottobosco* (the land beneath the woods) for new porcini mushrooms. Because much of Liguria borders on Emilia-Romagna and Piedmont, two regions that favor egg noodles, it is not surprising that they are eaten in the inland areas of the Riviera as well. A difference worth noting is that while Emilia-Romagna and Piedmont would usually use butter in their sauce, in Liguria olive oil is king. Ideally, you will want to make your own tagliarini (see the recipe for Pasta Sfoglia on page 203), but you may also use better-quality store-bought fresh noodles or dried egg noodles imported from Italy. It is also possible to substitute thicker tagliatelle, but the impact on the mouth would be less delicate. In the absence of fresh porcini or other edible wild mushrooms, you may combine fresh cultivated and dried porcini mushrooms as explained in the note below.

1 pound/450 g tagliarini
½ pound/225 g fresh funghi porcini*
2 tablespoons/30 ml Ligurian extravirgin olive oil
1 clove garlic, with the green heart removed, minced
2 sprigs fresh Italian (flat) parsley, minced
⅜ cup/3 ounces/½ glass/45 ml dry white wine

> * Note: If fresh porcini, cremini, or other special mushrooms are unavailable, you may make this dish using 8 ounces/225 g cultivated mushrooms in combination with 2 to 3 ounces/60 to 75 g dried *funghi porcini* that you have soaked. After soaking the dried mushrooms, strain the liquid and then soak the sliced cultivated mushrooms in the liquid for 10 minutes so that they will absorb some of the flavor.

Makes
4 servings

If you are making fresh pasta, prepare the tagliarini. Then set a large pot of cold water to boil. When it reaches a boil, add a pinch of sea salt. In the meantime, gently wipe the fresh mushrooms to remove dirt and impurities. Cut into medium-slim slices, but be careful not to make them too narrow or they will fall apart. (If you are using dried mushrooms, soak them until they are soft and then squeeze out the excess liquid. Clean and slice the fresh mushrooms you are combining them with.) Once the mushrooms are ready, gently heat the oil in a skillet and then add the garlic and parsley. Cook until the garlic is golden but not brown and the oil has begun to take on the fragrance of the garlic. Then add the mushrooms to the pan and sauté. About 30 seconds later, add the white wine. At the same time, you should put the tagliarini in the pot of boiling water to cook them until al dente. In the meantime, watch the sauce. The mushrooms should cook just until they soften and the sauce should take on a little thickness. When the pasta is cooked, drain it carefully and add to the skillet. Quickly combine the ingredients with a spoon or fork, all the while shaking the pan. Serve immediately. (Grated Parmigiano-Reggiano might weigh down this delicate, oil-based preparation, so I would omit it in this case.)

This dish would be well matched by the white wine you use in the sauce, or a medium- to full-bodied red such as Dolcetto, Chianti Classico, or Barbaresco. A Barolo or a Brunello di Montalcino would be overpowering.

Tagliarini alle Erbe Fresche

Tagliarini with Fresh Herb Sauce

Ideally, you would want to use fresh tagliarini here, but you may also employ dried tagliarini, especially if they are made with eggs. While this sauce also works with a non-egg pasta such as penne, it is not quite as enchanting. The portions here are for a delicate first course to a meal rather than a heaping bowl of pasta.

1 pinch sea salt (optional)
¼ cup/4 tablespoons/30 g fresh basil leaves, preferably tiny ones
⅛ cup/2 tablespoons/15 g fresh marjoram
⅛ cup/2 tablespoons/15 g fresh rosemary needles
⅛ cup/2 tablespoons/15 g fresh sage
⅛ cup/2 tablespoons/15 g fresh thyme
1⁄16 cup/1 tablespoon/7 g fresh mint (optional)
1 cup/½ pint/225 ml light cream
12 ounces/¾ pound/350 g tagliarini or penne

Makes
4 servings

Set a large pot of cold water to boil. Once it reaches a rolling boil, you may, if you wish, toss in a pinch of sea salt. This will be the water in which you cook the pasta. In a mortar combine all of the herbs and *gently* pound them until they break into little pieces. You are not making a paste, so there should be minimal pounding of the herbs. Once this is accomplished, you have a decision to make. If you are using dried pasta that requires longer cooking, add the pasta to the boiling water. If you are using fresh pasta that only cooks for about 30 seconds, make the sauce first. To make the sauce, pour the cream into a heavy-bottomed pot, add the herbs, and heat very gently. It should never approach a boil. Once you have begun to make the sauce, you should then cook the fresh pasta. If you are using dried pasta, make the sauce about 1 minute before the pasta is expected to be done. (Read the package instructions carefully to cook the pasta al dente, and check the noodles periodically as they boil.) Once the pasta is cooked, drain it in a colander (never rinse!), and immediately transfer the noodles to the pot with the sauce. Stir just enough so that the ingredients combine, but do not cook this combination further. The key to the successful preparation of this dish is that the herbs retain their fresh flavor, which is why there is minimal pounding and cooking. Serve immediately.

NOTE: You might be tempted to add grated cheese, but I would actively discourage this — the cheese will overwhelm the delicate flavor of the herbs.

Ligurian Impressions
of an Eighteenth-Century Traveler

"In some places on those desolate mountains, olives grow in abundance, furnishing France with good quantities of oil. . . . The Genoese also collect a few mushrooms which they manage to make a small business out of. . . . The countervailing wind prevented my arrival in Portovenere, as I had hoped. So I slept in Portofino, 20 miles from Genoa. With my ship battered by the winds, I wound up with a frightening case of seasickness. I set my stomach right in a little inn, where I found good mullet, good wine and good oil."

— Charles-Louis de Montesquieu,
1728

Spaghetti "Poveri"
"Poor" Spaghetti

Poverty is a relative concept. This dish is an old specialty of Portofino, a place that may have the highest per capita wealth of any town in Italy. It is not that these rich people are all Ligurians. Portofino has been a haven for wealthy industrialists, movie stars, and titled royalty for decades. The most dazzling yachts and cruise ships drop anchor throughout the year, and many of the super-rich with a Portofino address keep their yachts in the larger harbor of nearby Santa Margherita. During high season, every young and eager Portofinese man seems to find himself in the service — in one form or another — of a contessa with a lot of time and money on her hands. So the word *poor,* as regards spaghetti, has nothing to do with money. Time was, in the early years of the twentieth century, when Portofino was indeed a simple fishing village in which families eked out a subsistence based on what they could draw from the land and the sea. "Poor" ingredients, in fact, imply simplicity — these are foods that were readily available, and often at little or no cost. But "poor" has nothing at all to do with quality. The genuine flavors of yesterday are still the ones preferred today, even in fancy Portofino. I love the touch of combining tomatoes and lemon juice in a pasta sauce, something I have never before encountered.

5 ripe plum tomatoes, washed, peeled, cut into small cubes, seeds removed
Juice of ½ lemon
3 tablespoons / 45 ml Ligurian extravirgin olive oil
2 cloves garlic, cut in half, with the green heart removed
12 small or 6 larger fresh basil leaves, wiped clean
1 sprig Italian (flat) parsley, torn into large pieces
1 leaf fresh sage, torn into 3 or 4 pieces
2 anchovy fillets, well rinsed, bones removed, chopped into bits
¾ cup / 6 ounces / 1 glass / 85 ml dry white wine, preferably Ligurian
Sea salt
Freshly ground black pepper
1 pound / approximately 450 g spaghetti, trenette, or linguine
2 teaspoons / 5 g pinoli
1 tablespoon / 7 g freshly grated Pecorino Romano

*Makes
4 to 6 servings*

Set a large pot of cold water to boil. When it reaches a rolling boil, toss in a pinch of sea salt. While the water is coming to a boil, prepare the sauce. Start by peeling and cutting the tomatoes. A good shortcut for peeling the tomatoes is to place them on a slotted spoon, one at a time, just above the boiling water. This will allow the peel to slip off or be cut away more readily. Once they are cut and seeded, place the tomato cubes in a bowl and toss with the lemon juice. Then take a large, heavy-bottomed pan and place it over medium heat. Add the olive oil and, when it is somewhat hot but not splattering, add the garlic, basil, parsley, sage, and anchovies. Stir the ingredients continuously for 2 or 3 minutes, or until the garlic is golden but not in any way brown. Then add the wine and cook for 2 or 3 minutes, or until the alcohol has evaporated. This process will be aided by continuous, though not violent, stirring. Season with salt and pepper. Turn off the flame and remove the pan from the heat. Cook the pasta according to the directions on the package, making sure that you do not overcook it. About 30 seconds before the pasta is al dente, return the pan with the sauce to medium heat. When the pasta is cooked, drain it thoroughly in a colander (do not rinse it!) and add it to the pan. Immediately add the tomato/lemon mixture and toss everything in the pan. After 10 seconds of tossing, add the *pinoli* and the Pecorino Romano, toss another 10 seconds, and serve immediately. It is traditional to bring the pan to the table and serve the dish directly to your eager guests. The wine served should be the same one you used for cooking.

Spaghetti con Pomodoro e Porri

Spaghetti with a Sauce of Tomatoes and Leeks

A family recipe of a certain Anna Rossi, who lives not too far from La Spezia.

3 medium-size leeks
4 tablespoons/60 ml Ligurian extravirgin olive oil
28-ounce/800-g can peeled Italian plum tomatoes, preferably San Marzano type
12 small basil leaves, wiped clean with paper toweling
1 pinch sea salt
Freshly ground black pepper to taste (optional)
Slightly more than 1 pound/500 g spaghetti
2 tablespoons/15 g freshly grated Parmigiano-Reggiano (optional)

*Makes
4 to 6 servings*

Set a large pot of cold water to boil. In the meanwhile, carefully wash the white parts of the leeks and cut them into thin strips. Heat the oil in a large saucepan and then sauté the leeks for 3 to 4 minutes, making sure the oil does not get too hot and that the leek strips do not burn. Then add the tomatoes, which you should coarsely chop with a fork. Add the basil, salt, and optional pepper and heat the whole combination on a high flame for 5 minutes. Use a fork to break the tomatoes into small pieces. While this is cooking, cook the spaghetti according to the package directions just until the strands are al dente (you must test one every minute or so to be sure). Once the noodles are done, drain them in a colander and then add them to the saucepan until spaghetti and sauce are thoroughly integrated. If you wish, you may add up to 2 tablespoons of freshly ground Parmigiano-Reggiano at the moment you toss the spaghetti and the sauce. Serve immediately.

Noli

Noli, in the province of Savona, is yet another small gem on the Ligurian necklace. It is a fishing port that was once difficult to reach by any means except boat. Yet Margaret Gardiner Blessington, that intrepid traveler of the early nineteenth century, reached Noli by land and wrote charmingly of it.

"Many of the chains of rocks that bound the coast of the Mediterranean, between Finale and Noli, are of stupendous height; some large chasms on them resembling immense portals and windows; while the road, which is formed on a ledge, appears like a balcony overhanging the sea. Seen by moonlight, they give the idea of some gigantic palace, the residence of the genii of the place.

"Noli is about a mile from the last and largest of the grottos, and is a long straggling village built on the beach, immediately fronting the sea. The inn was crowded with guests, who were occupied in supping, singing, and smoking, and was redolent of the mingled odours of garlic, tobacco, and fried fish. At one table a party were devouring maccaroni in a similar manner to that in which an Indian juggler swallows steel; and at another were seated half a dozen persons partaking the contents of a large earthen bowl, the savoury steams of which proclaimed that garlic was one of its principal ingredients. Various small circles were celebrating their bacchanalian orgies round separate tables, and sang, or more properly speaking, roared a sort of wild chaunt, compensating by animation and noise for the great deficiency of harmony."

Pasta ai Pinoli con Ricotta e Rosmarino

Pasta with Pine Nuts, Baked Ricotta, and Fresh Rosemary

In the *entroterra* of the province of Imperia this dish is usually prepared with a soft goat's milk cheese similar to ricotta, but tangier. Another cheese that is used is Bruss, a sort of fermented ricotta that is used inland from the coast of the western Riviera. As these cheeses are not available beyond the confines of Liguria, there is a way to adapt this recipe. If you want the tangy flavor that the goat's milk or the fermentation implies, you may stir ½ teaspoon white wine vinegar into the ricotta before using the cheese. Then proceed according to the directions of the recipe. The dish is also very tasty using traditional ricotta cheese, which is to say the soft sweet cheese known as ricotta romana.

1 cup / 115 g fresh ricotta
½ teaspoon / 2.5 ml white wine vinegar (optional)
1 pound / 450 g pasta*
4 tablespoons / 30 g unsalted butter
2 long sprigs fresh rosemary (gently wipe with paper toweling, then remove
    all of the needles and discard the stems)
2 tablespoons / 15 g pinoli
1 to 2 tablespoons / 7 to 15 g freshly grated Parmigiano-Reggiano (optional)
1 pinch sea salt

> * There are various types of pasta that you may use in this dish, but they should all be of the small, tubular variety. Among your choices are *garganelli,* penne, and *maccheroni* (from Italy, of course).

Makes
4 to 6 servings

Preheat your oven to 350°F / 180°C. If you are adding vinegar to your ricotta, stir it in well (do not be concerned if the cheese softens). Place the cheese in an ovenproof dish (enamel, terracotta, or pyrex, for example) and bake for 15 minutes. Remove from the oven. When the cheese has cooled slightly, chop it coarsely into many little pieces. While the cheese is cooling, set a large pot of cold water to boil. When the water reaches a boil, you may add a little salt if you wish, although I would not recommend it in this case. Then cook the pasta according to the directions on the package. Your goal is that the pasta be quite al dente when you drain it. While the pasta is cooking, melt the butter in a large saucepan over low to medium heat until it is foamy but does not turn color.

Then add the rosemary needles and the *pinoli* and give the pan a couple of good shakes so that the butter is flavored, and remove from the heat. When the pasta has cooked, drain it thoroughly and add it to the pan. Return the pan to the heat, add the ricotta, the optional Parmigiano-Reggiano (be stingy!), and the pinch of sea salt. Stir so that the cheese softens and combines with the pasta, rosemary, and *pinoli*. Serve immediately.

Pasta al Forno con le Olive Nere e Capperi

Baked Pasta with Black Olives and Capers

A typical home recipe from a family near La Spezia.

1 large onion, sliced into thin rings
⅜ cup / 6 tablespoons / 85 ml Ligurian extravirgin olive oil
8 canned, peeled tomatoes
Sea salt to taste
Freshly ground black pepper to taste
20 small basil leaves, wiped clean and torn
Scant 4 ounces / 100 g black olives (preferably Taggia or Gaeta),
   pitted and cut into pieces
1 teaspoon capers (if packed in salt, rinse first)
1 pound / 450 g penne or maccheroncini
½ pound / 225 g fresh unsalted mozzarella, cut into dice-size cubes
2 tablespoons / 15 g freshly grated Parmigiano-Reggiano
Unflavored bread crumbs
A few curls butter

Makes
4 to 6 servings

Set a large pot of cold water to boil. After slicing the onion, heat the oil in a saucepan and then add the onion. Sauté until the onion slices are translucent and fragrant and then add the tomatoes, salt, pepper, basil, and olive pieces. Cook over relatively high heat for about 10 minutes, gently breaking up the tomatoes with a fork or wooden spoon. The sauce should not rapidly boil, but should also not simmer. After 10 minutes, stir in the capers thoroughly and then turn off the heat. While the sauce is cooking, add the pasta to the boiling water. When the noodles are quite al dente, drain them in a colander and place them in a lightly oiled, ovenproof baking dish. Top with the mozzarella and Parmigiano-Reggiano cheeses, then add the sauce and toss thoroughly so that the mozzarella begins to melt. Top this combination with a thin layer of bread crumbs and a few curls of butter. Bake in a preheated 350°F/180°C oven for 10 to 15 minutes, or until the crust is lightly golden.

Conchiglie al Paté di Polpo

Pasta Shells with Octopus Sauce

This is a preparation that speaks of the sea in its use of shell pasta and a wonderful octopus sauce. I first tasted it in Sestri Levante.

12 ounces/350 g pasta shells
1 jar or portion of Paté di Polpo (see page 105)
A few fresh basil leaves (optional)
A little freshly ground black pepper to taste (optional)
2 tablespoons/30 ml hot Fresh Tomato Sauce (see page 82) (optional)

Set a large pot of cold water to boil. When it reaches a rolling boil, add a pinch of sea salt. When the water returns to a boil, add the pasta and cook until al dente. Drain and place the pasta in a serving dish into which you have already added the octopus sauce, which can be cool or, if you wish, heated slightly before combining with the pasta. Toss well and serve. You may add either basil leaves or a little pepper, but not both. As an interesting option, you may stir two tablespoons of hot fresh tomato sauce into the *paté* and add, if you wish, basil or pepper.

Makes 4 servings

Lasagne al Pesto

Lasagne with Pesto

In Liguria, sheets of pasta tend to be very thin and delicate, and when lasagne dishes are prepared, they usually use fresh rather than dried pasta. If you use dried lasagne for this dish, try to use a high-quality Italian brand that is as thin as possible. Preferably the lasagne should be flat rather than curly.

1½ pounds/650 g lasagne, preferably fresh
1 cup/115 g (100 g plus 1 tablespoon) pesto
½ cup/60 g freshly grated Parmigiano-Reggiano or ½ cup/60 g fresh ricotta
½ cup/60 g freshly grated Pecorino Romano

Makes
6 servings

If you are using fresh lasagne, make them first. Then set a large pot of cold water to boil. Grease a lasagne pan with sweet butter. When the water reaches a rolling boil, cook the lasagne a few sheets at a time only until they are al dente. Remove each sheet with a flat slotted spoon and set aside, and then cook more lasagne. Once the sheets are cool enough to handle (but not cold), you should prepare the dish. Thoroughly stir a tablespoon of the hot pasta water into the pesto, and then spoon a thin layer of the sauce in the pan. Place one layer of lasagne atop this sauce. Then add a thin layer of pesto, a little Parmigiano-Reggiano or some fresh ricotta. Then top with a little Pecorino Romano. Continue this process, making a thin layer of noodles, pesto, and cheeses until all the ingredients are used and Pecorino is on top. Once this is done, bake for 20 minutes in a preheated 325°F/170°C oven.

Lasagne Portofino

Lasagne with Pesto and Gorgonzola Cheese

Here is an example of a culinary hybrid. The good people of Portofino (and much of Liguria) lived contentedly for centuries on pasta with pesto. Then, following World War II, the towns of the Portofino Peninsula became a popular winter refuge and summer resort for affluent people from Lombardy and Piedmont. These people brought along their taste for rich cow's milk cheeses, and one of them, Gorgonzola, wound up combined with pesto in lasagne. This is not nouvelle-style fusion, but really a blissful combination of ingredients that works very well. There are classicists (and I suppose I count myself among them) who prefer the pure flavor of pesto with pasta, but I confess to liking this preparation, too, and it has proved popular with guests. If you use dried pasta for this dish, try to use a high-quality Italian brand that is as thin as possible. If you are making fresh pasta (see the recipe for basic *sfoglia* on page 203), prepare it before assembling the ingredients (assuming, of course, that the pesto is already made).

1½ pounds / 650 g lasagne, preferably fresh
1 tablespoon / 7 g sweet butter
¾ cup / 85 g pesto
⅔ pound / 300 g Gorgonzola dolce (the yellow type), foil and rind removed; the cheese should be cut into thumbnail-size pieces
Freshly grated Parmigiano-Reggiano (optional)

If you are using fresh lasagne, make them first. After they have dried for about 10 minutes, set a large pot of cold water to boil. Grease a lasagne pan with the butter. When the water reaches a rolling boil, add a pinch of sea salt and then let the water return to a boil before adding the lasagne. Cook the lasagne a few sheets at a time only until they are al dente. Remove each sheet with a flat slotted spoon and set aside, and then cook more lasagne. Once the sheets are cool enough to handle (but not cold), you may begin to assemble the dish. Thoroughly stir a tablespoon of the hot pasta water into the pesto, and then spoon a thin layer of the sauce on the bottom of the pan. Place a thin layer of lasagne atop the pesto. Spoon on another thin layer of pesto, and then put a few pieces of Gorgonzola on top of the sauce, with enough distance apart that they will melt into the pesto without overwhelming it. Continue the process, making thin layers of noodles, sauce, and cheese, finishing with a layer of Gorgonzola. Many people like to add some Parmigiano-Reggiano on the top layer, either before or after the lasagne has been baked, but I am not one of them. Once the lasagne dish has been assembled, bake for about 15 to 20 minutes, or until the cheese has melted satisfactorily, in a preheated 325°F / 170°C oven.

Makes 6 servings

Lasagne al Pesto Bianco
Lasagne with White Pesto

If you use dried pasta for this dish, try to use a high-quality Italian brand that is as thin as possible. If you are making fresh pasta (see the recipe for basic *sfoglia* on page 203), you should prepare it first, then make the sauce, then cook the noodles and combine with sauce and Parmigiano-Reggiano.

1½ pounds / 650 g lasagne, preferably fresh
Pesto Bianco (the recipe on page 76 is sufficient)
1 tablespoon / 7 g sweet butter
1 cup / 115 g (100 g plus 1 tablespoon) freshly grated Parmigiano-Reggiano

Makes
6 servings

If you are using fresh lasagne, make them first. Then make the Pesto Bianco. While doing that, set a large pot of cold water to boil. Once it has reached a rolling boil, add a pinch of sea salt. When it returns to a boil, you are ready to cook the noodles. Cook the lasagne a few sheets at a time only until they are al dente. Remove each sheet with a flat slotted spoon and set aside, and then cook more lasagne. While they are cooking, grease a lasagne pan with the butter. Thoroughly stir a tablespoon of the hot pasta water into the Pesto Bianco, and then spoon a little of the sauce on the bottom of the pan. Once the sheets of pasta are cool enough to handle (but not cold), place one layer of lasagne on the bottom of the lasagne pan. Then spoon a thin layer of the sauce on top of the noodles. Then add some Parmigiano-Reggiano. Continue the process, making thin layers of noodles, sauce, and cheese, ending with a layer of cheese. Once this is done, you may serve as is or bake for no more than 3 minutes in a preheated 325°F/170°C oven.

This dish goes well with a light to medium-bodied red wine such as Dolcetto, Rossese di Dolceacqua, Ciliegiolo, or Chianti (a fair amount of this last is consumed in the province of La Spezia, which borders Tuscany and is the apparent place of origin for pesto bianco).

Rotolo Maria Pia

Mushroom–String Bean Roll

This delicious preparation is from the Osteria dell'Acquasanta, in the province of Genoa. It is simple to make, although a bit labor-intensive, and it makes a strong impression when served. The owners of the *osteria* suggest serving this dish with either a Sylvaner or Gewürztraminer wine, but in their absence a Vermentino, Pigato, or Gavi will be fine.

FOR THE PASTA
4½ cups / 500 g unbleached all-purpose flour
5 large eggs, lightly beaten
2 cups / 200 ml water

FOR THE FILLING
½ pound / 225 g slender string beans, tips cut off
1½ cups / 170 g fresh funghi porcini or 2 ounces / 60 g dried mushrooms, soaked,
    plus 2 ounces / 60 g fresh cultivated mushrooms, sliced
1½ tablespoons / 10 ml Ligurian extravirgin olive oil
1 clove garlic, peeled, green heart removed, minced
3 tablespoons / 20 g fresh Italian (flat) parsley, minced
3½ cups / 400 g fresh ricotta
½ cup / 60 g freshly grated Parmigiano-Reggiano
1 large egg

FOR THE TOPPING
½ cup / 60 g freshly grated Parmigiano-Reggiano
4 tablespoons / 30 g unsalted butter, melted

Make a mound of flour on a work surface. Add the beaten eggs to a crater you create in the center of the mound. Start combining egg and flour to incorporate the ingredients. Then make another crater and add some of the water. Combine with the flour, then add more water, until you have made a smooth, firm dough. If it is too moist, add a little more flour. Cover with a cloth and set aside for 10 minutes.

Makes
5 servings

Boil the string beans in lightly salted water for 10 to 12 minutes, drain, and let cool. Once cooled, mince the string beans.

Clean all the mushrooms carefully. If you have soaked any dried mushrooms, squeeze out the excess liquid. Slice all of the mushrooms. Sauté them in olive oil for 2 minutes, then toss in the garlic and parsley. Cook until the mushrooms soften and give off some liquid. Remove to a bowl and let cool. Once cooled, chop the mushrooms, garlic, and parsley into small bits.

Combine the string beans, mushroom mixture, ricotta, Parmigiano-Reggiano, and egg in a bowl. Mix until all the ingredients are thoroughly combined.

Cut the dough into three pieces. Roll out each piece of dough to make a long, tongue-shaped sheet of pasta about ¼ inch/.6 cm thick. Spread half the filling on one sheet of pasta, making sure not to get the filling too close to the edges of the dough. Top with another sheet of dough. Spread the rest of the filling on the second sheet. Top with the third sheet. Roll the whole thing up and gently tie it with string.

Set a large pot (8 quarts/8 liters) of cold water to boil. Once it reaches a boil, add a pinch of salt and a drop of olive oil. Carefully immerse the roll and boil for 10 minutes, taking care to turn it gently every so often, so it cooks evenly. Then lift the roll out and place it into a colander to cool. Let it sit for 30 minutes.

Cut the roll into 5 slices, and place them in a lightly buttered baking dish. Bake in the oven for 10 minutes at 350°F/180°C. Two minutes before you remove the baking dish, generously sprinkle freshly grated Parmigiano-Reggiano atop each slice and add some melted butter. Bake 2 more minutes, then serve immediately.

Ravioli

❧

Ravioli, now world-famous, were invented in Liguria. There are various stories, none fully verifiable, as to who first folded a rectangle of pasta dough over a filling of meat, cheese, or vegetables to create a *raviolo*. One story holds that the name comes from the Italian verb *ravvolgere,* which means to fold over. Other people insist that the name comes from the family in the town of Novi Ligure who first invented this pasta. It is generally conceded that ravioli were first prepared at or near Novi Ligure, which is in a valley north of Genoa on the Piedmont border. Ravioli are also popular in Piedmont, where they are often larger and called *agnolotti.*

Ravioli were among the first Italian pastas to travel to other countries because they were part of the larder in Genoese vessels. It was found that cheese ravioli could be dried and stored, so that ever-so-important taste of home could be had by sailors at sea. North Americans know them at least as well when they are filled with meat (and out of a can), but meat-filled ravioli, once upon a time, were only consumed with any regularity by families that could afford meat. There is an expression in Genoese dialect: "*O l'è staeto battezzou in te l'aegoa di ravieu,*" or "He was baptized with the water that cooked the ravioli," suggesting that a baby was born wealthy.

In middle-class families meat ravioli often appeared on Monday or Tuesday, when leftover meat from Sunday lunch was minced and combined with cheese and herbs to fill ravioli. Elsewhere in Liguria a cook filled ravioli with whatever was available, be it cheese, herbs, vegetables, or fish, or sometimes a combination of ingredients. A variation of the herb- and vegetable-filled ravioli are *pansôti,* which are shaped slightly differently and are always dressed with a walnut sauce.

There is no definitive or authentic version for the filling of ravioli. This is definitely grandma food, made with great love and a reliance on personal preference and family tradition. So fillings vary significantly, and I can only give you some suggestions about how to fill your own ravioli. I have been with many Ligurian grandmothers, and each made ravioli in her own way, treating her preparation like a family secret. But there was always a love of the craft, a love of creating food for children and grandchildren, and I am sure that the warmth of grandma's hands as she folded the ravioli gave additional sweetness to them.

Making Ravioli

The key words here are *sfoglia* (the sheets of pasta) and *ripieno* (the filling). Whenever you set about to make ravioli, prepare the *ripieno* first. Once this is done, cover it and set aside. When you make the dough, roll it out into pasta sheets one at a time, and only as you need them. If pasta sheets sit for too long in the open air, they will dry out. In making ravioli, the *sfoglia* should be thinner than for noodles. An average of ⅛ inch/.3 cm is desirable. It is not a problem if the *sfoglia* is transparent after it has been filled — Ligurians consider this a virtue. There are three methods to prepare ravioli you may consider. I will list them in my order of preference.

Method 1

1) Roll out a rectangular or square sheet of *sfoglia*.

2) Distribute olive-sized portions (about ½ teaspoon/slightly more than 1 g) of *ripieno* about 1½ inches/3.75 cm apart in a single line parallel to the edge of the sheet of *sfoglia*. The row of *ripieno* portions should be 1½ inches/3.75 cm from the edge of the *sfoglia*.

3) Carefully lift the edge of the *sfoglia* and fold it over the little balls of *ripieno* so that they are completely covered.

4) Take a knife, fluted ravioli wheel, or small pastry wheel and cut along the line where the edge meets the *sfoglia*.

5) Using your fingertips, gently press down the pasta in between the balls of *ripieno* so that you have completely sealed them off from one another. (See notes below.)

6) Use the ravioli wheel to cut rectangles of pasta, which, as you now see, are ravioli.

7) If necessary, gently press the edges of the ravioli with your fingertips to assure that they are sealed.

8) Put the ravioli on a lightly floured dishcloth or towel, making sure they do not touch one another. Sprinkle on a bit of flour so they will not stick together and can dry (though not dry out) for 15 to 30 minutes.

Repeat this process until this sheet of *sfoglia* is used up. If you have more dough, roll out another sheet. Continue until all the materials (*sfoglia* and *ripieno*) have been used.

NOTES: You can do steps 1 through 3 and then form the ravioli with a ravioli press. These are available in square or round shapes, are quite inexpensive, and can cut and crimp individual ravioli. If you use the round press, little scraps of *sfoglia* will be left over. You can use these arc-shaped noodles in minestrone or broth.

Method 2

1) Roll out two rectangular or square sheets of *sfoglia* of equal size.

2) Distribute olive-size portions (about ½ teaspoon/slightly more than 1 g) of *ripieno* in single lines. The balls of *ripieno* should be at least 1½ inches/

3.75 cm apart and no closer than ¾ inch/just under 2 cm from the edge of the *sfoglia*.

3) Carefully place the second sheet of *sfoglia* atop the first.

4) Press down with your fingertips to separate the rows of *ripieno* so that each individual raviolo may be formed.

5) Cut along the rows with a knife or ravioli wheel in straight vertical and horizontal lines to produce the ravioli. You may also use a square ravioli press.

6) If necessary, gently press the edges of the ravioli with your fingertips to assure that they are sealed.

7) Place the ravioli on a lightly floured dishcloth or towel, making sure that they do not touch one another.

8) If you have enough dough to make two more sheets of *sfoglia*, roll them out and repeat steps 2 through 7. If not, make the rest of the ravioli according to Method 1.

NOTE: This method may seem easier than the first. However, it requires much more precision in quickly cutting equal rectangular sheets of *sfoglia*, in lining up even rows of *ripieno* the proper distance apart, in quickly working so that the sheets of *sfoglia* do not dry out, and in accurately cutting the rows of ravioli so that they end up more or less of equal size.

Method 3

This method requires ravioli trays (*raviolatrici*), a relatively recent invention meant to give the pasta their shapes. These are inexpensive metal trays, not un-like shallow ice trays except that they have 36 separate compartments. This method yields perfectly formed, identical ravioli, but the process is slow and fussy. You can try a shallow ice tray if you don't have a ravioli tray, but I do not guarantee classic results.

1) Roll out two equal-sized rectangular sheets of *sfoglia* that are slightly larger than the ravioli tray.

2) Put 1 layer of *sfoglia* in the tray and press gently until the *sfoglia* takes the form of the tray.

3) Distribute little balls of *ripieno* (about ½ teaspoon/slightly more than 1 g each) into each compartment.

4) Roll the second sheet of *sfoglia* around your rolling pin.

5) Unroll the *sfoglia* over the tray, pressing down with the handles or edge of the rolling pin until the two layers of *sfoglia* adhere and separate ravioli are formed.

6) Carefully turn over the tray and let the ravioli fall onto a lightly floured

dishcloth or towel. Cut them into individual ravioli with a knife or ravioli wheel.

7) Repeat steps 1 to 6 until all the materials are used.

Cooking Ravioli

Like other folded pasta, ravioli must be cooked with delicacy. As always, you should use a large pot of cooking liquid. For ravioli filled with cheese, vegetables, herbs, or fish, the cooking liquid is lightly salted water. For meat-filled ravioli, you may use water or, better yet, broth made of capon, chicken, or beef.

Fresh ravioli usually take 5 to 8 minutes (shorter for cheese, fish, and vegetables; longer for meat fillings). Dried ravioli take 2 or 3 minutes longer. The only real way to determine doneness is to taste one. The *sfoglia* should be cooked through and the *ripieno* should be hot.

Using a slotted spoon, fish cooked ravioli out of the pot. Transfer them to a serving dish, top with a small amount of sauce, and serve immediately.

Ravioli di Pesce
Ravioli Filled with Fish

These ravioli should be made when there is leftover fish from another preparation or when you have boiled fish to make a broth. They are very delicate, and pair nicely with pesto, a light tomato sauce, or a very small amount of olive paste. They also can be dressed with seafood sauces or artichoke sauce.

FOR THE *RIPIENO*
2½ cups / 280 g leftover cooked fish, minced
1 cup / 115 g ricotta romana
1 egg, beaten
1 teaspoon grated lemon peel

FOR THE *SFOGLIA*
4 cups / 450 g unbleached all-purpose flour
4 large eggs, beaten
About 3 ounces / ¾ cup / 85 ml Ligurian extravirgin olive oil

Makes 4 to 6 servings

Combine all of the ingredients for the *ripieno,* and set aside. Then make the *sfoglia,* according to the directions on page 208, bearing in mind that the additional liquid for the dough will come from the olive oil. Add the oil a bit at a time until you reach the desired texture. Make the ravioli following the directions on page 248. Let the ravioli rest for 30 minutes before boiling them in a large pot of water. They should cook in about 7 minutes.

Ravioli di Carne (Ravieu)
Meat Ravioli

Ravioli di carne are inextricably linked to Genoa where, it seems, every citizen has his or her own secret recipe for the filling. Even Niccolò Paganini, the legendary violinist from Liguria's capital, had a recipe, and he enjoyed preparing it on tour when he was not playing his fiddle. The recipe you find here is a composite of how ravioli are made in Genoa nowadays. In the past, one usually found calf's brains, sweetbreads, udder, and other parts of the calf as the foundation of meat for the filling, and some ground veal and pork would be added. This is a delicious and delicate preparation, but many home cooks use these ingredients less nowadays. If you choose to use offal, apply these ingredients in the percentages that appeal to you so that they total about 1½ pounds/700 grams of meat. What follows is a modern version of ravioli that will be similar in taste to what one once might have sampled.

FOR THE *RIPIENO*
½ pound/225 g (or a little more if you want less meat) spinach and/or borage
½ tablespoon/4 g sweet butter
1 pound/450 g ground veal
¼ pound/115 g ground pork or minced pork sausage
¼ pound/115 g minced chicken liver or calf's liver
1 tablespoon red or white wine (optional)
1 tablespoon/7 g pinoli
A few currants (optional)
2 large eggs, plus 2 more yolks, beaten
2 to 3 tablespoons/15 to 22 g unflavored bread crumbs
3 tablespoons/22 g freshly grated Parmigiano-Reggiano
1½ tablespoons/10 g minced fresh marjoram
1 pinch sea salt

FOR THE *SFOGLIA*
4½ cups/500 g unbleached all-purpose flour
3 large eggs
Water (possibly)

Makes
6 servings

First make the *ripieno*. Wash the greens well and then steam them in the water that clings to the leaves until they are soft. Carefully squeeze all of the liquid out of the greens and then mince them very very fine. Melt the butter in a skillet and add the veal, pork, and liver. Sauté over medium heat until the meats are light brown, fragrant, and have not given off much liquid. If they do give off liquid, drain the pan and add a little wine. Sauté so that the flavor of the wine is incorporated. Even if the meat does not give off much liquid, you may add a dash of wine for flavor. Once the meat is cooked, add the *pinoli* and optional currants. Give the ingredients a quick stir to combine them and then remove from the heat. Once the ingredients have cooled enough, mince them well and put them in a mixing bowl. Add the minced spinach/borage, and then add the eggs and egg yolks, bread crumbs, Parmigiano-Reggiano, marjoram, and salt. Remember the purpose of the bread crumbs is to absorb some of the egg, so do not overdo it with the crumbs, too much of which will make the filling heavy.

Then make the *sfoglia,* using the proportion of flour and eggs indicated above, and following the instructions for *sfoglia* making on page 203. If the eggs do not provide enough liquid to the dough, judiciously add a little water.

Once the *sfoglia* dough is ready, make the ravioli according to the instructions on page 248. Let the ravioli rest, covered, for 30 minutes.

Boil the ravioli in water or broth for about 10 minutes, and dress in a mushroom sauce, light meat sauce, or a sauce of melted butter and fresh sage.

Ravioli di Magro
Fast-Day (Cheese) Ravioli

This is easier to prepare than meat ravioli, and if you are still acquiring your pasta-making skills, start with this one. *Ravioli di magro* were designed to be consumed on days when religious observances proscribed the consumption of meat. Pesto is a perfect sauce for these ravioli, as are sauces made with either fresh or sun-dried tomatoes, or other vegetable sauces.

FOR THE *RIPIENO*
1 large egg
1 pinch salt
A little freshly ground black pepper to taste
12 ounces / 1½ cups / 350 g fresh ricotta romana
4 tablespoons / 30 g freshly grated Parmigiano-Reggiano

FOR THE *SFOGLIA*
3½ cups / 400 g unbleached all-purpose flour
3 large eggs

Makes
4 servings

Make the *ripieno* first. Beat the egg with the salt and pepper in a mixing bowl. Then fold in the ricotta and the Parmigiano-Reggiano until the ingredients are thoroughly combined.

Now make the *sfoglia* dough. Combine the flour and eggs as described in the instructions for *sfoglia* making on page 203, remembering that when you make ravioli you should roll out sheets of dough only as needed.

Next, make the ravioli as described on page 248.

Let the ravioli rest for 30 minutes before boiling them in a large pot of water. They are cooked when they balloon slightly. Remove them gently from the pot using a slotted spoon, and dress them immediately and serve.

VARIATION: Instead of using all ricotta, make a combination that is ⅔ ricotta and ⅓ *prescinseua*.

Ravioli di Verdura e Formaggio

Vegetable and Cheese Ravioli

This is similar to Ravioli di Magro, except that it contains greens. Sauces made with either fresh or sun-dried tomatoes, or other vegetable sauces, are best, although pesto is all right, too.

FOR THE *RIPIENO*
8 ounces / 1 cup / 225 g borage or beet greens
1 large egg
1 pinch salt
A little freshly ground black pepper to taste
4 ounces / ½ cup / 120 g fresh ricotta romana
*   with an optional bit of* prescinseua *spooned in*
4 tablespoons / 30 g freshly grated Parmigiano-Reggiano

FOR THE *SFOGLIA*
3½ cups / 400 g unbleached all-purpose flour
3 large eggs

Make the *ripieno* first. Wash the greens carefully and then steam them in the water that clings to them. If borage or beet greens are unavailable, then consider spinach or Swiss chard. Once the greens are soft, squeeze the liquid from them thoroughly and mince them fine. Let cool. Beat the egg with the salt and pepper in a mixing bowl. Then fold in the greens, ricotta, optional *prescinseua,* and the Parmigiano-Reggiano until the ingredients are thoroughly combined.

Makes 4 servings

Now make the *sfoglia* dough. Combine the flour and eggs as described in the instructions for *sfoglia* making on page 203, remembering that when you make ravioli you should roll out sheets of dough only as needed.

Next, make the ravioli following the instructions on page 248.

Let the ravioli rest for 30 minutes before boiling them in a large pot of water. They are cooked when they balloon slightly. Remove them gently from the pot using a slotted spoon, dress them immediately with your choice of sauce, and serve.

Ravioli di Zucca

Pumpkin Ravioli

Pumpkin is another one of those ingredients that came to Italy after Columbus's voyages to the Americas. In Liguria, they sometimes substitute *trombetti,* horn-shaped squash that have a light orange pulp. Serve with pesto.

FOR THE *RIPIENO*
12 ounces / 1½ cups / 350 g cooked pumpkin or orange-colored squash
1 large egg, beaten
1 pinch salt
Freshly ground nutmeg to taste
4 tablespoons / 30 g freshly grated Parmigiano-Reggiano
2 tablespoons / 15 g pinoli
A couple of drops Ligurian extravirgin olive oil

FOR THE *SFOGLIA*
3½ cups / 400 g unbleached all-purpose flour
3 large eggs

Makes
4 to 6 servings

Make the *ripieno* first. Steam or bake the pumpkin until it can easily be scooped from the shell. Cool completely (this may be done the night before). Combine the pumpkin and all the other ingredients thoroughly.

Now make the *sfoglia* dough. Combine the flour and eggs as described in the instructions for *sfoglia* making on page 203, remembering that when you make ravioli you should roll out sheets of dough only as needed.

Next, make the ravioli as described on page 248.

Let the ravioli rest for 30 minutes before boiling them in a large pot of water. They are cooked when they balloon slightly, after approximately 5 to 7 minutes. Remove them gently from the pot using a slotted spoon, dress them immediately with pesto, and serve.

Barbagiuai

Fried Pumpkin Ravioli

Here is an unusual pasta from the province of Savona. You must first make the ravioli and then let them sit for 4 to 6 hours to dry before frying them. When eating, dip them into pesto or another sauce of your choice. While these are pastas, you might also consider them as an unusual antipasto in a meal in which soup rather than pasta or rice will be the first course.

FOR THE *RIPIENO*
6 cups / 700 g cooked or canned pumpkin
3 cups / 350 g ricotta romana
1 large egg, beaten
1 pinch salt
A little freshly ground nutmeg to taste
¾ cup / 85 g freshly grated Parmigiano-Reggiano
1 tablespoon / 7 g minced fresh marjoram

FOR THE *SFOGLIA*
3½ cups / 400 g unbleached all-purpose flour
6 ounces / 85 ml Ligurian extravirgin olive oil (plus more olive oil for deep-frying)
Ligurian white wine

Make the *ripieno* first. Steam or bake the pumpkin until it can easily be scooped from the shell. Cool completely (this may be done the night before). Combine the pumpkin and all the other ingredients thoroughly.

Makes 6 servings

Now make the *sfoglia* dough. Combine the flour and oil as described in the instructions for *sfoglia* making on page 208. The difference here is that oil is the primary liquid to combine with flour. You will find that by itself the oil is not liquid enough, and you will make up for this by adding white wine a little at a time until you get an elastic consistency. Set the dough aside for a few minutes to rest.

Next, make the ravioli as described on page 248. Remember that when you make ravioli you should roll out sheets of dough only as needed.

Let the ravioli rest for 4 hours. Then heat a skillet filled about 1 inch / 2.5 cm with good olive oil. When the oil is hot, fry the ravioli a few at a time until they puff out and are light gold in color and somewhat crunchy to the bite. Let drain on absorbent toweling and serve immediately with the sauce of your choice.

Pansôti

Pasta Filled with Herbs and Greens

Here is one of the greatest pasta preparations in Liguria, or anywhere, for that matter. *Pansôti* in Ligurian dialect mean *panciuti,* or potbellied, in Italian. The name describes the shape of these ravioli that are jam-packed with filling. Unlike all the other ravioli, to which you should add ½ teaspoon of filling, *pansôti* should receive a heaping teaspoon. They will be bigger than other ravioli in order to contain the extra filling. *Pansôti* once contained *prebôggion* (see page 433), an ancient mixture of spring herbs, but now one finds this mixture only when the chef makes an effort to have them near at hand. Most *pansôti* in Liguria are filled with a mixture of beet greens, borage, and spinach. For your *pansôti* to be special, there must be variety in the fillings. A single green simply will not do. I would encourage you to select from as many of the following as you have available and to make a subtle mixture: beet greens, borage, spinach, watercress, arugula, fennel, chicory, parsley, escarole, Savoy cabbage, Swiss chard, chervil, acacia, fresh marjoram, nettles, and a little basil. Chervil can appear in a slightly larger amount than the others.

   Pansôti must always be dressed with walnut sauce. It is a perfect combination of taste and texture, and after all the effort you go through to make the pasta, you should not want anything less.

FOR THE *RIPIENO*
6 cups/nearly 800 g mixed greens, washed, lightly steamed, minced*
2 cups/225 g fresh ricotta romana
1 medium egg, beaten
1 pinch freshly ground nutmeg
3 tablespoons/20 to 25 g Parmigiano-Reggiano

> * Variation: Instead of steaming all the greens and herbs together, only steam the greens, and add fresh herbs after. This will give a livelier taste to the filling.

FOR THE *SFOGLIA*
3½ cups/400 g unbleached all-purpose flour
2 large eggs
A little white wine or olive oil

Makes 6 servings

Wash the greens and then steam them in the liquid that clings, just until they are soft. Squeeze out all of the liquid, mince, and let cool. Combine the greens and herbs in a mixing bowl, add all of the other ingredients, combine thoroughly, and set aside.

Make the dough for the *sfoglia* as indicated on page 208. Note that the eggs alone will not make the dough soft enough, so you will need to add a judicious amount of wine or olive oil. Once the dough is ready, roll out sheets of *sfoglia* one at a time, making *pansôti* according to Method 1 of the ravioli instructions (page 248) before rolling out the next sheet. Remember to put a generous teaspoon of *ripieno* in each.

VARIATION: Nowadays most *pansôti* are made in triangular forms. Instead of cutting the *sfoglia* to make ravioli, proceed as follows: Cut the *sfoglia* into squares with 2-inch/.8-cm sides. Place the *ripieno* in the center of the squares and then fold the squares diagonally to form triangles. Gently run your finger along the seam to seal them shut.

However you make *pansôti,* you should dust them lightly with flour and let them sit for 30 to 45 minutes, covered, in a draft-free environment.

Boil in a large pot of water for 8 to 10 minutes, fish them out gently with a slotted spoon, and dress with Walnut Sauce (see page 77).

Risotto Valpolcevara

Risotto with Mushrooms, Tomatoes, and Basil

The Val Polcevara is a valley north of Genoa where the flavors of the hills meet those of the shore. So rice with fresh mountain *funghi porcini* are congenially matched with the flavors of tomato and basil from near the coast. You will have used several pots and pans in the execution of this dish, but the results are worth the effort.

2⅔ quarts/11½ cups/2½ liters cold water
1 pinch coarse sea salt
10 ounces/300 g fresh ripe tomatoes or a 16-ounce can of
  Italian peeled tomatoes, drained
2 tablespoons/15 g unsalted butter
3 tablespoons/45 ml Ligurian extravirgin olive oil
10 ounces/300 g small fresh funghi porcini *(or 2 oz/60 g dried* funghi
  that have been soaked) carefully washed and sliced thin
1 tablespoon/7 g finely minced fresh Italian (flat) parsley
Freshly ground black pepper
1 small onion, minced
14 ounces/1¾ cups/400 g Arborio, Vialone Nano, or other fine Italian rice
2 tablespoons/15 g freshly grated Parmigiano-Reggiano
16 small fresh basil leaves, wiped clean and torn into pieces

Makes
4 servings

Put the cold water and salt in a stockpot and set to boil. This water will be used for the risotto, but you can also use it to skin the tomatoes. If you are using fresh tomatoes, dice them into bite-size pieces and drain so that the liquid and the seeds are removed. If you prefer to eat tomatoes without the skin, use a slotted spoon to dip them into the boiling water for about 30 seconds. When you remove the tomatoes from the water, the skin should slip off easily. Then dice them. If you are using canned tomatoes, chop them into bite-size pieces. Set the tomato pieces aside.

In a small pot or pan (that you will later need to cover) place 1 tablespoon of butter, the olive oil, the mushroom slices, and the parsley and cook over medium-high heat for 4 to 5 minutes, or until the mushrooms begin to yield some of their liquid. Add the tomato pieces and some freshly ground black pepper to taste. Gently combine the ingredients, reduce the heat to very low, cover the pot, and simmer for 5 minutes.

In a large stockpot melt 1 tablespoon of butter and then add the minced onion. Sauté for 2 minutes. Add the rice and "toast" it by stirring with a wooden spoon. Then add 2 ladlefuls of the hot water with one hand and continuously stir the rice with the other hand. Once the rice has absorbed all of the water, add another ladleful. Continue this process for 10 minutes, continuously adding water once the previous water has been absorbed. Then add the mushroom-tomato mixture, including all of the pan liquid. Keep stirring so that this liquid is absorbed. Stir for another 10 minutes, judiciously adding water if the dish seems to be getting too dry. The result should be slightly creamy but not awash in liquid.

After the rice has cooked, remove from the heat and stir in the Parmigiano-Reggiano and torn basil leaves. Serve immediately.

From Act IV of
Anton Chekhov's *The Seagull*

MEDVEDENKO: In your travels abroad, doctor, what was your favorite city?

DR. DORN: Genoa.

MEDVEDENKO: Why Genoa?

DR. DORN: In Genoa there is a splendid street life. When you step out of your hotel in the evening, you become part of the throng. You find yourself moving along with it, with no particular goal, first one way, then another, with no special pattern. You breathe with the crowd, you lose yourself in it, and you begin to believe that a single world spirit could actually be possible.

Polenta Incatenata
"Enchained" Polenta

I can assure you, from a great deal of personal experience, that one of the most challenging aspects of writing seriously about the food of a place I love is that so much that one reads in print is just plain wrong. This becomes especially grievous when other writers read this misinformation and cite it and quote it repeatedly until most people just assume that it is truth. My approach has always been to go to the source in at least two ways. First, I must find the earliest available reference in print, in the original language, to read it for myself. Then I try to go to the place where the dish is from and talk to as many people as possible to gather a consensus about what the dish really is. *Polenta incatenata* has been misinterpreted so often that I fear it will be hard to redeem. First of all, some references to this dish in English call it "enchanted" polenta (which would be *polenta incantata*) and not "enchained" polenta, which is what the name means. The English-language descriptions then proceed to wax poetic about the enchantment of this dish, but I ask: Do beans, cabbage, and cornmeal bespeak enchantment to you?

Yet the question remains, why is the polenta enchained? I journeyed to the Lunigiana, the area just south of La Spezia, in search of an answer. The general answer (although I was not able to find original printed documentation — this is simple cooking passed down verbally through the generations) is that because the cabbage and beans are cooked first and the cornmeal is added after, the cornmeal becomes chained or fettered to the cabbage and the beans. In the wintertime, this dish was a one-course meal for poor families.

2⅔ *cups/300 g fresh* borlotti *or red kidney beans*
   or 1¼ cups/200 g dried beans that have been soaked
1 Savoy cabbage, washed, dried, coarsely chopped
3 medium potatoes, washed, peeled, chopped into chunks
1 carrot, washed, peeled, cut into chunks
1 medium onion, coarsely chopped
1 clove garlic, peeled, with the green heart removed, minced
2½ quarts/2½ liters cold water
6 ounces/170 ml plus 1 tablespoon Ligurian extravirgin olive oil
1 pinch coarse sea salt
2⅔ cups/300 g golden polenta flour
Freshly grated Parmigiano-Reggiano

Makes
6 servings
   Once the beans are ready to use (that is, previously soaked if necessary), place them in a large, heavy-bottomed pot. Add the cabbage, potatoes, carrot, onion,

garlic, water, 6 ounces/170 ml olive oil, and salt. Partially cover and cook over medium heat for 30 minutes. By the end of this time, the water should be boiling. Then add the polenta a bit at a time, sprinkling it into the pot from higher above than usual so that it falls to all corners of the pot and "enchains" itself to the other ingredients. All the while, as you add the polenta, you should keep stirring with a wooden spoon. Once the polenta has all been added, keep stirring for another 40 to 45 minutes. The result should be that the polenta is very creamy. If it gets too thick, add a bit of tepid water to the pot. Serve immediately, topped with a few drops of olive oil and a generous amount of Parmigiano-Reggiano.

The Countess Blessington in Genoa

Margaret Gardiner Blessington, an Englishwoman who had acute sensibilities and a wonderful way of turning a phrase, produced a three-volume set of travel writing, *The Idler in Italy* (1839-1840), that remains one of the most delightful and insightful accounts of a visit to Italy. Because of her status and charm, she met anyone who was anyone during her tours (of Lord Byron, whom she met in Genoa on April 1, 1837, she wrote, "I have seen Lord Byron; and I am disappointed! But so it ever is, when we have heard exaggerated accounts of a person; or when, worse still, we have formed a *beau idéal* of him."). She spent a great deal of time in Liguria, and her descriptions of places, local people, and their customs, are as relevant today as they were in her time. Her description of the mountains of Genoa brings to mind the words of John Ruskin: "Mountains are the beginning and the end of all natural scenery."

"Nothing could be more beautiful than the position of Genoa, were it not for one blemish; but even this, at a distance, adds to the beauty of the general effect. I refer to the near vicinity of the bold and bleak range of the Apennines, that form its background. When beheld from a distance, the city, which is built on an amphitheatre, with the fine bay bathing its foundations, looks as if placed

on an island between two seas; the mountains behind it being as blue as the
Mediterranean in front, and both mingling, as it were, with the horizon. The
white buildings rising one above the other between these vast masses of blue
have a beautiful effect, until viewed on the spot; when the contrast offered by
the splendid palaces and the bleak sterile mountains, at whose base they rear
their heads, is violent and disagreeable; the one offering a view of nature in her
roughest, wildest form, and the others presenting specimens of all the refine-
ments and graces of wealth and art. On looking at the Apennines from the
ramparts to-day, I was reminded of the truth of Rogers' lines in the 'Pleasures
of Memory': —

> 'Tis distance lends enchantment to the view,
> And robes the mountain in her azure hue.

For this chain of mountains, so 'beautifully blue' in the distance, are, when seen
near, of a cold greyish tint, and have a cheerless and frowning aspect. It is not
mountains alone to which distance lends charms, it gives a halo to anticipated
happiness, that reality dissolves; gilds the visions of hope, and disarms grief of
its stings; subduing the memory of sorrow to a pensive, but not unpleasing
recollection."

Soups

Suppa d'Agliu (Zuppa di Aglio)	Garlic Soup
Menestron	Minestrone, Genoese-Style
Mesc-Ciùa	Grain and Bean Soup
Crema di Ceci con Funghi Porcini	Chickpea Puree with Porcini Mushrooms
Zuppa di Funghi e Patate	Mushroom and Potato Soup
Zuppa di Porcini e Lumache	Mushroom and Snail Soup
Brodo di Pollo alla Ligure	Ligurian Chicken Stock
Lattughe Ripiene in Brodo	Stuffed Lettuce Rolls in Broth
La Pagioada	Marjoram Noodle Soup
Brodo di Pesce	Fish Broth
Minestra di Bianchetti	Whitebait Soup
Ciuppin	Fish Soup

*S*OUP HAS, for centuries, been the worldwide food of the cold and the poor. It serves as a catchall for miscellaneous ingredients that make better music as part of an orchestra of flavors than they do as soloists. This is no different in Liguria, with a couple of exceptions. The first is that Ligurian ingredients are usually of superior quality, so one does not feel compromised by eating a bowl of soup there. Where else are soups made with such a bounty of *funghi porcini?* The second is that there are several Ligurian soups that have relatively few ingredients, such as Zuppa di Aglio or La Pagioada, but nonetheless stint neither on flavor nor the pleasure they give.

I have not included a recipe for La Sbira, a tripe soup consumed by Genoese stevedores. It, and minestrone, are often sold at the port of Genoa, and on a cold wintry day it is very satisfying. Outside the Mercato Orientale in Genoa, there are *tripperie,* tripe sellers, who make La Sbira and other types of cooked tripe. The recipe has been omitted for two reasons. The first is that, unfortunately, most North American readers recoil at the prospect of tripe, so they would likely turn the page that contains the tripe recipe. But this, by itself, would not be sufficient reason. I have found that butchers and food sellers on our side of the ocean do not always handle tripe with sufficient care, and I would be loath to encourage a reader to purchase what might be less than perfect tripe and then unknowingly cook it improperly. If your travels take you to Genoa, however, treat yourself to La Sbira.

As you get to know Ligurian soups better, you might want to experiment with stirring in a little bit of one of this book's many sauces. The classic example is pesto in minestrone, but I have also enjoyed Sun-Dried Tomato Sauce (page 83) in soups such as Mesc-Ciùa, Zuppa di Aglio, and Zuppa di Funghi e Patate.

These Ligurian soups make good snacks or light lunches when accompanied by a wedge of fresh focaccia or a slice of vegetable torta. At supper, a Ligurian soup is often a good substitution for a bowl of pasta.

Suppa d'Agliu (Zuppa di Aglio)
Garlic Soup

I find it very interesting that this soup is typical of Triora, that town in the province of Imperia that supposedly has been a hideout for witches since ancient times. I wonder whether this soup gives the witches their staying power or if the normal citizens eat it to have some breathing room from the witches. Whatever the reason, this is a wonderfully healthful brew.

10 (8 + 2) cloves garlic, peeled
8 cups / 2 liters cold water
Sea salt to taste
1 tablespoon / 7 ml Ligurian extravirgin olive oil
1 slice slightly stale Italian bread per person, toasted
1 teaspoon / 15 ml Ligurian extravirgin olive oil per slice of bread
Freshly grated Parmigiano-Reggiano (optional)
Freshly ground black pepper to taste

Makes 4 to 6 servings

Smash 8 cloves of garlic and boil in a stockpot with the cold water. You should start the heat at medium and let the water come to a boil at its own pace. When it has reached a boil, toss in a fair amount of sea salt and then let the soup return to a boil. Turn off the heat and stir in a tablespoon of olive oil. Toast the bread and then place a slice in each bowl. Top with a teaspoon of olive oil. Top with a little bit of grated cheese, if you wish, and pepper to taste. Reheat the soup only until it comes to a boil. Then pour some over the toasts and serve immediately. The hot soup should melt the cheese.

VARIATION: I once used leftover rosemary focaccia (page 132) with this soup and did not add cheese or pepper. This is a delicious option.

Menestron

Minestrone, Genoese-Style

The word *minestrone* means "big soup" and certainly this one is. When most North Americans think of minestrone, it is closer to the vegetable soup popular in Milan, in which one can still readily recognize the different ingredients. By contrast, Ligurian minestrone (*menestron* in dialect) cooks gently until the ingredients come apart. This is a more homogeneous vegetable soup, but one that is complex in subtle flavors. Ligurian minestrone is always finished with a spoonful of pesto stirred in just before it is served. As always, the pesto is never heated, and the pesto used in soup is traditionally made without either *pinoli* or walnuts.

This is real old-fashioned Genoese soup, the kind eaten by the dock workers in the harbor. Use the pasta and beans and then select as many ingredients as possible. They should all be fresh, so, for example, frozen peas just will not do. You will note the use of a crust of Parmigiano-Reggiano cheese. This bespeaks frugality as well as taste. After grating cheese down to the crust, wipe it with paper toweling and then wrap it tightly in plastic and store it in the refrigerator. When heated, it will impart wonderful flavor to the soup.

2 to 2½ quarts / 2 to 2½ liters cold water
3½ ounces / 100 g fresh **borlotti** *or red kidney beans*
3½ ounces / 100 g raw cauliflower
3½ ounces / 100 g pumpkin or yellow squash
2 ounces / 50 g thin string beans
2 medium potatoes, washed, peeled, coarsely chopped
2 carrots, washed, peeled, coarsely chopped
1 stalk celery, washed, chopped into little bits
2 leeks, washed, chopped into chunks
2 plum tomatoes, peeled and seeded, chopped into chunks
2 medium zucchini, washed, chopped into bite-size pieces
A few leaves of borage or spinach, washed
½ cup / 60 g fresh peas
½ cup / 60 g fresh fava beans
1 baby eggplant, washed, chopped into bite-size pieces
Crust of wedge of Parmigiano-Reggiano (if available)
5 ounces / 150 g dried pasta, broken into little pieces
1 pinch coarse sea salt
1 medium onion, coarsely chopped
1 clove garlic, with the green heart removed, chopped into bits

1 sprig fresh Italian (flat) parsley, torn into pieces
2 tablespoons / 15 g freshly grated Parmigiano-Reggiano
6 ounces / ⅔ cup / 170 ml Ligurian extravirgin olive oil
1 tablespoon / 15 ml nut-free pesto per bowl of soup

Prepare all of the ingredients. Set the pasta, salt, onion, garlic, parsley, cheese, olive oil, and the pesto to one side. Add the water to a large soup pot and bring to a boil. Then, all at once, add all of the ingredients except those that were set aside. Cook at high heat for 5 minutes, stirring every so often. Then cover the pot, lower the flame to just above a simmer, and cook for 1 hour. You should open the pot every 10 minutes and give the ingredients a stir so that they do not stick to the pot. After 1 hour stir in the olive oil and add the crust of cheese. Break up any large pieces of food, such as the potatoes or cauliflower, that may assert its flavor individually if eaten. Then add the pasta, salt, onion, garlic, and parsley, and cook for another hour, stirring every 10 minutes to prevent sticking. The resulting soup should be quite dense. Remove the crust of cheese and discard. Add the Parmigiano-Reggiano, then serve a bowl to each diner, stirring in some pesto just before the soup is eaten.

Makes
4 to 6 servings

    The Genoese eat this soup hot, tepid, and cold, and it is delicious all three ways.

Mesc-Ciùa
Grain and Bean Soup

If pesto and ravioli are linked inextricably with Genoa and *focaccia col formaggio* and *trofie* with Recco, say *mesc-ciùa* (mess-choo-ah) to any Ligurian and the answer will be "La Spezia." The word is local dialect and means *mescolanza,* or mixture. This soup provided substance and sustenance to people who could never afford meat. It is, of course, a humble dish in terms of the cost and prestige of the ingredients, but it is not merely another typical "dish of the poor." First of all, though the ingredients are not too unusual (certainly not for Liguria), they nonetheless require a certain sophistication and skill to transform them into a memorable dish. Second, *mesc-ciùa* is closely linked with La Spezia. In olden days, when stevedores and dock workers loaded and unloaded wares that arrived in the port of La Spezia, sacks of certain food staples always managed to "disappear" before reaching their destination. Another trick was that a cut would "accidentally" be inflicted on a sack of large dried chickpeas or beans, with the result that they would spill all over the ground. They could no longer be delivered to their destination, and the women of La Spezia always somehow knew when there would be a bean spill in the harbor. Miraculously, they would all appear at the scene of the disaster wearing aprons, ready to gather up provisions. Rustic though this soup is, it remains a popular staple in and around La Spezia because it tastes good. A *sagra* (feast) is held each year in the city to celebrate its favorite dish. Note: If you cannot find spelt, use buckwheat or kasha.

2¾ cups/300 g dried large chickpeas (locally called Morocco peas)
1 cup/100 g spelt (farro)
2 pinches baking soda
2¾ cups/300 g dried white cannellini beans
Water
Fine sea salt
Olive oil
Freshly ground black pepper

Makes
6 servings

On the night before you plan to eat the soup, place the chickpeas, the spelt, and the baking soda in a bowl and cover with warm water. Let soak overnight. In another bowl, soak the cannellini with a pinch of baking soda and abundant warm water. The following day, 4 hours before you plan to eat the soup, drain the chickpeas and spelt and place them in a pot with 1 quart/1 liter of cold water with a very little bit of added salt. Bring to a boil and cook at a slow boil. After 30 minutes, drain the cannellini and place them in another pot with

¾ quart/¾ liter of cold water with very little salt. Boil each pot for 3 more hours. Then, combine the two, adding the white beans to the pot with the chickpeas and spelt, stir well, adjust the salt with care, and cook for 15 more minutes. Serve immediately. Each diner should add a healthy amount of delicate olive oil and freshly ground black pepper — these two elements will give the soup extra character and freshness.

Crema di Ceci con Funghi Porcini

Chickpea Puree with Porcini Mushrooms

This is a delicious soup that I tasted several times in small towns in the province of La Spezia. It is soothing, homey, and quite elegant, and it meets with great favor whenever I serve it.

½ pound/2½ cups/225 g dried chickpeas or four 16-ounce cans chickpeas
1 bay leaf
4 to 5 sprigs fresh Italian (flat) parsley
2 sprigs fresh thyme
1 small onion, minced
1 medium carrot, cut into bite-size pieces
1 stalk celery (from which you have cut the tough white end), sliced thin
2 teaspoons extravirgin olive oil
1 clove garlic, with the green heart removed, finely minced
7 to 8 ounces/200 g fresh funghi porcini *(you may substitute 1½ ounces dried*
   funghi that you have properly soaked)
Freshly cracked black pepper

Makes
6 servings

If you are using dried chickpeas, it is necessary to soak them overnight. Place them in a large bowl and fill with warm water, covering the chickpeas by 2 inches/5 cm. Cover the bowl and put it in a warm place. The next day the chickpeas will be ready to cook. Put them in a medium-size pot. Fill with cold water so that the liquid is 1 inch/2.5 cm higher than the chickpeas. Add the bay leaf, parsley, and thyme, all of which you have tied into a bunch. Also add the onion, carrot, and celery. Cover and cook over a very low flame until the chickpeas are quite soft (about 1 to 1½ hours). Drain the cooking water, reserving it for possible future use. Discard the bunch of herbs. Remove the pieces of carrot and set aside. It is customary to remove the skins from each pea, but many cooks skip this time-consuming and laborious procedure.

Note: If you are using canned chickpeas, you will not have to do the steps described above. Instead, combine the canned chickpeas and all of the ingredients mentioned in the above paragraph in cold water and simmer over slow heat, covered, for 15 to 20 minutes. Then reserve the water, discard the herbs, and set aside the carrot as indicated above.

Whichever procedure you have done, your next step is to put the chickpeas, onion, and celery in a food processor, blender, or manual food mill. If you are using electric equipment, blend until you have a velvety cream. The same texture is desirable if you are using the food mill. If you feel that the soup is too thick, you may judiciously add a bit of the cooking liquid that you have set aside. Return the chickpea puree to a saucepan and add the carrot pieces. Heat slightly.

In a skillet heat the olive oil, add the minced garlic and then the mushroom slices. Sauté until the mushrooms begin to release their liquid. Pour puree into warmed soup bowls and then, using a slotted spoon, add mushroom slices to each bowl of puree, making sure not to add too much of the mushroom pan juices. Into each bowl add a drop or two of extravirgin olive oil and some freshly cracked black pepper. Serve immediately.

Zuppa di Funghi e Patate
Mushroom and Potato Soup

This soup can be made with either fresh *funghi porcini* or dried ones. If necessary, you can combine dried mushrooms that you have soaked with fresh *funghi porcini* or with cremini or cultivated mushrooms.

14 ounces/350 g fresh mushrooms (a mixture of funghi porcini, *cremini, and cultivated mushrooms is acceptable; you may substitute 3 ounces/75 g dried* funghi *that you have properly soaked in combination with 4 ounces/100 g of fresh mushrooms)*
2 tablespoons/30 ml extravirgin olive oil
1 large yellow or Vidalia onion, minced
1 ounce/25 g prosciutto crudo, cut into bits
1 pound/450 g floury potatoes (such as Idaho baking potatoes),
peeled and cut into 1-inch/2.5-cm cubes
4¾ cups/1 liter broth (see note below)
Sea salt (optional)
12 thin slices Italian bread, preferably a bit stale
3 sprigs fresh Italian (flat) parsley, coarsely chopped

Makes
6 servings

If you are using any dried mushrooms, you must properly soak them (see instructions on page 230). Then squeeze out much of their liquid before using them for cooking. For all fresh mushrooms, wash them carefully and then slice them rather thick. Put the olive oil in a large stockpot and place over medium heat. Add the onion and prosciutto, sauté for 1 minute using a wooden spoon. Then add the mushrooms and the potatoes. Sauté for 3 or 4 minutes and then add the broth. Bring to a boil, then lower the flame, cover, and cook for 25 minutes. While the soup is simmering, lightly toast the bread in a toaster or in the oven, and place the pieces of toast at the bottom of warmed soup bowls. When the soup has cooked thoroughly, add a bit of sea salt, if you wish, and then break up the potato pieces with the wooden spoon. Stir thoroughly and then use a ladle to serve the soup. Top with chopped parsley and serve.

COOK'S NOTE ABOUT BROTH: Even cooks in Italy who should know better often make broth by dissolving bouillon cubes (known as *dadi,* or dice) in hot water. This is such a common practice that eyebrows are no longer raised when this shortcut is taken. However, cube-based broth is never as good as the real thing. They are always much too salty, and sometimes have gums, preservatives, and monosodium glutamate to make them more flavorful and substantial. As in North America, there are cubes flavored with beef, chicken, fish, or vegetables, but in Italy there are also cubes designed to impart the essence of *funghi porcini*. There are two options you can take to have a flavorful broth (or a reasonable substitute). The first, of course, is to make a broth from scratch, using beef, chicken, or vegetables (with a drop of olive oil added to the latter). Another approach, somewhat less classic but also reasonable, is to store certain cooking liquids in a jar in the refrigerator. These can be lengthened with water and, if there is no fat in the liquid yet, enlivened with a couple of drops of olive oil. For example, if you have cooked several dishes from this book, you might have some liquid from steaming greens, cooking beans, or sautéing mushrooms, onions, carrots, or celery. If stored in the cold part of the refrigerator, these liquids can last for two days. If frozen, they will last longer. Combine liquids that you think will go well together. Remember that this "broth" is meant to give an additional flavor base — in liquid form — to this soup, but that the dominant flavors and texture will come from the mushrooms and the potatoes.

Zuppa di Porcini e Lumache

Mushroom and Snail Soup

Snails are popular in Liguria, especially in the provinces of Imperia and Savona. When combined with the porcini that appear in profusion in the hills, you have a soup that is considered traditional cooking of the poor in old Liguria but fancy cuisine just about everywhere else.

3 tablespoons/45 ml Ligurian extravirgin olive oil
1 tablespoon/7 g unsalted butter
½ onion or 1 very small onion, minced
2 cloves garlic, peeled
7 to 8 ounces/200 g snails that have been removed from their shells and thoroughly soaked and then individually rinsed with cold water to assure that they are clean, cut in half lengthwise
14 ounce/400 g fresh funghi porcini, *carefully washed and then sliced to medium thickness (or 3½ ounces dried porcini that you have soaked)*
Freshly cracked black pepper
7 tablespoons/1¾ ounces/50 g unbleached all-purpose flour
6 ounces/170 ml/1 glass dry white wine, preferably Ligurian
6 cups/1½ liters vegetable broth (see note about broth on page 280; if you are using dried porcini, you may choose to strain the liquid they soaked in and add this liquid to the broth you use)
4 sprigs fresh Italian (flat) parsley, coarsely chopped

Makes
4 to 6 servings

After you have prepared all of the ingredients, gently heat the olive oil and butter in a large stockpot. Add the minced onion and garlic cloves to the pot. When the garlic cloves turn golden, remove them from the pot and discard (or save, perhaps, for another use). Add the snails and sauté for 4 minutes. Then add the mushrooms and sauté for 3 to 4 minutes. Add some fresh black pepper to taste, then the flour. Move the ingredients around briefly with a wooden spoon, and add the wine. Let the wine evaporate for 2 to 3 minutes and then add the broth. Stir so that the ingredients are combined and any clumps of flour are broken up. Cover and simmer for 30 minutes. Add the parsley, give the soup a quick stir, and serve.

Brodo di Pollo alla Ligure
Ligurian Chicken Stock

In Liguria it is customary to use *pollo ruspante* (free-range chicken) for stocks because the flavor will invariably be superior and these things count in Riviera kitchens. If you cannot locate a free-range chicken, select an organic chicken or a kosher one. The recipe for Ligurian chicken stock can be found on page 361 as part of the preparation of Gallina Lessa Ripiena (boiled stuffed chicken). The chicken is filled with greens and herbs, so that the flavor of the broth is outstanding. This is the perfect liquid to boil ravioli (page 250), although they may also be cooked in water with less dazzling results. Always remember, when using chicken stock that you have chilled, to skim off much of the fat before heating the stock.

Lattughe Ripiene in Brodo
Stuffed Lettuce Rolls in Broth

1 recipe for Stuffed Lettuce Rolls (see page 298)
3 quarts / 3 liters beef broth (or chicken or vegetable broth)

Prepare the lettuce rolls as described on page 298. Cook them in hot broth for 6 or 7 minutes and serve immediately, in the broth.

*Makes
6 servings*

La Pagioada

Marjoram Noodle Soup

Here is another example of frugal country cookery that results in a simple, delicious dish. I tasted this soup on a family farm near La Spezia, an area where marjoram is prized and Parmigiano-Reggiano cheese is historically present because of the trade route from La Spezia to Parma. As with all dishes, the quality of the ingredients is the key to the success of this dish. So fresh herbs and Italian Parmigiano are essential. Similarly, using superb homemade broth will produce an infinitely more satisfying soup than canned broth or one made from cubes. This dish might also be acceptable with vegetable or beef broth, if that is what you have at hand, but in every case the broth you select should be fresh and fragrant.

The classic pasta to use in this dish are *fedelini*, very thin strands of pasta that are thicker than angel hair but thinner than spaghettini. If your store does not have *fedelini*, then opt for the slightly thinner or thicker pasta that is available to you. The name *fedelini* connotes fidelity, which is something that is better understood when you see the strands of this pasta entwine in a bowl. *Fedelini* are traditional Ligurian pastas, and they also marry well with pesto. Because there was so much maritime commerce in the western Mediterranean, *fedelini* traveled in Ligurian ships to other countries and are often seen in the cuisines of Iberia and North Africa. They are especially central to several regional recipes in Spain, where they are known as *fideos*. I cannot give you detailed etymology about the name of this dish. The word did not exist in the Italian dictionaries I consulted, nor could I find it in dictionaries of Ligurian dialects. The closest thing I could think of is the word *paggio*, which means pageboy and also suggests the thin curls of a pageboy haircut. Perhaps this is meant to suggest the delicate strands of *fedelini?*

2 large eggs
2 tablespoons/30 ml Ligurian extravirgin olive oil
3 tablespoons/45 ml cold water
1 pinch sea salt
4 to 5 tablespoons/30 to 35 g minced fresh marjoram
1 cup/115 g (100 g plus 1 tablespoon) freshly grated Parmigiano-Reggiano
6 ounces/150 g fedelini
6 cups/1½ liters superb chicken broth

Makes
6 servings

In a large bowl, beat the eggs with the olive oil, water, salt, marjoram, and Parmigiano. Cook the *fedelini* in the broth until they are al dente (taste periodically to check). Once the noodles are cooked, add the egg mixture and beat with a whisk only until all of the ingredients are thoroughly combined. Serve immediately.

Brodo di Pesce

Fish Broth

This recipe goes hand-in-hand with Pesce al Vapore (page 326). This is a simple preparation but it useful for several purposes. It provides a meal of fish, but also broth that can be used in cooking or to drink on its own. Many seafood preparations call for broth, and it is better to use fish broth than one made from chicken or beef. Sometimes I use vegetable broths in seafood preparations, but if the broth contains juice from a strong vegetable such as spinach or cabbage, it will overwhelm the delicate nature of the final dish. The best equipment to use here is a fish poacher, but when I have had to do without one a good stockpot was acceptable if you use small fish. You have a fair amount of latitude as to what fish to use. Whichever it is will surely be consumed as part of a meal, so make it one that is to your liking. A general rule is that it should be a white-fleshed fish (cod, monkfish, hake, whiting, for example). Preferably the fish should be whole, including head and bones, as this will result in a more flavorful broth. You may then eat the fish hot or cold, accompanied by boiled potatoes and any of several sauces that strike your fancy. The most traditional is Salsa alla Genovese (page 86), but you should also consider Salsa Verde all'Antica (page 101); Salsa di Pinoli, Capperie e Acciughe (page 102); Agliata (page 97); Marò (page 90); Paté di Ortaggi (page 85); Rattatuia (page 84); or even a small amount of Pasta di Olive (page 94). You may also use the cooked fish to stuff in Ravioli di Pesce (page 251).

6 sprigs fresh Italian (flat) parsley, washed
1 medium onion, peeled, coarsely chopped
1 sprig fresh rosemary, split into 2 pieces
1 tablespoon / 7 g strips fresh lemon peel from untreated or organic lemons
2¼ pounds / 1 kilo white-fleshed fish, gutted and cleaned
Cold water
1 to 2 tablespoons / 15 to 30 ml Ligurian extravirgin olive oil

Place the parsley, onion, rosemary, and lemon peel in a fish poacher or broad pan or stockpot that can be covered. Place the fish on top of these ingredients, giving each part of the fish direct contact with the bed of flavors below. Add cold water just until the fish is completely covered. Then cover the pot and slowly bring to a boil. The water should never reach a rapid boil but should gently simmer. Cook the fish until it is done. This means that the flesh should be opaque but should not be tough or falling apart. The cooking time varies, depending on the size of the fish, although a smallish fish should cook for about 10 to 15 minutes. The way to tell if fish is cooked is to probe with a fork near the bone. If the flesh is no longer raw looking and pulls away from the

Makes
6 to 8 cups

bone easily, then the fish is cooked. Remove the fish from the poacher. You may serve the fish with head, tail, and bones intact, or you may wish to remove the head and fillet it to save your more squeamish guests the trouble. To make the broth, simmer for another 5 to 7 minutes, and then strain it, discarding all of the ingredients from the pot. Stir in 1 to 2 tablespoons of olive oil and then reserve the broth for other uses. It can be frozen in a plastic container (leave a little room at the top — the stock will expand as it freezes).

Minestra di Bianchetti

Whitebait Soup

This is an exquisite soup, one that is delicate and gratifying. I tasted it first in Savona, and order it whenever I see it on menus, mostly in the stretch of coast from Savona to Alassio. Your goal in preparing Minestra di Bianchetti is to strive for delicacy of texture and taste.

6 to 8 cups / 1½ to 2 liters Brodo di Pesce (see page 285)
1 tablespoon / 15 ml Ligurian extravirgin olive oil
1 medium zucchini, cut into small cubes
½ cup / 60 g fresh baby peas (or thawed frozen peas if fresh are unavailable)
8 ounces / 225 g fresh capelli di angelo *or other thin egg noodles*
½ pound / 8 ounces / 225 g fresh whitebait or redbait
1 extra-large egg, beaten with 1½ tablespoons / 12 g fresh marjoram leaves

First have the fish broth at hand. Bring it to a near boil and keep it at that temperature. Then, in a skillet in which you have heated the olive oil, sauté the zucchini cubes until they are soft, about 2 minutes. Add the baby peas and sauté for another minute. Add the contents of the skillet and the *capelli di angelo* to the soup and cook for a minute. Add the whitebait and cook for a minute, stirring continuously. Then turn off the heat and whisk in the beaten egg and marjoram. Serve immediately. Optionally, you may omit the egg and serve the soup garnished with marjoram leaves added at the last moment.

Makes
4 to 6 servings

Sestri di Levante

Sestri di Levante, midway between Genoa and La Spezia, is a typical Levante town: vibrant, bustling, fragrant with herbs, focaccia, and the spray of the sea. There are mountains hemming bays to the north and south. A strip of land projecting from the shore is the heart of Sestri. It has the particular characteristic of being surrounded on three sides by water, with the effect that there is an omnipresent murmur of waves, the cry of sea birds, and dazzling sunrises and sunsets over water.

"Sestri di Levante is a little town pleasantly situated on the sea-side, but has not the conveniency of a harbour. The fish taken here is mostly carried to Genoa. This is likewise the market for their oil, and the paste called *macaroni,* of which they make a good quantity."

— Tobias Smollett,
Travels Through France and Italy, 1765

"I exulted at seeing that piece of land extending from the shore: what a fabled night I spent in Sestri Levante! The inn was very close to the sea and a strong backwash licked against it. In the skies above the clouds were like fire and in the mountains there alternated the most vivid colors."

— Hans Christian Andersen, 1854

Ciuppin

Fish Soup

This famous chunky fish soup is found throughout Liguria but it is unquestionably a specialty of Sestri di Levante. Many men from Sestri sailed on Ligurian ships to faraway places, and a fair number of them wound up in San Francisco, where this soup mutated into the much heartier cioppino. In Sestri, it was made to use leftover ingredients, such as stale bread and random pieces of fish. The name comes from the word *sûppin*, meaning little soup.

1½ pounds/1.2 kilos assorted pieces of fish,
  preferably with the skin on and the bones in
7 (6 + 1) tablespoons/100 (85 + 15) ml Ligurian extravirgin olive oil
1 medium onion, coarsely chopped
1 stalk celery, chopped
1 large carrot, chopped
4 garlic cloves, 1 minced, the others cut in half with the green heart removed
½ cup/115 ml dry white wine
7 cups/1600 ml boiling water
⅞ cup/200 g canned, peeled tomatoes, with their liquid
3 tablespoons/22 g minced fresh Italian (flat) parsley
Salt and pepper to taste
4 to 6 slices stale country-style bread (1 slice per person)

Carefully wash and dry the pieces of fish. In a large, heavy-bottomed pot, heat 6 tablespoons of olive oil and then add the onion, celery, carrot, and the minced garlic clove. Sauté gently for about 5 minutes, and add the fish. Cook over medium-high heat for 5 minutes, turning often. Add the wine, boil rapidly, and let the wine cook down to half. Add the boiling water, then the tomatoes, parsley, salt, and pepper. When it returns to a boil, simmer for 20 minutes. In the meantime, toast the bread (or at least warm it if it is quite stale) and rub each slice with the halved garlic. Add a couple of drops of olive oil to each slice. Then place a piece of toast at the bottom of each soup bowl. Top with soup, when it is ready, and serve. Remember to warn your guests if there are bones in the fish.

*Makes
4 to 6 servings*

Richard Wagner in Liguria

Richard Wagner was a frequent traveler in Italy, starting with his first visit in July 1852 to Lago Maggiore in Piedmont. He traveled down from Zurich, the place he had been living in exile from Germany, where there was a warrant for his arrest for radical political activities. The first Italian town he stayed in was Formazza, which that coincidentally was near the birthplace of the mother of Giuseppe Verdi. Wagner had been working on the text for the Ring Cycle, and was suffering from writer's block. At the time, Wagner was writing the libretto for *Das Rheingold*. Although this is the first of the four operas in the cycle, he wrote the libretti in reverse order, beginning with *Götterdämmerung,* then *Siegfried,* and then *Die Walküre.* Italy inspired him and he managed to finish the libretto of *Das Rheingold* by the shores of Lago Maggiore.

On his second visit to Italy, in 1853, Wagner returned to Piedmont, this time visiting Torino, where he saw a performance of Rossini's *Il Barbiere di Siviglia* at the Teatro Regio. He was, in his word, "dissatisfied." He proceeded to Genoa, where he caught his first sight of the Mediterranean Sea. "I felt a sense of exaltation," he wrote of this experience. That mood would change, however, when he set sail for La Spezia. The voyage was quite rough and Wagner became very seasick. When he reached La Spezia, he checked into a hotel at Via del Prione 45, on one of the busiest thoroughfares in town. As he lay in

bed during the afternoon siesta, he later wrote, "I thought I was falling down in a whirlpool — this abyss into which I was falling — and I awakened having heard the opening chords of *Das Rheingold*." These E-flat chords that suggest the powerful churning of the Rhine River, are among the most vivid and evocative chords in all of opera. This music, which came to him in a bed in La Spezia, was the launching point for compositional labors that would occupy Wagner for more than twenty-five years as he wrote the extraordinary music for this epic tetralogy.

Outside Via del Prione 45, you will see a plaque that reads *"Qui, nell'estate del* MDCCCLIII *in una antica locanda dell'antico borgo, a Richard Wagner si rivelò uno splendido accordo musicale e prese forma il preludio dell'Oro del Reno."* That indicates that on a summer day in 1853 this splendid set of musical chords "revealed themselves" to Wagner at an old inn at this location.

Wagner again stopped at Lago Maggiore on the way home and, full of Italian inspiration, set about composing the Ring Cycle. Wagner returned to Italy numerous times, making many visits to Venice (where he would die in 1883), but also to Bologna, Florence, Rome, Naples, the Amalfi Coast, Sicily, and many return visits to the Italian Lake District. He wrote much of *Tristan und Isolde* and *Parsifal* in Italy, and unstintingly praised the country for the inspiration it offered him. But never, as far as we know, did Wagner return to Liguria, the place that gave him the earliest inspiration for his greatest achievement.

Vegetables
&
Salads

Condiggion	Mixed Vegetable Salad
Spinasci a-a Zeneize	Genoese Spinach with Raisins and Pine Nuts
Lattughe Ripiene al Pomodoro e Basilico	Stuffed Lettuce Rolls with Tomato and Basil
Involtini di Bietola	Beet Green Rolls
Polpettone	Potato–String Bean Tart
Torta di Zucchine	Zucchini Tart
Zucchine Ripiene	Stuffed Zucchini
Verdura Ripiena	Stuffed Vegetables
Cipolle Ripiene	Stuffed Onions
Funghi Porcini con Pinoli	Porcini Mushrooms with Pine Nuts
Funghi Porcini al Pesto con Pinoli	Fresh Porcini Mushrooms with Pesto and Pine Nuts
Funghi Porcini e Patate al Forno	Baked Porcini Mushrooms and Potatoes
Zimino di Carciofi e Piselli	Casserole of Artichokes and Peas
Pomodori Secchi	Sun-Dried Tomatoes

*"What was Paradise, but a garden full of vegetables
and herbs and pleasure? Nothing there but delights."*

— William Lawson,
seventeenth-century writer

HE SUN AND SEA AIR of Liguria, combined with the skillful agricultural abilities of the local populace, have made this region heaven on earth for vegetarians. There is an infinite variety of greens and herbs, all of superb quality and flavor, and one can live happily for months without ever eating meat.

Essentially, Ligurians do as little as possible to their vegetables, understanding that Nature made them perfect already. Usually, a bit of steaming or sautéing in olive oil is all that most greens might require. You should devote yourself to getting to know when greens and other vegetables are at their peak — this will deliver the most flavor as well as the most nutritional content.

Similarly, try to seek out farmers' markets that offer freshly picked greens and herbs of all types. If you become a steady enough customer, you might be able to have them put aside the choicest produce for you when it is picked. Remember that if you have an abundance of a particular vegetable, it can be stuffed, or baked into a torta, or turned into a sauce. You can also adapt a *polpettone* recipe (see page 302) to use up almost any vegetables you might have around. But no vegetable should ever go to waste.

What follow are some classic Ligurian vegetable preparations, although you should always remember that Ligurians eat vegetables just as you would want to: in perfect condition, close to their natural state, and usually dressed with a few drops of divine olive oil.

Condiggion
Mixed Vegetable Salad

Anyone who knows Italy can tell you that fresh salads are a standard side dish at many meals. Where *condiggion* (*condiglione* in Italian) differs is that it functions as a main course. While in the rest of Italy this is a new concept, Ligurians have eaten main course salads for centuries. *Condiggion*, eaten throughout Liguria, is particularly popular in the Ponente.

4 gallette del marinaio (see page 151)*
2 cloves garlic, cut in half, with the green heart removed
2 (1 + 1) tablespoons/30 (15 + 15) ml red wine vinegar
4 (1 + 3) tablespoons/60 (15 + 45) ml Ligurian extravirgin olive oil
2 (1 + 1) pinches fine sea salt
4 firm beefsteak tomatoes
1 large cucumber, peeled
3 tablespoons/22 g pitted Taggia or Niçoise olives
1 green or yellow pepper, cleaned, sliced into thin strips
2 small onions, coarsely chopped
3 sprigs fresh oregano or thyme, torn into bits
1 small handful small fresh basil leaves

* If you absolutely cannot locate *gallette del marinaio*, Uneeda biscuits are an acceptable though inferior substitution.

Makes 4 servings

Rub the *gallette del marinaio* with garlic and then discard the cloves. Place the *gallette* in the bottom of a salad bowl and top with 1 tablespoon of red wine vinegar and 1 tablespoon of olive oil and a pinch of salt. Set aside. In the meantime, slice the tomatoes and cucumber into thin slices, and prepare the olives and the yellow or green pepper. Once everything is ready, break up the *gallette del marinaio*. Then add the tomatoes, onions, green or yellow pepper, the oregano or thyme, and the olives. Toss well, adding the additional oil, vinegar, and salt. Set aside for about 10 minutes. Then top with some fresh basil leaves, leave for about 10 minutes, and serve.

Spinasci a-a Zeneize

Genoese Spinach with Raisins and Pine Nuts

This combination goes well with cooked meats, especially *tomaxelle,* as well as simply prepared fish. The combination of spinach, raisins, and pine nuts is a classic in this stretch of the Mediterranean and is ubiquitous in Barcelona.

1 pound / 450 g fresh spinach
2 tablespoons / 30 ml Ligurian extravirgin olive oil
1 clove garlic, with the green heart removed, minced
1 tablespoon / 7 g golden raisins (sultanas) or currants,
   soaked in warm water for 5 minutes
1 tablespoon pinoli
1 pinch fine sea salt
6 slices toast, each cut into 4 triangles, if serving as an appetizer

Carefully wash the spinach, removing all of the sand. Steam the spinach for 5 minutes, using only the water that clings to the leaves. Then remove the spinach and carefully squeeze out all of the liquid. Chop coarsely. Heat the olive oil gently in a pan or skillet. Add the garlic and let the oil become fragrant (the garlic should not turn color). Add the spinach, sauté for 3 minutes, then add the raisins, *pinoli,* and salt, and sauté for 4 to 5 minutes, turning the ingredients frequently so that nothing sticks or burns.

*Makes
4 servings
as a side dish,
6 servings
as an antipasto**

* This spinach is a popular appetizer when served on triangles of toast.

Lattughe Ripiene al Pomodoro e Basilico
Stuffed Lettuce Rolls with Tomato and Basil

Stuffed lettuce is a specialty of La Spezia. The stuffed lettuce rolls as presented here can be cooked in broth for 6 to 7 minutes and then served as a very nice soup (see page 283). Or you may prepare this dish as an appetizer or main course, using tomatoes and basil. You should use a soft buttery lettuce such as Bibb or Boston.

FOR THE LETTUCE ROLLS
24 leaves of Bibb or Boston lettuce,
* unblemished and quite fresh*
½ pound/225 g mortadella, cut into
* 1 piece, then minced*
½ ounce/15 g dried funghi porcini,
* soaked in 3 changes of water,*
* squeezed dry, then minced*
½ cup/60 g unflavored bread crumbs
3 large eggs, beaten
½ pound/225 g freshly grated
* Parmigiano-Reggiano*
½ cup/60 g minced fresh Italian (flat)
* parsley*

1 pinch fresh thyme, torn into bits
1 pinch fresh oregano, torn into bits
1 clove garlic, green heart removed, minced

FOR THE SAUCE
4 (2 + 2) tablespoons/60 (30 + 30) ml
* Ligurian extravirgin olive oil*
1 pound/½ kilo fresh ripe tomatoes,
* washed, chopped, seeds removed*
20 small basil leaves (or 10 larger leaves,
* torn in half), carefully wiped*

Makes
4 to 6 servings

Set a pot of cold water to boil. When it reaches a boil, quickly dip in each lettuce leaf, just to soften it. Remove the lettuce leaves to a cloth to dry. Now make the filling. Mince the mortadella and place it in a mixing bowl. Add all of the other ingredients, one or two at a time, and combine thoroughly. Take each lettuce leaf and put on it a small amount of filling in the shape of a little sausage. Then roll each leaf like a little cigar, completely enclosing the filling. The leaf should remain wrapped. If you are concerned that it will open, you may plunge a toothpick through it. Once this is done, set the rolls aside for a few minutes. To make the sauce, heat 2 tablespoons of olive oil in a pot, then add the tomatoes and stir vigorously to break them up into small pieces. Toss in about half of the basil leaves and shut off the heat. In a skillet, heat the remaining 2 tablespoons of olive oil and then add the little lettuce rolls. Toss in the rest of the basil leaves. Cook the rolls until the fillings become firm (about 5 to 7 minutes). Add the tomato sauce, simmer for 3 to 4 minutes, then serve.

Involtini di Bietola

Beet Green Rolls

Bietole, or beet greens, are a delicious and essential vegetable in Liguria, and they figure prominently in other regional Italian kitchens as well. This particular dish is easy to prepare and immensely pleasing to the palate.

¼ pound / 4 ounces / 115 g ground beef or veal
1 clove garlic, with the green heart removed, minced
½ small onion, minced
4 (3 + 1) cups / 450 (340 + 110) g beet greens
Sea salt to taste
Freshly ground black pepper to taste
3 large eggs
7 tablespoons / 50 g freshly grated Parmigiano-Reggiano
2 sprigs fresh Italian (flat) parsley, minced
2 sprigs fresh marjoram, torn into small pieces
2 tablespoons / 30 ml Ligurian extravirgin olive oil

Set a large pot of cold water to boil, first adding a generous pinch of sea salt. In a skillet, heat the ground meat gently for a minute and then add the garlic and the onion. Turn up the heat slightly and sauté more vigorously until the meat gives off some juice and the onion becomes slightly transparent. Then remove the pan from the heat. Wash the beet greens carefully and select the largest, most perfect leaves — they should be about one-quarter of the total. Dry these carefully and set aside. Boil the other greens in the large pot of water for 3 or 4 minutes, just until they become soft but still retain their vibrant color (and flavor). Try to fish the greens out of the water and into a colander so that you can save the cooking water for later. Once all the greens are out of the pot, turn the heat down very low under the water. Press the excess liquid out of the greens and mince them very fine. Transfer the minced greens to a mixing bowl and add the meat mixture and stir. Then add the salt, pepper, eggs, Parmigiano-Reggiano, parsley, marjoram, and olive oil. Combine thoroughly and then take the beet greens you set aside and open them up. Add enough filling to make each look like a small cigar. Roll the leaves tightly to enclose the filling and then tie them shut with string. Bring the water in the pot back up to a boil and then cook the *involtini* (beet green rolls) for 1 hour. Serve immediately. If you have made very large rolls, they can be sliced; smaller rolls can be served whole and cut by the diner.

Makes
4 servings

Lerici as Seen by
Shelley and D. H. Lawrence

Lerici, near La Spezia, sits on a bay that is one of the most fabled in the Mediterranean. Writers have been drawn here for centuries, and their words about the place tend to be florid, impassioned, and sometimes laced with the question of "What does it all mean?" that is born of their response to the jaw-dropping beauty of this area. The bays of Lerici and La Spezia are known together as the Gulf of Poets, attracting them, seducing them, confounding them. Indeed, this is the place where Shelley drowned.

> I sat and saw the vessels glide
> Over the ocean bright and wide,
> Like spirit-winged chariots sent
> O'er some serenest element
> For ministrations strange and far;
> As if to some Elysian star
> Sailed for drink to medicine
> Such sweet and bitter pain as mine.
> And the wind that winged their flight
> From the land came fresh and light.

> — Percy Bysshe Shelley,
> "Lines written on the Bay of Lerici," 1822

"I am so happy with the place we have at last discovered, I must write smack off to tell you. It is perfect. There is a little tiny bay half shut in by rock, and smothered by olive woods that slope down swiftly."

> — David Herbert Lawrence, from a letter, 1913

D. H. Lawrence moved a bit beyond Lerici to the enchanting town of Tellaro, where he wrote a charming and slightly chilling story about the Octopus of Tellaro. This particular octopod liked to swim to the base of the beautiful church at the water's edge, grab hold of a rope connected to the church bells, and ring them incessantly to disturb and alarm the citizenry. As a sort of revenge, the people of Tellaro dote on octopus dishes.

The tiny harbor of Tellaro

Polpettone
Potato–String Bean Tart

This popular dish, called *porpetton de faxolin* in dialect, is irresistible. *Polpettone* in the rest of Italy means meat loaf, but in vegetable-crazy Liguria there is no meat in sight. This tart is wonderful as a snack, an antipasto, or a main course. For Ligurians it has the particular association of being the food that is packed to take along for hikes and country outings.

1¼ pounds / 1 kilo boiling potatoes, peeled, cut into pieces
¾ pound / 340 g string beans, preferably slender
1 tablespoon / 15 ml Ligurian extravirgin olive oil
1 clove garlic, green heart removed, minced
2 tablespoons / 15 g fresh Italian (flat) parsley, minced
1 tablespoon / 7 g fresh oregano or thyme, torn into small pieces
1 cup / 115 g freshly grated Parmigiano-Reggiano
3 large eggs, lightly beaten
½ cup / 60 g prescinseua *or ricotta*
Fine sea salt to taste
Freshly ground black pepper to taste
1 cup / 115 g fine unflavored bread crumbs

Makes one 12-inch / 30-cm tart

Preheat oven to 350°F/180°C. Set two pots of water to boil. Add a little salt to one of them. Then add the potatoes to that pot, cook for about 20 minutes, drain, and mash. In the other pot, cook the string beans for 12 to 15 minutes (thin ones less, thicker ones more). Drain, and then chop them coarsely. Heat the olive oil in a skillet, add the garlic, cook for 1 minute, then add the string beans, parsley, and oregano or thyme. Cook for 2 minutes, until all of the flavors have combined. Remove from heat and let cool. Once the beans and the potatoes have cooled, combine them in a bowl. Add the Parmigiano-Reggiano, eggs, *prescinseua* (or ricotta), salt, and pepper, and combine the ingredients well. Grease a 12-inch/30-cm round glass ovenproof baking dish with a little olive oil. Sprinkle in some bread crumbs, but not too many (perhaps one-quarter of the total amount). Then spoon in the string bean mixture and smooth the top with a spatula. If you wish, you can score the top to form a pattern — Ligurians typically create diamonds. Top evenly with the rest of the bread crumbs. Bake for about 45 minutes and serve hot, warm, or cool.

Torta di Zucchine
Zucchini Tart

Zucchini is another vegetable that arrived in Europe with Columbus. In Liguria there is an expression in dialect, *ese unn-a succa veua,* which translates literally as "that's an old squash," a common way of referring to a slow-witted or foolish person. Yet zucchini (*zucchine* in Italian) are among the most popular vegetables in the region. Traditionally, the smallest possible zucchini are purchased for cooking. They have more flavor and less liquid. This torta is not like those in the bread chapter in that it is a crustless tart made in a glass ovenproof baking dish (12 inch/30 cm round).

2¼ pounds / 1 kilo small to medium zucchini, sliced very thin
1 medium onion, minced
10 tablespoons / 70 g unsalted butter
1 tablespoon / 15 ml Ligurian extravirgin olive oil
4 large eggs
2¾ cups / 300 g cooked rice (it should be slightly chewy)
2 tablespoons / 15 g freshly grated Parmigiano-Reggiano
1 tablespoon / 7 g freshly minced Italian (flat) parsley
1 tablespoon / 7 g freshly minced marjoram
1 pinch fine sea salt
3 to 4 tablespoons / about 25 g unflavored bread crumbs

Preheat oven to 350°F/180°C. After slicing the zucchini and onions, melt 8 tablespoons/55 g butter and the olive oil in a frying pan. Add the onion and sauté until transparent. Then add the zucchini, sauté just until the disks become soft, cover the pan, and turn off the heat. Let cool. In a large bowl beat the eggs, then add the rice, Parmigiano-Reggiano, parsley, marjoram, salt, and finally the zucchini mixture. Grease the baking dish with a little butter and add a thin coating of bread crumbs. Then add the egg-zucchini mixture and use a fork or spoon to make the filling level. Top with a thin layer of bread crumbs and curls made from the remaining butter. Bake for about 1 hour. Serve hot, tepid, or cold.

Makes
4 to 6 servings

Zucchine Ripiene
Stuffed Zucchini

Ligurians have a penchant for stuffing vegetables and none is more popular than zucchini. In their ongoing pursuit of flavor perfection, though, Ligurians inevitably use baby zucchini, which have more flavor and less water. However, if baby zucchini are unavailable, select the smallest, narrowest zucchini you can find.

4 medium zucchini or, preferably, 8 baby zucchini
1 tablespoon/7 g unsalted butter
3 tablespoons/20 g finely minced onion
⅓ pound/150 g ground veal or lean beef
⅛ pound/35 g prosciutto crudo, minced
2 large eggs, lightly beaten
¼ cup/4 tablespoons/30 g unseasoned bread crumbs
½ cup/8 tablespoons/60 g freshly grated Parmigiano-Reggiano
¼ teaspoon/1½ g freshly ground black pepper
¼ teaspoon/1½ g fine sea salt (optional)
A few fresh basil leaves, carefully wiped and torn into small bits
1½ cups/350 ml tomato sauce or puree
Ligurian extravirgin olive oil

Makes 2 servings as a main course, 4 servings as an antipasto

Preheat oven to 350°F/180°C. Set a large pot of cold water to boil. When it reaches a boil, add the zucchini and cook for 5 minutes. Remove them from the pot, let cool for a couple of minutes, and then slice them in half lengthwise. Carefully scoop out the pulp, making sure not to break the shell of the zucchini. Place the pulp in a large mixing bowl. Melt the butter in a skillet. Add the onion and sauté for a few seconds. Then add the veal or beef and cook gently for one minute, pushing the meat around the pan so that it cooks evenly and does not stick. Then add the prosciutto and continue cooking until the meat is thoroughly browned. Drain all the cooking fat and then add the meat and onion mixture to the zucchini pulp. Add the eggs, bread crumbs, Parmigiano-Reggiano, pepper, salt, and basil leaves to the bowl and combine with a wooden spoon. Once the mixture is well-blended, spoon it into the eight zucchini halves. Pour the tomato sauce into a large baking dish that has been lightly greased with olive oil. Carefully place the stuffed zucchini into the dish and bake for 15 to 20 minutes, or until the filling is browned but not overdone.

Trenette col Pesto

(Dana Gallagher)

*Pesto and Pasta di Olive,
two of Liguria's great sauces and condiments*

(Dana Gallagher)

*Pansôti Con Salsa di Noci
(Herb-filled Ravioli with Walnut Sauce)*

(Dana Gallagher)

Pesce alla Ligure (Fish, Ligurian-style)

(Dana Gallagher)

Accuighe all'Agro (Marinated Fresh Anchovies)

(Dana Gallagher)

Taggia olives,
the source of Liguria's sublime oil

(Dana Gallagher)

Pesche Ripiene (exquisite Stuffed Peaches)

(Dana Gallagher)

San Fruttuoso, a niche of paradise

An olive oil press in Cervo

There are snow-topped mountains
only a few miles from the sea in Liguria

The ingredients of pesto:
basil, garlic, cheese, pinoli, olive oil

Ligurian staples:
pasta, olives, herbs, olive oil, wine

Honeys and sauces from Triora

*Painted houses in Liguria
can fool the eye*

Camogli

Sunset in paradise

Serve hot, warm, or at room temperature with a bit of the tomato sauce from the dish.

VARIATION: I like to add a little fresh lemon zest or a few drops of fresh lemon juice to the mixture. Some cooks like adding a few sultanas to the mixture as well.

Verdura Ripiena
Stuffed Vegetables

The procedure and filling for zucchini may be used for other vegetables, including baby eggplant and beefsteak tomatoes. Simply substitute eggplant or tomato pulp for the zucchini. To stuff yelllow, red, or green peppers, cut them in half (either horizontally or vertically), remove all of the seeds, and mince whatever pepper is remaining in the cavity. Add this to the stuffing. If you feel the stuffing is too dry, add a little fresh lemon juice. Bake the stuffed vegetables as you would the zucchini. A platter of mixed stuffed vegetables makes a wonderful appetizer or main course.

Cipolle Ripiene
Stuffed Onions

This exquisite preparation succeeds when you use the best onions available, preferably a sweet variety such as Vidalia. These may be served as an antipasto all by themselves, or as part of a larger platter of stuffed vegetables in an antipasto or a main course. As with all Ligurian stuffed vegetables, they may be served hot, tepid, or cold.

12 medium onions, outer skins removed
4 ounces / 1 cup / 115 g freshly grated Pecorino cheese
Approximately 7 ounces / 200 g small potatoes, boiled and cooled, then minced
6 ounces / 1½ cups / 175 g finely minced prosciutto cotto *(boiled ham)*
1 egg
2 teaspoons / 4 to 5 g fresh oregano, minced
¼ teaspoon / ½ g nutmeg
1 tablespoon / 7 g unflavored bread crumbs
Sea salt and freshly ground black pepper to taste
¼ cup / 60 ml (total: 24 half-teaspoons) Ligurian extravirgin olive oil

Makes
24 half onions

The customary approach to cooking the onions for this dish is to boil them. I have tried it this way and it is acceptable (boil for 8 to 10 minutes), but I would recommend that you steam the onions. The way to do this is to set a large pot of water to boil. Once it reaches a rolling boil, place the onions in a colander and set the colander over the boiling water. Then cover the colander with the lid that belongs to the pot you are using. Depending on the size of the onion, you should steam them from 10 to nearly 20 minutes. The objective is that the onions be translucent and somewhat soft.

Once the onions are cooked, remove them and, as soon as they are not too hot to handle, cut them in half *horizontally*. Remove the heart of each onion and about 6 to 8 of the inner layers. The idea is that there be a big enough cavity to stuff, but not so big that the onion falls apart. Finely mince all of the onion pieces you have removed. In a mixing bowl combine the onion pieces, Pecorino, minced potato, *prosciutto cotto,* egg, fresh oregano, nutmeg, salt, and pepper. Once all the ingredients are combined but not overworked, put some of this filling into each of the 24 onion cavities. The key concept here is to put in enough filling so that the onion half is full, but do not press the filling down! This will cause the onion to fall apart and will also make the filling taste too heavy. Top each onion with a few bread crumbs — not so it is entirely covered, which is how Italian-American recipes would have it, but just enough to give the filling a little crunch. Top each onion half with ½ teaspoon of olive oil, place them in a baking dish lightly greased with olive oil, and bake in a pre-heated 350°F/180°C oven until the tops of the filling are golden but not browned (about 8 to 10 minutes).

Funghi Porcini con Pinoli

Porcini Mushrooms with Pine Nuts

A nice side dish for simple fish preparations.

1 tablespoon/15 ml Ligurian extravirgin olive oil
1 tablespoon/7 g sweet butter
1 pound/450 g funghi porcini, *carefully washed and cut into pieces about*
   ¼ inch thick
½ small onion, minced
2 ounces/55 g pinoli
1 tablespoon/7 g minced fresh Italian (flat) parsley

Makes
4 servings as
an appetizer,
6 servings as
a side dish

Put the olive oil and butter in a saucepan, and melt over low heat so that the oil and butter combine but do not burn. Add the mushrooms and cook gently for about 3 minutes, all the while stirring gently. Then add the minced onions and keep stirring so that all the flavors combine and none of the ingredients sticks to the pan. Then add the *pinoli,* and continue stirring and cooking for another 4 minutes. Add the minced parsley, and keep stirring for another minute so that the parsley is completely integrated. Serve immediately, either as an appetizer or as a side dish to cooked steak or veal chops.

Funghi Porcini al Pesto con Pinoli

Fresh Porcini Mushrooms with Pesto and Pine Nuts

This versatile preparation can serve as an appetizer, as a side dish for roast veal or other meats, or it can be used as the filling for a frittata (page 360) or a *torta di frittate* (page 185).

1 pound/450 g fresh funghi porcini, *carefully washed and sliced thin*
2 tablespoons/30 ml olive oil
2 to 3 tablespoons/30 to 45 ml pesto, *according to taste*
2 teaspoons/5 g pinoli
A few small fresh basil leaves, carefully wiped

After preparing the mushrooms, heat the olive oil in a skillet over medium heat. Add the *funghi* and sauté until they release their liquid. If these are older, drier mushrooms, you may need to add a teaspoon or two of cool water. Then add the pesto, turn up the heat to medium high, and sauté vigorously for 1 to 2 minutes. Serve on individual plates topped with some *pinoli* and garnished with a couple of basil leaves.

Makes 4 servings as an appetizer, 6 servings as a side dish

Funghi Porcini e Patate al Forno

Baked Porcini Mushrooms and Potatoes

This dish can serve as an accompaniment to a meat or poultry course, and also marries well with seafood such as octopus or scallops. I like it too as a vegetarian main course, accompanied by a glass of red wine and a salad.

Extravirgin olive oil, preferably Ligurian
1 pound / 450 g small to medium potatoes, washed, peeled, and sliced the same
* thickness as the mushrooms*
4 to 6 cloves fresh garlic, peeled
Sea salt and freshly ground pepper to taste
1 pound / 450 g fresh funghi porcini,* carefully cleaned, sliced not too thin
20 fresh basil leaves, carefully wiped clean, coarsely torn (or, if you prefer, about
* 8 to 10 sprigs fresh marjoram, torn)*
Freshly grated Parmigiano-Reggiano

> * Note: If fresh porcini, cremini, or other special mushrooms are unavail-
> able, you may make this dish using 8 ounces/225 g cultivated mushrooms
> in combination with 2 to 3 ounces/60 to 75 g dried *funghi porcini* that you
> have soaked. After soaking the dried mushrooms, strain the liquid and then
> soak the sliced cultivated mushrooms in the liquid for 10 minutes so that
> they will absorb some of the flavor.

Makes
4 to 6 servings

Preheat your oven to 350°F/180°C. After preparing all of the ingredients, take an ovenproof baking dish and grease it lightly with olive oil. Arrange the potato slices in a layer or two, distributing the garlic cloves throughout. Add salt and pepper to taste, and then top generously with olive oil (at least 2 tablespoons). Place the mushrooms on top, and cover with the torn basil leaves. Top with at least 1 more tablespoon of oil. Cover the dish tightly with aluminum foil and bake for 40 to 45 minutes. Take the pan from the oven and then remove the foil to let the steam escape. Serve immediately. Although it is not traditional in Liguria to top this dish with Parmigiano-Reggiano, some people do enjoy the addition of a judicious amount of this cheese when this dish is eaten as a main course (it would be overkill when having this dish as an accompaniment to meat, poultry, or seafood).

Zimino di Carciofi e Piselli
Casserole of Artichokes and Peas

In Liguria, the term *zimino* means a combination of ingredients (usually vegetables) that are cooked in a pan. A *zimino* typically serves as a side dish, but may also be a sauce or condiment for boiled or roast meats.

4 tablespoons / 60 g Ligurian extravirgin olive oil
2 ounces / 60 g pancetta (unsmoked bacon), cut into small cubes
2 small onions, thinly sliced
6 small artichokes, outer leaves removed, then cut into quarters or sixths
¾ cup / 6 ounces / 1 glass / 175 ml dry white wine, preferably Ligurian
⅔ pound / 300 g fresh peas
2 fresh basil leaves, torn into bits

Gently heat the olive oil in a frying pan, then add the *pancetta* and onions. Sauté until the onions are soft and the *pancetta* does not brown. Add the artichokes and continue to cook gently. After a couple of minutes, add a little wine and then add the peas. Continue to stir gently as the *zimino* cooks, adding the rest of the wine a little at a time. If necessary, add a little warm water so that the vegetables do not stick, but be sure not to give them a bath. When the peas are cooked, the dish is ready. The success of this dish depends on employing the freshest ingredients, which will be soft and tender when cooked. Once the dish is done, stir in the torn basil leaves and serve.

Makes 6 servings

Pomodori Secchi
Sun-Dried Tomatoes

This classic Ligurian ingredient has become one of the most abused foods in international cooking. In the 1980s many American chefs with more pretense than knowledge threw sun-dried tomatoes on just about everything in sight. Never mind that the tangy, intense flavor and slightly leathery texture corrupted most foods the sun-dried tomatoes came into contact with. The idea of the sun-dried tomato is one of preservation of a particular flavor for the seasons when it is not available. It is supposed to be used sparingly as a minor note in a sonata full of flavors. The only time a Ligurian might consider eating a whole sun-dried tomato would be as an appetizer, placing it over a slice of crusty bread, and washing it down with a glass of young red wine.

It is traditional in Liguria to make sun-dried tomatoes on the days before and after the feast of San Lorenzo on August 10. It is in these days that there are many shooting stars in the night sky, and after the intense summer sun sets the tomatoes are stored until the following morning. Families sit outside late into the evening to observe the stars, and then the mother rises at dawn to put the tomatoes back into the sun. This recipe was given to me by Signora Marta, an elderly lady in Manarola in the Cinqueterre, whose old house above the sea enjoys many hours of exposure to the sun. Ideally, you should pick a place to dry your tomatoes that has as many hours as possible of direct sunlight. Of course, the best tomatoes to use are those that have just been picked.

The procedure to make sun-dried tomatoes is the same whether you dry one tomato or one thousand. In Liguria, the women often store the tomatoes in larger jars if they use the tomatoes frequently, but I would advise you to use jars that hold about 8 ounces/225 g and then store them until you are ready to use them. Once a jar is opened, the tomatoes must be used rather quickly. The rule of thumb is that 1⅛ pound/about 18 ounces/500 g of fresh tomatoes will be needed to produce the right amount of sun-dried tomatoes to fit in the jar I have recommended.

Plum tomatoes or small round tomatoes, at the peak of ripeness
Fine sea salt, or coarse salt pounded in a mortar
Basil leaves, gently wiped with paper toweling
Ligurian extravirgin olive oil

Early on a sunny morning, wash the tomatoes carefully and then dry them with paper toweling. Cut them in half vertically and try, if possible, to leave them attached at one end rather than cutting all the way through the skin. Place the tomatoes on a rack with their interiors facing up. (You must use a rack — such as a cake rack — that has slats so that any liquid can fall through. This may also be the sort of metal rack that you use to hold something hot out of the oven that you do not want to touch a counter. The key thing is that the tomatoes be slightly off the ground or else the skins may adhere on a very hot day. If you do not have something slatted, try a slab of marble or terracotta and check the tomatoes periodically.) Sprinkle all of the tomato halves generously with salt and then place them out in the sun. As you go about your chores, pay attention to the changing position of the sun. If the tomatoes are no longer in direct light, move them so they receive as much exposure as possible. Also mind the weather: If rain is imminent, you will have to bring the tomatoes indoors because the higher humidity will cause mold to develop. As dusk approaches, bring the tomatoes indoors and cover them with plastic. On the following morning, place the tomatoes back into the sunshine and let them continue to dry. In general it takes four days for the tomatoes to dry but still remain soft to the touch. Inferior sun-dried tomatoes — those that are too often found in the United States — are those that are allowed to become leathery. Signora Marta told me that for the first two days the tomatoes should be arranged so that their interiors face the sun. On the third day they should be turned so that their exteriors face the sun. On the fourth day they should be turned again so that their interiors face the sun one last time.

On the evening of the fourth day, have your jars clean and ready to use. Also have the basil and olive oil at hand. If the tomato halves have remained attached, place a basil leaf on one side and then fold the other half over it. Then press gently so that the halves join, but do not press too firmly or the result will be denser, heavier, and chewier. If the halves have separated, you will need to put them together, with 1 basil leaf in between. Place each tomato in the jar, side by side and then one on top of another, without pressing them together. Fill the jar about 85 percent to 90 percent with tomatoes, and then pour in enough olive oil so that the tomatoes are moistened without being immersed. It is important that oil be on top of the tomatoes in such a way that it forms a layer between the lid and the tomatoes. Close the lid tightly and store in a cool, dark place. The jars should remain closed for at least six weeks before the tomatoes are eaten. In general, jarred sun-dried tomatoes can last for about a year, or just in time for the next crop of fresh tomatoes.

A FEW WORDS ABOUT SEEDS: It is customary in many Ligurian households to leave the seeds in when the tomatoes are cut, and therefore when they are dried. I mention this so that you know what has been the tradition. I, however, would encourage you to remove the seeds, taking care not to let the liquid spill out of the tomatoes. This is not for reasons of aesthetics, but rather because seeds impart a bitter taste which is only intensified during the drying process.

Men at Sea

*"In mare irato, in subita procella   "On wrathful seas, in sudden storms
    invoco te, nostra benigna stella"   I call to you, our kindly star"*

There is, throughout Liguria, a collective memory of hardships suffered at sea. This information is passed down from one generation to another in stories told as nets are mended, as fish are cleaned, as prayers are said and meals are served, as old and young fishermen sit patiently in their small craft waiting for the fish to bite.

The words above are part of a hymn sung to the Stella Maris by sailors and fishermen in Savona. Across the region there are similar gestures of devotion to the star that has guided mariners since antiquity. The most beautiful, I believe, is held each summer in Camogli as part of the Festa della Stella Maris. As darkness overtakes the sky, the lights of town are dimmed and all the fishermen put out to sea with only a small light on each boat. The townspeople stand on the beach in the dark and peer out at the hundreds of small lights in the distance that look like so many fireflies against a carpet of black velvet. Then, at an assigned moment, everyone — on land and at sea — looks to the Stella Maris and recites prayers of gratitude.

In Camogli and throughout Liguria, the churches are full of objects and artifacts of the sea, and there are special saints who are venerated because of the protection they provide. The adjacent picture is an old mass card (1954) from a church in the port of Genoa that has a large following among seamen.

In late July, Levanto, in the province of La Spezia, holds a Festa del Mare that honors San Giacomo, another patron saint of fishermen. La Spezia itself holds a similar festival in early August, as does Ventimiglia. A week later, in San Remo, is the Festa del Marinaio, with a special sailor's mass held in the sanctuary of the church of Nostra Signora della Costa (Our Lady of the Coast).

As part of the San Remo *festa,* there is a re-creation of the election of the Consoli di Mare (Consuls of the Sea). These would be three seafarers who would be elected to devote themselves for two years to the public good, the improvement of business, and the conservation of the shoreline. (This enlightened

N. S. della Fortuna
venerata nella Chiesa di S. Carlo
in GENOVA (via Balbi)

A typical mass card for men at sea

environmentalism predates our own awareness by centuries.) The first reference to the Consuls of the Sea was in a document dated March 12, 1430, although they were thought to have existed since the late fourteenth century. The consuls would create law, set policy, adjudicate disputes, coordinate harbor traffic. They were an essential part of San Remo life and commerce well into the nineteenth century. The tradition was revived following the Second World War, although now only two consuls are selected and their functions are purely ceremonial.

Camogli (the name means "Home of Wives," for the women who stayed behind) has another famous festival of recent vintage, the Sagra del Pesce, which is held on the second weekend of May. This is to thank San Fortunato, one of the patron saints of fishermen, for his protection during the Second World War. It seems that after praying to the saint for help in feeding the starving town, the fishermen went to sea, which was heavily laden with German mines, for an entire night. A very generous catch was taken and every fisherman returned to the port unharmed. The fish was preserved or turned into sauces and spreads, and the people of Camogli were able to live through the rest of the war on the provisions gathered that night.

Each May, on the second Saturday night, solemn processions walk through the streets of town, and all of the citizens gather in the church to pray for the safety of its fishermen and sailors. Then the fishermen of town go to sea and return the following dawn with boats full of fish. On Sunday, there is a feast in which an immense frying pan (13 feet/4 meters in diameter with a handle that is 19½ feet/6 meters long) is set up in the harbor and the fishermen fry thousands of kilos of fish that are distributed free to the people of the town.

After all of the townspeople have been served, the ever-increasing number of tourists who come to observe the feast are then fed. This is a sacred feast that has strong significance for the *camogliesi*. Their choice to feed their own first is not a lack of generosity, but rather a desire to assure that every citizen, young and old, feels connected to the history and tradition of Camogli. In my first year in town, I was asked to eat when the tourists are fed, but since then I have been included with the townspeople, which is an honor indeed.

The oldest fisherman in Camogli, eighty-nine years old when the photograph of him in the first section of color illustrations was taken in the summer of 1995, is nicknamed "Napoli." No one seems to know, or remember, what his real name is. He began working in 1918 as a cabin boy on ships and at some point in his adolescence lost an eye. Soon after, he became a fisherman and did it for decades before moving on to the typical occupation of old *pescatori,* net-mending. Wherever you look in Camogli, nets are spread out on rocks hung to dry, or piled in majestic mountains on docks.

Although "Napoli" eats fish, as does everyone else in Camogli, he has a certain tenderness for them that many of his colleagues share. This is born of a love, respect, and fear of the sea. "Just think," he told me, "what a terrible life little fish lead. If they swim too deep they will be eaten by larger fish. If they come too close to the surface they will be devoured by sea birds. And if they manage to grow big, they will end up in my net. Is that any kind of life?"

On a cliff overlooking the port is the rest home for retired men of the sea. This place is part of the Ligurian tradition of caring for others in the community, which makes this region different from most other Italian regions, where the family is the social center and the source of protection and care. The men live in the rest home, awash in the sounds of the waves below that rock them gently back to memories of days and nights at sea.

A feast akin to Camogli's Sagra del Pesce is held each September in Badalucco, in the *entroterra* of the province of Imperia. Badalucco is, as my friend Philippa Davenport described it, the town that gives all praise to cod. More than six hundred years ago, the people of Badalucco survived a siege by the Genoese by living on stockfish, dried (unsalted) cod that can last for years. I am convinced that the fishy smell must have driven the Genoese away, but it is catnip to the people (and cats) of Badalucco. The fish is soaked for several days in running cold water, and then meticulously scrubbed by the women of town, all outfitted with bathing caps and rubber gloves (see the photo in the first section of color illustrations).

The men of town then cook the fish in giant vats in combination with divine local olive oil, plus hazelnuts, pine nuts, mushrooms, anchovies, white wine, garlic, and parsley. The combination cooks for sixteen hours, which explains why I have chosen not to provide you with a recipe in this book. The feast is held after a long night of cooking. There are always visiting Norwegians (who supply the stockfish) and usually 15,000 people turn out for this feast, which is offered by this charming town of 1,000 very healthy, happy people.

Ligurians who did not fish usually went to sea in commercial ships and, more recently, as staff on cruise liners. Tiny Camogli was not only a fishing port, but in the nineteenth century was a bigger shipbuilding center than Hamburg. It raised experienced mariners such as Simone Schiaffino, the man who organized the fleet of ships to carry Garibaldi and his men to Sicily and up the coast to forge a united Italy.

When Ligurians went to sea, they generally garnered the respect of the places they visited. People from Genoa still are accorded a great welcome at Black Sea ports owing to the civilized conduct of business by the Republic of Genoa six hundred years ago. The venerable title character of Joseph Conrad's *Nostromo* is a Ligurian. It is remarkable that Conrad, who never saw Liguria, understood the region so well — this is because of the frequent contact he had with Ligurian seamen in his travels on the oceans of the world.

Ligurian sailors in their denim outfits arrived in San Francisco for the Gold Rush of 1849, and Levi Strauss adapted the material to create blue jeans (from the name *blu di genova,* the Ligurian description of denim). The Ligurians who remained in California created wonderful farms and fisheries, and were among the founders of the California wine industry.

Many Ligurian sailors never came home. Many died of disease or drowning, while others created homes elsewhere. Left behind were parents, wives, girlfriends, and children. In just about every Ligurian home I have visited, there is a collection of vintage photographs of men who went to sea, many never to return. The one on the facing page, dated 1881, is from a family collection in Savona. Behind each of these photographs is a story of fortunes made, fortunes not made, occasions lost, dreams deferred. In the eyes of these ancient mariners, one sees the tortured, dramatic, yet noble history of the men of Liguria who went to sea and of the women who tilled the land and raised families while their men were away.

Giuseppe Fazzi

SAVONA

*Photographs like this one
are in many Ligurian homes.*

Fish
&
Seafood

Pesce alla Ligure	Fish, Ligurian Style
Pesce al Vapore	Poached Fish
Pesce alla Praese	Small Fish as Prepared in the Town of Prà
Branzino al Sale	Sea Bass Baked in Salt
Scaloppe di Branzino in Crema di Asparagi	Sea Bass Fillets in Asparagus Sauce
Rospo con Carciofi	Monkfish with Artichokes
Rospo al Vermentino	Monkfish in a Vermentino Wine Sauce
Frittata di Rossetti	"Redbait" Omelette
Bagnun di Acciughe	Fishermen's Anchovy Casserole
Capponadda	Capponadda
Cappon Magro	Cappon Magro
Buridda	Fish and Seafood Stew
Buridda di Stoccafisso	Stockfish Stew
Stoccafisso alla Chelbi	Stockfish with Vegetables
Seppie del Pescatore	Fisherman's Cuttlefish Casserole
Seppie in Umido con Patate	Stewed Cuttlefish with Potatoes
Seppie in Zimino	Stewed Cuttlefish with Greens
Moscardini in Umido all'Aglio	Stewed Baby Octopus

WHILE LIGURIA is a famously coastal region, it does not benefit from the same rich waters that one finds near Sicily, or the Atlantic coasts of Spain, France, Norway, Iceland, Canada, and the United States, or the Pacific coasts of North and South America, Asia, Australia, and New Zealand. The waters near Liguria have historically been rather poor, and the problem has only compounded in recent years as demand for fish has risen and portions of the Mediterranean have become polluted.

However, the clever Ligurians have always made the best of what they had, and found additional sources of fish further afield. The first thing to understand about Ligurian fish cookery is that they have mastered the use of *pesce azzurro* (which would translate inaccurately into English as "blue fish"). These are, in fact, the small fish such as anchovies and sardines that have blue or silver scales. These fish are eaten fresh in Liguria as often as they are preserved. In their fresh form they bear no resemblance to the strong-flavored salty fish that we think of coming in tubes or cans that can be opened with a key.

Pesce azzurro is remarkably nutritious, and Ligurians can ascribe some of their robust health to their regular consumption of this fish. Fresh sardines and anchovies are more readily found in our markets than ever before, especially if you live on the coast or in a major urban center. If you do not find them, ask your fishmonger to get them.

Ligurians have long enjoyed tuna, usually packed in their own olive oil. The tuna is usually caught off the coast of Tunisia in North Africa, where large Genoese trawlers have paid for fishing rights for hundreds of years. In addition, certain fish from the sea are caught in small numbers, and are usually steamed (*al vapore*) or prepared *alla ligure* (with olives and *pinoli*).

The other major Ligurian fish is stockfish (dried cod), which has been purchased from Norway for more than five hundred years. The most famous stockfish preparations are in Badalucco, in the province of Imperia. This is described on page 317. Sources to buy stockfish are listed on page 446 and page 456.

Do not confuse stockfish with *baccalà,* which is salt cod. *Baccalà* is more popular in the Veneto, in Spain, and in Portugal. It must be soaked in many changes of water to rid it of its saltiness, while stockfish (which is rock-hard), must be soaked at length to make it soft enough to cook. While I have had fun at the Stockfish Festival of Badalucco, the smell is not the memory I cherish. I remember a long table of smiling Ligurian women with rubber gloves singing as they cleaned the fish in preparation for the feast. But that was enough stockfish to feed thousands of people. The smell of one fish in your own kitchen is not a problem. If you prefer, you may use fresh cod, although that is considerably more expensive.

Ligurians have some seafood at their disposal, especially mussels (*muscoli*), clams (*datteri, mitili,* and *arselle*), octopus (*polpo*), and baby octopus (*moscardini*). Where Ligurians far exceed most other peoples in fish and seafood cookery is their ability to match the flavors of the land — herbs, potatoes, greens, even cheese, ham, and sausage — with certain fish and seafoods to make memorable dishes. You will find those and other recipes in this chapter. You should also consult the chapter on sauces, condiments, and spreads, beginning on page 57, for ideas about flavoring fish and seafood.

Remember also to look for more fish and seafood recipes in the antipasti chapter (page 169). Those recipes, and many in this chapter, may be used interchangeably because Ligurians are much more liberal than most Italians when it comes to deciding where particular preparations should appear in a meal.

Pesce alla Ligure

Fish, Ligurian Style

This is a simple but always delicious preparation that relies on the freshness of the fish being used. Although this preparation is done in a baking dish, there is a version used on fishing boats that employs a skillet. Typically, a Ligurian cook uses per serving one small whole fish that came from the sea only shortly before being cooked. Among the choices are *orata* (gilthead), *branzino* (sea bass), or *triglia* (red mullet). You may also use a small red snapper or another pink- or white-fleshed fish that is not too delicate in flavor. See the photograph in the second section of color illustrations.

2 whole fish, approximately 8 ounces / 225 g each
A few sprigs fresh marjoram, tarragon, or rosemary (optional)
½ cup / 110 ml dry white wine, preferably Ligurian
¼ cup / 55 ml Ligurian extravirgin olive oil
¼ cup / 110 g small black olives, preferably Taggia or Gaeta
1 pinch salt (optional)
2 teaspoons / 5 g minced fresh garlic
2 tablespoons / 15 g chopped fresh Italian (flat) parsley

Preheat oven to 350°F/180°C. Carefully gut, clean, and scale each fish, leaving the head and tail intact. If you choose to, place a little fresh marjoram, tarragon, or rosemary in the cavity of each fish. Then place the fish in a baking dish large enough so that the fish fit in snugly but without pressing up against the sides or against one another. Combine the wine and oil in a bowl or measuring cup and then pour this mixture over the fish. Add the olives and optional salt to the liquid. Cover with aluminum foil and bake for 15 to 20 minutes, or until the fish flakes easily at the touch of a fork. When the fish is cooked, toss on the garlic and parsley and serve the fish on a plate to which the olives and some cooking liquid have been added.

Makes 2 servings

COOK'S VARIATION: Whether you place some herbs in the fish's cavity is up to you. This decision is a personal one for every Ligurian cook. But one distinct variation in this dish is that in eastern Liguria, cooks tend to toss raw garlic on top of the finished dish while in western Liguria they add garlic to the uncooked dish (or even put it in the fish's cavity). The choice for you really depends on whether you prefer raw or cooked garlic.

Pesce al Vapore

Poached Fish

See the recipe for Brodo di Pesce (page 285) for details. This is a simple preparation that relies simply on your having the freshest possible fish and your dedication to seeing that the fish is not overcooked. It is preferable to select smaller fish, or in any event about ½ pound/225 grams per person. The poached fish is best served, hot or cold, with boiled potatoes and one or more sauces of your choice.

Cultivation of basil in Prà

Pesce alla Praese
Small Fish as Prepared in the Town of Prà

The town of Prà is just beyond the western boundary of Genoa and is reachable on the city's mass transit system. It is a slightly rough-and-tumble place on the periphery of a major metropolitan area, but cultists of basil know that this is the epicenter of great basil growing. The herb finds its way into just about every dish in Prà, yet no one seems to tire of it. I first tasted Acciughe (fresh anchovies) alla Praese at the Trattoria-Bar Le Caravelle, whose clientele is strictly local. It was prepared by Lidia Tassone, a small dark-haired woman who is very serious about her cooking. This simple dish, which can also be prepared with fresh anchovies, sardines, or almost any small silver or white fish, benefits from the unmistakable flavor and fragrance of *basilico di Prà*. If that is not available to you, select the most perfumed small leaf basil you can locate. In the United States this type of basil is sometimes called Genoese or Genovese basil.

½ pound / 225 g fresh anchovies, sardines, or other small silver or white fish
4 tablespoons / 2 ounces / ¼ cup / 60 ml Ligurian extravirgin olive oil
8 tablespoons / 4 ounces / ½ cup / 120 ml dry white wine, preferably Ligurian
2 tablespoons / 1 ounce / ⅛ cup / 30 ml fresh lemon juice (optional)
8 tablespoons / 2 ounces / ½ cup / 60 g tiny basil leaves, or larger basil leaves torn
into small pieces

Makes
4 servings
as an appetizer,
2 servings
as a main course

Thoroughly wash each little fish, cutting off the head but leaving the tail. Remove some of the skin from the upper part of the fish, although you do not have to do this too assiduously. Split the fish in half by cutting vertically along its belly. Lift out the skeleton and then rinse the inside of the fish thoroughly. Pat each fish dry with paper toweling. After all of the fish have been cleaned, heat the olive oil gently in a large, heavy-bottomed pan. When the oil is hot, place the fish in the pan in a single layer. Cook for 1 minute over medium heat and then pour in the wine. Cook for 1 more minute and then, if you want, add the lemon juice. Whether or not you use the juice, you should cook the fish for 1 more minute (a total of 3 minutes). Then add all of the basil leaves and swirl the pan for 1 minute so that the juices are infused with the flavor of the basil. Depending on the thickness of the fish you are using, the total cooking time should be between 4 and 6 minutes. Serve the fish hot with the sauce and basil leaves.

Branzino al Sale

Sea Bass Baked in Salt

There is a long tradition in several parts of the Mediterranean of baking fish in a salt crust, and Liguria is one of those places. The salt acts as a sealant and allows the fish to become very moist without drying. For the most part, the salt flavor does not penetrate the fish, so what you are left with is perfect fish flavor. While this recipe is for sea bass, you may also use other good, high-quality fish with white flesh, such as dentex, striped bass, trout, hake, gilthead bream, sea bream, striped bream, and red snapper. Because fish differ in size, the following formula is to use based on the weight of the fish: The amount of salt you use should be twice the weight of the fish.

1 sea bass or other fish (for example, 4½ pounds/2 kilos)
Coarse sea salt (for example, 8¾ pounds/4 kilos)

Gut and carefully wash the fish, but do not remove the scales. Do not remove the head or tail. Dry the fish gently with paper toweling. Spread half of the salt in a large baking dish. Place the fish on the salt bed and then top with more salt. The fish should be entirely encased. Place the dish in a preheated 475°F/ 240°C oven.

On average, a fish should bake for about 35 minutes for a salt crust to form. Every so often, add a few drops of water, which will help the salt crust form. The fish will be cooked when the crust is rock-hard. Remove from the oven and, using a hammer, break the crust and remove the fish. Remove the skin and then serve immediately.

Scaloppe di Branzino in Crema di Asparagi
Sea Bass Fillets in Asparagus Sauce

This recipe is an adaptation of the one served at the Locanda Miranda in Tellaro in the province of La Spezia. The original preparation, as made by chef Angelo Cabani, is quite delicious but very labor-intensive. I have made a few adjustments that will save you time and effort in the kitchen without sacrificing flavor and subtlety.

4 sea bass fillets, each about ½ pound/250 g, carefully washed and patted dry with paper toweling
5 (2 + 3) tablespoons/75 (30 + 45) ml delicate Ligurian extravirgin olive oil
1 tablespoon/15 ml fresh lemon juice
Sea salt to taste
Freshly ground black pepper to taste
2 cloves garlic, peeled and split in half, with the green heart removed
1 pound/500 g green or white asparagus, washed and gently scraped, with the tough ends cut off and discarded
2 scallions, finely minced
¾ cup/6 ounces/1 glass/85 ml Ligurian dry white wine
1 tablespoon salmon roe*
2 egg yolks**

* Signor Cabani's recipe calls for salmon roe, which does give a particularly subtle and delicious minor note in the palette of flavors. However, if you cannot locate salmon roe (which, after all, is not particularly Ligurian), you may make one of the following substitutions (in order of preference): ¼ ounce/7 g *bottarga* (dried mullet or tuna roe) or ¼ teaspoon/1½ g anchovy paste.

** Some readers of this book may live in areas where they do not have full faith in the safety of raw egg yolks. This is an unfortunate development in modern times, as less attention (and government regulation) has been devoted to protecting our food. If you would rather not use raw egg yolks, I suggest that you substitute a level teaspoon of mayonnaise.

Makes
4 servings

Set a large pot of cold water to boil. When it reaches a boil, add a pinch of salt. After setting the water to boil, gently wash and dry the sea bass fillets, and then marinate them in a dish with 2 tablespoons/30 ml olive oil, the lemon juice, and salt and pepper to taste.

As soon as the water returns to a boil, cook the split garlic cloves for about 15 seconds to soften them. Fish them out with a slotted spoon and mince them. Now immerse the asparagus in the boiling water and cook for about 6 minutes.

You need to save a few tablespoons of the cooking water for use later on. Carefully fish out the asparagus (so that you do not break the tips) and let them drain in a colander. Then transfer them to a clean cutting board and cut them 1 inch/2.5 cm below the tip. Set these smaller pieces with the tips aside in a warm spot and then chop the longer asparagus stems into little pieces.

Now cook the fish: Heat 3 tablespoons of olive oil in a heavy-bottomed pan and add the garlic and shallots. Sauté gently for 5 minutes and then add the wine and a tablespoon of the hot cooking water. Cook until the liquid reduces by half. Then add the sea bass fillets (having discarded the marinade) and cook for 5 minutes. Turn the fillets and cook for another 5 minutes.

While the fish is cooking, make the sauce. Place the chopped asparagus stems in a food processor or blender and run until the asparagus is reduced to liquid. If you are using egg yolks, add them to the asparagus and process just until the yolks and asparagus are combined. If you are using *bottarga* or anchovy paste instead of salmon roe, you should add these at the same time as you do the egg yolks. The sauce is now ready.

If you are using mayonnaise and salmon roe, you should liquefy the asparagus and then remove it to a mixing bowl. Stir in the mayonnaise and the roe and the sauce will be ready.

Once the sauce is made, pour a small amount in the center of individual plates for each diner. When the fish fillets are cooked, place one on each plate atop the little pool of sauce. Place 2 or 3 asparagus tips to one side of the fish. You might place 1 or 2 small boiled potatoes on the other side, and then serve immediately.

Rospo con Carciofi

Monkfish with Artichokes

I tasted this dish in Albenga, which is famous for its artichokes.

8 slices monkfish fillet, about 4 ounces / 100 g each
Unbleached flour
Freshly ground black or white pepper (optional)
1 tablespoon / 7 g unsalted butter
2 tablespoons / 30 ml Ligurian extravirgin olive oil
4 baby artichokes, washed, outer leaves removed, coarsely chopped
1 teaspoon / 2 to 3 g capers (optional)
1 clove garlic, green heart removed, minced
Scant ½ cup / 100 ml dry Ligurian white wine
2 sprigs fresh Italian (flat) parsley, minced

*Makes
4 servings*

Wash and carefully dry the monkfish fillets. Coat them thoroughly but not heavily with flour, to which you may have added some pepper to taste. Take a heavy-bottomed skillet and melt the butter with the olive oil over medium heat. Once the oil is hot but not smoky, add the monkfish fillets to the pan. Cook them for 1 minute, giving the pan a couple of vigorous shakes so the fish does not stick. Then add the artichokes, optional capers, and garlic. Cook for about 8 minutes, turning the fish fillets after 4 minutes. Then add the wine and parsley and cook for 3 minutes over medium-high heat until the wine evaporates.

Rospo al Vermentino
Monkfish in a Vermentino Wine Sauce

The key to the flavor of this dish relies almost entirely on the wine you use. If it is possible to find Ligurian Vermentino, that is your best bet. Failing that, Vermentino from Tuscany or Sardinia will do. If none of these is available, then use a dry white such as Orvieto or Vernaccia di San Gimignano, but this would then be only a faint approximation of what the dish tastes like in Liguria.

2 pounds / 1 scant kilo monkfish fillet, cut into 4 pieces
Unbleached flour
Freshly ground black or white pepper (optional)
6 tablespoons / ⅜ cup / 85 ml Ligurian extravirgin olive oil
1 tablespoon / 7 g unsalted butter (optional)
2 sprigs fresh Italian (flat) parsley, minced
1 large clove garlic, with the green heart removed, minced
1 bottle (¾ liter) Ligurian Vermentino wine

After washing and drying (in paper toweling) the monkfish fillets, flour them lightly on all sides. You may grind some black or white pepper into the flour if that suits your taste. In a large, heavy-bottomed skillet for which you have a cover, heat the oil (and, if you wish, melt in the optional butter, which will give the dish a richer flavor). When the oil is hot but not spattering, add the parsley and garlic and then immediately add the monkfish pieces. Quickly cook the fish on both sides so that it takes on a bit of color and absorbs the fragrances of garlic and parsley. Then pour in the wine gently, cover the pan, and cook over a low flame for about 10 minutes, or until the fish flakes at the touch of a fork. Serve each piece of fish on a warm plate, adding 2 tablespoons of sauce and garnishing, if you wish, with a lemon slice and a sprig of fresh parsley.

Makes 4 servings

Frittata di Rossetti
"Redbait" Omelette

The term *redbait* has a different and unattractive connotation in American English than *rossetti* in Italian, but there is not a proper English term to describe the fry (newborn fish) of red mullet. In Liguria, *bianchetti* (or *gianchetti* in dialect) are whitebait, or the fry of anchovies. *Rossetti,* to Ligurians, are just as delicious but they taste slightly different. This recipe was taught to me by an old fisherman who wears an eyepatch and is well known to the locals at the docks of Porto Maurizio (Imperia). Whenever I run into him, he takes a long time to tell some tall yarn of the sea before I can ask him a simple question such as "How are you today?" I have never been able to learn this man's name; I think he does not reveal it to maintain some air of mystery. Yet he has been a valuable, if somewhat garrulous, resource for how Ligurian fishermen did things in years past. This is a simple and wonderful dish that is made aboard boats and all along the Ligurian coast.

10 ounces / 2½ cups / 300 g rossetti (or bianchetti if rossetti are unavailable)
4 large eggs
2 tablespoons finely minced fresh Italian (flat) parsley
½ clove garlic, green heart removed, minced
2 tablespoons Ligurian extravirgin olive oil

*Makes
2 to 4 servings*

Wash the *rossetti* thoroughly and let them drain in a finely meshed strainer so that the water runs out but you do not lose the baby fish. Beat the eggs, parsley, and garlic in a bowl only until they are thoroughly combined. Then add the *rossetti* and gently stir so that all of the ingredients combine. Heat the oil in a heavy-bottomed pan or skillet over medium-high heat. Add the egg mixture and, as the fisherman said to me, "*Deve sentire prima un buon calore,*" or "The combination must feel some good heat." This should occur within 15 to 20 seconds of your adding the egg mixture to the pan. Then lower the flame and move the whole frittata about with a fork so that it does not stick and so that the interior cooks until firm. Slide the frittata onto a large plate and then flip it back into the pan so that the other side cooks until it is golden and firm. Serve hot or let cool to a tepid temperature. The frittata is typically cut into wedges before serving.

A Meager Catch

It is often said that the Mediterranean has been overfished and that demand for good fish far exceeds supply. This, however, is not a new phenomenon, and it was remarked upon in 1861 by J. Henry Bennet, M.D., in his book *Mentone and the Riviera as a Winter Climate.*

"The cold oceans and seas are those in which fish, especially good edible fish, thrive the most and are the most prolific. The cod, the mackerel, the herring, the sole, the salmon, all belong to northern latitudes. . . . The fish [in the Mediterranean] is in general neither good nor abundant, which accounts for the Roman Catholic inhabitants of its shores consuming so large a quantity of the product of the herring and the cod fisheries of Northern Europe" . . . a fisherman on the Riviera might pull in "but a few pounds weight of a minute transparent whitebait-looking fish, a few sardines and small red mullets, some diminutive sword-fish fry, and two or three crabs, the size of a five shilling piece, that have not been able to get out of the way."

Bagnun di Acciughe

Fishermen's Anchovy Casserole

Every night fishermen throughout Liguria set sail at dusk and fish until dawn. From the shore the small lights that hang from the edge of their small craft on the dark sea look like jewels displayed on black velvet. This is the nightly spectacle I have witnessed from my window in Camogli. One day I asked one of the fishermen what they eat during the night, and had the happy opportunity to learn firsthand. Many fishermen keep a small burner on board to make delicious one-pot meals, including this one.

2 pounds / 900 g fresh anchovies (often available upon request from better fish markets)
4 tablespoons / 60 ml Ligurian extravirgin olive oil
2 cloves garlic, green hearts removed, minced,
*   plus 2 more cut in half, green hearts removed*
1 medium onion, minced
5 fresh plum tomatoes, chopped coarsely, seeds removed and liquid drained
Sea salt
Freshly ground black pepper
¾ cup / 175 ml dry white wine, preferably Vermentino
3 sprigs fresh Italian (flat) parsley, minced
1 piece toasted white Italian bread per person
2 sprigs fresh oregano, minced

Makes
4 to 6 servings

Wash the anchovies and remove the heads. Split them down the middle and remove the bones and the internal parts. Wash them carefully and dry them with paper toweling. Heat the olive oil gently in a casserole or pot and add the minced garlic and onion. Sauté until the onions become transparent and then add the tomatoes, and salt and pepper to taste. Cook for 10 minutes, stirring gently every so often. Add half of the white wine and cook for about 5 minutes or until the wine has evaporated. Push the tomato mixture to the sides of the pot and place the anchovies in layers on the bottom. Push part of the tomato mixture on top of the anchovies, add the parsley and rest of the wine, cover, and cook gently for 10 minutes. While the casserole is cooking, toast the bread slices and rub them with the fresh garlic halves. Place a slice at the bottom of each serving bowl. When the casserole is ready, spoon some into each bowl and then top with some minced fresh oregano.

Serve accompanied by dry white wine, preferably Vermentino (or, alternatively, Pigato or Vernaccia di San Gimignano).

Santa Margherita

"Santa Margherita is an attractive small town linked with the harbour by a road on the very edge of the sea and a long colonnade, under the protection of which the fish market is conducted with voluble gossip. Scampi, triglia, prawns and all other ingredients of *frito misto* lie on black slate tables. The peasant women have their own personal scales, lifting them into the air as they measure the weight intently before telling the purchaser the price. Above the colonnade grow bougainvillaea, geraniums and red-hot pokers. A monument to six partisans and eighteen hostages shot by the Germans [during World War II] has a place of honour on the waterfront, near the monument to World War I. This represents a soldier whose steel helmet has fallen off. The little harbour is stuffed with sailing boats, row boats and small yachts.

"The surrounding houses are coloured terra-cotta or café au lait, all with green shutters. One of them is the Trattoria dei Pescatori, a regional eating place gay with bunting and consisting of two long narrow rooms leading into one another. Check table cloths, gay frescoes and a merry proprietor add to the enjoyment of the 'fish soup'. This consists of a mixed grill of red mullet, chicken fish, cuttlefish, mussels, priest fish, crayfish and capone served in an enormous bowl full of fish stock and crusts of bread — a meal in itself."

— Charles Graves, *Italy Revisited,* 1950

Capponadda

This is an ancient dish, one closely linked to Ligurian maritime tradition. It is the dish that sailors and fishermen ate at sea that was sort of a poor version of Cappon Magro, the recipe that follows. A key ingredient that is now difficult to locate is *mosciame,* which is dried tuna. In Liguria it has become rare, too. If you have access to tuna carpaccio (thin slices of sushi-quality raw tuna), which has become increasingly popular, you may substitute it. Otherwise, omit this ingredient. The saltiness of this dish was thought to be an antidote to seasickness. This recipe comes from the Trattoria a Cantinn-a in Cavi di Lavagna (Genoa).

4 gallette del marinaio *(rusks or Uneeda biscuits can make a marginally acceptable substitute)*
1 clove garlic, cut in half, with the green heart removed
2 tablespoons/30 ml water
2 tablespoons/30 ml red wine vinegar
8 ounces/225 g high-quality tuna packed in olive oil, drained, separated into bite-size pieces
1½ cups/170 g Ligurian olives packed in brine
4 salt-packed anchovies, cut into small bits
1 ounce/30 g capers packed in salt
1 tablespoon/7 g minced fresh oregano or thyme
2 large tomatoes, ripe but firm, cut into slices
12 thin slices mosciame or tuna carpaccio (if available)
20 small basil leaves or 10 large leaves, torn in half, wiped clean
Ligurian extravirgin olive oil

Makes
4 servings

Rub the sailor's biscuits with garlic and then douse each biscuit with a tablespoon of water mixed with vinegar. Then break them into large pieces and place them at the bottom of a bowl. Top with the tuna, olives, anchovies, capers, and oregano and toss to combine the ingredients. Top the bowl with a layer of tomatoes, *mosciame* (if available), and basil. Add a little olive oil and then toss the salad after presenting it at the table.

Cappon Magro

This dish is at once very Ligurian and yet not at all typical of any other food preparation. In its opulent show of excess it is antithetical to everything Ligurians hold dear. Yet in its attention to quality, to festivity, and to subtlety, it suits Liguria perfectly. With ingredients piled high like a maritime pyramid of Cheops, Cappon Magro is the extravagant consummation of the wedding of the land and the sea. In that this dish is food as architecture, which became all the rage among fancy American chefs in the early 1990s, it was far ahead of its time. Architectural food presentation is now chic in fancy American restaurants, but Cappon Magro has always been the ultimate expression of that aesthetic. It seems that many of the ingredients come in pairs, as if the dish had been invented by Noah. Cappon Magro is so unusual because it, more than any recipe I can name from any place, contains practically all of the nonsweet ingredients of a region, in this case from the land and the sea. It is not certain what the origins of this dish are. The name means, ironically, "lean cappone," a type of fish. This dish is anything but lean, although no single ingredient is terribly fattening. Cappon Magro is usually served at family feasts to celebrate the return of a sailor from a long period at sea, and the symbolism is that of uniting the sea and the land, which is in every way the essence of Liguria. In assembling this dish, you should use all of the aesthetic resources you have at your disposal. Pile the ingredients to create a pyramid and, if you place an ingredient in one spot, put the same ingredient in the diametrically opposing spot so that there will be a pleasing symmetry in the construction of this edible edifice.

FOR THE SAUCE
1 small piece soft white bread
1 ounce/2 tablespoons/30 ml red wine vinegar
1 cup/115 g fresh Italian (flat) parsley
1 clove garlic, peeled, with the green heart removed
1 pinch coarse sea salt
6 tablespoons/⅜ cup/40 g pinoli
3 tablespoons/³⁄₁₆ cup/20 g capers packed in vinegar or brine
2 large hard-boiled eggs
5 olives, pitted, or 1 tablespoon olive paste (see page 94)
3 ounces/⅓ cup/85 ml Ligurian extravirgin olive oil

1 2¼ pound / 1 kilo fillet of firm fish such as cod, scrod, gilthead, or dentex,
  cut into 3 pieces
8 baby artichokes, halved, doused in lemon juice
1¼ cups / 5 ounces / 140 g slender green beans
3 large carrots, peeled, cut into bite-size chunks
2 medium zucchini, cut into thick disks
2 medium potatoes, peeled, cut into bite-size chunks
½ head small cauliflower, cored, cut into florets
2 medium beets, peeled
3 gallette del marinaio (see page 151 for recipe, and page 446 for shopping sources;
  if you absolutely cannot obtain gallette del marinaio, *Uneeda biscuits make a*
  marginally acceptable substitute)
1 clove garlic, cut in half, with the green heart removed
½ cup / 115 ml red wine vinegar

FOR THE GARNISH

1 lobster, about 2 pounds / 1 kilo, boiled or steamed, cooled, cut into 8 pieces with
  the shell still attached
8 large shrimp or prawns, boiled, shells removed
8 raw oysters
8 whole mushrooms packed in oil
8 green or black olives

1) First make the sauce. Soak the bread in vinegar. Then, in a mortar, *Makes* pound the bread, parsley, garlic, salt, *pinoli,* capers, eggs, and olives (or paste). *8 servings* Once everything is combined, stir in the olive oil to make a velvety sauce.

2) Now prepare the ingredients for the pyramid and the garnish.

First, boil the lobster and the shrimp in different pots of water, then let cool. Cut the lobster into 8 pieces, and remove the shells from the shrimp.

Place the fish fillet, cut into 3 pieces, into a pan and add enough cold water just to cover the fish. Add a pinch of sea salt and cook over medium heat. The water should merely simmer. Cook for about 15 minutes, or until the fish flakes at the touch of a fork. Remove from the water.

Boil each vegetable separately until they are tender. Start with the artichokes, and end with the beets. Set each aside.

Open the oysters. Set aside.

3) Make the pyramid. Rub each *galletta del marinaio* with garlic and douse with vinegar. Place them in the center of a large platter, one next to the other.

Then place a piece of the fish fillet atop each biscuit. Add a coating of sauce atop each piece of fish. Then make a decorative mountain, starting from the extremes of the biscuits and working inward, using all of the cooked vegetables. With each layer of vegetables, add a coating of sauce. Some people like to make a layer of a single vegetable, starting with potatoes or beets or zucchini and ending with artichokes, while other people artfully combine all of the vegetables. The choice is up to you.

4) Garnish the pyramid. Place the 8 oysters strategically around the base of the pyramid. Then stick a mushroom into the side of the pyramid, just above each oyster. Above the mushroom stick an olive. Above the olive, stick a shrimp. Above the shrimp, place a piece of lobster, preferably vertical and giving the impression of reaching upward. Spoon any leftover sauce over the peak of the pyramid so that it runs down the sides, lightly coating the garnish ingredients.

5) Serve with great fanfare, and good Ligurian white wine.

The Sagra del Pesce,
Camogli's famous fish feast

Buridda
Fish and Seafood Stew

Buridda is often said to be the oldest way to cook fish in Liguria. While there is no absolute way to document this, I would think that simple frying or grilling of one type of fish would have occurred before the more complicated task of combining various fish. Also, the typical *buridda* preparation includes tomatoes, which have only appeared with any regularity in the Ligurian kitchen in the last two centuries. Nonetheless, *buridda* does have a place of honor in Liguria and in one way reflects how the cuisine has been transformed. In the past, *buridda* was a dish of the poor. It was made with the odds and ends left in the fish market at closing time that would be sold off at a lower price. Nowadays, a cook shopping for ingredients to make *buridda* can still purchase assorted pieces of fish that the fishmonger cannot otherwise sell because they are too small. However, many Ligurian cooks now buy fancier pieces of fish and costlier seafood. This results in a more princely dish that is often quite delicious, but contradicts the humble origins of a dish that is admirable on its own terms. Your objective while shopping is to buy the freshest fish, preferably ones with a firmer flesh, and to acquire small pieces of several different species. If you live in a place where typical Mediterranean fish are not sold, do not be concerned about authenticity. There are numerous variations on the theme of *buridda* throughout Liguria, and you can allow yourself some latitude based on the fish and seafood available to you. This recipe is rather typical of a *buridda* you might eat in Genoa, while the one that follows, Buridda di Stoccafisso, is notable because it uses only one fish rather than an assortment. That preparation is more frequently found in the Ponente. As with many Ligurian recipes, there is a corresponding dish to *buridda* in Nice, where it is called *bourride*.

Ligurian extravirgin olive oil
2¼ pounds / 1 kilo onions, peeled and sliced very thin
2 cloves garlic, with the green heart removed, minced
1 pound / ½ kilo ripe plum tomatoes, washed and cut into cubes
4 sprigs fresh Italian (flat) parsley, minced
2 sprigs fresh oregano, minced (or 2 small pinches dried oregano)
3½ pounds / 1½ kilos assorted pieces of white or pink firm-fleshed fish fillets (such as monkfish, hake, cod, dentex, grouper, tilapia, bream), carefully washed, dried, and cut into pieces about 2 inches / 5 cm wide
1 pound / ½ kilo assorted seafood (such as shrimp removed from its shell, baby octopus, cuttlefish; but not shellfish such as lobster, crab, mussels, or clams), all thoroughly washed or rinsed
Sea salt

Freshly ground black pepper
¾ cup / 6 ounces / 1 glass / 85 ml dry white wine, preferably Ligurian

Use a casserole or flameproof glass pot. Pour a very thin layer of the best olive oil (preferably Ligurian) that you can find. The oil provides a flavor base for this dish, and using mediocre oil will yield mediocre *buridda*. Place half the onions in the pot on top of the oil. Distribute one of the minced garlic cloves on the onions, and then half of the tomato pieces. Next add half of the parsley and oregano. Add all of the fish and seafood and then add sea salt and pepper to taste. Now add the rest of the onions, garlic, tomatoes, parsley, and oregano. Drizzle 2 tablespoons of olive oil over the whole dish and then pour in the wine. Cover and cook over a very low flame until the liquid in the pot becomes rather concentrated and the fish is soft and the seafood tender. Typically, the cooking time for this dish is about 2 hours.

Makes
6 servings

Buridda di Stoccafisso

Stockfish Stew

This is a typical preparation of the western Riviera and is distinct in that it is a fish stew with only one type of fish (aside from the minor flavor note of the anchovy fillets). If stockfish is unavailable, you may use salt cod (*baccalà*). In either case, the fish must be soaked in several changes of water until soft, then rinsed properly before using it. This recipe comes from Giorgio Delgrande and his sisters, who run the very likable Osteria Vino e Farinata in the old section of Savona. The food at this *osteria* is very genuine, and there is a great respect for Ligurian tradition.

¼ cup/2 ounces/4 tablespoons/60 ml Ligurian extravirgin olive oil
1 medium to large onion, sliced thin
3 cloves garlic, with the green heart removed, minced
½ cup/50 g minced fresh Italian (flat) parsley
4 anchovy fillets, rinsed and deboned, cut into bits
¾ ounce/3 tablespoons/20 g capers, well rinsed
3½ ounces/100 g small black olives, preferably Taggia, Niçoise, or Gaeta, pitted
¾ ounce/3 tablespoons/20 g pinoli
1 tablespoon/15 ml tomato sauce
3½ pounds/1½ kilos stockfish or salt cod that has been properly soaked and rinsed
1 pound/450 g medium potatoes, washed, peeled, and cut into cubes
Sea salt to taste
½ cup/4 ounces/115 ml (100 ml plus 1 tablespoon) dry white wine, preferably Ligurian

Makes 4 servings

Use a casserole or flameproof glass pot. Add the olive oil and gently heat. Add the onions and sauté until they turn golden in color, approximately 10 minutes. Then add the garlic, parsley, and anchovies and cook gently for another 10 minutes, stirring gently to combine all the flavors. Add the capers, olives, *pinoli*, and tomato sauce and cook for 5 minutes. Then add the stockfish and potatoes and a small amount of sea salt to taste. Finally, pour in the white wine, cover the pot, and cook gently for 50 minutes. Once done, the pot should sit for 30 more minutes, covered, before the *buridda di stoccafisso* is served.

Stoccafisso alla Chelbi

Stockfish with Vegetables

I sampled this dish at Da Genio restaurant in Genoa, whose owner, Giovanni Rifaldi, was kind enough to give me the recipe. The key to this dish's successful preparation is the proper selection and handling of the vegetables. They should be at the peak of freshness and ripeness, and should be cut according to the directions given. There will be several bowls, pots, and pans to wash after, but the effort is worth it.

1⅓ pounds / 600 g stockfish that has already been soaked and softened in water, cut
    into bite-size slices (or use salt cod that has been properly soaked and rinsed)
1 tied bunch fresh herbs, including parsley, basil, thyme, and others of your choice
    (I have used chervil and sorrel when available)
14 ounces / 400 g baby or Chinese eggplant, cut into dice-size cubes
14 ounces / 400 g sweet onions, cut into small chunks
9 ounces / 300 g baby zucchini, cut into small chunks
9 ounces / 300 g fresh string beans, washed, with the tips removed
6 ounces / ¾ cup / 175 ml Ligurian extravirgin olive oil
1 large red pepper, washed, seeded, cut into strips
1 large yellow pepper, washed, seeded, cut into strips
Slightly more than 1 pound / 500 g San Marzano plum tomatoes (or you may use a
    28-ounce can, setting aside the liquid), coarsely chopped, with the seeds removed
14 ounces / 400 g firm potatoes, washed, peeled, cut into thin slices
1 pinch paprika
1 pinch sea salt

Set two large pots of cold water to boil. After having previously soaked the *Makes* stockfish, cut it into slices and then boil in one of the pots for 10 minutes along *6 servings* with the bundle of herbs. When the fish is cooked, remove it to a dish and toss away the herbs. When the fish has cooled, remove any remaining skin and bones.

While the fish is cooking, use the boiling water in the other pot to separately steam certain vegetables until they are slightly soft, although not limp (typically this will take about 5 minutes). First do the eggplant; set aside. Then do the onions; then the zucchini, then the string beans. Set each aside. The reason each vegetable is steamed separately is that they all have different cooking times. In a large heavy-bottomed pot or Dutch oven heat the olive oil gently. Add the red and yellow peppers and, after another moment, the tomatoes, which have been coarsely chopped with the seeds removed. Simmer for 5 minutes, stirring occasionally. Add the potatoes, cover, and cook for 5 minutes. Then add the stockfish, cover, and cook for 5 minutes. Then add all of the other vegetables, and cook uncovered for 5 minutes. Toss in the paprika and sea salt, give a quick stir, and serve.

Seppie del Pescatore

Fisherman's Cuttlefish Casserole

This is another of those one-pot stews favored by fishermen, which can be prepared aboard their boats while waiting for the fish to bite. This dish is popular in the Levante side of Liguria.

3½ ounces / scant ½ cup / 100 ml Ligurian extravirgin olive oil
1 medium onion, minced
1 stalk celery, minced
1 small carrot, minced
1 clove garlic, with the green heart removed, minced
1 salted anchovy
1¾ pounds / 800 g cuttlefish, carefully washed and cut lengthwise into ribbons
½ cup / 50 ml dry white wine
4 medium potatoes, peeled, cut into small cubes
1 red pepper, washed, seeds removed, cut into strips
2 plum tomatoes, chopped coarsely and seeded (you may substitute canned tomatoes)
Scant ½ cup / 200 g fresh peas or zucchini cut into cubes
1 dash freshly ground pepper (but not too much)
1 tablespoon pesto (optional)

After preparing all of the ingredients, heat the olive oil in a large, heavy-bottomed pot. Add the onion, celery, carrot, and garlic and sauté. After 1 minute add the anchovy, which you should proceed to mash up with the slotted spoon you are using. When the ingredients become fragrant and the onions translucent, stir in the cuttlefish and sauté for 2 minutes so that all sides are slightly golden yellow. Then add the white wine, cover the pot, and cook over low heat for 10 minutes. Add the potatoes, red pepper strips, tomatoes, the peas or zucchini, and very little black pepper. Cover and cook on low heat for 45 minutes. The stew is now ready to serve. Some fishermen stir a tablespoon of pesto into the pot just before serving to lend a taste of terra firma. This is up to you, but I recommend tasting the dish without pesto before taking the leap.

Makes 4 servings

Seppie in Umido con Patate

Stewed Cuttlefish with Potatoes

The dish will be more successful if you endeavor to use Ligurian products — olive oil, wine, Taggia olives — that will impart the flavors that you would encounter if you ate this dish in Genoa or San Remo.

¾ cup / 175 ml Ligurian extravirgin olive oil
1 clove garlic, with the green heart removed, minced
2 sprigs fresh Italian (flat) parsley, minced
1¾ pounds / 800 g cuttlefish, carefully washed and cut lengthwise into ribbons
1 pound / 450 g medium potatoes, washed, peeled, cut into bite-size chunks
¾ cup / 175 ml Ligurian dry white wine
1 pinch sea salt (optional)
2 plum tomatoes, coarsely chopped, seeds removed
12 black olives, preferably Taggia or Gaeta
4 basil leaves, gently torn
Freshly ground black pepper to taste

Makes
4 servings

Gently heat the olive oil in a heavy-bottomed pot (preferably a terracotta pot with a flameproof bottom, although stainless steel is fine). Add the garlic and parsley and heat for 1 minute. Then add the strips of cuttlefish and cook for a couple of minutes, until they turn light gold in color. Add the potatoes, wine, and optional sea salt, give everything a good stir to combine the ingredients, and then cover and cook over low heat for 20 minutes. Add the tomatoes, olives, and basil, combine the ingredients with a quick stir, cover, and cook for 10 more minutes. Serve, with black pepper available for those who want it.

Seppie in Zimino
Stewed Cuttlefish with Greens

The original Ligurian term *zemin* has been changed in Italian to *zimino*. It is thought that the word derives from the Turkish *semin* and the Arabic *saminun*. Its original significance was a dish cooked with greens, but in Liguria a *zimino* might also be cooked with chickpeas or, for that matter, other legumes and vegetables. But the idea of slow-cooked vegetables with the possible addition of meat or seafood has endured. Traditionally this dish is made with *bietole* (beet greens), but you can also use Swiss chard, spinach, or these three greens in combination. I once made this dish at home in New York using collard greens and, although they are not especially Ligurian, the results were outstanding.

6 tablespoons/85 ml Ligurian extravirgin olive oil
1 large onion, cut into small pieces
1 small bunch fresh Italian (flat) parsley, minced
2 cloves garlic, with the green hearts removed, minced
1 stalk celery, minced
1¾ pounds/800 g cuttlefish, carefully washed and cut lengthwise into ribbons
¾ cup/1 glass/175 ml Ligurian white wine
2¼ pounds/1 kilo greens of your choice, carefully washed and with tough ends cut
    away, then coarsely chopped
1 tablespoon/15 ml tomato sauce or 1 plum tomato, seeds removed, minced (optional)
Scant ⅓ cup/150 g canned chickpeas, drained of their liquid (optional)
1 ounce/30 g pinoli, lightly toasted, if you wish (optional)
1 ounce/30 g raisins (optional)

Heat the olive oil in a large, heavy-bottomed stew pot. Add the onion, parsley, garlic, and celery and sauté for 1 minute, being careful not to burn them. Then add the cuttlefish and cook for 5 minutes so they gather the flavors of the pot. Add the wine, cover, and cook over low heat for 10 minutes. Add the greens, cover, and cook for 30 to 40 minutes, or until the cuttlefish pieces are tender. This is the basic preparation and is very good. There are local variations throughout Liguria and you may add any or all of the optional ingredients. If you wish to add the tomatoes and/or the chickpeas, they should be added 10 minutes before cooking is completed. If you wish to add the *pinoli* (wonderful when toasted!) and/or the raisins, they should be tossed in when cooking is completed and the stew should be given a thorough stir before the dish is served.

Makes
6 to 8 servings

Moscardini in Umido all'Aglio
Stewed Baby Octopus

Toss aside your preconceptions about these little creatures, which are succulent and delicious. They are easy to find in better seafood shops. This dish is also very easy to prepare.

2 pounds / 1 scant kilo fresh baby octopus,
*   about 1 inch / 2.5 cm in size, carefully washed*
3 tablespoons / 45 ml Ligurian extravirgin olive oil
4 to 5 garlic cloves, cut in half, with the green heart removed
2 plum tomatoes, seeds removed
1 stalk rosemary (optional) or dried hot red pepper to taste (optional)

Makes
4 servings
as a main course,
6 to 8 servings
as an antipasto

Wash the octopus and set them aside without drying them. In a heavy-bottomed pot place the olive oil, garlic, tomatoes, and, if you are using them, either the rosemary or the hot red pepper. Place the octopus on this combination. Wrap the lid of the pot with a clean, light cloth and close the lid tightly on the pot. Cook over medium heat for 20 minutes without lifting the lid. Every few minutes you should shake the pot to prevent the contents from sticking. When the cooking time has elapsed, serve the octopus and sauce piping hot.

Moscardini *(baby octopus)*

The Hard-Headed Women
of San Remo (1879)

It is still common, in the Liguria of today, to see women carry baskets on their heads, especially women in the Cinqueterre who are bringing newly picked grapes in from the vineyards. In the town of Lavagna (Genoa), it is possible to see women transport sheets of slate on their heads without seeming terribly put upon. William Miller, in his book *Wintering in the Riviera with Notes of Travel in Italy and France and Practical Hints to Travellers* (1879), described the talents of the women of San Remo, whose formidable heads seem to have no modern rivals. Note too his swipe at American behavior.

"The women, when young, are good-looking; many have the dark Italian eye, but, like the Mentone women, soon acquire, from the drudgery to which they are exposed, a hard-looking and dried-up appearance. They are treated as very beasts of burden, and are accustomed from the early years to carry enormous loads upon their heads, far more so than at Mentone, and they glory in the amount they can carry. I have beheld one carrying an enormous log of wood on her head; and barrels, and every description of heavy articles, are constantly seen to be so carried. A lady told me she had a heavy oak table carried home to her house by her gardener's wife, and it was thought nothing of. Such a thing as a rope and pulley, much less a crane or rope to lift stones from the ground to the floors where masons are building a house, are utterly unknown. The women are employed as day-labourers, at something like a shilling a day, to carry the stones aloft on their heads. I have seen a woman, time after time, carrying a stone or a couple of uneven stones balanced, the one on the top of the other, on her head, up ladders nearly perpendicular, to a height of two storeys, to the stage where the masons were working. All they do is just twist a handkerchief in a coil on the head, and then, with a most extraordinary power of balancing, they convey the load to where it is wanted. Men very seldom undertake the drudgery. If they do, they carry a lighter load, not, however, on their heads, but on the bent back or shoulders, protected by a sack. I have observed a woman carrying a stone on her head which it took four of them to lift. Their skulls and spines no doubt thicken and acquire some strange amount of hardy strength, but any nobler faculty must be crushed out of them; yet they never seem to feel their degradation and would resent, I presume, the introduction of appliances by which their labour would be saved, and at the same time a means of livelihood taken from them.

"Of all the instances, however, of this nature which I witnessed, the most marvellous was that of carrying a pianoforte on the head. On our second visit to San Remo, a lady informed me that she had seen this sight. It seemed truly incredible, and perhaps, as she was an American, I was at first inclined to set it down to the national tendency to imaginative exaggeration. I looked anxiously for visual corroboration, seeing being in such a case believing, and I was not disappointed. The very day of leaving I had the good fortune to witness the scene, and thus was enabled to give full credit to the story. Happening to be in town, I met three women walking steadily along the street, their bodies erect, one in front and two behind, with the huge load of a heavy cabinet piano on their heads. I think each had one hand, at least, raised to steady it — a very painful exertion of itself to most people. Apparently, keeping pace together, this burden was sturdily carried as if it cost them no effort; while by their side marched a man in charge, who, I was thankful to observe, . . . carried no instrument of flagellation in his hand. Probably he would condescend to assist in raising the piano at starting, and in lowering it at its destination."

Miller later observes that "I am told that it is quite usual for a woman to carry 100 kilogrammes (220 lbs.) up to the mountains, and this every day; she will also bring a heavy bundle of grass or something back again. The men walk beside them empty-handed, or oftener still ride the mules and donkeys. If a man has to transport a heavy weight, he takes his wife with him to carry it. . . . The men consider it a disgrace to carry anything, a parcel even, and a woman's highest ambition is to keep her husband in perfect idleness."

Egg, Poultry, & Meat Dishes

Frittata	Frittata
Gallina Lessa Ripiena	Boiled Stuffed Chicken
Involtini con Carciofi	Veal Rolls with Artichokes
Tomaxelle	Little Veal Rolls
Manzo Negretto	Stewed Beef with Onion Sauce
Cima Ripiena	Stuffed Veal Breast
Fegato alla Genovese	Genoese Calf's Liver with Garlic Sauce
Maiale alle Olive	Pork Loin with Black Olives
Agnello con Carciofini	Lamb with Baby Artichokes
Agnello con Olive e Funghi	Lamb Stew with Olives and Mushrooms
Coniglio alle Mandorle	Rabbit with Almonds
Coniglio all'Aggiada	Rabbit with Garlic Sauce

"An egg is always an adventure."

— Oscar Wilde

EGGS ARE EATEN in Liguria with some regularity in omelettes and frittatas, in noodles, and in baked goods. They are probably the animal protein most consumed in Liguria, a region that eats less meat than just about any in Italy, certainly in the regions from Naples to the Alps. Up until not very long ago, meat consumption in Liguria was reserved for Sundays and special occasions. On Mondays and Tuesdays one would eat ravioli or vegetables stuffed with meat left over from the feast day. Otherwise, meals were made with vegetables, herbs, and cheese.

Rabbit is popular in the Ponente, and it marries well with Ligurian wine and traditional flavorings. Beef and veal are not used often; perhaps the most famous meat dish is *cima ripiena,* stuffed veal breast. There also are *tomaxelle,* little veal rolls stuffed with vegetables, rice, or herbs. Certain other specialty dishes using veal, beef, or poultry are listed below.

Frittata

This is a basic preparation in the Italian kitchen and central to Ligurian cookery. You must become adept at making a frittata to successfully make certain recipes in this book. The recipe given here is the basic one, but there is some room for variation. You can add minced fresh herbs and, perhaps, a teaspoon or two of grated Parmigiano-Reggiano or Pecorino to the eggs before making the frittata. You should not burden the frittata with too much cheese or it will stick to the pan. A frittata may be eaten hot, but in Italy, as often as not, it is eaten at room temperature or even cold. If you intend to cool your frittata, cover it with a clean cloth or paper toweling to protect it from bacteria.

1 tablespoon Ligurian extravirgin olive oil
2 extra-large eggs
1 or 2 drops of cold water (optional)

Take a 7- or 8-inch/17- to 20-cm omelette pan and grease it with 1 tablespoon of olive oil. Heat the pan over medium heat and then add 2 eggs that you have beaten, with, perhaps, a drop or two of cold water. Let the eggs set and cook them longer than you would a typical omelette or scrambled eggs. To do this effectively, you need to shake the pan periodically so that the frittata does not stick. You may also lift it with a spatula (made of metal or rubber, according to the needs of your omelette pan). Once the frittata has a rather firm skin on one side (after about 4 to 5 minutes, typically), slide the frittata out of the pan and onto a plate. The less-cooked side should be facing upward. Now lift the plate with one hand and, with the other hand, grab the handle of the pan and cover the frittata with the pan. In one motion, flip both hands in an arc so that the plate is now on top of the pan and the less-cooked side of the frittata is now face-down in the pan. Return to the heat and cook for 3 to 4 minutes until the bottom side is firm. As before, you need to shake the pan continuously to prevent sticking. The result should be a firm egg "pancake" that is slightly golden brown on both sides. Slide the frittata out of the pan and onto a plate. Serve immediately, or let cool. This process may be repeated if you need more than one frittata, such as in the recipe for Torta di Frittate con Funghi Porcini, Pesto e Pinoli on page 185.

Gallina Lessa Ripiena
Boiled Stuffed Chicken

This dish is simple, good food made special by the typical flavors of Liguria. This recipe comes from the Trattoria Garibaldi in the small town of Ne in the province of Genoa. The town is so small its name could hold only two letters! This chicken is delicious when served with Paté di Ortaggi (page 85) or Salsa Verde all'Antica (page 101).

2 cups / ½ pound / 225 g borage (or beet greens or spinach), carefully washed, boiled, cooled, and chopped
6 quarts / 5½ liters cold water
1 chicken, preferably free range, organic, or kosher, approximately 3 to 3½ pounds / 1½ kilos, with the liver and giblets removed
1 bunch fresh basil leaves, carefully wiped, torn into pieces
A few sage leaves, torn into pieces
A few sprigs fresh marjoram, torn into pieces
A few sprigs fresh Italian (flat) parsley, minced
½ cup / 60 g freshly grated Parmigiano-Reggiano
½ cup / 60 g unflavored bread crumbs
2 eggs
Sea salt to taste
Freshly ground pepper to taste
1 to 2 tablespoons milk (optional)
1 clove garlic, split, with the green heart removed
1 onion, peeled and cut into quarters
1 large carrot, washed, scraped, cut into large chunks
1 stalk celery, washed, trimmed, cut into 3 pieces

First cook the borage, beet greens, or spinach and let cool. Chop them when they are cool. Then set the water to boil in an 8- to 10-quart stockpot. Add a generous pinch of coarse sea salt to the water. Carefully wash and dry the chicken, removing large pieces of fat from under the skin and the cavity. Wash the liver and giblets and mince them before placing them in a large mixing bowl. Add the chopped borage, plus the basil, sage, marjoram, parsley, Parmigiano-Reggiano, bread crumbs, eggs, salt, and pepper. Combine the mixture thoroughly. If it is too dry you may add some milk to moisten it. Fill the cavity of the chicken with this mixture. Then, using needle and thread, sew the chicken tightly at both ends. When the water in the pot reaches a boil, add

Makes 1 chicken and 5 to 6 quarts / 5 to 6 liters stock

the garlic, onion, carrot, and celery. Then add the chicken, cover the pot, and cook over low heat for about 90 minutes. When it is done, remove the chicken from the stock and let it cool. Open at one end and remove the filling. Serve a scoop of filling on each plate. Slice the chicken, starting with the breast, and serve accompanied, if you wish, by a sauce of your choosing. At the Trattoria Garibaldi this dish is traditionally followed by a good mixed salad.

To use the stock, remove the onion, garlic, carrot, and celery pieces and, if you wish, strain the stock. Pour into glass jars or a bowl and refrigerate. Once the stock is chilled, you should skim the fat before heating it. This is one of the richest, most flavorful stocks you will ever taste because of all of the flavors in the stuffing of the chicken.

Involtini con Carciofi

Veal Rolls with Artichokes

I first tasted this dish in Finale Ligure in the province of Savona, but there are versions of it throughout Liguria. It is really worth making only with fresh artichokes, because those packed in oil or brine are either too heavy and soggy or too pungent. Only small- to medium-size artichokes (that are easily cut) will do.

1½ pounds / 650 g tender veal, sliced into 12 thin slices
6 small to medium-size fresh artichokes
1½ lemons
6 tablespoons / 40 g sweet butter
Fine sea salt
Freshly ground black pepper
1 tablespoon / 7 g unbleached all-purpose flour
6 ounces / 1 glass / 175 ml beef stock

First slice the veal, if this work has not been done for you by a butcher. Clean the artichokes well and remove the outer leaves and the stem. Chop each artichoke into 4 to 6 pieces and put them in cold water that has been acidulated with the juice of ½ lemon. Take a slice of veal, place on it a piece or two of artichoke, a little butter, and salt and pepper to taste. Roll the veal slice tightly, pass it lightly in flour, and secure with a toothpick. Repeat the process until all 12 rolls have been made. Melt the remaining butter in a pan over medium heat and then add the rolls and start to sauté them. Immediately after, add all of the remaining artichoke pieces and let cook for 30 seconds. Then gradually add the broth so that the rolls will remain moist. When cooking is complete (in less than 5 minutes total), add the juice of 1 lemon, quickly raise the heat below the pan, give the pan a couple of good shakes to spread the lemon flavor around, and serve immediately.

Makes about 12 rolls

Tomaxelle
Little Veal Rolls

Tomaxelle, once upon a time, were products of the Ligurian penchant to not let anything go to waste. These are rolls of leftover slices of roasted or braised veal or beef that are filled with various delicious ingredients. The name derives from the Latin *tomaculum,* meaning "little sausages." Around 1800, when there was an Austrian occupation of Genoa, some Austrian soldiers were taken prisoner and were served *tomaxelle.* While to the Genoese these were leftovers, to the Austrians they were delicate and beguiling, especially as prison fare. The modern version does not typically use leftovers, but is still of interest because of its flavor and delicacy.

2 ounces / 60 g dried funghi porcini, *soaked, drained, and chopped*
6 ounces / 175 g ground veal
1 clove garlic, green heart removed, minced
¼ cup / 4 tablespoons / 60 ml dry red or white wine
2 to 3 tablespoons / 15 to 20 g unflavored bread crumbs
3 tablespoons / 20 g pinoli
3 tablespoons / 20 g freshly grated Parmigiano-Reggiano
2 tablespoons / 15 g fresh marjoram, torn
1 tablespoon / 7 g fresh Italian (flat) parsley, torn
2 large eggs, beaten
Sea salt and pepper to taste
8 (about 2 ounces / 60 g each) thin slices of veal loin (the slices must be very thin)
1 to 1½ cups / 225 to 340 ml Fresh Tomato Sauce (see page 82)

*Makes
4 servings*

After having soaked the mushrooms and gathered the ingredients, sauté the ground veal, mushrooms, and garlic in a large skillet for a few minutes, just until the veal has given off some liquid and turns a light brown color. No butter or oil should be necessary. Drain the liquid and add the wine. Cook for another minute or so, until the wine has given off some of its alcohol. Transfer the veal-mushroom-wine mixture to a bowl and let cool for a few minutes. Then add, in order, the bread crumbs, *pinoli,* Parmigiano-Reggiano, marjoram, parsley, eggs, salt, and pepper. Combine the ingredients thoroughly with your hands or a wooden spoon. Lay out the veal slices and put a little cylinder of filling in the middle of each cutlet. Then flatten the filling so that it covers almost the entire surface of the veal slice. Roll the slice and then secure it with string, or perhaps with a toothpick. Add the tomato sauce to the same skillet, heat it slightly, then add the veal rolls. Cook gently until the veal slices are cooked through, usually about 10 minutes. Serve with mashed or boiled potatoes and either a salad or cooked greens such as the *spinasci* on page 297. Some Ligurian cooks omit the tomato sauce and instead sauté the rolls in olive oil or butter over high heat. This is tasty, but adds unnecessary calories. I prefer the homier flavor of braising the veal rolls in tomato sauce.

Manzo Negretto

Stewed Beef with Onion Sauce

Here is a fragrant and delicious way to stew beef that is typical of the area around Sarzana, near the border of Tuscany and the province of La Spezia. The sauce that is derived from this preparation is delicious with tubular pasta such as penne and *maccheroni* or when combined with rice. Of course, you may also use some of this sauce to accompany the beef.

1¾ pounds / 800 g onions, cut into slices of medium thickness
1¾ pounds / 800 g boneless beef such as flank steak or another economical cut
Sea salt to taste
Freshly ground pepper to taste*
6 tablespoons / ⅜ cup / 80 g unsalted butter
4 ounces / ½ cup / 115 ml (100 ml plus 1 tablespoon) tomato sauce

> * Variation: I have used a teaspoon or so of whole peppercorns in this dish instead of ground pepper and have had felicitous results.

Makes 6 to 8 servings

Slice the onions and put them in a casserole. Place the beef in the center of this bed of onions. Add the salt and pepper and then add enough cold water to the pot so that the beef is entirely covered. Cook over medium heat for 5 minutes and then cover and reduce the heat to low. Cook until all the water is absorbed. This may take anywhere from 90 minutes to 2½ hours or even more depending on the cut of beef you are using, so check the pot periodically. Once all the water is absorbed, remove the meat, add the butter and tomato sauce, and cook over medium heat only until the butter has melted and combined thoroughly with the onions and tomato sauce. The sauce will keep in the refrigerator for at most two more days after it has been made.

Cima Ripiena
Stuffed Veal Breast

This is an adaptation of a recipe given to me by Laura Rossana, a smiling fruit and veg-etable seller at stand 54 of the San Remo market. *Cima* means "summit" in Italian, and indeed *cima* is the summit of the school of cooking that says "*Non si spreca niente*" ("Nothing should ever be wasted"), which is what Laura admonishes. *Cima* can be served tepid or cold, accompanied by a Salsa alle Erbe Fresche (page 232) or some other herb sauce. Leftover *cima* can be sliced thin and served as an antipasto, or lightly coated in bread crumbs and fried gently in butter.

2 small artichokes, outer leaves removed, sliced thin, and doused with a bit of
  fresh lemon juice
1 medium carrot, washed, peeled, grated into long thin strips
1 medium zucchini, washed, cut into long thin strips
1 medium red pepper, washed, seeded, cut into thin strips
Scant ¼ pound/100 g prosciutto cotto, *in ⅛ inch/.3 cm slices (cut these slices*
  into julienne strips)
½ cup/115 ml Ligurian extravirgin olive oil
3 ounces/¾ cup/85 g beet greens, stems removed, steamed in the water that clings
  to the leaves after washing
½ cup/60 g shelled fresh peas (or canned, if fresh are not available)
4 large eggs
½ cup/115 ml whole milk
4 tablespoons/30 g freshly grated Parmigiano-Reggiano
2 tablespoons/15 g fresh marjoram, torn into pieces
Fine sea salt to taste
Freshly ground pepper to taste
1 boneless breast of veal, about 5½ pounds/2.5 kilos, with a pocket cut into it
  (ask your butcher to prepare the meat for you)
4 large hard-boiled eggs
Cold water
1 tablespoon coarse sea salt
1 medium onion, sliced
1 carrot, chopped
1 stalk celery, chopped
1 bay leaf

Prepare the artichokes, carrot, zucchini, red pepper, and prosciutto. Heat the olive oil in a pan, then add the artichokes, carrot, zucchini, beet greens, and

Makes
8 servings

peas and sauté for 3 to 4 minutes, until the carrot has softened slightly. Remove from the pan and let cool. In a bowl, beat the raw eggs and milk lightly. Briefly heat them in the skillet, only until they are loosely scrambled. Remove from the pan and gently mince. Add the cooked vegetables, prosciutto, Parmigiano-Reggiano, marjoram, salt, and pepper. Let cool. After having washed and dried the veal breast, carefully insert the egg-vegetable-cheese-prosciutto mixture, and gently place the hard-boiled eggs at different places in the mixture. (Remember that when the *cima* is sliced, the result will be a mosaic-like cross-section, so there will be thin slices of hard-boiled egg along with flecks of artichoke, carrot, zucchini, red pepper, beet green, and prosciutto.) It is very important that the pouch not be more than two-thirds full. The reason for this is that the filling will expand with cooking and you do not want it to burst.

Once you have filled the pouch, cut a long piece of butcher's twine, which you will use to sew the pouch shut with a trussing needle. Then — very important — use the needle to poke 10 to 12 holes at various points in the veal breast. This will let hot air out of the veal breast so that it does not burst. Make sure that you have just punctured the veal, but not driven a hole so far that the filling will escape. Wrap the veal breast in a layer of cheesecloth and, if you wish, tie the whole package with more butcher's twine. Using the cloth and twine, shape the veal breast into a sort of barrel-shaped cylinder.

Take a large deep pot and fill it halfway with cold water. Add sea salt, onion, carrot, celery, and bay leaf. Heat until the water begins to simmer, then gently lower the veal breast into the water. Cover and simmer for 2 to 2¼ hours, skimming fat as necessary. Check it every so often by poking the veal with a skewer, just enough to check the veal but not to create a hole through which the filling can escape.

When the *cima* is cooked, lift it carefully from the liquid and place it on a marble surface or a plate. Laura says to then place a weight, such as a thin slab of marble or a plastic board with cans of food (e.g., tomatoes or beans), so that the total weight will be about 4 pounds/just under 2 kilos. Let it sit for about 3 hours (Laura leaves it overnight), then remove the weight. Slice and serve with sauce.

The cooking liquid will make a wonderful broth for other uses.

COOKING VARIATION: Laura Rossana also cooks *cima* in an unusual way. Boil the *cima* over relatively high heat for 30 minutes. Then unwrap it and roast for about 40 minutes at medium heat (about 350°F/180°C) in a covered casserole to which you have added a generous amount (about 2 cups/450 ml) of red or white wine that you have brought almost to a boil in a separate pot. According to Laura, cold wine toughens meat while hot wine makes it more tender. Once this *cima* is cooked, let it cool before serving.

Fegato alla Genovese

Genoese Calf's Liver with Garlic Sauce

The most famous liver dish in Italy is probably *fegato alla veneziana,* Venetian calf's liver cooked with onions. Less well known, but just as delicious, is Genoa's take on calf's liver, which is classically married to *agliata* or *aggiada* (garlic sauce). This is a much more subtle dish than you would imagine. The bread in the sauce tones down the garlic, while the vinegar in the sauce tempers those particularly characteristic flavors in liver that make it unsavory to certain diners. Approach this dish with an open mind and I think you will be pleasantly surprised. The key is to cook the liver very quickly to assure that it is not overdone, or it will toughen.

1½ pounds / 700 g calf's liver, cut into very thin strips
2 tablespoons / 30 ml Ligurian extravirgin olive oil
1 cup / 115 g (110 g plus 1 tablespoon) agliata (see page 97)
Sea salt to taste (optional)

In Italy butchers gladly cut thin strips of liver or other meats upon request. If you are so favored, this will save you work. Otherwise, you will need to purchase one whole piece of liver and, using a very sharp knife, cut thin slices across the grain of the liver. This is much easier than it sounds and should not deter you from preparing this dish. Heat the olive oil to medium-high heat (it should not splatter, however) in a heavy-bottomed skillet. Add the liver and sauté rapidly for 2 or 3 minutes, using a wooden spoon. Then push the liver to one side of the pan and spoon the garlic sauce into the other side. Continue to move the liver and sauce around with the spoon until they are thoroughly combined. This should take another 3 to 4 minutes, but you must watch attentively that the liver does not overcook. Serve immediately, adding a pinch of sea salt if you wish.

Makes 4 servings

VARIATION: In preparing this dish, I sometimes add a dash more vinegar after adding the garlic sauce, to spike it up a bit. I have also given it a different twist by adding ½ teaspoon of excellent balsamic vinegar instead of the white wine vinegar that would be used in Genoa.

Maiale alle Olive

Pork Loin with Black Olives

This dish is popular in the hills and mountains on the border of the Levante and the region of Emilia-Romagna. It combines the use of pork so typical of Emilia-Romagna with flavors that are typically Ligurian. In some towns, it is customary to use pork chops (about 1 inch/2.5 cm thick) instead of a pork loin.

4 tablespoons/¼ cup/60 ml Ligurian extravirgin olive oil
1 tablespoon/½ ounce/15 ml white wine vinegar
¾ cup/6 ounces/175 ml dry white wine, preferably Ligurian
Sea salt to taste
Freshly ground black pepper to taste
1 clove garlic, cut into slivers
1 tablespoon/7 g minced fresh thyme
2 bay leaves
1½ pounds/650 g boneless pork loin or pork roast (or 6 chops)
2 tablespoons/15 g unsalted butter
4 ounces/1 cup/115 g pitted black olives, preferably Taggia or Gaeta

Makes
4 to 6 servings

Combine the first eight ingredients in a deep bowl or dish to make a marinade. Add the pork, cover with plastic wrap or with the dish's cover, and let marinate for 2 hours in a cool, dark place. If you have a warm kitchen, it is advisable to put the pork and its marinade in the refrigerator even though this will rob the preparation of some of its flavor. After the 2 hours, remove the bay leaves from the marinade and discard. Then melt the butter in a Dutch oven or a deep pan that has a cover. Add the pork and brown on all sides over medium-high heat. Then add the marinade and the olives, reduce the heat, cover, and cook for 30 minutes. Serve topped with some of the sauce.

NOTE: This is the traditional way of making this dish. For chops, the cooking time may be sufficient, but I have found that when I use an American pork loin, it may take another 15 to 20 minutes for it to be completely done. The goal is that the meat slice easily and be pinkish-white through and through. It should have reached an internal temperature of 350°F/180°C, which you may check by using a meat thermometer.

Agnello con Carciofini

Lamb with Baby Artichokes

I tasted this dish in a farmhouse in the Valle d'Impero, heartland of delicious olive oil and artichokes. It is popular throughout Liguria. To make it successfully, you must use fresh baby artichokes.

2 tablespoons / 30 ml Ligurian extravirgin olive oil
1 medium onion, minced
2¼ pounds / 1 kilo lean lamb chunks
1 sprig fresh rosemary
¾ cup / 6 ounces / 170 ml Ligurian dry white wine
4 baby artichokes (hard leaves and stems cut away), cut into 4 to 6 pieces
1 tablespoon / 7 g sweet butter

Heat the olive oil in a good skillet. Add the onion and sauté until golden yellow. Add the lamb pieces and cook gently, shaking the pan periodically so that the pieces do not stick. Pull the needles of rosemary off the stem and toss them into the pan, combining them with the lamb chunks. Cook for 3 or 4 more minutes. As the lamb begins to render some of its fat, pour in the wine. As the wine begins to evaporate, add the artichokes. A moment later, add the sweet butter and finish cooking (just until the lamb is tender and the artichoke pieces are slightly soft), moving all of the ingredients about so that the flavors blend. Serve with Pigato or Vermentino, or another medium-weight dry white wine.

Makes 4 to 6 servings

COOK'S VARIATION: When they are available, I add ½ cup of fresh baby peas along with the artichokes. You might use the same amount of drained, canned baby peas, but the taste is not as impressive. However, the first time you make *agnello con carciofini,* you should make it only with artichokes to know what the real taste is. The next time, for contrast, add peas.

Agnello con Olive e Funghi

Lamb Stew with Olives and Mushrooms

Simple country cooking with honest yet subtle flavors.

4 (3 + 1) tablespoons/60 (45 + 15) ml Ligurian extravirgin olive oil
1 medium onion, cut into thin rings
2¼ pounds/1 kilo lamb chunks, preferably from the shoulder
1 tablespoon/7 g unbleached flour
12 ounces/1½ cups/340 ml/dry white wine, preferably Ligurian
1 clove garlic, peeled
1 bay leaf
1 sprig fresh thyme
¾ cup/6 ounces/170 ml hot water
Freshly ground pepper to taste
10 to 12 ounces/300 g small cultivated mushrooms, carefully washed
Scant ¼ pound/100 g black olives, preferably Taggia or Gaeta (if you prefer green
  olives, you may substitute them, but the flavor of the dish will be different)

Makes
4 to 6 servings

Gently heat 3 tablespoons olive oil in a large pot or saucepan. Add the onions and sauté until golden. Then add the chunks of lamb and brown on all sides. Add the flour and move the pieces of lamb around so they all are covered with some flour. Add the wine, bring to a slow boil, then add the garlic clove, bay leaf, thyme, hot water, and pepper. Cover, turn the heat all the way down, and simmer for 30 minutes. In a small skillet, gently heat 1 tablespoon olive oil and then sauté the small whole mushrooms for 2 to 3 minutes. After the stew has cooked for 30 minutes, remove the garlic clove and the bay leaf. Add the olives and then the mushrooms with their pan liquid. Stir to combine the ingredients, cover, and then cook for another 10 to 12 minutes.

The famous artichokes of Albenga

Coniglio alle Mandorle

Rabbit with Almonds

This recipe comes from the Ristorante Dâ Casetta in Borgio Verezzi in the province of Savona, and is wonderfully delicious. Rabbit abounds in the Ponente and is popular in the local cuisine. Here is a fine preparation. (If rabbit is unavailable, chicken may be substituted, although this will yield a different result.)

1 cleaned rabbit, approximately 3 pounds / 1.3 kilos, reserve the liver
1 clove garlic, green heart removed, minced
1 sprig fresh rosemary
1 sprig fresh thyme
3 tablespoons / 20 g minced fresh Italian (flat) parsley
1 pinch freshly ground nutmeg
3 tablespoons / 22 g coarse sea salt
1 pinch freshly ground white pepper
2 tablespoons / 15 g unsalted butter
7 tablespoons / 100 ml Ligurian extravirgin olive oil
½ cup / 55 g minced onion
1⅞ cups / 200 ml dry white wine such as Vermentino
⅓ cup / 85 ml Fresh Tomato Sauce (see page 82)
3⅓ cups / 750 ml beef broth or chicken or vegetable broth
1 rabbit liver, cooked in butter, minced
½ cup / 60 g peeled whole almonds (unsalted)
¼ cup / 30 g toasted hazelnuts (unsalted)
¼ cup / 30 g pinoli

Makes 6 servings

Ask your butcher to clean the rabbit for you, reserve the liver, discard the head, and cut the rabbit into 18 pieces (with the bone still attached). When you get the rabbit home, rinse the pieces well in cold water and let them drain in a colander. While the rabbit is draining, pound garlic, rosemary, thyme, parsley, nutmeg, salt, and pepper together in a mortar and set aside. Place the rabbit pieces in a flameproof casserole dish, about 15 to 16 inches / 40 cm in diameter and 4 inches / 10 cm in height. Cover the pot and place it over a very low flame. During this process, the rabbit will give off most of its liquid, which you should drain two or three times. While this is occurring, heat the butter and oil in a separate pan and then sauté the onions until they are soft and fragrant. When the rabbit is dry (after about 20 minutes), add the onions, butter, and oil to it. Then add the contents of the mortar and stir well. Cook over medium heat so that the rabbit turns slightly pink. Then add the wine and tomato sauce, lower the flame, and cover. Cook gently for 1 hour, periodically adding broth to keep the dish moist. You will find that the rabbit becomes tender during cooking.

While the rabbit is cooking, make the almond sauce. After having cooked the liver (which you may omit if it does not appeal to you, although it adds an important flavor element), pound the almonds, hazelnuts, and *pinoli* in a mortar until they have formed a paste or powder. Then add the rabbit liver and pound just until all the ingredients are combined. Add a little broth to make this a thick paste. Five minutes before the rabbit is finished, stir in the almond sauce, continue to cook, then serve. A nice accompaniment to this dish is cooked buttered carrots. Serve with a red wine such as Rossese or Dolcetto.

Coniglio all'Aggiada

Rabbit with Garlic Sauce

This preparation comes from the Ristorante Dâ Casetta in Borgio Verezzi, as does the Rabbit with Almonds that precedes this recipe. (Chicken may be substituted.)

1 cleaned rabbit, approximately 3 pounds/1.3 kilos, reserve the liver
2 cloves garlic, green heart removed, minced
1 sprig fresh rosemary
1 sprig fresh thyme
3 tablespoons/22 g coarse sea salt
2½ tablespoons/20 g minced peperoncino *(hot red pepper)*
7 tablespoons/100 ml Ligurian extravirgin olive oil
2 ounces/50 g pancetta or prosciutto cotto, cut into cubes
1⅞ cups/200 ml dry white wine such as Vermentino
2¼ cups/500 ml beef broth or chicken or vegetable broth
1 rabbit liver, cooked in butter, minced
1 large clove garlic, with the green heart removed, minced
½ cup/60 g unflavored bread crumbs
7 tablespoons/100 ml white wine vinegar

Makes
6 servings

Ask your butcher to clean the rabbit for you, reserve the liver, discard the head, and cut the rabbit into 18 pieces (with the bone still attached). When you get the rabbit home, rinse the pieces well in cold water and let them drain in a colander. While the rabbit is draining, pound garlic, rosemary, thyme, salt, and *peperoncino* together in a mortar and set aside. Place the rabbit pieces in a flame-proof casserole dish, about 15 to 16 inches/40 cm in diameter and 4 inches/10 cm in height. Cover the pot and place it over a very low flame. During this process, the rabbit will give off most of its liquid, which you should drain two or three times. While this is occurring, heat the oil in a separate pan and then sauté the cubes of *pancetta* or *prosciutto cotto* until they are soft and fragrant. When the rabbit is dry (after about 20 minutes), add the *pancetta* and oil to it. Then add the contents of the mortar and stir well. Cook over high heat for a few minutes until the rabbit turns slightly pink. Then add the wine, lower the flame, and cover. Cook gently for 1 hour, periodically adding broth to keep the dish moist. You will find that the rabbit becomes tender during cooking.

While the rabbit is cooking, make the garlic sauce. After having cooked the liver (which you may omit if it does not appeal to you, although it adds an important flavor element), pound the garlic and bread crumbs in a mortar and then add the vinegar. Add the rabbit liver and pound just until all the ingredients are combined. Five minutes before the rabbit is finished, stir in the garlic sauce, continue to cook, then serve. A nice accompaniment to this dish is cooked buttered carrots. Serve with a white wine such as Vermentino.

Hemingway Has Bananas in La Spezia

In "Che Ti Dice La Patria?" a short story by Ernest Hemingway, the characters drive through Liguria from La Spezia to Genoa to Ventimiglia, eating spaghetti, steak, potatoes, bananas, and wine. While they probably could have eaten more classical Ligurian cuisine, there is an interesting detail that Hemingway caught: When the characters dine at a trattoria in La Spezia, the only fruit available for dessert is bananas. This is not a native fruit, but La Spezia has long been the chief port of delivery of exotic fruits for central and northern Italy. The city has numerous fancy fruit shops offering dried fruits from the Middle East and North Africa, bananas from Africa and Central America, pineapples from Hawaii and the Philippines, and all sorts of luscious fruits from Brazil. While most Ligurians enjoy their divine local fruit, the people of La Spezia also enjoy magnificent fruits from all corners of the world. My favorite shop is Giuseppe Panattoni at Piazza Garibaldi 23, where ancient posters from Chiquita, Del Monte, and Dole bespeak a time when bananas were an exotic and precious commodity.

Fruits
&
Desserts

Pesche Ripiene	Stuffed Peaches
Salame di Albicocche	Apricot Salami
Camogginn	Camogli Cherries
Marrons Glacés	Candied Chestnuts
Castagne al Profumo di Viola	Violet-Scented Chestnuts
Mietti	Chestnut Cream Cups
Pacciugo	Portofino Ice Cream
Pandöçe (Pandolce)	Sweet Genoa Cake
Spungata Ligure	Ligurian Fruit Pie
Sciumette	Little Meringue Sponges
Genoise	Genoese Sponge Cake
Amaretti	Bitter Almond Cookies
Friscêu di Mele	Apple Fritters
Friscêu Cö Zebibbo e Pinoli	Raisin–Pine Nut Fritters
Friscêu di Frutta Secca	Dried Fruit Fritters

*L*IGURIA, LUSH GARDEN that it is, is favored with a bounty of extraordinary fruits and nuts. Because these are of such high quality, the most classic Ligurian dessert remains a perfect piece of fruit at the peak of its ripeness. There is seldom the need to adorn this fruit with toppings such as syrup, ice cream, or whipped cream, although all of these elements combine in *pacciugo,* an extravagant dessert from Portofino.

The region has most of the major fruits found in Italy. Unlike most other northern Italian regions, in Liguria there is a profusion of citrus, whose juice gives flavor to sauces and cooking juices and whose peel, when dried, forms a subtle backdrop when grated or a more forceful one when served candied. Lemon and orange waters often give subtext to certain dishes, and are popular as perfumes and liquids to cleanse the skin.

Most Ligurian citrus comes from the Ponente, although some good lemons can be found in the province of La Spezia. Until 1855, when Nice was part of Liguria, the town of Menton, at the border with Ventimiglia, was a major citrus-producing zone. In 1825 the English began buying lemons and olives near Ventimiglia and Bordighera. Word returned to England about the beauty of the place, and soon it became the preferred winter resort for lords and ladies, dukes and duchesses.

After Nice was ceded to France, the Ventimiglia to San Remo area was developed for floriculture by the English and the Germans. Fabulous gardens were built, especially the Hanbury garden in Ventimiglia in 1890. Yet the cash crops were still citrus and olives. It was at the beginning of the twentieth century that flowers were planted for cultivation and sale. Carnations were originally the most popular flower, although the rose is now predominant. It is notable that the flavors and fragrances of flowers find their way into honeys, sauces, and desserts in Liguria, and you will find a couple of examples in this chapter.

As in much of Italy, particular towns in this region become known for certain fruits: Camogli for cherries, Volpedo for peaches, Arenzano for strawberries, Ventimiglia for lemons, and so on. La Spezia, a large port of entry for fruit from Asia and the tropics, has always had a profusion of exotic fruit to combine with traditional Ligurian fruits (see page 378). As you might expect, the selection of fruit ice creams in La Spezia is especially enticing. This town is also a center for dried fruit, such as berries, apricots, peaches, and bananas.

In selecting fruit at home, you should pay less attention to seeming physical perfection and concentrate instead on fragrance. Develop a Ligurian nose. Every fruit has a natural fragrance, whether it is cantaloupe, lime, apple, pear, banana, or anything else. Even hard-shelled fruits, such as coconut, have fragrances; all it takes is more effort and concentration to identify them. Fruit that is normally washed should not touch water until just before it is served, so that as much residual perfume will remain as possible.

Genoa, with its ancient links to Asia, North Africa, and the Americas, has long been a port of entry for sweets. The Arab penchant for ice and fruits in combination found congenial ground in Liguria, where the native fruit was so special. The Genoese are big ice cream and sorbet eaters. The most typical and popular ice cream of Genoa is *pànera,* which is intensely flavored coffee ice cream.

The two most famous Genoese contributions to the world of desserts are genoise (sponge cake), and candied fruits and nuts. Because genoise and marrons glacés (candied chestnuts) have French names, there has long been the mistaken assumption that they are of French origin. Another popular local dessert is *pandolce,* a dense sweet bread that is something of a cousin of the more eggy and yeasty panettone of Milan.

Ligurians love little cookies such as amaretti, and also enjoy fritters made with apples or raisins. But nothing can match a perfect piece of fruit.

Pesche Ripiene

Stuffed Peaches

In Liguria the peaches are of unsurpassed flavor and fragrance. They fairly drip with nectar and, in my view, are the perfect summer dessert just as they are. There are golden peaches and delicate white ones, but the most typical Ligurian peach, which has an almost orange flesh, comes from the town of Volpedo and bears its name. This is the peach that is often used for stuffing. You should select the most voluptuous peaches you can get your hands on. See the photograph in the second section of color illustrations.

2 ounces / 60 g raisins
Rum or vin santo
7 large peaches
12 amaretti cookies, pounded into little crumbs (see page 401)
1 tablespoon / 7 g minced candied orange or lemon peel
* (or a combination of the two)*
2 to 3 tablespoons / 15 to 20 g sugar
6 ounces / ¾ cup / 175 ml dry white wine

Soak the raisins in some rum or vin santo for 1 hour, and then drain. Wash six of the peaches, cut each in half, and remove the pit. Wash the seventh peach, peel it and mash it or run it through a food mill to create a pulp. Combine this pulp with the raisins, amaretti crumbs, and orange or citrus peel. Stuff the peaches with the filling. You now have a choice of how to bake the peaches. Some cooks bake the stuffed halves. Others, after filling the halves, rejoin them and bake the peaches whole. Whichever way you choose, you should top the peaches with a little sugar and then place them in a large baking dish in which the white wine has been poured before adding the peaches. If you choose to bake peach halves, they should be placed filling-side up. Bake for 25 to 30 minutes in a preheated 350°F/180°C oven. During baking, baste every so often with the cooking liquid. Serve hot, tepid, or cold.

Makes
6 servings

Salame di Albicocche

Apricot Salami

I tasted this special dessert in the home of a lovely Genoese lady who said the recipe had been in the family for as long as anyone can remember. It was created because the family had a small plot of land in the countryside with apricot trees that gave so generously that new ways had to be found to use up all of the fruit in its very short season. If you do not have fresh apricots available, you may substitute dried apricots that you have poached and then cooled.

FOR THE FILLING

2¼ pounds / 1 kilo fresh apricots, pitted, or 1½ pounds / 675 g dried apricots
6 tablespoons / ⅜ cup / 40 g granulated sugar
3 tablespoons / 20 g sweet butter, melted
2 tablespoons / 15 g lemon zest
1 tablespoon / 8 g cinnamon powder
2 tablespoons / 15 g unflavored bread crumbs
4 ounces / 115 g (100 g plus 1 tablespoon) peeled almonds, pounded in a mortar

FOR THE DOUGH

1¾ cups / 200 g unbleached flour
4 tablespoons / ¼ cup / 30 g granulated sugar
4 tablespoons / ¼ cup / 30 g sweet butter, softened
1 large egg
1 tablespoon / 15 ml Ligurian extravirgin olive oil
Juice of ½ lemon
6 tablespoons / ⅜ cup / 85 ml whole milk

Makes
6 to 8 servings

If you are using fresh apricots, wash them carefully, cut them in half, and discard the pits. Immerse them in boiling water and cook for a few minutes, until they are soft but not mushy. Check them every minute to make sure. Once they are cooked, drain and let the apricots cool. If you wish, you may place them in a dish covered with plastic wrap and refrigerate. If you are using dried apricots, rinse them in tepid water and them cook them in boiling water for about 10 minutes. Cool them as you would the fresh apricots.

While the apricots are cooling, make the dough. Combine the flour, sugar, and softened butter in a mixing bowl. Then add the egg, olive oil, and lemon juice and work the mixture with your hands just until everything is combined. Transfer the dough to a clean surface and then roll out the dough with a rolling pin to form a thin circle of dough. This should be done by rolling directly away from you, rather than at angles, and turning the dough so that it will be rolled evenly. The dough should be as thin as possible, but not so thin that it will tear when you fold it. Cover the dough with a cloth and set aside.

To make the filling, combine the sugar, melted butter, lemon zest, cinnamon powder, bread crumbs, and pounded almonds in a mixing bowl. Then carefully add the cooked apricots and gently fold the combination so that the apricots incorporate the other flavors without breaking into little pieces. Preheat your oven to 350°F/180°C.

Take the cloth off the dough and then carefully spoon the apricot mixture along the diameter of the circle, forming a cigar-shaped cylinder that goes almost from one end of the circle to the other. Leave enough dough at the ends so that you can fold them, like two flaps, over the ends of the apricot cylinder. Then roll one whole side of the dough over the filling and continue to roll it so that you form a neat wrapper of dough around the filling. It should look like a strudel or, in local terms, a salami.

Gently place the "salami" in a buttered baking dish. Brush the top with a little melted butter and then with the milk. Place in the oven and bake for 45 to 50 minutes. Serve hot, tepid (my preference), or cool. Let stand for at least 5 minutes before slicing. Cut a slice for each serving.

Camogginn

Camogli Cherries

A visitor to Camogli today would not understand the genesis of this recipe. Many years ago, in the hills above town there were numerous cherry trees that produced a small and highly flavorful cherry. This was known as the *camogginn,* or Camogli cherry. These delicious cherries gained fame in the region and numerous plantings were done, especially in the hills north of Genoa on the road to Piedmont. While one can now eat these cherries elsewhere in Liguria, the custom of combining them with anise flavor is unique to my beloved little town. Anise also grew near Camogli (and still does), and a spirit made with anise seed used to be a popular local libation for sailors and fishermen. Generally the only Italian anise liqueurs available outside of Italy come from Trieste, Rome, Sicily, Naples, or the Marche. You should select one that has a pronounced taste of anise but is not overbearing. These cherries preserved in alcohol, made in June, were packed in jars and provided a taste of home for mariners far from home. You might consider packing these in four 1-cup jars or two 2-cup jars. These cherries can be eaten with dry cookies, over sponge cake, with vanilla ice cream, or all by themselves. The cherry-anise liquid is ambrosial, but you should not plan on driving after consuming it.

1 quart / 1 liter bottle of anisette liqueur
1 tablespoon / 7 g sugar
4 cloves
1⅓ pounds / 600 g small red cherries, washed, cut in half, pitted
Skin of 1 small lemon, cut into about 15 strips
1 small cinnamon stick for each jar

Makes approximately 4 cups

Place 1 tablespoon of anisette, the sugar, and the cloves in a large bowl. After washing, cutting, and pitting the cherries, place them in the bowl and stir. Then stir in the strips of lemon rind. Pack this mixture in wide-mouthed sterile jars, adding a small cinnamon stick to each jar. For every cup of cherries, add ¾ cup/6 ounces/175 ml of anisette and then seal the jars. Let stand in a dark, cool place for two weeks before using.

Marrons Glacés
Candied Chestnuts

It is generally accepted that marrons glacés, or candied chestnuts, were invented somewhere in Liguria, probably in either the province of Genoa or Savona. It is thought that during one of the many French occupations of Genoa during the eighteenth century that the delicacy was discovered, renamed, and carried off to France. To be frank, I was never much of a fan of marrons glacés. I found the taste muddy, the sensation in the mouth cloying, and I always had a terrible sense that my teeth needed brushing for three days after. That was until I tasted the marrons glacés as prepared at the Pasticceria Helvetia in Finale Ligure (in the province of Savona). One afternoon in late fall, as I walked past this bakery, a rack of marrons glacés sat in the window. Given my past history with them, I just walked by. But I later returned, and am I glad! I bought one, which in the past would have been more than sufficient, but it was not enough. I tried a few more, and never was there the sense of heaviness or oversweetness. Maurizio Zaniboni, the owner of Pasticceria Helvetia, has kindly shared his recipe, which I pass on to you. Needless to say, this recipe is rather labor-intensive (it takes five days, and then more work three months later), but it is worth the effort. A small package of these makes a wonderful gift at holiday time or if you are someone's dinner guest.

Cold water for boiling the chestnuts
1 generous pinch sea salt
4½ pounds / 2 kilos fresh-picked chestnuts of the highest quality

FOR THE SYRUP
6¾ cups / 54 ounces / 1½ liters water
   (I recommend spring water)
4½ pounds / 2 kilos granulated (caster)
   sugar
2 drops vanilla extract

FOR THE GLAZE
1 cup / 8 ounces / 225 ml liquid sugar
   (alternative: ½ cup / 4 ounces / 60 g
   confectioner's sugar plus 4 tablespoons
   syrup)

Day 1: Set a large pot (at least 8 quarts/8 liters) of cold water to boil. Once it reaches a rolling boil, add the salt and let it return to a boil. In the meantime, use a small sharp knife to make a cut in the peel around the total circumference of each chestnut. This is not about cutting into the nut, which would be quite difficult, but just about the first loosening of the peel. When the water reaches a rolling boil, add all of the chestnuts. Once the water returns to a boil, cook for 25 to 30 minutes (if you are using larger chestnuts, it takes a little more time). Drain the chestnuts in a colander and then, when they are just cool enough to handle, remove the peels from each chestnut (they should slip off easily).

Makes
4½ pounds /
2 kilos

(Cook's note: Although Signor Zaniboni did not indicate this, I found that after peeling the chestnuts, it helped the process to then take the sharp little knife and cut a little bit of chestnut from one end, making a small hollow. This allows the syrup to penetrate the inside of the chestnut, which is delicious. You might choose to do some this way, and others without the incision, and then come to your own decision about which you prefer.)

Now make the syrup. Take a large pot (preferably of copper, although this is not essential) and add the spring water, sugar, and the vanilla and heat over medium-high heat, stirring continuously with a wooden spoon. When it reaches a boil, turn down the heat somewhat and boil for 5 minutes, stirring continuously. Now add all of the chestnuts and stir well so they are entirely covered. Turn the heat down to low and cook for 10 minutes. Turn off the heat and transfer to a large bowl or dish that has a cover that fits snugly. Cover entirely and set aside for 24 hours, preferably in an area without too much light, drafts, or temperature changes.

Day 2: Carefully pour all of the syrup back into the pot, striving to leave as little in the bowl with the chestnuts as is possible. Boil the syrup for 10 minutes, and then pour the hot syrup back over the chestnuts. Cover and set aside for 24 hours under the same conditions as Day 1.

Day 3: Repeat the process of Day 2.

Day 4: Repeat the process of Day 2.

Day 5: Use a spoon to place the chestnuts, one by one, in sterile jars. They should be packed so that they gently touch, but should not be pressed down in any way. Pour the syrup over the nuts in each jar, then close tight. Store the jars in a dark, cool place for 90 days.

Day 90: The final process. It is time to glaze the chestnuts. If you have liquid sugar, this is what you will use. If not, you will need to separate the chestnuts from the syrup and then combine about 4 tablespoons of the syrup with ½ cup/60 g confectioner's sugar. Heat this gently until the sugar dissolves.

Preheat your oven to 425° to 450°F/220° to 230°C. Take one or two large pans and place racks in them so that when you put your marrons on them they will not stick to the pan. Hold each marron at both ends, using the thumb and index finger of one hand. Take a small brush and apply a thin coat of liquid sugar or sugared syrup on each side. Place each glazed chestnut on the rack in the pan. Once you have done this, bake for 3 to 4 minutes. The marrons will acquire a transparent glaze and an inviting sheen. Let cool before eating.

(The Zanibonis often make huge batches of chestnuts in syrup which they store, then glazing only a few dozen at a time in anticipation of demand.)

Eating Marrons Glacés: Although these marrons do not have the heaviness one usually encounters, they are still rich in flavor and should be savored. Let your tongue and palate warm the nut in your mouth so that the glaze will be the first thing you taste before the chestnut dissolves, releasing its flavor and that of the syrup. Even after you have swallowed the dissolved nut, do not reach for another. Let the afterglow of flavor transfix and delight you for another 15 minutes.

The Strawberries of Arenzano

The town of Arenzano, in the western part of the province of Genoa, is famous for its strawberries. They are small, delicate, and intensely fragrant, reminding me of Bardolino wine. Twenty kilos (44 pounds) of Arenzano strawberries were shipped to Japan in 1959 for the wedding of the crown prince and princess.

Each year since 1952 the town has held a strawberry festival to celebrate the harvest. A Strawberry King and Queen are selected, and they arrive at city hall in a golden carriage to initiate the festivities. The fame of these berries has far outstripped the local ability to meet the demand. There has always been a small amount of arable terrain, and as Arenzano became a desirable weekend place for people from Genoa, Turin, and Milan, many farmers sold their land. So most of the berries consumed at the strawberry festival actually come from the regions of Trentino and Veneto in northeastern Italy. But if you visit Arenzano on your own, particularly in June, you will be able to sample *le fragole di Arenzano,* and you will then know what a strawberry is supposed to taste like.

Castagne al Profumo di Viola
Violet–Scented Chestnuts

Chestnuts and violets are a marriage made in heaven, and here is your chance to perform the ceremony.

Slightly more than 1 pound / ½ kilo fresh chestnuts
3 tablespoons / 20 g sea salt or coarse salt
1 cup / 225 ml violet honey (see page 111)

Makes
approximately
1 pound / ½ kilo

Select only fresh chestnuts in pristine shape. The most desirable are ones that were very recently harvested. Set a large pot of cold water to boil to which you have added the salt. Once it has reached a rolling boil, add the chestnuts and boil for 45 minutes, with the pot partially covered. Drain the water and, when the chestnuts are not too hot to handle, slip off their skins. Cover the chestnuts with a light cloth or wax paper and let cool. Once they are cool, you have two options. The first is to dip the chestnuts in the honey and then serve at some point on the same day. The other option is to place the chestnuts in a large-mouthed sterile jar and then pour in the violet honey and close tightly. They may be kept, unopened, for several months in a cool, dark spot.

Mietti

Chestnut Cream Cups

I first tasted *mietti* in Pigna, a mountain resort town in the Valle di Nervia in far western Liguria, near the borders of Piemonte and the French Maritime Alps. This is simple country cooking of once upon a time, but all good foods inevitably resurface and now *mietti* are slowly reclaiming their place at the Ligurian table. There has been a significant change in the recipe. In decades past, the terrain of this area was too rugged to herd cattle, so goats were kept to provide milk for drinking and for cheese. On special occasions, a goat would be slaughtered to serve at a feast. *Mietti,* in their classical preparation, were made with goat's milk, although now they are almost always made with cow's milk, which is readily available in markets. Another possible variation is that you may wish to add some sugar to the pot when you cook the *mietti*. In the past, sweetness came from fresh raw milk, but commercial, pasteurized milk does not have the same sweetness. I would recommend a teaspoon of fine brown sugar as a sufficient base amount, although I expect that some readers of this book would want their *mietti* sweeter. But remember: The dominant flavor here is chestnut and the primary texture is silkiness, so to make these *mietti* into an overly sweet pudding is inadvisable.

1 quart / 1 liter fresh whole goat's or cow's milk
1 small pinch finely granulated sea salt
11 ounces / 2¾ cups / 300 g chestnut flour
1 teaspoon / 2.5 g fine brown sugar (optional)

Put the milk and the salt in a large, deep saucepan and gently warm it over medium-low heat for about 30 seconds. Then gradually add the flour, holding the measuring cup in one hand while consistently stirring with a wooden spoon with the other. After a few minutes, add the optional sugar and keep stirring gently. You must continuously stir or the cream will stick to the bottom. After about 10 minutes, the cream will begin to thicken. You must continue stirring until you have created a silken, pudding-like cream without any lumps. The total cooking time is typically 30 minutes. Once the contents of the pot are rather thick and creamy, pour it into 4 pretty dishes, preferably of glass, and serve tepid.

Makes
4 servings

WINE SUGGESTION: Although this is a rustic dessert for which wine was seldom intended, I have discovered that *mietti,* when served with a small glass of superior Sicilian Marsala, is a blissful combination even if Marsala is not often consumed in Liguria.

Pacciugo
Portofino Ice Cream

Pacciugo (sometimes spelled *paciugo*) is an opulent ice cream specialty popular in the towns of the Portofino Peninsula. It is thought to have been invented in the 1930s in Portofino, although there is no definitive documentation. In some ways it is like an American ice cream sundae, except that it is customarily created in a tall, globe-shaped glass rather than in a dish, and there is a stricter definition of what the finished product should contain. Unlike a sundae, *pacciugo* does not contain nuts. As always, the success of this preparation rises and falls on the quality of the ingredients used. For example, maraschino cherries are not an acceptable substitute for brandy-soaked *amarena* cherries, and any sort of whipped cream substitute cannot replace the real thing. For the chocolate ice cream, I try to use bitter or semisweet chocolate ice cream rather than the sweet type — this results in a better balance of bitter and sweet tastes.

1 to 2 tablespoons / 7 to 15 g brandy-soaked amarena *cherries (the Fabbri brand is widely available, although you may use any high-quality brand you have at hand)*
2 to 3 tablespoons / 30 to 45 ml fresh whipped cream that has been chilled (though not frozen) in your freezer
2 scoops chocolate ice cream
1 ripe peach, cut into bite-size pieces
Strawberry or raspberry syrup*

> * In Italy, fine berry syrups are not icky-sweet and loaded with artificial colors, flavors, and preservatives. Some of the best are made by Romanengo in Genoa and they are sold abroad. If you cannot find a berry syrup that is pure of flavor and intention, it is best to make a berry coulis. You may do this by taking fresh (preferably) or frozen strawberries or raspberries and, after cleaning them carefully, pureeing them in a food processor or blender. If the raspberries have seeds, strain the coulis before serving.

Makes
1 serving
Take a large wide-mouthed glass (making sure it is not so delicate that it will break under the spoon of an enthusiastic eater). Spoon the brandied cherries into the base. Top the cherries with the whipped cream. Then add the 2 scoops of chocolate ice cream. Top the ice cream with the pieces of peach. Finish by pouring a generous amount of berry syrup on top and serve immediately, perhaps accompanied with a few amaretti cookies (see page 401) or a dry almond biscuit.

Pandöçe (Pandolce)
Sweet Genoa Cake

The Genoese do not like their pandolce compared with the panettone of Milan. They assert that their cake has medieval origins, while panettone is more recent. Pandolce arrived in London in the luggage of nineteenth-century British travelers who wintered in Liguria, and came to be known in England as Genoa Cake. Pandolce was originally prepared in Genoese homes at Christmastime and only more recently did it appear in bakeries. Every Genoese woman had her own secret ingredients that went into the cake, which is a combination of candied fruit, nuts, citrus waters, and a hint of herbs or spices. I have heard that it used to be traditional that the women would take the doughs to bed with them to warm them and encourage the action of the yeast. Several loaves of *pandolce* would be prepared in the days leading up to Christmas Eve, with the intention that there be enough to last through Epiphany (January 6). The first cake to be served would have a laurel or olive branch poked in the top, and it was up to the youngest child to remove the branch and cut the cake. The first piece would then be wrapped in a cloth and given to the first alms-seeker who knocked at the door.

1 teaspoon/2.25 g active dry yeast
½ cup/60 g warm milk (about 110°F/43°C)
½ cup/60 g unsalted butter, softened
¾ cup/85 g granulated sugar
2 teaspoons/30 ml Marsala
4 teaspoons/60 ml orange or lemon flower water
1 tablespoon/7 g fennel seeds
1 large egg, lightly beaten
3½ cups/500 g unbleached flour
⅓ cup/40 g dried currants
⅔ cup/80 g golden raisins (sultanas)
⅓ cup finely chopped candied citron peel (lime, orange, or lemon)
½ cup/60 g pinoli

Let the yeast dissolve in the milk in a bowl until it becomes foamy (about 10 to 15 minutes). In a large bowl, soften the butter with a wooden spoon and then add the sugar, a little at a time, stirring until the mixture is airy. Add the Marsala and citrus water, stirring gently. Add the fennel seeds and egg. Mix everything together until homogeneous. Then add the milk/yeast mixture. The next step requires close observation. Add the flour a little at a time with one hand while stirring well with the other. The dough should be moist. If you feel it is too wet, add a little more flour, but do this with great care. Once this is done, add

Makes 1 cake for 6 to 8 servings

the currants, sultanas, citron peel, and *pinoli*. Transfer to a much larger bowl that has been lightly greased with unsalted butter. Cover with a clean towel and set aside in a warm spot that is free of drafts. Let sit for 4 to 6 hours. It will rise somewhat, but not nearly as much as you might expect.

One-half hour before baking, preheat oven to 425°F/220°C. Place the dough on a cookie sheet greased with butter. Form a round loaf that is about 6 inches/15 cm in diameter. Use a knife to score three slits in the crown in such a way that you form a triangle. Bake for 50 to 55 minutes, or until golden. Cool entirely on a wire rack before serving. The cake can last up to two weeks when wrapped well.

Pandolci *on a baker's shelf in Genoa*

Spungata Ligure
Ligurian Fruit Pie

It is a bit inaccurate to call this a pie. A *spungata* is flatter than a pie and is really closer to what is known in other parts of Italy as a *crostata*. This good basic preparation comes from Bacchus, a popular drinking and eating place in San Remo. Bacchus is a combination wine bar, wine shop, and restaurant, and you may go there for any or all of these reasons. The best *spungata* is the one made with homemade preserves or, at the very least, the finest commercial preserves you can locate. The recipe Bacchus gave me, and one I am deeply fond of, is for a *spungata* made with *visciole*, a delicious dark red or black cherry typical of the Italian regions of Liguria, Emilia-Romagna, and Lazio. They also make *spungata* with other jams and preserves and you may do so as well. However, you should remember that not many fruit flavors combine well with pine nuts, almonds, and candied fruit, so you should not be indiscriminate. I have enjoyed *spungata* made with apricot, peach, quince, and sweet orange preserves.

FOR THE FILLING
1 cup / 120 g black cherry or other
   preserves
¼ cup / 1 ounce / 30 g pinoli
¼ cup / 1 ounce / 30 g peeled almonds
¼ cup / 1 ounce / 30 g fine candied citrus,
   cut into small bits

FOR THE DOUGH
2¼ cups / 250 g unbleached flour
2½ teaspoons / 5 g salt
⅞ cup / 100 g granulated sugar*
1 large egg
5½ ounces / 150 g sweet butter,
   softened

* Note that I prefer less sugar in the dough; follow your taste.

*Makes one
12-inch / 30-cm pie*

Place the jam, *pinoli,* almonds, and candied citrus in a bowl and stir so that all the ingredients are combined. Set aside. On a lightly floured surface, combine the flour and salt into a small hill. Stick your palm on top, flatten it, and make a crater in the center. Add the sugar and open the egg on top of it. Then add the butter, which you have gently softened with your hands, and then start working the flour so that all the ingredients combine. One of your objectives should be to work the dough as little as possible, because this will give your *spungata* a more delicate crust. Make the dough into a ball. If the dough seems a bit hard (perhaps because of the flour you are using), you can add a little water, but not more than 2 teaspoons. Cut the dough into two pieces, one larger than the other. Using a rolling pin (preferably a simple wood cylinder about 22 inches / 56 cm long), roll out the dough to about ¼ inch / 0.6 cm thick. Lightly butter a baking dish or pie plate 12 inches / 30 cm in diameter. Line the dish with the larger of the two sheets of dough and toss in a little bit of flour. Spoon in the jam mixture evenly. Carefully place the other layer of dough on top and, with moistened fingers, join the two pieces of dough. You may simply seal them, as an Italian baker might do, or crimp them, as an American would. In either case, cut away and discard the excess dough. Bake in a preheated 350°F/180°C oven for 30 minutes. Let cool before cutting or serving. *Spungata* can be served tepid or at room temperature, but it does not taste good if it has been refrigerated.

Sciumette
Little Meringue Sponges

Just up the road from where I live in Camogli is the town of Recco, arguably the best food town in Liguria. Although it is most famous for *focaccia col formaggio*, *trofie al pesto*, and *cappon magro*, the particularly deft hand of the typical Recco chef is also suitable for the preparation of *sciumette*, the Ligurian word for "little sponges." They are not unlike the French dessert *oeufs à la neige*, which look like icebergs floating in a dark yellow sea. While I would be hard put to tell you which version came first, I can tell you that *sciumette* have been part of the Ligurian dessert table at Easter and Christmas for at least three hundred years. This recipe was kindly given to me by the owners of Manuelina restaurant, one of Liguria's culinary shrines. Note that I encourage you to use organic lemons and eggs to avoid chemicals that will change the flavor of this dish and perhaps be harmful to your health.

5 cups / 1200 ml whole milk
Rind of 1 organic (without coloring, sprays, or wax) lemon, grated
2 tablespoons / 15 g sugar
5 extra-large eggs (preferably organic), separated
1 teaspoon / 5 ml fresh lemon juice (from the organic lemon)
⅝ cup plus 1 tablespoon / 125 g and ⅝ cup plus 1 tablespoon / 125 g sugar
1 teaspoon / 2.3 g and 1 teaspoon / 2.3 g powdered cinnamon
½ ounce / ⅛ cup / 2 tablespoons / 15 g pistachio nuts, chopped

Makes
6 to 8 servings

Using a large, heavy-bottomed pot and very low heat, slowly bring the milk to a low boil. Gently stir in the lemon rind and 2 tablespoons/15 g of sugar.

While the milk is slowly coming to a boil, place 4 of the egg whites (you may reserve or discard the fifth) in a chilled glass or metal bowl and beat (with an eggbeater or a whisk) until they form peaks. Gently stir in the lemon juice, ⅝ cup plus 1 tablespoon/125 g sugar, and 1 teaspoon powdered cinnamon. Beat until the combination is stiff.

As the milk starts to simmer (it should never reach a violent boil), use a clean teaspoon to take a heaping spoonful of egg white mixture. Slide it carefully into the milk. Repeat the process three more times so that four *sciumette* will be cooking at one time. Make sure that there is space between them because these "little sponges" will enlarge. After 90 seconds, turn each *sciumetta* so that it will poach on the other side for another 90 seconds. At Manuelina they recommended handling the *sciumette* with two forks (spoons would break them), but I have had more success with one fork and a slotted spoon, although

I try to emulate the delicacy of hand found in Recco. After they have poached on both sides, remove the *sciumette* to a dish or tray lined with paper toweling.

Then whip the egg whites again and make four more *sciumette,* repeating the procedure until all of the egg white mixture is used up. Always make sure that the milk simmers but never really boils. Once done, pause for a few minutes and let the pot cool.

Then, while the *sciumette* drain, make a sauce for them. Strain the milk of any impurities. Pour the milk into a measuring cup until you have 3 cups/675 ml. If there is not enough from the milk you used for poaching, add more whole milk.

Beat the 5 egg yolks in a bowl and pour them into the pan you used to heat the milk. Add ⅝ cup plus 1 tablespoon/125 g of sugar and combine thoroughly. Place the pot over very low heat and start adding the milk a little at a time. As you add the milk, stir constantly with a wooden spoon. Cook until it thickens into a custard (about 3 or 4 minutes), but make sure it does not boil. (If the sauce is overcooked, it will curdle. If it does, you have two options: one is to make another sauce. The second is to place the curdled sauce in a blender and run it at medium speed for about 15 seconds.)

Once the sauce is ready, place the pot in a large dish of cold water so that the sauce will cool. Stir the sauce every so often.

To serve, place some sauce on individual dishes and carefully place 2 or 3 *sciumette* on each plate. Garnish with a little cinnamon and a few chopped pistachio nuts. Alternatively, you may place all of the sauce and *sciumette* (and garnish them) on a platter and then serve each diner. This makes a more dramatic presentation but, to me, the extra handling required to serve them can alter the look and flavor of the *sciumette,* and you have labored too much to want that to happen.

Genoise

Genoese Sponge Cake

Here is one of the most classic cake preparations. Most bakers assume that because of its French name that this is a French creation. The French have always been especially adept at incorporating the best things they find elsewhere into their own cuisine and culture, and genoise is no exception. I am sure that during one of the many French occupations of Genoa (in the eighteenth century, I would guess in this case), this recipe was discovered and brought home to France. In Genoa it is typically used as the bed for an artfully made preserve of apricot, peach, or cherry. I have also enjoyed it topped with pureed marrons glacés. It is also possible to slice your genoise horizontally and make it a sandwich for one of these fillings. You may freeze a genoise, carefully wrapped in plastic or stored in a plastic container, for up to two months.

3 large eggs, beaten
¾ cup / 3 ounces / 85 g granulated sugar
¾ cup / 3 ounces / 85 g pastry flour, sifted
4 tablespoons / 2 ounces / 55 g sweet butter, melted and cooled

Makes one 7-inch / 18-cm round cake

Preheat oven to 350°F/180°C. Lightly butter a 7-inch/18-cm cake pan. In a large mixing bowl, beat the eggs and the sugar with a whisk until they have almost doubled in volume. This may also be done with an electric hand mixer, but I do not find that the mixing attachment for the food processor does the trick. Now comes the delicate part. Sift about one-third of the flour and add it to the egg mixture, folding it in very lightly with a whisk or rubber spatula. You should stir as little as possible. Do not use the electric mixer for this procedure. Then sift the second third of the flour, and add as you did the first third. Then add the last third in the same manner. Now pour the cooled melted butter down the side of the bowl, stir quickly, and pour the mixture into the pan. Bake for about 20 to 25 (or up to 30) minutes. The cake should be firm to the touch (and slightly spongy) and should have pulled away from the pan. Let set for 5 minutes and then carefully slide a dull knife around the sides of the pan to loosen the genoise. Carefully turn it out onto a wire rack to cool.

Amaretti

Bitter Almond Cookies

These well-known Italian cookies are produced commercially in Saronno, in Lombardy, but this is the recipe from Sassello, in the province of Savona, whose amaretti are homemade and more memorable. In Liguria, amaretti are typically served with tea, with fruit, with wine, and as a stuffing for peaches (see the recipe on page 383). You must understand that these are not bitter cookies with almonds, but rather cookies made with sweet almonds (the type you are used to) and bitter almonds (which you can find in pastry shops, good fruit-and-nut sellers, and some health food stores).

2 teaspoons/5 g sweet butter
1 tablespoon/7 g unbleached flour
⅔ cup/75 g peeled, blanched bitter almonds
  (available in health food stores and specialty shops)
¾ cup/85 g peeled, blanched sweet almonds
¾ cup/85 g granulated sugar
4 egg whites
1 tablespoon/7 g confectioner's sugar

Grease a cookie sheet with the butter and then top with the flour. Tap the tray to dislodge any excess flour. Place the bitter almonds, the sweet almonds, and the granulated sugar in a mortar and pound until you have created a powder (this procedure may also be done in a blender or food processor, but the traditional method, of course, is in the mortar). Whisk the egg whites in a cold glass or metal bowl until you see peaks. Use a wooden spoon to add the whipped egg whites into the mortar. Then stir for about 5 to 8 minutes, or until the mixture is smooth.

Makes 24 cookies

Now make the cookies. There is a family way to do it, and I have also devised a slightly more professional adaptation. To do it as a family cook would, take a heaping teaspoon of the mixture and plop it onto your greased cookie sheet. Each little mound of batter should be about 1 inch/25 mm in diameter, and should be spaced 1 inch/25 mm apart. The more professional way to do this is to put the mixture into a pastry bag with a plain tip. Squeeze out enough batter to form mounds 1 inch/25 mm in diameter. No matter how you make the mounds, when you are done, set the tray aside in a cool, draft-free spot for 3 hours. The mounds will expand as they sit.

Baking: 15 minutes before you are ready to bake, preheat your oven to 350°F/180°C. Dust the confectioner's sugar over all the mounds and then bake the cookies for about 20 minutes, until they are crunchy and light gold in color. Let cool thoroughly on a wire rack. Serve at room temperature. They may be stored in an airtight plastic container for about ten days, although I doubt such good cookies will be allowed to last that long.

Dessert Fritters

Fritters are endlessly popular in Liguria because of their ease of preparation and addictive quality. Before setting about to make fritters, read the hints about frying on page 177.

Frisceu di Mele
Apple Fritters

½ cup / 115 ml* warm whole milk
1 package (2½ teaspoons) / 6 g active dry yeast
4 cups / 450 g unbleached flour
1 large egg
1 cup / 225 ml tepid water
1 cup / 225 ml white wine
Extravirgin olive oil or peanut or canola oil
2 cups / 225 g apples, washed, cored, seeded, and sliced into thin crescents
Confectioner's sugar or vanilla-scented confectioner's sugar (optional)

* Note: 115 ml equals 100 ml (or 1 dl) plus 1 tablespoon.

Makes 4 to 6 servings

Place the warm milk in a large mixing bowl, add the yeast, and leave for 15 minutes so that the yeast may activate. Add the flour, egg, water, and wine. Combine the ingredients using a wooden spoon so that you make a very soft, slightly liquidy batter. Cover the bowl with a damp cloth and set aside for 1 hour. Slice the apples just before they will be used so they do not oxidize.

When you are ready to make the fritters, take a large, heavy-bottomed pan or a wok and fill it ½ inch/1.25 cm high with olive oil. Heat the oil over medium heat. As the oil is heating, add the apple slices to the batter and combine well. When the oil is hot (but not sputtering or smoking), dip a tablespoon into the oil and then into the batter. Start spooning tablespoonfuls of batter into the oil. As the fritters begin to take shape and expand, turn them with a slotted spoon so that they cook evenly. Typically, it should take about 1 minute to cook each fritter. Once they are golden in color, remove them with the slotted spoon to paper toweling, where they will drain. Keep spooning batter into the oil until it is all used up. Serve the fritters immediately, topped, perhaps, with confectioner's sugar.

Friscêu Cö Zebibbo e Pinoli

Raisin–Pine Nut Fritters

½ cup/115 ml* warm whole milk
2½ teaspoons (1 package)/6 g active dry yeast
4 cups/450 g unbleached flour
1 large egg
1½ cups/235 ml tepid water
½ cup/115 ml Marsala
1 tablespoon granulated sugar
1 grated lemon peel or 2 tablespoons minced candied lemon peel
2 tablespoons/15 g pinoli
1 cup/110 g mixed brown and golden raisins (sultanas)
Extravirgin olive oil or peanut or canola oil
Confectioner's sugar or vanilla-scented confectioner's sugar (optional)

*Note: 115 ml equals 100 ml (or 1 dl) plus 1 tablespoon

*Makes
4 to 6 servings*

Place the warm milk in a large mixing bowl, add the yeast, and leave for 15 minutes so that the yeast may activate. Add the flour, egg, water, Marsala, and granulated sugar. Combine the ingredients using a wooden spoon so that you make a very soft, slightly liquidy batter. Cover the bowl with a damp cloth and set aside for 1 hour. Then stir in the lemon peel, *pinoli,* and raisins, and combine well.

When you are ready to make the fritters, take a large, heavy-bottomed pan or a wok and fill it ½ inch/1.25 cm high with olive oil. Heat the oil over medium heat. When the oil is hot (but not sputtering or smoking), dip a tablespoon into the oil and then into the batter. Start spooning tablespoonfuls of batter into the oil. As the fritters begin to take shape and expand, turn them with a slotted spoon so that they cook evenly. Typically, it should take about 1 minute to cook each fritter. Once they are golden in color, remove them with the slotted spoon to paper toweling, where they will drain. Keep spooning batter into the oil until it is all used up. Serve the fritters immediately, topped, perhaps, with confectioner's sugar.

Friscêu di Frutta Secca

This is a variation I have devised, one that I have not encountered in Liguria, but which is in keeping with the ideas of the Ligurian kitchen. The recipe is identical to the one for Friscêu Cö Zebibbo e Pinoli, except that I have removed the raisins and replaced them with 1 cup/110 g finely minced dried fruit. You may vary these as you choose, but I particularly enjoy combining dried apricots and dried cherries. Other dried fruits I have used are pears, apples, bananas, pineapple, cranberries, currants, peaches, and figs. Let your palate and taste be your guide.

From the Diary of
Claude Monet (1884)

17 February: "We have arrived in the Valle Nervia at an extraordinarily picturesque little borgo (Dolceacqua)."

18 February: "The place is superb, there is a bridge that is a jewel of lightness."

Western Liguria has dozens of stone bridges that span brooks and rivulets. Perhaps none is more famous than the bridge at Dolceacqua, a town in the *entroterra* of Ventimiglia and Bordighera where Liguria's best-known red wine, Rossese di Dolceacqua, is produced. This bridge was built after a previous one collapsed in the fifteenth century. It is remarkably delicate, especially given that it is 107 feet/33 meters long. To me it looks as if it is made of spun sugar — its ethereal nature has always captivated visitors, at least as much as the delicious local food and wine, about which Monet did not comment.

The stone bridge of Dolceacqua

The Wines
of Liguria

$\mathcal{L}$IGURIA, with its steep slopes, difficult soil, and limited arable terrain, is not a region that produces a great quantity of wine. It would be possible to cultivate more vines if Ligurian farmers would choose to do so, but that would mean sacrificing precious soil that is used for fruit, vegetables, and herbs. This has not happened, in part, because Liguria borders on Piedmont and Tuscany, which along with Friuli-Venezia Giulia produce the highest quality wine in Italy. These wines are regularly found on Ligurian tables, although the biggest reds (Barolo, Barbaresco, Brunello di Montalcino, and Vino Nobile di Montepulciano) are less often seen because they are quite costly and would overpower the delicate flavors of Ligurian food.

The nearness of these great wine-producing regions means that many grape varieties are available in Liguria: More than one hundred varieties may be found in the region's small vineyards. The foremost Ligurian grapes are Pigato, Vermentino, Rossese, and Dolcetto. Pigato is a round, pleasing white, while Vermentino is slightly more prickly, though equally gratifying. Rossese is a nice medium-weight red that is described below. It may surprise you to see Dolcetto listed as a Ligurian grape, since it is so intimately associated with southern Piedmont. In fact, the Dolcetto grape is native to Cáiro Montenotte in the province of Savona. It is probably the Ligurian red of choice, even though much of it is acquired from the neighboring Piedmontese province of Alessandria.

Vermentino is the most versatile white wine grape in Liguria. It can vary in fragrance and flavor, based largely on the terrain in which it is grown, the amount of sun it receives, and its proximity to either sea or woods. It can also vary according to who makes the wine and the preference he or she has. I have tasted many Ligurian Vermentinos (there are also good ones from Sardinia and Tuscany, and you should seek them out if hard-to-find Ligurian ones are not available).

One type of Ligurian Vermentino, found in the area above Sestri Levante in the province of Genoa, has a pronounced fragrance of anise, pine, rosemary, or sage. This Vermentino is rich and structured, and I enjoy drinking it with vegetable tarts or such fish as sardines, fresh anchovies, or sea bass. Another Vermentino, found in the area where the provinces of Genoa and La Spezia meet, has a fragrance reminiscent of peaches and lavender. I like this wine by itself, or with young, milky cheeses.

Ligurian wine is influenced by its neighbors in another important way. In Piemonte (Piedmont) most wines are made from a single grape (Dolcetto or Nebbiolo, for example) as are the wines of western Liguria (Riviera di Ponente). Tuscan wines are usually blends of several grapes, as are those in eastern Liguria (the Lunigiana and the Cinqueterre).

As in most of Italy, winemaking in Liguria dates back to ancient times. Grapes arrived in Liguria (especially around Dolceacqua) with the Phoenicians. In most cases, Ligurian grape growers have a small patch of land and production is limited to what is consumed and sold locally. When Liguria was under Napoleon, and each stretch (or "department") of land moving from west to east was devoted to growth of a particular product, the terrain from Arma di Taggia to Albenga was the department of vines. In contrast, the stretch from Arma to Nice was for palms. Only a few Ligurian wines — particularly Rossese di Dolceacqua, Pigato, Vermentino, and the whites of the Cinqueterre — have achieved fame beyond the region, but because of limited production they are hard to find and often pricey. The visitor to Liguria should make an effort to sample the region's wines, most of which marry perfectly with its delicious and delicate cuisine.

Wine figures centrally in Ligurian gastronomy and social customs. One drinks white wine (especially Pigato or Coronata, the white wine of Genoa) while consuming freshly baked focaccia. Many Ligurian dishes feature a splash of wine to give flavor to the recipe. Until recently, one would see a *pirrone,* a typical wine bottle, on every fishing boat. A *pirrone* has an unusually long neck and narrow mouth. It is designed so that one could drink from it without placing one's lips on the rim. The *pirrone* provided wine for all of the fishermen and would be passed around while waiting for the fish to bite.

In describing Ligurian or any Italian wine, it is necessary to understand a couple of terms. The main one is D.O.C. (which stands for Denominazione di Origine Controllata). This means that a particular wine is produced according to standards of typicity and quality that have been set by the regional and national agricultural governmental authorities. Italy has hundreds of grape varieties and thousands of wines, and in the early 1960s it was deemed necessary to codify these, in part to guarantee quality and in part to preserve historical and cultural distinctions.

While the D.O.C. designation implies a good minimum standard of quality, there can be a great range of difference among wines that bear the same name and place of origin. Similarly, if a wine does not have a D.O.C. designation, this does not mean that it is bad. Rather, it simply suggests that the wine is a combination of grapes that is an expression of the taste and preferences of the winemaker.

The other term to understand is D.O.C.G. (Denominazione di Origine Controllata e Garantita). The designation is a more specialized one that refers to very few wines in Italy (about twenty at this writing) that are of such particular quality or character that they receive a special "guaranteed" designation. Most D.O.C.G. wines are among Italy's best and most famous, such as Barolo and Brunello di Montalcino, but there is one in Liguria, which was designated in 1995. This is the Sciacchetrà made in the Cinqueterre in the province of La Spezia. This is a fortified dessert wine made in minute quantities from the grapes that are used to make typical Cinqueterre whites. Its alcohol content is 17 percent (while a typical white wine might be 11 percent), and there is so little of it that you might not even find it if you go to the zone of production.

There are four D.O.C. zones in Liguria (from west to east): Rossese di Dolceacqua; Riviera Ligure di Ponente; Cinqueterre; and Colli di Luni. These zones cover much of the provinces of Imperia, Savona, and La Spezia, but almost entirely ignore the province of Genoa, where little D.O.C. wine is produced.

Rossese di Dolceacqua

This wine is often referred to simply as Dolceacqua, referring to the town where almost all Rossese is produced. Dolceacqua, north of Ventimiglia and a stone's throw from the French border, produces a flavorful, full-bodied D.O.C. red that goes well with the rabbit dishes popular in the area. When the Rossese is aged for at least a year and its alcohol content rises from 12 percent to 13 percent, the wine can be called Rossese Superiore. Rossese di Dolceacqua was a great favorite of Napoleon Bonaparte, that well-known Frenchman of Ligurian origin (his family was from near La Spezia).

Riviera Ligure di Ponente

The provinces of Imperia and Savona produce most of the top wines in Liguria. As mentioned above, most are made almost entirely of one grape variety. One often finds geographical subdivisions on some of the Ponente wines, such as Albenganese (from the area around Albenga), Finalese (from the area around Finale Ligure) and Riviera dei Fiori (from the area stretching from Ventimiglia to Porto Maurizio).

PIGATO is made of a grape of the same name. Some Pigato wines have up to 5 percent other added grapes grown in the same designated area. This lightly fragrant, straw yellow white wine with a slightly bitter almond taste goes beautifully with Ligurian seafood dishes and savory baked goods. Good Pigato comes from near Albenga and will be called Pigato Albenganese. The minimum alcohol content is 11 percent.

VERMENTINO from this area is slightly more fragrant and fruity than its cousin in the Lunigiana. It is a perfect match with antipasti and fish, and typically has a minimum alcohol content of 11 percent.

ROSSESE DELLA RIVIERA DI PONENTE is a light ruby red made with the same grape as in Dolceacqua, but grown in different climate and terrain. It is dry, delicate, with a winy nose, and is quite drinkable. Minimum alcohol content is 11 percent.

ORMEASCO is made from Dolcetto and can contain up to 5 percent other red grape varieties. It has been made in a small area of the province of Imperia since 1300. It has a winy nose, ruby red color, slightly bitter taste, and moderate body. It goes well with most foods. It has a minimum alcohol content of 11 percent and when it has been aged for one year and has an alcohol content of at least 12.5 percent it is labeled Ormeasco Superiore. Ormeasco Scia-trac is a lighter, pinker version of the red with a minimum alcohol content of 11 percent. Ormeasco is honored with a festival in late August in the town of Pornassio.

Quiliano is a major wine-producing town in the province of Savona. The local wine is a white called Buzzetto, but the town also makes good Vermentino, Pigato, and two particular reds: Granaccia (Grenache) and Sangiovese.

Cinqueterre

The wines of the Cinqueterre, five beautiful little villages in the hills just north of La Spezia, require great effort to produce. Tiny vineyards dot the slopes. Grapes are collected by hand and placed in small baskets that are carried to wineries by workers or on the backs of donkeys. I have occasionally seen Ligurian women carry these baskets on their heads.

Typical Ligurian wines

In October 1995 I was invited to pick grapes during the harvest above Manarola. The wine of this area has taken on mythic status in part because the Cinqueterre have become so overrun with tourists in recent years and people want to taste the local wine. In truth, the wine is very pleasant, but it is not better than other Ligurian whites. Part of what makes these wines so prized is the difficulty entailed in producing them. Because the grapevines are planted on what little level ground can be found on the steep mountains that rise from the sea, the cultivation and picking of the grapes and the maintenance of the vines require hard work. Years ago, a tiny railway was installed with great effort to transport workers and grapes up and down the hills. The little cars remind me of something from a ride in an amusement park, and it can be a tad frightening going up and down. The grapes are 350 meters (more than 1,150 feet) above sea level. They are all gathered by hand and loaded into the little cars, which then are sent down the hills to be transported to the Cantina Sociale, the winery cooperative that produces the wine for most of the area's growers. The backbreaking work is no longer appealing to younger Ligurians, who can make more money through tourism than in cultivating grapes. I worked with two women, one in her late twenties, the other around forty years old. They told me that in a few years there will be little crop left because no one will want to tend the grapes — the labor is exhausting and there is little financial reward. I noticed that many other types of vegetation had sprouted among the trellises that held the grapevines. Soon what little Cinqueterre wine is left will be made by private growers on their small plots of land. If these growers have any grapes left over, they will sell them to the Cantina Sociale. This passing of a beloved way of life is a by-product of what we call progress. It is understandable that people would want to earn more money with less labor, but soon the particular taste of this wine, whose grapes drew flavor from the sea air as well as the spontaneous vegetation of the Ligurian hills, will be but a memory.

BIANCO DELLE CINQUETERRE A delicate straw-colored D.O.C. white wine made of Albarola, Bosco, and Vermentino grapes. It is light in flavor and fragrance, and matches well with most local dishes.

CINQUETERRE SCIACCHETRÀ, mentioned above, is a dessert wine that is at least 17 percent alcohol. It is amber in color with an alluring honeyed bouquet and ranges in flavor from sweet to almost dry. It must be aged at least one year before being sold. It is found almost exclusively in the Cinqueterre, plus a few places in La Spezia and Genoa. It is sold by the bottle or half-bottle and, rarely, by the glass in a few bars and cafés.

Colli di Luni

The zone known as the Lunigiana is a mountainous area covering the point where Liguria, Tuscany, and Emilia-Romagna meet. The wines here tend to be blends of several grapes, and show some Tuscan influence. The wines of the Lunigiana were renowned in Roman times and were a particular favorite of Pliny.

ROSSO DEI COLLI DI LUNI, a ruby-colored fragrant red, is made of Sangiovese and other available grapes, including Canaiolo, Pollera Nera, and Ciliegiolo. There can be an addition of up to 25 percent other red grapes, with the result that there are great differences in the D.O.C. Rosso dei Colli di Luni from one producer to another. In effect, it is a cousin of Chianti. The minimum alcohol content is 11.5 percent, and when it is 12.5 percent and has been aged for two years it is labeled Riserva.

BIANCO DEI COLLI DI LUNI is made of Ligurian Vermentino, Trebbiano Toscano, and can contain up to 30 percent other white wine grapes. This wine is light straw-colored and is delicate and dry. The minimum alcohol content is 11.5 percent.

VERMENTINO DEI COLLI DI LUNI, a wine made entirely of the grape of that name, is a delicious, dry white with a slightly almond taste. The minimum alcohol content is 11.5 percent.

There are numerous non-D.O.C. wines produced in Liguria, often made with well-known grapes from other regions. These include Chardonnay, Gewürztraminer, Pinot Bianco, Sauvignon Blanc, and Tocai among the whites, and Bracchetto, Merlot, and Sangiovese among the reds. Among the non-D.O.C. wines that are typically Ligurian one finds whites such as Biancolella, Buzzetto, Coronata, and Lumassina, and the red Granaccia.

While Ligurian wines have begun to travel, and you should favor them in your wine selections if you have the choice, I want to give you some options if you cannot locate Ligurian wines:

For *whites,* you should look for a Vermentino from either Tuscany or Sardinia. If these are unavailable, you may substitute a Vernaccia di San Gimignano from Tuscany or a Gavi from Piedmont.

For *reds,* you should first select a Dolcetto from Piedmont. These are easily found, so you should not have to look further. If necessary, however, other red substitutions could be a lighter Chianti or Chianti Classico (although not a Riserva), or a Sangiovese from Emilia-Romagna or Tuscany.

Salute!

Curing One's Ills
in Alassio

In doing my research for this book, I discovered an amazing subset of travel literature, most of it written in the last four decades of the nineteenth century, dedicated to readers who go to warmer climates in the winter to restore and preserve their health. Some of these books are written by doctors, others by travel writers. Catering to these "snowbirds" became a major industry and Liguria, paradise that it is, was the favored destination for many of these visitors, especially from Britain, Germany, Switzerland, and Russia.

Eustace A. Reynolds Ball's *Mediterranean Winter Resorts: A Practical Handbook to the Principal Health and Pleasure Resorts on the Shores of the Mediterranean,* published in London in 1899, is typical of these books. The author goes into explicit, almost gruesome, detail about where to go depending on what medical complaints you report. The following is part of the entry for Alassio, written in 1895. The author also informs us that Rev. T. Hewitt, B.D., conducts church services twice daily and that the church has a circulating library, by subscription for the winter season. Dr. Boon and Dr. Names (who speaks English), are there for medical problems. Mr. Walter Congreve serves as banker and House Agent, and also supplies wines and English stores. We are told that Alassio is extremely cheap, provisions are plentiful, and that servants are easily procured and will accept moderate wages.

"The class of cases for which the climate of Alassio is best suited are those with limited disease and feeble circulation; and those suffering from overwork often find the warmer air of the Riviera suits them better than the tonic air of the higher Alps. Cases, which have recurring attacks of hæmorrhage, form a prominent feature, and generally do well at Alassio. . . . The influence of the climate of Alassio on chronic rheumatism varies with the different cases; some persons are entirely free from any symptoms, while other patients, again, do not seem to gain any benefit at all from the climate. Gout is usually benefited, as are its milder manifestations. Owing to its fine sandy beach, Alassio forms a very admirable winter resort for strumous or weakly children. For the same reason it forms a very excellent resort for sufferers from nervous diseases. In partial paralysis, the sufferers are enabled to spend a large proportion of their time by the sea, and to take what little exercise they are capable of on a level surface. Patients showing any marked tendency to hysteria and melancholia should, however, on no account be sent there, as the almost invariable tendency of the climate is to aggravate those complaints. That large and common class of ailments, known as nervous breakdown, frequently receive very great benefit from a prolonged stay there. Caution, however, should be exercised in sending any case in which sleeplessness forms a prominent symptom, as but little benefit is likely to be obtained in such cases. In diseases of the heart a great alleviation of symptoms may be reckoned on in consequence of a winter spent in Alassio. Not only does the open-air life improve the general nutrition, but also those great dangers bronchitis and broncho-pneumonia may be warded off."

A Ligurian Larder

"There is no love sincerer than the love of food."

— George Bernard Shaw

*I*N THE INTEREST of love, here is a selective, but by no means exhaustive, list of essential ingredients of the Ligurian kitchen. Most of these foods are described in more detail elsewhere in this book. I cannot be emphatic enough in my insistence that you use the very best ingredients available to you. While this philosophy is applicable to all types of cooking, it is especially so as regards Ligurian food because it is based entirely on the outstanding and distinct flavors of its raw materials.

Anchovies *Acciughe*

When we think of these fish, invariably it is the brown, salt-cured anchovy that comes to mind. A Ligurian might just as likely think of fresh anchovies or even *bianchetti,* the transparent newborn anchovies that they boil or put in omelettes or fritters. Fresh anchovies have become increasingly available in our markets, especially those near the coasts. Anchovies in Liguria are also conserved in salt or converted into sauces. Many of these products are now available, some from Liguria, others from Sicily or other Italian regions.

Artichokes *Carciofi*

The artichokes of Liguria and Lazio (Rome's region) are considered Italy's best. They are a harbinger of spring, and between February and April they are conspicuous in Ligurian dishes. North Americans are used to seeing huge artichokes, the type that are more often seen in Lazio. Ligurians prefer baby artichokes that look like flowers waiting to blossom. They are much more delicate and require less pruning before cooking. These baby artichokes can almost be eaten whole, and are delicious raw as well as cooked. Most Ligurians say that the best artichokes come from Albenga. In addition to the traditional green artichokes, there are also exotic little purple ones, but they are difficult to find outside the region. Ligurians make a sauce, *paté di carciofi* (also called *crema di carciofi* or *salsa cynara*), that helps them impart the flavor of artichoke throughout the year. Ligurian artichoke sauce has become increasingly available in our better food stores, so that we can have the flavor of real Ligurian artichokes at any time.

Basil *Basilico*

Basil is the emblematic leaf and fragrance of the Ligurian kitchen. While it is not originally a native of this region, it found particularly congenial soil when planted there. The herb is of Asian origin, having been cultivated in India (Krishna and Vishnu considered basil sacred), China (where it is little used), and in Vietnam, Thailand, and Laos, where it is very popular. It has long been popular throughout the Mediterranean (the Greek word *basilikon* means royal), and is used in much of Italy. While Italians are proud of their combination of basil and tomatoes, they would probably hesitate to acknowledge that the herb came from Asia and the fruit came from the Americas. Keats, who knew his Ligurian basil, had his heroine Isabella bury her murdered lover's head in a pot of basil, which she watered with her tears.

The glory of pesto in Liguria is that the fragrance and taste of basil is so extraordinary. Ligurians tell you that this is because of the particular soil combined with the sea air. They insist that basil grown on the other side of those mountains, in Piedmont, Lombardy, and Emilia-Romagna, just does not taste the same. And they are right. Basil does taste different depending on where it is grown, and Liguria, for the above-mentioned reasons, is that paradise where basil grows best. There are even distinct differences in basil grown in one part of Liguria or another. People in the province of Genoa willingly pay more to have basil grown in the tiny suburb called Prà, which can be reached on the Genoese public transit system. This very urban-looking place, where highways connect and which seems quite rundown, has for centuries grown the basil that makes the best pesto. In Liguria the preferred basil for just about every application is the small, round-leaf type called *basilico genovese,* which is what is planted in Prà. Seeds for this basil are available outside Italy, usually sold under the name

Genovese basil. These produce a sweeter, milder basil than the one most North Americans know. What is typical basil in most countries, the large-leaf, highly fragrant, minty-tasting variety, is used in Liguria only for stuffing (see Basilico Ripieno, page 182) and would appear in pesto only if the small-leaf kind were unavailable. On most terraces in Genoa and throughout the region, families who do not have their own land grow basil and other herbs in flower pots and coffee cans, so they have an abundant supply for most of the year. If you live in a temperate or warm climate, you can do the same.

Ligurians say that the best basil appears in April and May, and they often make a lot of pesto at that time to store in jars for the months when the basil is less vivid. Some Ligurians place basil leaves in olive oil, close the container tight, and store them for several months. In my view, basil does not freeze well, and certainly dried basil, those pathetic black little leaves, should not even have a place in your kitchen.

Beet Greens *Bietole*
These are variously called beet tops or beet roots. They are often discarded in the markets of North America, which is a major error. They are delicious, and loaded with vitamins and minerals. Get to know your vegetable seller and ask that beet greens be kept for you. They are moderate in cost and are an essential filling in Ligurian vegetable tortes and pastas.

Butter *Burro*
Butter is not a major protagonist in the Ligurian kitchen, which is unique in Northern Italy in that and many other regards. Yet it has always been used in baking and, because Liguria borders on the major dairy regions of Piedmont, Lombardy, and Emilia-Romagna, butter has always been available. Olive oil is the cooking fat of choice, but when Ligurians use butter it is always unsalted. When you use butter for any recipes in this book, it must be unsalted.

Cheeses *Formaggi*
See individual listings for Crescenza, Parmigiano-Reggiano, Pecorino Romano, *Prescinseua,* and Ricotta.

Chestnuts *Castagne*
Chestnuts, now a somewhat rare and luxurious commodity, have long been foods for the poor in Liguria and other parts of Italy. They are turned into pastes that provide sustenance and dried to make flour. When wheat flour was too expensive, breads and pasta were often made with a combination of wheat

and chestnut flour. Of course, chestnuts are the key ingredient in marrons glacés (candied chestnuts), which are a specialty of Genoa. You may be able to acquire fresh chestnuts in the fall, and chestnut flours are available by special order (see pages 444-445).

Chickpeas *Ceci*

Chickpeas serve the same function as chestnuts in Ligurian cooking: to provide flour and bulk to dishes when other ingredients are too expensive. Chickpea flour is the essential ingredient in *farinata*.

Crescenza

Crescenza is the fundamental cheese for *focaccia col formaggio,* the great bread from Recco. It is often confused with Stracchino cheese and, while they are similar, they are not the same. Stracchino is from Lombardy, has a thin white rind, and is slightly sweeter. Crescenza has no rind and is tangier. *Stracchino* is the local Ligurian word for Crescenza. If you cannot locate Crescenza, which has recently become available in North America, you may use Stracchino and stir in a bit of yogurt or buttermilk to give it more tang.

Eggs *Uova*

Eggs in Italy are smaller than those in North America and have much darker yolks. They are often called *rossi di uova* or egg reds. They give the golden color to egg pasta. For the purposes of this book, you should select large (as opposed to medium, extra-large, or jumbo) eggs. If you are making pasta, you might choose to eliminate some of the whites and just use the yolks.

Fish and Seafood *Pesce e Frutti di Mare*

Although Liguria is a coastal region and has long been a maritime republic, the sea has represented trade and transport much more than a food resource. Ligurians do eat fish, and quite a bit of it, but it is so-called poor fish rather than prized varieties such as tuna or swordfish. They feast on fresh anchovies and sardines, as well as newborn fish such as whitebait (*bianchetti* or *gianchetti*), "redbait" (*rossetti,* from mullet), sea bass (*branzino*), hake (*nasello*) and gilthead bream (*orata*). Ligurians do eat canned tuna because they have a long tradition of fishing off the coast of Tunisia. Mussels (called *muscoli* in Liguria; *cozze* in the rest of Italy) are the foremost shellfish of the region, although large red crayfish are found in the waters off Santa Margherita. Clams (*arselle* or *mitili*) are consumed in moderate amounts. Octopus (*polpo*) and baby octopus (*moscardini*) also turn up on Ligurian tables.

Flour *Farina*

Italians are jealous of North Americans for the quality of our wheat flours. The most prized flour in Italy is from Canada and goes by the name Manitoba, for the province of its origin. The standard Italian wheat flour used to make focaccia, bread, and fresh pasta is called tipo 00. You may safely use unbleached all-purpose flour for all of the recipes in this book that call for flour. For chestnut flour and chickpea flour, look under their individual listings.

Fruit *Frutta*

Ligurian fruits are divine. Read more about them on page 381.

Funghi Porcini (Wild Boletus Mushrooms)

In thinking about fancy Italian mushrooms, it has become the norm to refer to them as *funghi porcini*. In fact, there are many varieties of wild mushrooms that are safe to eat that can be used in cookery. It is true, however, that *funghi porcini* are the most prized and, in the Ligurian kitchen, the most ubiquitous. Porcini are most commonly found in spring and fall, although they appear in summer and, in Liguria at least, during the winter. The key is rainfall. During one autumn visit not long ago, I found the region besieged by torrential rain. Difficult as this was — and, sadly, quite damaging to property and livestock — many Ligurians found some consolation in the knowledge that there would be a plethora of *funghi porcini* awaiting them when the sun returned.

It is possible to find *funghi porcini,* or similar varieties, in wooded areas throughout North America. For example, I have collected them in the ski basin northeast of Santa Fe following one of the brief but frequent rain showers that sweep across northern New Mexico. Of course, you must be fully acquainted with mushrooms before collecting and eating them because there are many poisonous varieties. In Italy many police departments have trained mycologists (mushroom experts) on staff, especially in mountain areas. Such experts are harder to find in North America, although many nature preserves have rangers who know about mushrooms. Most fancy food shops, and even some supermarkets, now sell dried *funghi porcini* from Italy. For some recipes in this book, you may combine fresh cultivated mushrooms with dried *funghi porcini* that have been soaked.

Porcini mushrooms come with the Latin name *boletus*. The popular autumn porcino is the *Boletus edulis*. The cold-weather porcino is *Boletus pinicola,* the summer porcino is the *Boletus reticulatus,* the red porcino is the *Boletus rufus,* and the black porcino is the *Boletus aereus*.

CLEANING *FUNGHI PORCINI:* These mushrooms are very delicate and if not handled correctly they will lose many of the qualities that make them so prized. Once picked, they should be used quickly. In Italy it is customary to cut and trim the mushrooms at the place they are picked. This simply means cutting away some of the dirt and other materials from the stem and leaving them on the ground. The cap or crown of the mushroom — which contains much of the flavor and aroma — should be handled with great care and should not be detached from the stem.

Once the mushrooms are brought to the kitchen, they should be carefully wiped with a damp cloth to remove any dirt. Then give them a quick rinse in cool water. If they are washed at length in cold water, their perfume will vanish. Then proceed to use them in the recipe you have selected.

CUTTING *FUNGHI PORCINI:* Most recipes require that *funghi porcini* be sliced before cooking them. In many cases, especially when eaten raw, they should be sliced paper-thin using a sharp paring knife. Other preparations, such as when the mushrooms are sautéed or baked, may call for thicker slices. When consumed this way, they have an agreeably beefy texture. To slice the *fungo,* gently place it cap-down on a cutting board. If it has a large crown, you will probably want to cut a few slices of the crown before reaching the stem. Then slice from the stem down to the cutting board, all the while trying to assure that the whole slice will be more or less of equal thickness.

SAUTÉING *FUNGHI PORCINI:* Typically one sautés *funghi porcini* in olive oil or sweet butter. There is a good deal of debate as to whether the oil or butter should be heated before the mushrooms are added. I have tried it both ways and believe that both methods are suitable, but with a difference. I find that *funghi* sliced paper-thin cook better in oil or butter that has been heated. Thicker, beefier mushroom slices often cook better with oil or butter that is room temperature. In either case, the sautéing should be done over medium-high heat. You will know when the mushrooms are done if you do the following: Watch as the mushrooms release their water. Continue to cook. Once the water has evaporated and the oil or butter seems clear, the mushrooms are done. If you are using minced garlic and parsley, as is often the case, you also have a choice. If you add the garlic along with the mushrooms, the garlic will cook and flavor the mushrooms. It will also be milder. You may also cook the mushrooms alone and then toss in garlic and parsley once the mushrooms are done.

FREEZING *FUNGHI PORCINI:* If you have collected a lot of mushrooms and cannot use them all at once, there is a means of keeping them for up to seven days. Slice the *funghi* and sauté them (with garlic and parsley, if you wish). The only difference is that you should not let the water evaporate completely. Rather, let about 50 percent of the water evaporate and then remove from the heat. This extra water will help protect the mushrooms when you freeze them.

USING DRIED *FUNGHI PORCINI:* As a standard rule, 1 ounce of dried *funghi porcini* becomes 1 cup of mushrooms when soaked.

Herbs *Erbe*

Herbs are, more than anything else, what sets Ligurian cookery apart from any other regional Italian cuisine. Of course, readers of this book will probably not have access to the profusion of fresh herbs found on the hillsides of Liguria, but things are no longer as dire as once upon a time in the kitchens of North America and northern Europe. Cooking with herbs no longer must connote cooking with dried herbs that have grown musty from long residence on a spice rack. Good fruit and vegetable vendors invariably sell fresh herbs, as do the merchants at farmers' markets that are now a staple in so many cities. Many supermarkets now sell herbs in plastic Ziploc bags, and while these herbs taste and smell somewhat generic — more of the nursery and less of the land — they are acceptable if there is no alternative. Anyone with a little land can set aside space for an herb garden — I would encourage you to try to buy seeds from Italy, especially basil. In North America, this is often called Genovese Basil, and the result is the small-leaf type that is preferred in Liguria. It is invariably more fragrant and delicate, and requires less pounding in a mortar to produce delicious pesto. City-dwellers can grow herbs in a small pot or coffee can on a ledge or windowsill, or even on a counter in a sunny room. Herbs are also used in Liguria for medical purposes. For example, leaves of basil, lavender, parsley, or sage that are steeped in hot water are used to ease mosquito bites. Other applications are described on page 43. Also see individual listings for basil, rosemary, marjoram, and *prebôggion*.

Garlic *Aglio*

One of the secrets of the healthful properties of Ligurian food is the presence of garlic. This cuisine is not "garlicky" in the Southern Italian sense, but is made flavorful and fragrant in judicious amounts. There are some instances, such as *aggiada* (garlic sauce), garlic soup, and *bruschetta* rubbed with garlic, in which the flavor is the protagonist. In using fresh garlic, always cut out and discard the green heart (also called the germ) — this creates a bitter taste during cooking.

Lettuce *Lattuga*

Ligurians like soft buttery lettuces. Boston or Bibb lettuce is the type to look for when you want to make *lattuga ripiena* (stuffed lettuce) or a typical Ligurian salad.

Marjoram *Maggiorana*

Marjoram grows wild and fresh throughout Liguria and is probably the most typical Ligurian herb after basil. It can be found fresh in markets, and is easy to grow.

Mushrooms *Funghi*

Basic cultivated mushrooms, the white ones that you buy in the Styrofoam boxes in the supermarket, do not have much appeal in Liguria, where spectacular wild mushrooms abound. Read about *funghi porcini* above. Yet cultivated mushrooms may be combined with *funghi porcini* if the latter are scarce.

Mussels *Muscoli or Cozze*

Most of the mussels consumed in Liguria are found in the bays of La Spezia and Lerici, where they have been cultivated for many years. In selecting mussels, find out how recently they were taken from the waters and examine them carefully. You want to choose ones that are closed tight and have a sparkling shell. Any mussels that open before you cook them should be discarded. Always scrub mussels well and discard the beards before steaming. Any mussels that do not open during steaming should be discarded.

Nuts *Noci*

In most of the Mediterranean, nut trees and bushes form an important part of the topographical and culinary landscape. Liguria has a profusion of nuts, and their meats and oils give taste and substance to many regional dishes. This is seldom acknowledged by people who speak of the cooking of this area, but imagine pesto without pine nuts (and sometimes walnuts), or *pansôti* pasta without walnut sauce. Almonds and hazelnuts are often matched with fish, or provide flavorings for desserts and baked goods. Nuts provide the crunch, the dryness, and the body that contrasts with the sharp, the sweet, the bitter, and the sour of other ingredients. The most popular are *pinoli* (pine nuts), regular almonds (*mandorle*), bitter almonds (*mandorle amare;* available in some health food stores), hazelnuts (*nocciole*), walnuts (*noci*), and chestnuts (*castagne* or *marroni*).

Olive Oil *Olio d'oliva*

Olive oil is the preferred cooking fat of Liguria (unlike the rest of Northern Italy, which favors butter or lard). It is also used as a condiment, and has found numerous other applications in the region.

Many of these are for medical purposes:

- For a blister or mole, one uses a compress of hot oil and chamomile tea.
- As a purgative: 2 or 3 tablespoons of oil in the morning.
- For burns: Beat oil with an equal amount of water. This is used before exposure to the sun or after a burn to treat it. (Of course, using oil alone would burn the skin. But when beaten with water it becomes sort of a protective cream.)
- The oil is often used for massage.
- When dabbed on a cotton ball, it is used to paralyze and lift a tick from the skin.
- Mosquitoes are less likely to bite skin covered with oil.

Olive oil is also used to give last rites. Until the 1950s it was used as lamp oil in some few seaside and mountain towns that were not yet wired for electricity. Olive oil has always been an essential element for Ligurians: Columbus allotted a daily ration of a quarter liter of olive oil (about 1 cup) per sailor.

The province of Imperia produces 70 percent of Ligurian olive oil. A saying in that area holds that from the moment a grape is crushed a wine grows, while from the moment an olive is crushed, its oil dies. There is a great love for the fruity fresh flavor of young oil made with Taggia olives. Another saying states: *A veitae e l'euio vegna de lungo a galla* (Truth and oil always emerge).

Olives *Olive*

Olives in Liguria are exquisitely flavored. The most famous variety is the *taggiasca,* a small black, brown, or red olive from around the town of Taggia (Imperia). These olives make what many consider the finest olive oil in the world. Ligurian olives are also delicious and delicate enough that they find their way into antipasti, breads, salads, pasta sauces, and fish and meat preparations. When ground to a pulp they become *paté d'olive* (olive paste), which is also called *pasta d'olive, crema d'olive,* or *olivada.* This pulp is an exquisite flavoring sauce that is a versatile fundamental for the Ligurian cook. It is now easily found in better food markets and by mail order, although you should make sure the product is from Liguria.

Oregano *Origano*

When North Americans speak of oregano in Italian cuisine, it is dried oregano that we think of. In Liguria it is just as likely that fresh oregano will be used. You will find that this is a different taste, and one that is pleasing indeed. The classic use for fresh oregano is in combination with anchovies that have been preserved in salt. To this you add a couple of drops of excellent olive oil, and you have a perfect antipasto.

Oneglia and Olive Oil

Oneglia, which with the town of Porto Maurizio, makes up the larger city of Imperia, has always been a place of commerce rather than recreation. It is the chief port for the agricultural bounty of the Valle dell'Impero, where much of Liguria's finest food is grown. The olive oil has always been exceptional, and in recent years demand and production have both grown. This is remarkable because, according to this account written in 1931, things were very different. If you go to Oneglia, be sure to visit the Museo dell'Olio, the Olive Oil Museum.

"The town of Oneglia makes quite a different impression on the visitor from that made by all the other towns of the district. The main streets are wide, with an arcaded footpath on the other side; there is a sense of space and, one almost might say, grandeur, in the numerous *piazze*. . . . Near the port, with its picturesque quays where the motley collection of people move about and jostle one another — sailors and fishermen, peasants from the upper valley, sharp-eyed men of business, supervising the loading and unloading, or exportation, of their goods, women selling fish, and children playing at marbles — one finds that Oneglia is nothing but a commercial city, with a population composed of factory hands, and that its character is entirely unlike that of the other Riviera towns of this neighbourhood. . . . The oil of Oneglia has been famed for centuries for its special excellence, and this industry formed one of the principal occupations of the inhabitants. Until the general destruction of the trees during the Great War (1915-1918), the hillsides in the neighbourhood of Oneglia, Porto Maurizio and Diano were covered with olives, and cultivated with assiduity, as one of the chief sources of incomes. Now that carnations and stocks have occupied the terraces in the place of the olive trees, the manufacture of oil has diminished, and pure olive oil, with adulteration of cotton or nut oil, is rarely found."

— Edward and Margaret Berry,
At the Western Gate of Italy, 1931

A stone frantoio *(olive oil press)*
in Pontedassio

Parmigiano-Reggiano

This cheese, commonly called Parmesan in English, is perhaps the greatest of all. It is produced in four provinces in Emilia-Romagna — those of Parma, Reggio Emilia, Modena, and Bologna — and in the province of Mantua in Lombardy. True Parmigiano-Reggiano has the consortium's seal on its crust, and you should accept no substitute, certainly not the so-called Parmesan that comes from the United States or Argentina. Just as the salt of La Spezia is used to make prosciutto (see below), it is used for production of Parmigiano-Reggiano, so historically the cheese found its way to Liguria through exchange for salt. It is used in pesto and to top some pastas, and as part of fillings for stuffed vegetables and mussels.

Pasta

Liguria is considered one of four classic pasta heartlands of Italian pasta, along with Sicily, Campania, and Emilia-Romagna. Documents show that pasta was produced and sold commercially in Liguria, in fresh and dry forms, as far back as 1279. Ligurians like to tell you that pasta as we think of it today was born in their region and, while that is certainly possible, Neapolitans could probably make a similarly persuasive case. I suspect that the true story of pasta's origins are permanently lost in the mists of history. While Neapolitans and Sicilians favor dried pasta and the people of Emilia-Romagna use primarily fresh egg pasta, Liguria is unique in that both types of pasta play important roles in the cuisine. There are many native Ligurian pastas, including *trenette*, ravioli, *pansôti*, *trofie*, and *corzetti*. There is a special traditional Ligurian pasta dough that is made with white wine instead of water (see Pasta Sfoglia alla Ligure, page 208).

Pecorino

Pecorino, in Ligurian terms, is the hard sheep's milk cheese that is used for grating. For more than a thousand years, active trade has brought excellent sheep's milk cheese from Sardinia to Genoa, and that cheese still is used in Liguria today, primarily to give a sharp bite to pesto. The cheese is also popular served in chunks accompanied by Taggia olives. There is also Pecorino from Lazio, the central Italian region where Rome is located. This is traditionally called Pecorino Romano. Do not accept substitutes called "Romano Cheese" that come from North or South America.

Pine Nuts *Pinoli*

What are luxury items in other parts of the world are basic components of Ligurian cooking. Ligurians buy *pinoli* abundantly because they are readily available, and use them freely. In addition to their use in pesto, they go with sauces, fish, and desserts. Good *pinoli* must smell fresh and buttery. If you have had some in a jar for years, they are rancid. Discard them and buy a small bag full of fresh *pinoli* from a Mediterranean grocer and then make your first batch of pesto. You will soon discover what pine nuts can do.

Polenta

Corn, yet another of the many foods Columbus brought from the Americas, is thought to have first been planted in Italian soil in the Veneto around 1530, brought there by Venetian merchants. It gradually became the preferred meal for polenta, which in one form or another (usually of millet, barley, or sorghum) was a sort of cereal eaten in Italy since ancient Roman times.

Potatoes *Patate*

Columbus cannot take credit for finding potatoes (he only brought back yams). It was with the Conquistadors who brought the potato from South America to Europe. Potatoes first arrived in Liguria many years later in the backpacks of Napoleon's armies, who came to Genoa in the early nineteenth century. The Ligurians and the Piedmontese were probably the first Italians to use potatoes in gnocchi. Potatoes also substituted for fava beans in many dishes. For example, it was traditional to cook stockfish with fava beans, but now one invariably finds it paired with potatoes. The potatoes from Badalucco and Triora in the province of Imperia are especially famous. They only arrived in that area around 1887. Potatoes have enriched Ligurian cuisine, winding up in focaccia, gnocchi, and combined with string beans in *polpettone,* and with pesto.

Prebôggion

A combination of herbs sold in Ligurian markets that is used to stuff in ravioli and *pansôti*. Typically *prebôggion* includes sorrel, borage, wild chicory, chervil, lovage, and sometimes pimpernel, dandelion, and thistle. They are boiled, then sautéed in a pan with oil, anchovy fillets, and garlic. Eaten as a vegetable side dish, or combined with rice or in omelettes.

Prescinseua

This dairy product, something between sour milk and cheese, is a fundamental ingredient of Ligurian cooking. The name comes from *prezû,* the Ligurian word for rennet. Recipes appear on pages 79-80. A reasonable substitution can be created by combining ricotta cheese with either buttermilk or tangy yogurt.

Prosciutto

Prosciutto is a product of the neighboring region of Emilia-Romagna, with the best coming from the province of Parma. Yet Liguria plays an important role in making these hams. There is an ancient trade route between Parma and La Spezia, which serves as the port of Parma. La Spezia also has been an historic producer of excellent sea salt, which is sent to Parma to cure the hams. Similarly, it is the air from the Ligurian Sea that blows through the valleys of the Apennine Mountains that is used to air-cure the hams. When one visits the storerooms where the hams hang, invariably windows are opened to the west and east to allow cross ventilation from the sea. There are two types of prosciutto. *Crudo* is raw, air-cured ham and is the more prized of the two. It becomes deep pink to almost red, and is delicious when combined with figs or cantaloupe. You should look for it in your store as Prosciutto di Parma — it has a characteristic star-shaped logo on its side. *Prosciutto cotto* is boiled ham, but much better than what one usually finds. It is carefully seasoned with Ligurian salt and boiled to an exquisite tenderness. Ask for it in your market under the name Parmacotto. When you purchase either *crudo* or *cotto,* it is essential that the ham be sliced almost transparently thin so that it melts in your mouth. The goal is that you not chew it much, in which case you focus on texture, but rather to let it dissolve so that you focus on taste. Prosciutto does not figure too much in Ligurian dishes, except as part of the stuffing for vegetables and mussels.

Rabbit *Coniglio*

Rabbit is popular in the Ponente because it is inexpensive, flavorful, and abundant thanks to the animals' penchant for free love. Better butchers in North America can provide you with rabbit and cut it to your specifications. Ligurians separate the head, heart, and liver and boil them to make a rabbit broth that is added to the meat as it cooks to keep it tender.

Rosemary *Rosmarino*

Consider using only fresh rosemary. This has become a popular herb around the world and it is easy to buy fragrant sprigs. It is also possible to grow at home. You should remove the needles from the sprig as needed and discard any that are gray or brown. If the rosemary you have is not compellingly fragrant, get rid of it.

Ricotta

This soft cow's milk cheese is an essential in Italian cookery. It is made of small curds that are twice-cooked (*ri-cotta* = cooked again). In supermarkets it often comes in containers and tastes somewhat bland and gelatinous rather than fresh and milky. Find a good cheese shop that has a supplier of fresh ricotta. The best is usually called ricotta romana.

Salt *Sale*

"Salt is white and pure. There is something terribly holy in salt" (Nathaniel Hawthorne). One of the touchstone tastes of Liguria is of the sea, whether it is fish, shellfish, the sea air that gives special flavor to the herbs and vegetables that grow near the coast, or salt, that most fundamental of sea flavors. While most recipe books simply advise you to use salt and leave it at that, I want you to experience the taste of Liguria as you would if you were there. For this reason, all recipes where salt is required in this book call for sea salt. It has a more direct salt taste than iodized commercial salt, so you should use it sparingly. Note that there are two types of sea salt you should have available. One is coarse, and it is essential to put atop focaccia. The other is the traditional fine salt that looks like table salt.

Stockfish *Stoccafisso*

Stockfish has long been a staple in Ligurian cuisine, especially in the provinces of Imperia and Savona on the Ponente. The town of Badalucco holds a festival (*la sagra del stoccafisso*) each September in which the town cats go into sensory overdrive from the fishy fragrance that wafts through the streets. Stockfish is dried cod, mostly from Norway and Iceland. It is like a fish-shaped baseball bat, and is as hard as a stick (which is thought to be the origin of its name). Do not confuse it with *baccalà,* which is salt cod. This is more popular in Spain, Portugal, and the Veneto region of Italy. The Ligurians have always favored stockfish, and seem not to mind the long soaking and scrubbing required to bring it back to life. If you cannot locate stockfish, you may substitute *baccalà,* although it will take many more soakings to rid it of all of its saltiness. If you feel flush, you can also make the stockfish recipes in this book using fresh cod, although the cooking times will be much shorter.

Stracchino

See Crescenza, above.

Tomatoes *Pomodori*

Ligurians grow beautiful fresh tomatoes in their gardens, and are among the leading producers of sun-dried tomatoes (*pomodori secchi*). These were not intended to be a faddish ingredient, as they are in the rest of the world, but were devised as a means of preservation for when tomatoes are out of season. There is a recipe on page 312. You may also pound sun-dried tomatoes to make a very potent sauce (see page 83).

Vegetables *Verdura*

Vegetables are described in more detail in the chapter devoted to them. The key, as always, is freshness, ripeness, and careful handling. You should always want the best possible vegetables on your plate. If you planned to make a dish using a particular vegetable and there are only inferior examples available, opt instead to use a different one instead of producing a mediocre vegetable dish that will make you and your guests frown.

Vinegar *Aceto*

In general, Ligurians use white wine vinegar when vinegar is called for. Herb-infused vinegars are not popular in Liguria for the simple reason that there is such an abundance of fresh herbs all the time.

Wine *Vino*

Wine is described in more detail on page 409. The four leading Ligurian grapes are Pigato and Vermentino (both whites) and Rossese and Dolcetto (reds). If you cannot locate Ligurian wines, you may use a Dolcetto from Piedmont as a red and either a Vermentino or a Vernaccia di San Gimignano from Tuscany as a white. It is often stated that the Vernaccia originated near Vernazza in the Cinqueterre in Liguria, but I have not seen enough credible documentation to verify this assertion.

Zucchini *Zucchine*

More than with most vegetables, it is important to select zucchini carefully when making Ligurian food. The goal is to get the smallest, tenderest ones available. These are sweeter and have more flesh and less water. Ligurians like to buy zucchini with the flower still attached. They remove the pistil and the stamen and then fill the flower with herbs and either ricotta or *prescinseua,* dip the flower in batter, and deep-fry it. Delicious!

Stockfish for sale in Badalucco

Sources for Ligurian

Ingredients & Products

*T*HE FOLLOWING is a listing of some reliable sources of food, wine, and equipment available to readers of this book. I have also included many sources in Liguria, for two reasons. The first is that I hope you will go there at the earliest possible moment. It is a place I love, and I trust you will, too. Moreover, when you sample the flavors of Liguria *in situ,* you will acquire what I call touchstone tastes, those that you will use as a point of reference when you cook at home. But these sources are also listed for the benefit of importers of food, wine, and housewares, so that they can bring these products home to you. (Note: When calling or faxing from outside of Italy, remember to use the country code [39] and to drop the first zero in the Italian phone number. So a call to Genoa from the United States would begin 011-39-10.)

Williams-Sonoma has some Ligurian food, products, and equipment. Another fine source for Ligurian foods is Corti Brothers in Sacramento, California, which is described under "Leading Food Purveyors" (see page 446).

Cakes, Cookies, and Sweets
Most Ligurian baked goods are fragile and perishable, and while I can send you to some very good places if you are traveling in the region (and I might direct you to some of the listings in my book *Italy for the Gourmet Traveler,* in which

Liguria is the first chapter), there are very few commercial bakeries whose quality I can endorse that also do shipping for export. One, however, is Panarello, which makes an excellent *pandolce genovese*. If you do not wish to make one yourself (although you should attempt to) Panarello is the perfect source. The store is near Genoa's Mercato Orientale and the Brignole train station. The business address, and the one importers should contact, is on Via Carso. Other shops listed in Liguria are admirable for their individual products and are worth visiting if you are in the area.

PASTICCERIA HELVETIA
Via Pertica 16
17029 Finale Ligure (SV)
tel 019/692900

Sells the best marrons glacés I have ever tasted. The recipe is on page 387. There are other excellent baked goods as well.

KLAINGUTI
Piazza Soziglia 98R
Genova
tel 010/296502

This has been Genoa's most famous bakery since 1887. Giuseppe Verdi came here often and they created a Falstaff cake in honor of the protagonist of the composer's last opera. He wrote them a note that "Your Falstaff is better than mine!" I am not a fan of that very rich cake (although I adore that opera), but I would send you to Klainguti for the *canditi* (the wonderfully delicate candied fruit that you can use to make *pandolce* and other sweets and cakes). The marrons glacés here are also very good.

PANARELLO
Store: **Via Galata 67R**
(closed Sunday afternoon and Monday)
Factory: **C.I.D.A.G. (the acronym for the owners)**
Via Carso 111, Genova
tel 010/8310660

Panarello sells a full range of Ligurian baked goods, starting with *pandolce genovese,* and including cookies such as amaretti (from Sassello), biscotti del Lagaccio, Canestrelli, and other delicacies.

PIETRO ROMANENGO
Via Soziglia 74 (other branches at Via Roma 51 and Corso Buenos Aires 16)
Genova
tel 010/297869

Since 1780 Romanengo has produced outstanding *canditi* (candied fruits), often called the best in Italy. They also use exquisite Ligurian fruit to make jams, syrups, and chocolates. They also make *sciroppo di rose* (rose syrup) and *acqua di fiori di arancio* (orange flower water), which lend their fragrance to genoise, the famous local cake that is now made round the world.

ROMEO VIGANOTTI FABBRICA
CIOCCOLATO
Vicolo dei Castagna 14R
Genova
tel 010/208561

You may not know that the city of Turin in Piedmont (Piemonte) is credited with having invented the chocolate bar. From the time that cocoa (yet another food that came to Europe after Columbus went to the Americas) was shipped to the chocolate makers of Turin and Switzerland, its port of entry was Genoa. Viganotti became one of the premiere chocolate makers of Genoa, and everything is still handmade. They also have chocolate-covered Ligurian chestnuts (fitting for a place whose address is on what we would call Chestnut Lane).

PASTICCERIA FRANCESCA
SCALVINI
Via Colombo 3
Noli (SV)
tel 019/748201

A wonderful old bakery in a charming, out-of-the-way seaside town that merits a visit. There is *pane del pescatore* (a sweetish cake for fishermen), as well as amaretti, chocolates, *pasticcini di pinoli* (pine nut cookies), and many other cookies.

Cheese

While there is very little cheese produced in Liguria and almost none of it goes abroad, you should pay close attention to the cheeses you do buy for the recipes in this book. So-called Parmesan cheese, which is really Parmigiano-Reggiano, is clearly identifiable by the imprint of the cheesemakers' consortium on the rind of each wheel of cheese. Accept no substitute from the U.S., from Argentina, or even from other regions of Italy. This cheese is made only in a delimited zone in Northern Italy, and nothing else can compare. For hard sheep's milk cheese, look for Pecorino Romano or Pecorino Sardo. They have an imprint on the rind of a sheep's head and droopy ears. As for the cheese to put in your *focaccia col formaggio,* if at all possible you want Crescenza, not the *Stracchino* for which it is usually mistaken outside of Liguria (see Fairway and Zabar's, listed under Leading Food Purveyors, page 446). If you want to make your own *prescinseua,* Genoese cheese curds, you will need rennet, a source for which is indicated on page 456. Also see La Bottega di Angelamaria listed under Honey.

Coffee

Because the Italian Riviera borders on Piedmont, which vies with Friuli as the great coffee region of Italy, Liguria has been a traditional point of entry for coffee beans that arrive in the ports of Genoa and Savona and then are sent to Turin for roasting. This is different from Friuli, where the port of Trieste is also one of the great coffee roasting centers in the world. For the most part, Ligurians drink coffee roasted in Piedmont, which is excellent. But there are two

Ligurian coffee roasters I hold in high esteem. One is Torrefazione Fratelli Pasqualini in Villanova d'Albenga in the province of Savona. Here is a fine, established firm that receives its beans at the port of Savona, then selects and roasts them with care, and sells them in the zone from Savona to Alassio. Crastan Caffè is in Arcola, just beyond the port of La Spezia. Because this area is closer to Emilia-Romagna and Tuscany, beans that arrive here go to those regions. But Crastan has established itself as a small, reliable importer of beans from major coffee-growing nations that are personally selected and roasted by the owners. To my knowledge, Crastan coffee is not sold outside of Italy, but it is worth looking for if you are there, and importers should consider acquiring it.

TORREFAZIONE FRATELLI
PASQUALINI
Via Roma, 143
Villanova d'Albenga (SV)
tel 0182/582591

CRASTAN CAFFÈ
Località Romito Magra
Arcola (SP)
tel 0187/988492

Cooking Equipment: See Traditional Ligurian Housewares (page 457).

Flours
While you should have no problem finding unbleached, all-purpose wheat flour in your local markets, others may take more looking. Chickpea flour is found in many Middle Eastern stores, while chestnut flour and spelt (farro) are really only found at excellent gourmet shops, including those listed under Leading Food Purveyors. Here are some flour suppliers you may want to know about. Some will sell directly to you; others will tell you where you can buy their products in your area.

ARROWHEAD MILLS
P.O. Box 866
Hereford, TX 79045
tel 713/364-0730

A good range of stone-ground flours.

THE BAKER'S CATALOGUE
RR2, Box 56
Norwich, VT 05055
tel 800/827-6836

Part of King Arthur Flour Company. They are very responsive and stock high-quality products.

LA BOTTEGA DI ANGELAMARIA:
see listing under Honey

PAMELA'S PRODUCTS
156 Utah Avenue
South San Francisco, CA 94080
tel 415/952-4546

A good selection of flours, plus sea salt.

PURITY FOODS, INC.
2871 West Jolly Road
Okemos, MI 48864
tel 517/351-9231

A good source for spelt (farro).

WALNUT ACRES
Penns Creek, PA 17862
tel 800/433-3998

A catalog offering various grains, flours, and nuts.

Honey

Liguria is one of the leading flower growing zones in the world, especially the province of Imperia. With all of the fabulous gardens and hothouses in the area, it should not surprise you that Liguria produces divine honey. It is often sold by producers of wine or olive oil, and you need only choose the honey drawn from the flower that most appeals to you.

GIUSEPPE FERNANDEZ
Via Calice 186
Località Perti
Finale Ligure (SV)
tel 019/687042

This firm sells honey from the hills just inland, where spectacular flowers produce delectable honeys. Many come with individual denominations for the flower, such as acacia, rose, and orange, or mixed honeys that come under the name of *millefiori* (a thousand flowers). This is also a wonderful source for almonds, pine nuts, walnuts, and hazelnuts, all packed in honey.

LA BOTTEGA DI ANGELAMARIA
Piazza Roma 26
Molini di Triora (IM)
tel 0184/94021

People come from all around to this famous and singular shop. Angelamaria herself is a leg-end. Triora is famous for two things — its bread and its witches. Supposedly witchcraft has been practiced in these parts, but all I can say on that score is that Angelamaria is be-witching in the very best sense. As to the bread, Molini di Triora means Mills of Triora. This area used to be dotted with mills to make flour from the local wheat, a rare commodity in Ligurian agriculture. *Pane di Triora* is a thick crusty whole wheat round more akin to what we call peasant bread than to any other Ligu-rian bread. Its recipe is secretly guarded, and the townspeople sell the bread throughout the Ponente. Angelamaria sells this bread, plus excellent flour, fresh mushrooms, cheeses (including *bruss,* the fermented cow or goat's milk ricotta), books, witch-related parapher-nalia, plus some of the best honey I have encountered in Liguria. If you are in the Imperia–San Remo area, a trip to Molini di Triora will be rewarding.

Leading Food Purveyors

BALDUCCI'S
424 Avenue of the Americas
New York, NY 10011
tel 212/673-2600 or 800/225-3822
tel 800/247-2450 (for catalog within New York State)
tel 800/822-1444 (for catalog outside New York State)

Balducci's does not particularly emphasize Ligurian food, but they have a wide range of Italian products, some of which may be of use to you for this book.

BRISTOL FARMS
1570 Rosencrans Avenue
Manhattan Beach, CA 90266
tel 213/643-5229

837 Silver Spur Road
Rolling Hills Estates, CA 90274
tel 213/541-9157

606 Fair Oaks Avenue
South Pasadena, CA 91030
tel 818/441-5588

All three Bristol Farms stores have good selections, and they do ship.

CORTI BROTHERS
P.O. Box 191358
Sacramento, CA 95819
tel 916/736-3800

Darrell Corti is a proud Ligurian-American who has imported a great range of products from his ancestral region. He was also helpful in sending me down numerous delicious paths during my research. Corti Brothers is probably the place I would tell you to contact first if you cannot locate the necessary ingredients for a Ligurian larder where you live. Ask about flours, stockfish, tuna packed in olive oil, dried *funghi porcini,* pine nuts, beans, olive oil, olives, vegetable sauces and pastes, cheese, and even *gallette del marinaio* (the sea biscuits that are so typical of Ligurian coastal cuisine).

DEAN AND DELUCA
560 Broadway
New York, NY 10012
tel 800/221-7714 or 212/431-1691

A fancy shop that has a good range of food, equipment, and books related to everything gastronomic.

FAIRWAY MARKET
2127 Broadway at 74th Street
New York, NY 10023
tel 212/595-1888

2328 12th Avenue at 133rd Street
tel 212/234-3883

This famous New York store has long stocked Ligurian oils, spreads, and pastes, plus good fresh herbs. It was also one of the first stores to carry Crescenza cheese, the secret to *focaccia col formaggio.*

SORRENTO MARKET
5518 Sepulveda Boulevard
Culver City, CA 90230
tel 310/391-7654

A good source in Southern California.

TODARO BROTHERS
555 Second Avenue
New York, NY 10016
tel 212/532-0633

A well-stocked traditional purveyor in New York that will ship.

VIVANDE
2125 Fillmore Street
San Francisco, CA 94115
tel 415/346-4430

Write for a catalog — they stock many of the products you will want.

WILLIAMS-SONOMA
P.O. Box 7456
San Francisco, CA 94120
tel 415/421-4242; catalog 800/541-2233

Many fine Ligurian and Italian food products,
and an excellent source for kitchen equipment.

ZABAR'S
2245 Broadway
New York, NY 10024
tel 212/787-2000

This famous emporium has a good selection of
cooking equipment, and some Ligurian food-
stuffs. They carry Crescenza cheese for your
focaccia.

ZINGERMAN'S
422 Detroit Street
Ann Arbor, MI 48106
tel 313/769-1625

Ari Weinzweig is one of the more knowledge-
able and likable food sellers around, and he
goes to great lengths to procure great products
and sell them to you by mail in peak condition.

Meats

Most Italian groceries outside of Italy stock what they call Genoa salami, which
is made entirely of pork. This bears only the most distant connection to *salame
di Sant'Olcese,* which is the salami Ligurians eat. This salami is made of ground
veal and pork, and is unmistakable in flavor and delicacy. It is not currently
available in North America, but some importers may soon bring it in. If you
live in a country in which you can import salamis without problems, consider
acquiring some if you are in Genoa. My favorite source is Fratelli Centanauro,
which is near the Oriental Market (the market too has good salami and cheese
sellers). For importers reading this book, I also include the address of Salumificio Parodi, which makes the best *salame di Sant'Olcese* I have tasted. If you cannot get *salame di Sant'Olcese,* substitute a soft, sweet, slightly garlicky salami. If
you need certain specialty meats for some recipes in this book, in North America contact D'Artagnan.

FRATELLI CENTANAURO
Via San Vincenzo 103R
Genova
tel 010/580841

SALUMIFICIO PARODI
Località Berti
Sant'Olcese (GE)
tel 010/709827

D'ARTAGNAN, INC.
399-419 St. Paul Avenue
Jersey City, NJ 07306
tel 201/792-0748 or 800/327-8246

While most of the meats you will need for this
book will probably be easily located where you
live, if rabbit, hare, or capon is necessary, you
may need to contact D'Artagnan. They have a
catalog.

Mushrooms

While it is possible to find dried *funghi porcini* from Italy from any of the leading food purveyors I indicate above, with Ligurian mushrooms there is also the possibility of getting them packed in either oil or vinegar. While the latter have a distinct taste that does not lend itself readily to most prepared dishes (although it is wonderful with poached fish), oil-packed Ligurian mushrooms are versatile and delicious. One good source is the Serafina Sottoli e Funghi store in Genoa, listed under Sauces, Spreads, and Packed Vegetables (page 456). Also see La Bottega di Angelamaria under the listings for Honey (page 445). Also:

ARCOS MUNOS VICTORIA
Corso Montecarlo 46
Località La Mortola Inferiore
(just outside Ventimiglia [IM])
tel 0184/229331

A wonderful supplier of mushrooms,
dried and fresh, plus truffles.

Olive Oil and Other Products Packed in Oil

If there is one product that is indispensable to your successfully becoming a Ligurian cook, it is olive oil. Ligurian oil was heavily exported in the early decades of the twentieth century, almost entirely from the port of Oneglia in the city of Imperia. That town has an excellent olive oil museum that you must visit if you are in the area. In former times, much of the olive oil went to Ligurian émigrés and other Italians who had moved to the Americas and Australia. In recent decades, as the descendants of these émigrés adopted eating habits more like those of the countries they lived in, much less Ligurian oil was exported. When olive oil's great virtues became better appreciated in the 1980s, the demand for top oil boomed and more has been sold abroad. While I am an admirer of oils from Tuscany, Umbria, Lake Garda, and other parts of Italy; France; Spain; Greece; and elsewhere in the Mediterranean, I unabashedly assert that Ligurian olive oil is the best. It is delicate, but with a very forward and fruity flavor. It is good for sautéing, giving its special flavor to sauces and to foods that cook in it, without adding weight or a greasy texture. Ligurian olive oil is also extraordinary because it is a sublime condiment. Whatever you put it on, from boiled potatoes to poached fish to fresh vegetables or stirred into minestrone, Ligurian olive oil will make your food taste exquisite.

In recent years, more olive oil has been exported from Liguria, and it is now possible to locate oil you will be pleased with. Rainieri, Isnardi, Ardoino, and Carli are leading exporters, and the fine products of companies such as Roi and Frantoio di Sant'Agata are also appearing abroad more regularly. Many of these companies also sell olive-based products such as *paté di olive* (olive paste), excellent Taggia olives packed in oil or brine (*salamoia*), and superb Ligurian vegetables packed in oil. There is even wonderful olive oil soap.

Although you will more readily find oil from the larger firms, I also have listed some oil makers whose products have not traveled outside their native region. Small producers clearly have more control over quality than would larger cooperatives and distributors, and their oils have more distinct personalities than the larger producers could ever achieve. Many of the small producers do not yet export, but if you are traveling in Liguria you should look for their oils. Similarly, I hope that food importers reading this list will be motivated to sample some of the oils and oil-packed foods I have listed. If you are only able to visit Genoa rather than the oil-producing zones, visit the Il Frantoio store on Via San Vincenzo.

Ligurian oil is distinct because it is one of the few oils you will find that use only one variety of olive rather than a blend of oils from different olives, such as you might find in Tuscany. This is not unlike drinking a wine made from one grape, such as Chardonnay or Cabernet Sauvignon, rather than a blend of grapes. What you discover when you taste a single-olive oil is a more direct contact with the fruit itself. The top Ligurian olive variety is the Taggiasca, named for the town of Taggia in the province of Imperia. Taggia olives make superb oil, and are also wonderful to eat. Other leading Ligurian olive varieties include Lavagnina (the Taggiasca equivalent on the Levante side of Liguria) and the Pignola. It is generally conceded that most of the top Ligurian oil is made in the province of Imperia and the adjoining province of Savona, so if you see IM or SV on the label, you will know where it came from. In every case you want oil that is extravirgin (*extravergine*). This means that the oil comes from the first cold pressing of olives in a stone olive press (*frantoio*). If you are used to oil that has been in the bottle for a few months, the taste of freshly pressed oil will surprise you. Frankly, you may be disappointed by its seemingly aggressive flavor, but it will soon smooth out.

FRANTOIO ROI
Via Argentina 1
18010 Badalucco (IM)
tel/fax 0184/408004

In addition to making delicate oil, Roi's Franco Boeri and his family also produce sauces such as *bagna cauda,* pesto, *salsa di noci, salsa di rucola* (rocket or arugula) and packed vegetables such as sun-dried tomatoes and small stuffed peppers. Roi products are among the few Ligurian brands that are found in many parts of North America.

OLEIFICIO G. BOERI
Via Stazione 40
Badalucco (IM)
tel 0184/43460

Good oil, very good olives, excellent sun-dried tomatoes.

FRANTOIO BORGOMARO
DI LAURA MARVALDI & C. S.N.C.
Piazza della Chiesa 1
18021 Borgomaro (IM)
tel 0183/54031

It is known that oil has been produced on this site since at least the year 1000, and the Marvaldi family have made oil here since 1784. I consider this one of the finest Ligurian oils, and it is also one of the most expensive. The production is limited and almost all of it is sold in the region, so you will have to go there to acquire it. The oil is used at Manuelina restaurant in Recco, one of the top places to eat in Liguria.

AZIENDA AGRICOLA NOCETI
Località Dotta 1, Frazione Paggi
16042 Carasco (GE)
tel 0185/350115

Roberto Noceti makes oil using Lavagnina olives (the Levantine equivalent of the more famous Taggia olive used in the Ponente). It is also possible to acquire a nice little white wine (Bianchetta Genovese), that is typical of the area.

G. CRESPI E FIGLI SRL
Corso Italia 81
18024 Ceriana (IM)
tel 0184/551013   fax 0184/551518

Crespi is one of the better-known producers of olive oil and other products, and Ceriana is one of the loveliest towns in all of Liguria. If you are nearby, it is certainly worth a visit. Crespi products are available throughout Liguria and also abroad. These include sauces such as pesto, Olivada (made with black olives), Oliverde (made with green olives), Salsina (made of sun-dried tomatoes), Carciofina (artichoke sauce), as well as packed olives, sun-dried tomatoes, and artichokes.

BRACCO
Via Cavour 11
Cervo (IM)
tel 0183/418140

Here is a good small producer in one of the most beautiful Ligurian towns of all. They have a wood olive press that is more than four hundred years old. In addition to oil, they sell sauces, packed vegetables, and delicious jams from local fruit, especially apricots and figs.

AZIENDA AGRICOLA
DOMENICO RAMOINO
Via XX Settembre, Frazione Sarola
18023 Chiusavecchia (IM)
tel 0183/52646   fax 0183/270610

One of the larger producers in the area.

CONFRATERNITÀ
DI SAN LORENZO
Via Principale
Diano Arentino (IM)
tel 0183/43397

Excellent olive oil produced in limited quantities. It can be shipped, although you will pay
dearly for the postage and handling.

AZIENDA FEOLA
Via San Pietro 17/23
18030 Diano Marina (IM)
tel 0183/495049

The Taggiasca olives grown in the Diano Valley
taste a little different from those grown in the
valleys to the west, with the result that the oil
produced by brothers Luigi and Nello Feola is
also distinct. As you become more adept at
tasting oils, you will begin to notice such distinctions. The Feolas also sell their olives
packed in brine and in a paste.

BARTOLOMEO VENTURINO
Via Messighi 10, Frazione Borganzo
18030 Diano San Pietro (IM)
tel. 0183/43274 (at the press);
0183/498341   fax 0183/43247

Excellent oil from the Diano Valley, as well as
pesto, olives, walnut sauce, olive paste, and
other delicacies.

ANTONIO PERRINO
Via Monsignora Laura 1
Dolceacqua (IM)
tel 0184/206267

Excellent, fragrant olive oil at a fair price.

FRANTOIO OLEARIO BENZA
Via Dolcedo 180
Dolcedo (IM–Porto Maurizio)
tel 0183/208132

The olives used by the Benza family come
from high in the Prino Valley and are delicate
in flavor and fragrance. Of particular note is
the oil they call *Primuruggiu,* which is oil made
from the very first olives of the season. For this
they do not use a press, but simple squeezing
or pressure that naturally yields the delicate oil.
They also sell olives in brine, *paté di olive,* and
sun-dried tomatoes packed in oil.

FRANTOIO ABBO DINO
Via Roma
18023 Lucinasco (IM)
tel 0183/52411

Their *oiu de sciappa,* sold in an elegant black
bottle, is intensely flavored, very enticing, and
richer than typical Ligurian oil.

LE DELIZIE DEL FRANTOIO
Via Don Bellone 8
18100 Borgo d'Oneglia (IM)
tel 0183/297880   fax 0183/297610

This company produces very good oil, and also
sells pesto, olive paste, sun-dried tomatoes in
oil, olives in brine, and artichoke paté. Their
products are widely available and can be
shipped, although this can prove costly if the
products are sent long distances.

AZIENDA AGRICOLA L'ALPICELLA
Via Diano Calderina, 284 bis
Oneglia (IM)
tel 0183/276082

Here is a lovely place to discover Ligurian flavors. This working farm is an agritourist destination, with nine beds. Delicious oil and vegetables are produced here, and much of the garden's output is packed in oil. Of particular note are *trombette,* seedless squash that are sliced thin and then packed. Also wonderful are *pomodori verdi,* green tomatoes prepared with oil according to a family recipe. I empty the jar over hot pasta and do not need to add a thing.

PAOLO GUARDONE
Via Garessio 52
18100 Oneglia (IM)
tel 0183/23371

A small producer with a good product.

RAINIERI S.P. A.
Via Tommaso Schiva 5
18100 Oneglia (IM)
tel 0183/290133

Rainieri is one of the largest Ligurian olive oil producers, and its products are found throughout the region and abroad. It is available in good stores in North America and was the first Ligurian oil I ever tasted. There is also a small amount of oil called Riserva di Prelà, which, I am told, is the preferred oil at the Vatican.

FRATELLI CARLI
18100 Oneglia (IM)
tel 0183/7080

If you visit Oneglia, you cannot help but notice the Carli building directly behind the train station. This oil is widely distributed and there are many households that maintain a standing order for Carli oil. You should be sure to visit the olive oil museum at the Carli plant, one of the finest of its type in Italy. You will see exhibits and documentation about the history of oil production in Liguria. If you buy Carli oil, be sure to specify that you want extravirgin oil.

FRANTOIO DI SANT'AGATA
DI ONEGLIA
Via Scuole 4, Frazione Sant'Agata
Oneglia (IM)
tel 0183/23472   fax 0183/20963

This firm produces excellent oils and a whole range of sauces and oil-packed vegetables, including *funghi porcini.* Their products are available in Italy and abroad. They also sell good pasta and coffee.

AZIENDA AGRICOLA CASTELLO
DI PERINALDO
Piazza Castello 1
18030 Perinaldo (IM)
tel 0184/632346

A fine small producer.

ANGELO & TOMMASO LUPI
Via Mazzini 3
Pieve di Teco (IM)
tel 0183/36161

ISNARDI
Via Torino 156
Pontedassio (IM)
tel 0183/279560 or 0183/279717
fax 0183/279719

An old family firm that makes excellent oil and many other products, including pesto, jar-packed olives and other vegetables, and even olive oil soap, which is wonderful for the skin. Isnardi products are widely available in Italy and can be found in good stores abroad. Pontedassio is 8 km north of Oneglia, and the ride up will give you a nice quick view of olive trees and typical Ligurian inland scenery.

AZIENDA AGRICOLA
"A MACCIA"
Via Umberto I, 56
18028 Ranzo (IM)
tel 0183/318003

Ferdinanda Fiorito and her daughter Loredana
tend their olives with great devotion, and this
is palpable in their final product.

FRANTOIO DA OLIVE GAZIELLO
Via San Secondo 14
18039 Ventimiglia (IM)
tel 0184/351456

A very old firm that produces good oil and
wine and sells pesto, sun-dried tomatoes, an-

chovies, mushrooms, and other products. From
November to mid-April it is possible to visit
and watch the oil being pressed.

FRANTOIO BARTOLOMEO MARTINI
Via Molini 1, Frazione Riva
18010 Villa Faraldi (IM)
tel 0183/41068

An old olive press that makes a fine oil with
Taggiasca olives.

OLIVE OIL PRODUCERS
IN THE PROVINCE OF SAVONA

ANTICO FRANTOIO SOMMARIVA
Via G. Mameli 7
Albenga (SV)
tel 0182/559222   fax 0182/541143

It is possible to visit here during the season
(typically mid-November to early February) to
watch the oil being made. In addition to Taggia olive oil, other products include Limolive, a
combination of ground olives and Ligurian
lemons; Oliverde, olives crushed with Ligurian
herbs; and Diavolino, olives crushed with hot
red peppers. There are also whole olives in
brine, homemade anchovy paste, artichokes
and other vegetables packed in oil, *formaggetta
sott'olio* (aged ricotta cheese packed in oil),
pesto, and *salsa di noci*. Olive oil has been made
at this spot for at least three hundred years.

AZIENDA AGRARIA ANFOSSI
Via Paccini 39
Località Bastia
Albenga (SV)
tel 0182/20024

Excellent oil and vegetables have been produced by the Anfossis since 1931. If I were to
single out one item, it would be the wonderful
Albenga artichokes that they pack in oil or use
to make *crema di carciofi,* an artichoke paste that
is good on bread, on pasta, with poached fish,
or to stir into soups and sauces to give exotic
flavor.

COOPERATIVA OLIVICOLA DI
ARNASCO
Piazza IV Novembre 8
17032 Arnasco (SV)
tel 0182/761178

FRANTOIO DA OLIVE
FRATELLI POZZO
Via Amedeo 31
Cisano sul Neva (SV)
tel 0182/595047

The Pozzo family has been making oil with great care since 1850. In the winter, when the oil is being pressed, you can call (0182/595154) to reserve a batch and come to watch it being made.

AZIENDA AGRICOLA CASCINA
DELLE TERRE ROSSE
Via Manie 3
17029 Finale Ligure (SV)
tel 019/698782

Vladimiro Galluzzo produces wine as well as good olive oil.

COOPERATIVA AGRICOLA FINALESE
Via Perti 106, Frazione Perti
17024 Finale Ligure (SV)
tel 019/695246

The cooperative makes two oils, one using Taggiasca olives, the other with Pignola olives.

OLIO PIZZO S.N.C.
Via Pieve del Teco 26
17036 Leca d'Albenga (SV)
tel 0182/21451

Operated by Giovanna Pizzo, whose father sold oil here for many years. She sells a fine oil, as well as olives in brine and olive paste.

OLEIFICIO NICOLÒ POLLA
Via Ghilini 46 (site of production)
Corso Europa 31 (point of sale to public)
Loano (SV)
tel 019/668027

The Polla family has been making oil since 1875. They are a big enough firm now that they also sell products from other regions, but you should look only for Ligurian products. The *olio extravergine di Liguria di olive taggiasche* is quite fine, as are the many vegetables, spreads, and sauces packed or made with this oil.

AZIENDA OLEARIA "L'ULIVO"
Via Roma 89
17030 Nasino (SV)
tel/fax 0182/77213

In addition to delicious oil, this firm sells pesto, olives in brine, sun-dried tomatoes, and *funghi porcini* packed in oil. They also say they will ship their products.

FRANTOIO OLEIFICIO
SANDRA ROSCIANO
Via Provinciale 1/A
17020 Toirano (SV)
tel 0182/98204

Good olive oil, plus pesto, mushrooms, honey, and sun-dried tomatoes.

AZIENDA AGRICOLA ETTORE VIO
Frazione Crosa, 16
17030 Vendone (SV)
tel 0182/76297

A wine producer that also makes a small quantity of delicate olive oil.

OLIVE OIL PRODUCERS AND SELLERS
IN THE PROVINCE OF GENOA

**AZIENDA AGRICOLA
BRUZZO FRANCESCO
Via Rivarola 69/2 (point of sale)
Chiavari (GE)
tel 0185/309795 (phone at the farm)**

Francesco Bruzzo makes an intense and memorable oil using Pignola and Taggiasca olives. The oil is available at the point of sale in Chiavari and is also sold abroad.

**IL FRANTOIO —
LA BOUTIQUE DELL'OLIO
Via San Vincenzo 158
Genova
tel 010/591725**

This shop, near the Brignole station and the excellent Mercato Orientale in Genoa, is one of the best sources I know for Ligurian products, especially olive oil. If you are unable to visit local producers but happen to be in Genoa, this is the place to come. They also sell sauces and vegetables in jars, plus excellent jams made of Ligurian fruit. The store is typically shut for most of August.

**COOPERATIVA OLIVICOLTORI
"DU FACCIÙ"
Frantoio della Località Facciù
Moneglia (GE)
tel 0185/49303**

A cooperative that produces the oil from the olives of fifty members.

**COOPERATIVA AGRICOLA
SAN COLOMBANO
Via D. Cuneo 22
16040 San Colombano Certenoli (GE)
tel 0185/358065**

This cooperative, with more than two thousand members, produces oil, cheeses, vegetables, honey, chestnuts, hazelnuts, and wine.

**COOPERATIVA OLIVICOLTORI
SESTRESI
Via Valle Ragone 32
16039 Sestri Levante (GE)
tel 0185/44341**

A cooperative with more than five hundred members.

OLIVE OIL PRODUCERS
IN THE PROVINCE OF LA SPEZIA

**COOPERATIVA AGRICOLA
DI LEVANTO
Località Le Ghiare 20
19015 Levanto (SP)**

This press is the cooperative that makes the oil of 320 local members. They also sell local honey.

Rennet

If you want to make your own *prescinseua,* you may acquire rennet from the New England Cheesemaking Supply Company, P.O. Box 85, Ashfield, MA 01331. Tel 413/628-3808, fax 413/628-4061.

Sauces, Spreads, and Packed Vegetables from Liguria

See the listings under Olive Oil (many of these foods are made or packed by olive oil producers) and Leading Food Purveyors. Also consider the listings below.

SERAFINA SOTTOLI E FUNGHI
Via Canneto il Curto 34
Genova
tel 010/203779

Here is a wonderful little food boutique specializing in vegetables packed in oil (*sottoli,* or "under oil") or in vinegar (*sottaceti,* or "under vinegar"). One of the real specialties here are all types of Ligurian mushrooms, which come dried or packed in either oil or vinegar.

GENUINA LIGURE
Corso Villaregia, 106C
18015 Riva Ligure (IM)
tel & fax 0184/487548

Decent products, including sauces, sun-dried tomatoes, olives, and mushrooms.

Stockfish

In addition to Corti Brothers (listed under Leading Food Purveyors, page 446), there are many sources for stockfish in ethnic food markets around the world, including those selling the food of Italy, Spain, Portugal, Scandinavia, West Africa, and the Caribbean. If you get on good terms with the owners, they may do the presoaking of the fish for you. In Liguria, try:

BOTTEGA DELLO
STOCCAFISSO
Vicolo Lavagna 13R
Genova
tel 010/296536

This store has been in business since 1936, and their products are first rate. Most of the stockfish comes from Norway or the Faroe Islands and is handled with loving care.

Traditional Ligurian Housewares (including *corzetti* stamps)

BUTTEGHINA MAGICA
Via della Maddalena 2R (at the corner of
Via Macelli di Soziglia)
16124 Genova
tel 010/296590

Daniela Tinello has a shop full of good
kitchenware, including many items that are
specifically Ligurian. For example, she sells the
wooden stamps used in the preparation of
corzetti pasta. There is also a selection of mortars and pestles in all sizes. Remember that it is
preferable to have a marble mortar with a
wooden pestle. Signora Tinello also sells the
pirrone, the glass vessel favored by Ligurian fisherman to carry wine when they are at sea. Mail
order is possible.

GRANONE & MONCHIERI
TORNITURE E PRODOTTI IN LEGNO
Vico del Filo, 10R
16123 Genova
tel 010/2471294

In the heart of the old quarter of Genoa is this
fine woodworking shop that produces beautiful
corzetti stamps. When I first inquired, they did
not yet do mail order, but seemed willing to
do so for readers of this book. The prices of
their stamps are half of those at Butteghina
Magica.

ARFINENGO
Via Cesarea 82
Genova
tel 010/592610

Sells *corzetti* stamps.

FRANCO CASONI
Via Bighetti 73
Chiavari (GE)
tel 0185/301448

Signor Casoni is one of the last remaining *in-
tagliatori,* artisans in Liguria who specialize in
the carving of *corzetti* stamps (*stampe per i
corzetti*) used to imprint designs on pasta. They
come in various designs, including crosses,
flowers, coats of arms, and iconography from
the heyday of the Republic of Genoa.

SOPRANO
Galleria degli Orti Shopping Center
Via Bonfante 39
Oneglia (IM)

Licia and Bruno Soprano own two wonderful
shops that are excellent sources for equipment
if you are in the Ponente. One shop has imaginative plates, china, and crystal. The other
shop is a superb collection of kitchenware that
has every piece of Ligurian kitchen equipment
you would want, except for *corzetti* stamps,
which are little known in the Ponente. This is
where I bought my farinata pan (*teglia di farinata*), which come in many sizes. They also sell
marble disks to use for flattening your *cima di
vitello,* along with specially designed wood
pieces that you can use to press the sides of the
cima. In addition, there are traditional Ligurian
pots (*pentole forma genovese*) that have two handles and round bottoms. There are also marble
mortars in all sizes and genuine wood pestles.

THE CHEF'S CATALOGUE
3915 Commercial Avenue
Northbrook, IL 60062
tel 312/480-9400; 800/338-3232

SASSAFRAS ENTERPRISES, INC.
1622 West Carroll Avenue
Chicago, IL 60612
tel 312/226-2000; 800/537-4941

Good for baking pans and stones.

WILLIAMS–SONOMA
P.O. Box 7456
San Francisco, CA 94120
tel 415/421-4242; catalog 800/541-2233

An excellent source for kitchen equipment.

ZABAR'S
2245 Broadway
New York, NY 10024
tel 212/787-2000

A source of mortars and pestles, baking pans, and Crescenza cheese.

Wine

Listed below are some of the better wine producers in Liguria. Because production in most cases is small, there is relatively little exportation of Ligurian wine. However, if your travels take you to Liguria or if you can arrange through your wine seller or an importer to receive some Ligurian wine, these are all solid choices. As I suggest on page 415, in the absence of Ligurian wines, you may substitute reds such as Dolcetto from Piedmont or a medium-bodied Chianti Classico from Tuscany, or whites such as Vermentino from Tuscany or Sardinia, or a Vernaccia di San Gimignano from Tuscany.

IN THE PROVINCE OF IMPERIA

FELICE FORESTI
Via Braie 223
18033 Camporosso Mare (IM)
tel 0184/292377; fax 0184/250922

Rossese di Dolceacqua, Pigato, Vermentino.

TENUTA GIUNCHEO
Località Giuncheo
18033 Camporosso (IM)
tel 0184/288639

Good Vermentino and Rossese di Dolceacqua.

TERRE BIANCHE
Località Brunetti
18033 Camporosso (IM)
tel 0184/31230

Good Pigato, Vermentino, and a blend of the two grapes called Arcana. Also good Rossese di Dolceacqua.

AZIENDA VINICOLA
DOMENICO RAMOINO
Via XX Settembre
Frazione Sarola
18023 Chiusavecchia (IM)
tel 0183/52646

Pigato, Rossese.

MARIA DONATA BIANCHI
Via delle Torri 16
18010 Diano Castello (IM)
tel 0183/498233 or 0182/85022

Good Vermentino and Pigato.

AZIENDA VINICOLA FEOLA
Via San Pietro 17
18013 Diano Marina (IM)
tel 0183/495049

Vermentino, Pigato, Ormeasco, and Rossese di Dolceacqua.

GIOBATTA MANDINO CANE
Via Roma 21
18035 Dolceacqua (IM)
tel 0184/206120

Very good Rossese di Dolceacqua.

CANTINA DEL ROSSESE
FRATELLI GAJAUDO
Via Roma 33
18035 Dolceacqua (IM)
tel 0184/206180

Pigato, Vermentino, and Rossese di Dolceacqua.

TENUTA COLLE DEI BARDELLINI
Località Sant'Agata
18100 Imperia
tel 0183/21370

Just outside the city of Imperia is this respectable producer of Pigato, Vermentino, and very good olive oil.

AZIENDA AGRICOLA
CASTELLO DI PERINALDO
Piazza Castello 1
18030 Perinaldo (IM)
tel 0184/290962 (also, there is a fax and phone in Genoa: 010/582779)

Good Rossese di Dolceacqua.

AZIENDA AGRICOLA ASCHERO
Piazza Vittorio Emanuele II, 7
18027 Pontedassio (IM)
tel 0183/23515

Good Vermentino and Pigato; also Rossese.

TOMMASO E ANGELO LUPI
Via Mazzini 9
18026 Pieve di Teco (IM)
tel 0183/36161 or 0183/21610

Among the better-known producers in Liguria, their wines are often available for export. They produce Pigato, Vermentino, Rossese di Dolceacqua, and Ormeasco (a popular local red).

A MACCIA
Via Nazionale 56
Frazione Borgo
18028 Ranzo (IM)
tel 0183/318003

Good Pigato.

RICCARDO & LENA BRUNA
Via Umberto I, 81
Frazione Borgo
18028 Ranzo (IM)
tel 0183/318082

Their "Le Rus Se Ghine" is probably the best Pigato I have tasted. Because Ranzo is about 2000 feet/600 meters above sea level, the result is a drier, more structured wine than is produced at lower elevations. Their other Pigato, called Villa Torrachetta, is also delicious.

ENZO GUGLIELMI
Corso Verbone 48
18030 Soldano (IM)
tel 0184/289042

Delicious Rossese di Dolceacqua.

IN THE PROVINCE OF SAVONA

AZIENDA AGRARIA SOMMARIVA
Via Patrioti 80
17031 Albenga (SV)
tel 0182/50823 or 0182/541524

Pigato and Rossese.

VITICOLTORE ENRICO DARIO
Via Massari 4
17030 Bastia d'Albenga (SV)
tel 0182/20548

Pigato and Rossese.

ANFOSSI
Via Paccini 39
17030 Bastia d'Albenga (SV)
tel 0182/20024

Good Pigato, Vermentino, and Rossese.

CASCINA FEIPU
Località Massaretti, 7
17030 Bastia d'Albenga (SV)
tel 0182/20131

Good Pigato and various reds, including Bracchetto d'Albenga, a slightly sweet wine.

AZIENDA AGRICOLA BOIGA
Via Maglio 4 — Frazione Perti
Finale Ligure (SV)
tel 019/687054

Lumassina, Vermentino, and a red, Rosso da Tavola, made with Sangiovese and Rossese. They also make excellent olive oil and grow wonderful peaches and apricots.

CASCINA DELLE TERRE ROSSE
Via Manie 3
17024 Finale Ligure (SV)
tel 019/698782

Good Pigato, Lumassina, Vermentino, and Rossese. There is a delicious dessert wine made of Vermentino grapes called Passito. This name denotes grapes that are dried like raisins to concentrate their sugars before the wine is made.

AZIENDA AGRICOLA
MARCELLA ISETTA
Via Dodino 24
17040 Quiliano (SV)
tel 019/887102

Quiliano Bianco, Buzzetto di Quiliano, Granaccia di Quiliano, and Sangiovese di Quiliano.

AZIENDA AGRICOLA
GIACOMO MONTALDO
Via Viarzo 6/2
17040 Quiliano (SV)
tel 019/887476

Buzzetto di Quiliano.

AZIENDA AGRICOLA SAN
DALMAZIO DI REPOSI
Via Grandi 11
17040 Quiliano (SV)
tel 019/884820

Pigato and Vermentino.

AZIENDA AGRICOLA
GIUSEPPINA SCARRONE
Via Tecci 34
17040 (SV)
tel 019/887010

Buzzetto di Quiliano, and the reds Granaccia
di Quiliano and Sangiovese di Quiliano.

AZIENDA AGRICOLA
TURCO INNOCENZO E DIONISIA
Via Bertone 7/1
17040 Quiliano (SV)
tel 019/887153 or 019/887120

Buzzetto (also in a sparkling wine), Pigato, Granaccia di Quiliano, and Sangiovese di Quiliano.

AZIENDA AGRICOLA CAPELLANIA
Via Laiolo — Località Capellania
17028 Spotorno (SV)
tel 019/746007

Pigato, Lumassina, and Rossese.

ETTORE & NATALINA VIO
Frazione Croisa 16
17030 Vendone (SV)
tel 0182/76297

Good Vermentino and Pigato.

IN THE PROVINCE OF GENOA

AZIENDA AGRICOLA NOCETI
Località Dotta 1
Carasco (GE)
tel 0185/350115

Nice Bianchetta Genovese; also makes good
olive oil.

ENOTECA BISSON
Corso Giannelli, 28/R
16043 Chiavari (GE)
tel 0185/314462

This may be the best-known wine store in Liguria. You should look for their own product,
although other wines are available too. The
best whites may be their Acinirari and
Caratello, but you should also consider the
lovely Bianchetta Genovese, the Vermentino,
and the rosé made with *ciliegiolo* grapes.

COOPERATIVA VITICOLTORI
CORONATA VALPOCEVERA
Via Monte Guano 1/A
16152 Cornigliano (GE)
tel 010/468933

Coronata, Vermentino della Valpolcevera, and
Bianco Valpolcevera.

CANTINE BREGANTE
Via Unità d'Italia 47
16039 Sestri Levante (GE)
tel 0185/41388; fax 0185/481456

Their Golfo Tigullio Vermentino is my basic
drinking wine at home in Camogli. It is light
and pleasant, not as rich and complex as some,
but makes for a good house wine to accompany Ligurian home cooking. They also produce, all with a Golfo Tigullio appellation,
whites such as Bianchetta, Moscato, and Mis-
santo; white, rosé, and reds under the name
Nostralino ("our own"), and a *ciliegiolo* rosé.

AZIENDA AGRICOLA MONTEVERDE
Via Ciro Menotti 21
19030 Castelnuovo Magra (SP)
tel 0187/28460

Vermentino, Rosso del Cervo (red), plus good honey and olive oil.

CASCINA DEI PERI
Via Montefranco, 71
19030 Castelnuovo Magra (SP)
tel 0187/674085

Good Colli di Luni Vermentino.

LA COLOMBIERA
Località Montecchio 92
19030 Castelnuovo Magra (SP)
tel 0187/674265 or 0187/601206

Good Lunigiana wines, including Vermentino and a red called Rosso Terrizzo.

OTTAVIANO LAMBRUSCHI
Via Olmarello 16/A
19030 Castelnuovo Magra (SP)
tel 0187/674261

A fine old family producer, well regarded for its Colli di Luni Bianco, its Vermentino, and a special "red label" Vermentino called Etichetta Rossa.

IL TORCHIO
Via Provinciale 202
19030 Castelnuovo Magra (SP)
tel 0187/674075

Good Colli di Luni wines, including Vermentino; a Bianco (a blend of Trebbiano, Malvasia, and Vermentino); and a Rosso.

FORLINI E CAPPELLINI
Piazza Duomo 6
19010 Manarola (SP)
tel 0187/920496

Up the hill from the train station is the cantina of this producer of good Cinqueterre wines.

COOPERATIVA AGRICOLA DI RIOMAGGIORE, MANAROLA, CORNIGLIA E VERNAZZA
Località Groppo — Frazione Manarola
19010 Riomaggiore (SP)
tel 0187/920435

This is the cooperative that produces most of the Cinqueterre white wine. I had the occasion to participate in the 1995 harvest, which involves taking a little train up and down the steep slopes of the mountains inland from the Cinqueterre. They also make small quantities of Sciacchetrà, the area's famous and powerful dessert wine (which is not to everyone's taste).

WALTER DE BATTÈ
Via Pecunia 9
19017 Riomaggiore (SP)
tel 0187/920127

A good and careful small producer of Cinqueterre and Sciacchetrà wines.

IL MONTICELLO
Via Groppolo 2/B
19038 Sarzana (SP)
tel 0187/621432

Makes Vermentino and a wine called Il Groppolo, which combines Vermentino and Albarola grapes.

Bibliography

While Ligurians are characteristically thorough in their self-examination, most of the books and resources they produce about the region do not travel beyond its borders. Many of the sources listed below are useful for readers fluent in Italian who wish to investigate further the region's history, culture, geography, food, commerce, and, that most elusive topic of all, the nature of being Ligurian. Much of the most interesting — if not the most accurate — documentation about Liguria has come from foreigners who have visited the region through the centuries. And it is their writings that might be most provocative for readers of this book. These too are listed below. Whenever I am in Liguria I read *Il Secolo XIX*, the newspaper of Genoa that appears throughout the region in local editions. More than any other Italian newspaper I know, this one speaks to its readers in local terms, and there is an animated ongoing dialogue in the editorials and the letters to the editor about topics large and small: shipping; port traffic; accomplishments of leading Ligurians; weather; advice on herb cultivation; fishing; where mushrooms are sprouting; which focaccia baker used less than perfect oil; and so on. *Il Secolo XIX* ("The Nineteenth Century") is a wonderful mirror of Liguria.

Accame, Franco. *Mandilli de Saea*. Genova, De Ferrari, 1990.

Agnati, Adriano, ed. *Guida Rapida d'Italia, vol I: Liguria, Piemonte, Valle d'Aosta, Lombardia*. Milano, Touring Club Italiano, 1992.

Agnesi, Vincenzo. *Alcune Notizie sugli Spaghetti*. Imperia, 1975.

————. *É Tempo di Pasta*. Torino, Gangemi, 1992.

Alford, Henry. *The Riviera: Pen and Pencil Sketches from Cannes to Genoa, by the Dean of Canterbury, with Twelve Chromo-Lithographic Illustrations and Numerous Woodcuts from Drawings by the Author*. London, 1869.

Anderson, Burton. *The Wine Atlas of Italy and Traveller's Guide to the Vineyards*. London, Mitchell Beazley, 1990.

Artusi, Pellegrino. *La Scienza in Cucina e l'Arte di Mangiare Bene*. Torino, Einaudi, 1974.

Bagnasco, Renzo, and Nada Boccalatte. *A Tavola!: Insolite Ricette Liguri di Ieri e di Oggi*. Genova, Sagep Editrice, 1995.

Ball, Eustace A. Reynolds. *Mediterranean Winter Resorts: A Practical Handbook to the Principal Health and Pleasure Resorts on the Shores of the Mediterranean*. 4th Edition. London, Kegan Paul, Trench & Co., 1899. 2 vols.

Balletto, Laura. "Dieta e Gastronomia nel Medievo Genovese," in *Saggi e Documenti*, Vol. II, Civico Istituto Colombiano, Genova, 1986.

Baring-Gould. *A Book of the Riviera*. London, Methuen & Co., Ltd. 1923.

Barozzi, Petro, et al. *Liguria*. Milano, Fabbri, 1985.

de Beatis, Antonio. Ed. J. R. Hale. *Travel Journal in Germany, Switzerland, The Low Countries, France and Italy, 1517-1518*. London, Hakluyt Society, 1979.

Belgrano, Luigi Tommaso. *Della Vita Privata dei Genovesi*. Genova, 1846 (reprinted by Multigrafica Editrice, Rome, 1970).

Bennet, J. Henry, M.D. *Mentone and the Riviera as a Winter Climate*. London, John Churchill, 1861.

————. *Winter in the South of Europe or, Mentone, The Riviera, Corsica, Sicily, and Biarritz, as Winter Climates*. 3rd Edition. London, John Churchill & Sons, 1865.

————. *Winter and Spring on the Shores of the Mediterranean: or, The Genoese Rivieras, Italy, Spain, Corfu, Greece, the Archipelago, Constantinople, Corsica, Sicily, Sardinia, Malta, Algeria, Tunis, Smyrna, Asia Minor, with Biarritz and Arcachon, as Winter Climes*. 5th Edition. London, John Churchill & Sons, 1875.

Bernardini, Enzo. *Images de l'Italie: Ligurie*. Genova, Sagep Editrice, 1994.

Berriolo, Sandra, et al. *Mangiarfuori: Come e Cosa Mangia il Mio Bambino?: Guida Pratica alla Refezione Scolastica per Genitori e Operatori*. Vignate, Associazione Consumatori Utenti/FCE, 1995.

Berry, Edward and Margaret. *At the Western Gate of Italy*. London, John Lane, The Bodley Head Limited, 1931.

Bertoldi, Maria Luisa Rosciano. *Guida ai Detti Genovesi e Liguri*. Milano, Sugar Editore, 1970.

Bini, Bruno. *Trattorie e Ristoranti Fuoriporta*. Genova, *Il Secolo XIX*, 1993.

Bini, Bruno, and Antonino, Ronco. *Genova e Liguria*. Milano, Mediolanum Editori Associati, 1990.

Blessington, Margaret Gardiner (Countess of). *The Idler in Italy.* London, Henry Colburn, 1839-1840. 3 vols.

Boddington, (Mrs.). *Slight Reminiscences of the Rhine, Switzerland and a Corner of Italy.* London, Longman, Rees, Orme, Brown, Green, and Longman; and John Rodwell, 1834. 2 vols.

Boero, Pino, and Maria Novaro, eds. *La Riviera Ligure: Momenti di una Rivista.* Genova, Sagep Editrice, 1986.

Borzani, Luca, and Antonio Gibelli, eds. *La Via delle Americhe: l'Emigrazione Ligure tra Evento e Racconto.* Genova, Sagep Editrice, 1989.

Bullock-Hall, W. H. *The Romans on the Riviera and the Rhone: A Sketch of the Conquest of Liguria and the Roman Province.* London, Macmillan & Co., 1898.

Byron, G. G. *The Poetical Works of Lord Byron.* Oxford, Oxford University Press, 1970.

Cabano, Gino, et al. *Piccola Guida di Portovenere, Lerici e Tellaro.* Massa, Città del Mondo di M.B., 1995.

Caraceni Poleggi, Fiorella. *Genoa: Sagep Guide.* 3rd Edition. Genova, SAGEP, 1989.

Cesaretti, Paolo, ed. *Le Valli dell'Olivo.* Cinisello Balsamo, Amilcare Pizzi, 1995.

Cesari Sartoni, Monica. *Dizionario del Ghiottone Viaggiatore "Italia."* Bologna, Tempi Stretti/Fuori Thema, 1994.

Cilento, Bruno, and Lorenzo Oliveri. *In Treno da Genova a Ovada.* Genova, Sagep Editrice, 1989.

Conrad, Joseph. *Nostromo.* Harmondsworth, Penguin Books, 1963.

Cricca, Gianfranco. *Antiche Ricette di Castelnuovo Magra.* Castelnuovo Magra, Comune di Castelnuovo Magra, 1981.

Cunsolo, Felice. *Guida Gastronomica d'Italia.* Novara, De Agostini, 1975.

David, Elizabeth. *I'll Be With You in the Squeezing of a Lemon.* London, Penguin, 1995.

Davidson, Alan. *Il Mare in Pentola.* Milano, Mondadori, 1972.

Del Conte, Anna. *The Classic Food of Northern Italy.* London, Pavilion, 1995.

Desio, Ardito (trans. Elisabetta Bernadini). *Monte di Portofino: Naturalistic Pocket Guide.* Genova, Stringa Editore, 1980.

Dickens, Charles. *Pictures From Italy.* London, Hazell, Watson and Viney, 1868.

di Lena, Pasquale, et al. *Il Paese del Vino.* Siena, Enoteca Italiana/Alsaba Grafiche, 1994.

Dolcino, Michelangelo. *Storia di Genova.* Genova, Francesco Pirella, 1989.

Donte, Vincenzo Guido, Giovanni Garibbo, and Paolo Stacchini, eds. *La Provincia di Imperia.* Imperia, Consiglio Provinciale dell'Economia Corporativa di Imperia, 1934.

Fedozzi, G., et al. *Cervo: A Historical and Tourist Guide.* Imperia, Dominici Editore, 1993.

Fernández-Armesto, Felipe. *Columbus.* Oxford, Oxford University Press, 1991.

Ferrando, Isabella, and Tiziano, Mannoni. *Liguria: Portrait of a Region.* Genova, Sagep Editrice, 1989.

Field, Carol. *The Italian Baker.* New York, HarperCollins, 1985.

———. *Focaccia.* San Francisco, Chronicle Books, 1994.

Fletcher, Geoffrey. *Italian Impressions.* London, George Allen & Unwin, 1974.

Gho, Paola, ed. *Osterie d'Italia 1994.* Farigliano, Slow Food Editore, 1994.

Giardelli, Paolo. *In Treno da Genova a Casella.* Genova, Sagep Editrice, 1993.

Goethe, Johann Wolfgang von. *Italian Journey,* from *Collected Works,* vol 6. Princeton, Princeton University Press, 1994.

Graves, Charles. *Italy Revisited.* London, Hutchinson & Co., 1950.

Grosso, Orlando. *Genoa and the Riviera of Liguria.* Roma, La Libreria dello Stato, 1953.

Guide Gallery, *La Spezia.* La Spezia, GG, 1989.

Hamilton, Frederick Fitzroy. *Bordighera and the Western Riviera.* London, Edward Stanford, 1883.

Hawthorne, Nathaniel. *Complete Works,* vol. 10. *Passages from the French and Italian Note-Books.* London, Kegan Paul, Trench, Trübner & Co. Ltd, 1893.

Hemingway, Ernest. "Che Ti Dice La Patria?" from *The Short Stories of Ernest Hemingway.* New York, Scribner Paperback Fiction (Simon & Schuster), 1995.

Hudson, Roger, ed. *The Grand Tour, 1592–1796.* London, The Folio Society, 1993.

Ibañez, Vicente Blasco (trans. Frances Douglas). *In the Land of Art (En el País de Arte).* London, T. Fisher Unwin Ltd., 1924.

Johnson, J. *Change of Air, or the Pursuit of Health: An Autumnal Excursion through France, Switzerland and Italy, In The Year 1829; With Observations on The Moral, Physical and Medicinal Influence of Travelling-Exercise, Change of Scene, Foreign Skies, and Voluntary Expatriation.* London, 1831.

Levati, Ombretta. *Cinqueterre.* Novara, Istituto Geografico De Agostini, 1992.

"Libro del Introito del Convento" (food purchases for a convent), Archivio di Stato, Genoa, 1696.

Lingua, Paolo. *La Cucina dei Genovesi.* Padova, Franco Muzzio Editore, 1989.

Lorieri, Pier Paolo. *Erbe Selvatiche delle Apuane e della Lunigiana.* Fivizzano, Tipocart Conti, 1994.

Marchese, Salvatore. *La Cucina Ligure di Levante: Le Fonti, Le Storie, Le Ricette.* Padova, Franco Muzzio Editore, 1990.

Marcenaro, Giuseppe, ed. *Viaggio in Liguria.* Genova, Sagep Editrice, 1992.

Martini, Mario Maria. *Mercanti e Navigatori Liguri.* Rome, Augustea, 1930.

de Maupassant, Guy. *La Vie Errant.* Paris, Louis Conard, 1889.

Melville, Herman. *Journal of a Visit to London and the Continent.* London, Coen & West Ltd., 1949.

Milioni, Stefano. *Columbus Menu: Italian Cuisine After the First Voyage of Christopher Columbus.* New York, Italian Trade Commission, 1992.

Miller, William. *Wintering in the Riviera, with Notes of Travel in Italy and France and Practical Hints to Travellers.* London, Longmans, Green, and Co., 1879.

Millon, Marc and Kim. *The Wine Roads of Italy.* London, HarperCollins, 1991.

Monteverde, Franco. *I Liguri: Un'Etnia Tra Italia e Mediterraneo.* Firenze, Vallecchi Editore, 1995.

More, Jasper. *The Land of Italy.* London, B. T. Batsford, 1949.

———. *The Mediterranean.* London, B. T. Batsford, 1956.

Morgan, Lady Sydney. *Italy.* London, Henry Colburn & Co., 1821. 3 vols.

Moryson, Fynes. *An Itinerary.* Glasgow, James MacLehose and Sons, 1907–1908. 4 vols.

Murray, John (publisher). *Handbook for Travellers in Northern Italy.* London, 11th Edition (1869), 15th Edition (1883), 16th Edition (1899).

Nuova Editrice Genova. *L'Antica Cuciniera Genovese.* Genova, 1983 (a reprint of one of the standard Ligurian cookbooks from the mid-nineteenth century).

O'Faolain, Sean. *A Summer in Italy.* London, Eyre & Spottiswoode, 1949.

O'Neill, Molly. "Bringing Up Basil," *The New York Times Magazine,* August 11, 1996.

Ortona, Giorgio. *A Tavola Prima e Dopo La Scoperta* (no. 12 in the series "Monografie su Temi Colombiani"). Genova, Edizioni Culturali Internazionali Genova, 1992.

Paganini, P. Angelo, ed. *Vocabolario Domestico Genovese-Italiano.* Genova, Schenone, 1857.

"Il Palio in Cucina." Published by Comune di La Spezia, 1993.

Pallavicino, Cammilo. *Libro di Spese* (accounting of family food purchases). Archivio di Stato, Genova, 1668.

Pastorino, Carlo. *La Mia Liguria* (Bruno Rombi, ed.). Genova, Edizioni Culturali Internazionali Genova, 1987.

Piccinardi, Antonio. *L'Olio a Tavola.* Milano, Giorgio Mondadori, 1988.

Pickles, Sheila, ed. *The Grand Tour.* London, Pavilion, 1991.

Pike, Ruth. *Enterprise and Adventure: The Genoese in Seville and the Opening of the New World.* Ithaca, Cornell University Press, 1966.

Plotkin, Fred. *The Authentic Pasta Book.* New York, Simon & Schuster, 1985.

———. *Italy for the Gourmet Traveler.* Boston, Little, Brown, 1996.

Prescott, William H. *History of the Reign of Ferdinand and Isabella the Catholic.* Philadelphia, J. B. Lippincott & Co., 1875. 3 vols.

Roberts, Cecil. *Portal to Paradise: An Italian Excursion.* London, Hodder & Stoughton, 1955.

Rossi, Emanuele. *La Vera Cuciniera Genovese Facile e Economica.* 1992 printing by Arnaldo Forni Editore of the 1865 original.

Rousseau, Jean Jacques. *Confessions.* London, William Glassher, 1874.

Rum, Piera, ed. *Guida ai Musei della Liguria.* Milano, Electa, 1987.

Scott, William. *Rock Villages of the Riviera.* London, Adam & Charles Black, 1898.

Schneer, Dr. Joseph. *Alassio: A Pearl of the Riviera.* London, Trübner & Co., 1887.

Serafini, Flavio, ed. *Il Museo Navale Internazionale di Imperia.* Trieste, Edizione LINT, 1994.

Smollett, Tobias. *Travels Through France and Italy.* Oxford, Oxford University, 1992.

Sparks, Edward I. *The Riviera: Sketches of the Health Resorts of the Northern Mediterranean Coast of France and Italy from Hyères to Spezia.* London, J. A. Churchill, 1879.

Spence, Joseph (Slava Klima, ed.). *Letters from the Grand Tour.* Montréal, McGill–Queen's University Press, 1975.

Spinola family. *Libro di Spese* (accounting of food purchases for a noble family). Archivio di Stato, Genova, 1732.

Stendhal (Henry Beyle). *Mémoires d'un Touriste.* Paris, Michel Lévy Frères, 1854.

Strasburger, Eduard. *Rambles on the Riviera* (in German, *Streifzüge an der Riviera*). London, T. Fisher Unwin, 1906.

Taviani, Paolo Emilio. *La Genovesità di Colombo.* (no. 1 in the series "Monografie su Temi Colombiani"). Genova, Edizioni Culturali Internazionali Genova, 1992.

Touring Club Italiano. *Guida Rapida d'Italia: Liguria, Piemonte, Valle d'Aosta, Lombardia.* Milano, TCI, 1993.

Twain, Mark (Samuel L. Clemens). *The Innocents Abroad, or The New Pilgrims' Progress.* New York, Grosset & Dunlap, 1911.

Varese, Carlo. *La Fidanzata Ligure, ossia Usi, Costumanze e Caratteri dei Popoli della Riviera ai Nostri Tempi.* Paris, Baudry, 1832.

Wilton, Andrew and Ilaria Bignamini, eds. *The Grand Tour: The Lure of Italy in the Eighteenth Century.* London, Tate Gallery, 1996.

Wright, Edward. *Some Observations Made in Travelling Through France, Italy, &c. in the Years 1720, 1721, 1722.* London, A. Millar, 1764. 2 vols.

What I love best in all the world
Is a castle, precipice-encurled,
In a gash of the wind-grieved Apennine.
Or look for me, old fellow of mine
(If I get my head from out the mouth
O' the grave, and loose my spirit's bands
And come again to the land of lands) —
In a seaside house to the farther South,
Where the baked cicala dies of drouth,
And one sharp tree — 'tis a cypress — stands
My sentinel to guard the sands
To the water's edge. For what expands
Before the house, but the great opaque
Blue breadth of sea without a break?
Italy, my Italy.
Queen Mary's saying serves for me
(When Fortune's malice lost her in Calais) —
Open my heart and you will see
Graved inside of it, 'Italy'.
   Such lovers old are I and she:
   So it always was, so shall ever be.

— Robert Browning, *"De Gustibus"*

Camogli

Index

Recipes are indicated in boldface page numbers. Photographic references to listings are indicated by an italicized page number.

Acciughe. See Anchovies
Acciughe all'Agro (Marinated Fresh Anchovies), **187**
Acciughe Fritte con Salsa (Fried Anchovies with Special Sauce), **190**
Acciughe in Tegame (Casserole of Fresh Anchovies), **188**
Acquasanta, 245
Adriatic Sea, 12
Aegean Sea, 12
Africa, 15, 20, 148, 284, 324, 378, 382, 456
Aggiada (agliata), 17, 90, **97–98**, 219, 285, 369, 427; Coniglio all'Aggiada (Rabbit with Garlic Sauce), **376–377**; Fegato alla Genovese (Genoese Calf's Liver), 97, **369**
Agnello con Carciofini (Lamb with Baby Artichokes), **371**
Agnello con Olive e Funghi (Lamb Stew with Olives and Mushrooms), **372**
Agnesi pasta, 200, *201,* 226

Agnesi, Vincenzo, 200
Alassio, 7, 25, 29, 40, 92–93, 152, 191, 287, 416–417, 444
Alassio: Pearl of the Riviera (Schneer), 152
Albenga, 7, 25, 28, 85, 332, *373,* 410, 412, 422
Alessandria, 409
Alford, Henry, 8
Almonds (*mandorle*), 9, 56, 72, 374–375, 396, 428; Amaretti (Bitter Almond Cookies), 44, 382, 383, 392, **401–402**; Coniglio alle Mandorle (Rabbit with Almonds), **374–375**
Alps, 359, 391, 417
Amalfi Coast, 291
Amaretti (Bitter Almond Cookies), 44, 382, 383, 392, **401–402**
Ameglia, 27
Anchovies (*acciughe*): 12, 40, 56, 102, 140–141, 142–143, 187–188, 189, 190, 323, 328, 334, 336, 410, 421, 433; Acciughe all'Agro (Marinated Fresh Anchovies), **187**; Acciughe Fritte con Salsa (Fried Anchovies with Special Sauce), **190**; Acciughe in

Tegame (Casserole of Fresh Anchovies), **188**; Bagnun di Acciughe (Fisherman's Anchovy Casserole), 187, **336**; Salsa di Pinoli, Capperi e Acciughe (Sauce of Pine Nuts, Capers, and Anchovies), **102**, 141
Andersen, Hans Christian, 288
Antipasti, 34, 56, 81, 85, **169–194**, 302, 309, 324, 429
Anise/anisette, 386, 410
Apennine mountains, 22, 266–267, 434
Appetizers, 34, 56, 81, 85, **169–194**, 302, 309, 324, 429
Apples (*mele*), 403, 405; Friscêu di Mele (Apple Fritters), **403**
Apricale, 24
Apricots (*albicocche,*), 9, 34, 382, 384–385, 400, 405; Salame di Albicocche (Apricot Salami), **384–385**
Arab and Islamic influence in Liguria, 12, 46, 62, 77, 127, 148, 351, 382
Arenzano, 382, 389
Argentina, 32, 85, 432
Arma di Taggia, 410
Artichokes (*carciofi*), 9, 14, 25,

34, 55–56, 85, 89, 144, 311, 363, 371, 373, 421–422; Agnello con Carciofini (Lamb with Baby Artichokes), **371**; Involtini con Carciofi (Veal Rolls with Artichokes), **363**; Rospo con Carciofi (Monkfish with Artichokes), **332**; Sugo (Paté or Crema) di Carciofi (Artichoke Sauce), **89**, 251, 422; Torta di Carciofi e Verdura (Savory Pies, with Greens), 35, 52, **157, 162–164**; Zimino di Carciofi e Piselli (Casserole of Artichokes and Peas), **311**
Asia, 323, 382, 422
Asparagus (*asparagi*), 330–331; Scaloppe di Branzino in Crema di Asparagi (Sea Bass Fillets in Asparagus Sauce), **330–331**
Atlantic Ocean, 10, 12, 130, 323
At the Western Gate of Italy (Berry), 430
Australia, 323
Austrians in Ligura, 25, 29, 88, 364
Authentic Pasta Book, The (Plotkin), 200, 203

Baccalà (salt cod), 12, 56, 324, 346, 435
Badalucco, 24, *61, 167, 180*, 317–318, 324, 433, 435, *437*
Bagna Cauda, **96**, 183
Bagnun di Acciughe (Fisherman's Anchovy Casserole), 187, **336**
Baking, 16, 22, 34–35, 117–123; *see also* Breads; Desserts
Baking stones, 123–125
Ball, Eustace A. R., 416–417
Ballet, 30
Balzi Rossi caves, 25
Bananas (*banane*), 378, 382, 405
Barbagiuai (Fried Pumpkin Ravioli), **257**
Barbaresco wine, 231, 409
Barbiere di Siviglia, Il (Rossini), 290
Barcelona, 14, 297
Bardolino wine, 389
Barley, 433
Barolo wine, 231, 409, 411
Basil (*basilico*), 16, 27, 60, 62–64, 66–71, 73–76, 82, 182–183, 232, 327, 328, 422–423, 427; Risotto Valpolcevara, **260–261;** Stuffed Basil Leaves (Basilico Ripieno), **182–183,** 423; *see also* Pesto
Basilico Ripieno (Stuffed Basil Leaves), **182–183,** 423
Bass, sea (*branzino*), 325, 329–331, 424; Branzino al sale (Sea Bass Baked in Salt), **329;** Scaloppe di Branzino in Crema di Asparagi (Sea Bass Fillets in Asparagus Sauce), **330–331**
Bass, striped, 329
Beans (*fagioli*), 14, 55–56, 65, 180, 226, 228, 245–246, 264–265, 272, 276–277, 295, 302; Frittelle di Fagioli (Bean Fritters), **180;** Mesc-Ciùa (Grain and Bean Soup), 272, **276–277;** Polenta Incatenata (Polenta, Beans and Cabbage), **264–265;** Polpettone (String Bean–Potato Tart), 228, 295, **302;** Rotolo Maria Pia (Mushroom–String Bean Roll), **245–246;** Trenette alla Genovese (Trenette with Pesto, Potatoes, and String Beans), 65, **226**
Beauty, 5–6, 8, 9, 14, 18, 24, 28–29, 35, 46, 112–113, 266–267, 300, 381
Beef, 33, 56, 107, 299, 364–366; Manzo Negretto (Stewed Beef with Onion Sauce), **366**
Beef and Onion Sauce (Sugo Negretto), 109, **366**
Beerbohm, Max, 27
Beet greens. *See* Bietole
Bennet, J. Henry, 335
Berio, Luciano, 24

Berlin, 29
Berries, 382, 389
Berry, Edward and Margaret, 430
Bianchetti (whitebait), 56, 287, 334, 335, 421, 424; Frittata di Rossetti ("Redbait" Omelette), **334;** Whitebait Soup (Minestra di Bianchetti), **287**
Bibliography, 463–468
Bietole (beet greens), 299, 351, 423; Beet Green Rolls (Involtini di Bietole), **299;** *See also* Greens
Biscuits (*biscotti*), 55–56, 60, 119, 120, 151
Bisteca Sanremasca (Tomato Bread), **174**
Bixio, Nino, 165
Black-eyed peas, 180
Black Sea, 12, 77, 318
Blenders, use in sauce preparation, 62, 75, 83, 102, 105
Blessington, Countess (Margaret Gardiner), 228–229, 237, 266–267
Blu di Genova, 32, 318
Blue jeans, origin of, 32
Boddington, Mrs., 46
Bogliasco, 117
Boletus mushrooms (Aereus, Edulis, Pinicola, Reticulatus, Rufus), 425; *See also Funghi porcini*
Bologna, 33, 107, 192, 291, 432
Bonaparte, Napoleon, 17, 88, 410, 411, 433
Borage (*Borragine*), 9, 181, 219, 255, 258–259, 433; Borage Fritters (Friscoë di Borragine), **181;** Borage and Cheese Gnocchi, **219;** Borage and Cheese Ravioli, **255;** Pansôti (Pasta Filled with Herbs and Greens), **258–259;** Pasta Sfoglia al Borragine (Green Pasta Flavored with Borage or Spinach), 199, **209**
Bordighera, 7, 9, 24, 29, 40, 72, 381
Borgio Verezzi, 374, 376
Boston, 10
Bottarga (dried tuna roe), 56
Bra cheese, 62
Branzino al Sale (Sea Bass Baked in Salt), **329**
Brazil, 378
Brazzi, Rossano, 24
Bread (*pane*), in Liguria, 14, 16, 35, 44, 51, 55–56, 59, 60, 73, 77, 81, 85, 96, 103, 105, **115–164,** 172, **174–176,** 199, 427, 429; with Olive Oil (Pane e Olio), **172;** *see also* Farinata; Focaccia; *Piscialandrea; Sardenaira;* Savory pies
Bread crumbs, 77
British Isles, 12, 33, 93, 148

British people: on French Riviera, 6, 7, 138, 354, 382, 393; in Liguria (Italian Riviera), 7, 8, 17, 25, 27, 29, 72, 138, 228–229, 266–267, 354, 381, 416–417
Brodo di Pesce (Fish Broth), **285–286,** 287
Broths and stocks, 33, 34, 280–281 (note about broth), 282–287, 326, 337, 361–362, 374, 376; beef broth, 285, 374, 376; chicken broth, 283, 284, 285, **361–362,** 374, 376; fish broth, **285–286,** 287, 326, 337; vegetable broth, 282, 283, 285, 374, 376
Browning, Robert, 469
Bruschetta, 73, 104, 175, 427; Bruschetta con Funghi Porcini (Toasts Topped with Porcini Mushrooms), **175**
Brunello di Montalcino wine, 231, 409, 411
Bruss cheese, 238
Buckwheat, 276
Buenos Aires, 60
Buridda (Fish and Seafood Stew), 17, **344–345**
Buridda (Stockfish Stew), 344, **346**
Butter (*burro*), 15, 32, 33, 40, 55, 63, 73, 78, 230
Buttermilk, 79, 126, 424, 433
Byron, George Gordon, Lord, vi, 29, 266

Cabani, Angelo, 330
Cabbage, 55–56, 264
Cáiro Montenotte, 409
Cakes, 22, 35, 56, 119, 148, 154, 382, 384–385, 393–394, 395, 396–397, 400, 441–442; *see also* Desserts
Calamari, 12, 191; Insalata di Calamaretti e Patate (Salad of Baby Calamari and Potatoes), **191;** *see also* Squid
California, Ligurians in, 32, 289, 318
Calvino, Italo, 24
Camogli, xiii–xiv, *xv,* 19, 25–27, 36, 46, 67, 69, 117–120, *121,* 123, 130–131, 133, 151, *153,* 166, 314, 316–317, 336, *339, 343,* 382, 386, 398, *418, 470;* Camogginn (Camogli Cherries), 382, **386;** Pesto di Camogli, **69**
Campania, 9, 18, 35, 199, 200, 432
Canada, 203, 323, 425
Cannellini, 180, 272, 276–277; Grain and Bean Soup (Mesc-Ciùa), 272, **276–277**
Cannes, 7, 8
Cardoons, 55
Cap d'Antibes, 7
Capers, 102, 240; Pasta al Forno con le Olive Nere e

Capperi (Baked Pasta with Black Olives and Capers), **240;** Salsa di Pinoli, Capperi e Acciughe (Sauce of Pine Nuts, Capers, and Anchovies), **102**
Cap Ferrat, 7
Capons, 56
Capponadda, 151, **338**
Cappon Magro, 120, 151, 338, **340–342,** 398
Capurro, Emanuela, 127
Carrara, 8
Carrots, 86
Caruggi (typical Ligurian alleyways), *21,* 35, *41,* 148
Casaregis, Giuseppe Maria, 165
Casoni, Franco, 222
Catalonia, 166
Cats, 27, *87,* 131, 165–166
Cavour, Camillo, 22
Celts, 7, 12, 17
Central America, 378
Cheese (*formaggio*), 14, 15, 17, 33–35, 40, 55–56, 60, 62, 64–67, 73, 76–77, 83, 118, 123, 126–128, 137–138, 148, 154, 199, 200, 202, 219, 238–239, 243, 324, 410, 443; *see also* Bra; Crescenza; Focaccette; Focaccia col Formaggio; Gorgonzola; Invernizza; Parmigiano-Reggiano; Pecorino; Prescinseua; Ricotta con le Cipolle; Stracchino; Taleggio
Cheese and Vegetable Gnocchi (Gnocchi Variegati), **219**
Cheese-Filled Ravioli (Ravioli di Magro), **254**
Cheese Focaccia, 34, 118, 123, **127–128,** *129,* 136, 276, 424
Cheese and Vegetable Ravioli (Ravioli di Verdura e Formaggio), **255**
Cheese Puffs (Focaccette), **137–138,** *139*
Chekhov, Anton, 262
Cherries, 382, **386,** 392, 396, 400, 405
Chervil, 9, 258–259, 433
Chestnut flour (*farina di castagne*), 10, 199, 200, 211, 218, 221, 391, 423–424, 444
Chestnut Cream Cups (Mietti), **391;** Chestnut Gnocchi, **218;** Chestnut Noodles, **211;** Chestnut *Trofie,* **221**
Chestnuts (*castagne*), 9, 10, 34, 55–56, 109, 148, 382, 387–391, 423–424, 428; Castagne al Profumo di Viola (Violet-Scented Chestnuts), **390;** Crema di Castagne al Profumo di Viola (Violet-Scented Chestnut Puree), **109;** Marrons Glacés (Candied Chestnuts), 10, **387–389,** 400, 424; Mietti (Chestnut Cream Cups), **391**

"Che Ti Dice La Patria?"
(Hemingway), 378
Chianti (and Chianti Classico)
wine, 231, 244, 414, 458
Chiavari, 9, 19, 144, *159*, 200,
222
Chicken (*pollo*), 85, 361–362;
Gallina Lessa Ripiena
(Boiled Stuffed Chicken),
283, **361–362**
Chicken broth, 283, 284,
361–362
Chickpea flour (*farina di ceci*),
10, 35, 56, 120, 144–145,
148, 444; Farinata (Chickpea
Tart) **144–145**, *146*, 148;
Paniccia (Chickpea
"Bread"), 144, **147**
Chickpeas (*ceci*), 10, 14, 56, 144,
148, 272, 276–277, 278–279,
424; Grain and Bean Soup
(Mesc-Ciùa), 272, **276–277**;
Chickpea Puree with
Porcini Mushrooms
(Crema di Ceci con Funghi
Porcini), **278–279**
Chicory (*cicoria*), 9
Chimes, The (Dickens), 195
China, 195, 422
Chives (*erba cipollina*), 81
Chocolate, 56, 392
Christ, Jesus, 35, 162
Christmas, 393, 398
Ciliegiolo wine, 244
Cima Ripiena (Stuffed Veal
Breast), 56, 359, **367–368**
Cinnamon, 55–56
Cinqueterre, 19, 28, 32, 40,
42, 192, 314, 354, 410–412,
414; wine, 28, 100, 192–193,
410–412, 414; *see also*
Manarola; Monterosso;
Vernazza
Cioppino, 289
Cipolle Ripiena (Stuffed
Onions), **306–307**
Ciuppin (Fish Soup), 32, **289**
Civiltà contadina (peasant
traditions), 36–44
Clams (*arselle, datteri, mitili,
vongole*), 12, 324, 424
Clabber, 79
*Classic Food of Northern Italy,
The* (Del Conte), 33
Cocoa (*cacao*), 14, 148
Cod (*merluzzo*), 12, 55–56,
285, 317–318, 324, 335,
346–348; *see also* Baccalà;
Stoccafisso; Stockfish
Coffee (*caffè*), 148, 382, 443
Colli di Luni wine, 411, 414
Colombia, 24
Columbus, Christopher, 12,
13, 14, 194, 215, 216, 256,
303, 429, 433; impact on
European cuisine, 14, 194,
215, 256, 433
Conchiglie al Paté di Polpo
(Pasta Shells with Octopus
Sauce), **241**
Condiggion (Condiglione;
Mixed Vegetable Salad),
103, **296**

Condiments. *See* Sauces
Conrad, Joseph, 318
Contadini, 39–44; *see also*
Liguria, traditions and
wisdom
Convents, 55–56
Cookies, 401–402, 441–442
Corn (*mais*), 14
Coronata wine, 124, 410, 414
Corzetti del Levante (Stamped
Corzetti), 35, 53, 56, 78,
104, 200, 203, 208, 210,
222, *223*, **224**, 457
Corzetti della Valpolcevara
(Figure-Eight Corzetti), 35,
78, 200, **225**
Corzetti stamps, 53,54, *223*,
224, 457
Crayfish (*gamberoni*), 424
Cream (*panna*), 15, 32, 33, 67,
80
Crema ai Pinoli e Maggiorana
(Pine Nut–Majoram
Sauce), 56, **78**
Crema di Castagne al Profumo
di Viola (Violet-Scented
Chestnut Puree), **109**
Crema di Ceci e Funghi
Porcini (Chickpea Puree
with Porcini Mushrooms),
278–279
Crescenza (cheese from
Liguria), 126–128, 132, 137,
423, 424, 443; *see also*
Liguria; Invernizzina;
Stracchino
Crostata (Fruit Jam Tart), 35,
396–397
Crostini con Spinasci (Spinach
Toasts with Raisins and
Pine Nuts), **176**
Cruise ships and cruise lines,
32
Cuttlefish (*seppie*), 7, 12, 56,
337, 349–351; Seppie del
Pescatore (Fisherman's
Cuttlefish Casserole), **349**;
Seppie in Umido con
Patate (Stewed Cuttlefish
with Potatoes), **350**; Seppie
in Zimino (Stewed
Cuttlefish with Greens), **351**

Del Conte, Anna, 33
Delgrande, Giorgio, 346
Denmark, 30
Denominazione di Origine
Controllata (D.O.C.) wines,
409–414, *413*; *see also Wine
and individual listings*
Denominazione di Origine
Controllata e Garantita
(D.O.C.G.) wines, 231,
409–411, 413
Dessert fritters, **403–405**
Desserts, 379–405, 428; *see also*
Fruits; Amaretti (Bitter
Almond Cookies), 44, 382,
383, 392, **401–402**;
Camogginn (Camogli
Cherries), 382, **386**;
Castagne al Profumo di
Viola (Violet-Scented

Chestnuts), **390**; Friscêu cö
Zebibbo e Pinoli (Raisin–
Pine Nut Fritters), **404**;
Friscêu di Frutta Secca
(Dried Fruit Fritters), **405**;
Friscêu di Mele (Apple
Fritters), **403**; Genoise
(Genoese Sponge Cake),
35, 382, 386, **400**; Marrons
Glacés (Candied Chestnuts),
10, **387–389**, 400, 424;
Mietti (Chestnut Cream
Cups), **391**; Pacciugo
(Portofino Ice Cream), 381,
392; Pandöce (Pandolce;
Sweet Genoa Cake), 382,
393–394, *395*; Pesche
Ripiene (Stuffed Peaches),
383; Salame di Albicocche
(Apricot Salami), **384–385**;
Sciumette (Little Meringue
Sponges), **398–399**;
Spungata Ligure (Ligurian
Fruit Pie), **396–397**
Detroit, 10
Diano Ligure, 7, 430
Diavolicchio, 16
Dickens, Charles, 25, 29, 195
Dogs, 27, 165–166, *167*
Dolceacqua, 24, 73, 405, *406*,
409–412, *413*; Rossese di,
wine of, 86, 244, 375, 405,
409–412, *413*, 436
Dolcetto wine, 86, 107, 231,
244, 375, 409–412, 436
Dorchester, 93
Doria, Andrea, 142, 165;
Andrea Doria Pizza, **142–143**
Doria family, 67, 222
Dumas, Alexandre, 20

Easter, 162, 398
Easter Pie (Torta Pasqualina),
35, 52, **162–164**
Eggplant (*melanzane*), 42, 84
Eggs (*uova*), 14, 55–56, 148,
185, 186, 203–209, 230, 334,
359–360, 398, 424; Frittata,
360; Frittata di Rossetti
("Redbait" Omelette), **334**;
Hard-Boiled Eggs with
Special Sauce (Uova Sode
con Salsa), **186**; Torta di
Frittate con Funghi Porcini,
Pesto e Pinoli (Frittata
"Cake" with Porcini
Mushrooms, Pesto, and Pine
Nuts), **185**, 309, 360; Torta
Pasqualina, 35, 52, **162–164**;
see also Pasta Sfoglia (Egg
Pasta)
Egypt, 9, 165
Elgar, Sir Edward, 25
Emerson, Ralph Waldo, 6
Emilia-Romagna, 8, 9, 12, 14,
22, 24, 28, 33, 35, 64, 107,
136, 192, 199, 200, 230,
370, 396, 415, 422, 423,
432, 434, 444
Enchanted April, 29
England, 33, 40, 381, 393; *see
also* British Isles; British
people in Liguria

Entroterra, 18–19, 24, 25, 32,
40, 42, 46, 120, 225, 230,
238, 317
Epiphany, 393
Equipment for cooking and
baking, 49–54, 203, 457
Europe, 60, 112, 138, 152, 165,
203, 216, 335, 427, 433

Falstaff (Verdi), 22
Fantozzi, 24
Farinata (Chickpea Tart), 17,
35, 52, 78, 120, **144–145**,
146, 424
Farro (spelt), 55, 272, 276–277,
444
Fascism, 23, 27, 28, 200
Fava bean flour, 150
Fava beans (*fave*), 10, 14, 56,
90, 171, 194, 195, 221, 433;
Fava Bean Sauce (Marò),
90, 150, 210, 216, 221, 285;
Fave, Salame e Pecorino
(Fresh Fava Beans, Salami,
and Pecorino Cheese), **194**
Favetta (Fava Bread), **150**
Fedelini (*fideli, fideos*), 55–56,
166, 284
Fegato alla Genovese (Genoese
Calf's Liver), 97, **369**
Fellini, Federico, 24
Fennel (*finocchio*), 56
Fennel, wild (*finocchio selvatico*),
69
Ferdinand, King of Spain, 12,
13
Festa della Focaccia (Recco),
118
Festa del Mare (La Spezia), 314
Festa del Marinaio (San
Remo), 314
Fideli (*fedelini, fideos*), 55–56,
166, 284
Field, Carol, 39, 123, 125
Figs (*fichi*), 9, 34, 44, 56, 72,
194, 195, 405, 434
Filling for pasta. *See* Ripieno
Finale Ligure, 19, 25, 158, 237,
363, 387, 412
First World War, 337, 430
Fish and seafood (*pesci e frutti
di mare*), 12, 14, 15, 17,
32–35, 40, 55–56, 59–60,
65, 67, 74, 83, 97, 99,
102–106, 118, 148, 177,
187–193, 199, 228, 233,
251, 285–286, 288, 289, 310,
321–352, *353*, 410, 428, 429;
Acciughe all'Agro
(Marinated Fresh
Anchovies), **187**; Acciughe
in Tegame (Casserole of
Fresh Anchovies), **188**;
Bagnun di Acciughe
(Fisherman's Anchovy
Casserole), 187, **336**;
Branzino al Sale (Sea Bass
Baked in Salt), **329**; Buridda
(Fish and Seafood
Stew), 17, **344–345**;
Buridda (Stockfish Stew),
344, **346**; Capponadda, 151,
338; Cappon Magro, 120,

Fish and seafood (*continued*)
151, 338, **340–342;** Fish
Broth, **285–286,** 287; Fish-
Filled Ravioli, **251,** 285;
Fried Anchovies with
Special Sauce, **190;** Frittata
di Rossetti ("Redbait"
Omelette), **334;** Insalata di
Calamaretti e Patate (Salad
of Baby Calamari and
Potatoes), **191;** Moscardini
in Umido all'Aglio (Stewed
Baby Octopus with Garlic),
352; Muscoli Ripieni
(Stuffed Mussels), **192–193;**
Pesce alla Ligure (Fish,
Ligurian-style), 324, **325;**
Pesce alla Praese (Small Fish
as Prepared in Prà), **328;**
Rospo al Vermentino
(Monkfish in a Vermentino
Wine Sauce), **333;** Rospo
con Carciofi (Monkfish
with Artichokes), **332;**
sauces for, 83, 86, 90,
97–102; sauces with,
103–106; Seppie del
Pescatore (Fisherman's
Cuttlefish Casserole), **349;**
Seppie in Umido con
Patate (Stewed Cuttlefish
with Potatoes), **350;** Seppie
in Zimino (Stewed
Cuttlefish with Greens),
351; Scaloppe di Branzino
in Crema di Asparagi (Sea
Bass Fillets in Asparagus
Sauce), **330–331;** Stoccafisso
alla Chelbi (Stockfish with
Vegetables), **347–348**
Fish Broth (Brodo di Pesce),
285–286, 287, 326
Fisherman's Anchovy
Casserole (Bagnun di
Acciughe), 187, **336**
Fisherman's Cuttlefish
Casserole (Seppie del
Pescatore), **349**
Fish Soup (Ciuppin), **289**
Fishing and fishermen, xv, 10,
16, 23, 26, 32, 36, 39–40,
42, 44–46, 59, 118, 119, 130,
153, 314–319, 324, 334, 336,
338, 339, 410, 430
Flaubert, Gustave, 18
Florence, 291
Flour (*farina*), 9, 14, 35, 199,
200, 203–207, 211, 425,
444; chestnut flour, 10, 199,
200, 444; chickpea flour,
10, 35, 444; fava flour, 150;
whole wheat flour, 199
Flower oils, 9
Flowers, 9, 10, 12, 24–25, 44,
72, 92, 110, 111, 382
Flower waters, 44, 110, 381
Focaccette (Cheese Puffs),
137–138, *139*
Focaccia, 9, 26, 33, 34, 49, 51,
65, 78, **117–136,** 171, 228,
272, 288, 410, 433, 435;
basic recipe, **123,** 130,
132–134; history and

description, 117–122; with
cheese (Focaccia col
Formaggio), 34, 118, 123,
127–128, *129,* 136, 276, 398;
with Gorgonzola cheese,
133; with herbs, 34, *132;*
with olive oil and white
wine, **123;** with olives, **133,**
135; with onions, **130;** with
potatoes, **134;** with
rosemary, **132;** with sage,
132; with sausage, **136;** with
truffle oil, **134**
Focaccia col Formaggio
(Focaccia with Cheese),
34, 118, 123, **127–128,** *129,*
136, 276, 424; Metodo
Antico (Old Method),
127–128, *129* ; Metodo
Moderno (Modern
Method), 127, **128,** *129*
*Focaccia: Simple Breads from the
Italian Oven* (Field), 123
Foggia, 97
Food conservation, 16, 39, 44,
53, 59–60, 78, 190, 312–313
Formagetta, 127
Formazza, 290
Fragrance, 33–35, 62, 118, 130,
148, 228–229, 382, 383, 410
France, 6, 7, 8, 17, 25, 30, 40,
72, 88, 120, 138, 233, 288,
323, 354, 382, 391, 448
Frantoio (olive press), 44, *431,*
449
French people in Liguria, 17,
18, 20, 88, 148, 233, 382,
387, 405
French Riviera, 6, 7, 17, 72,
138, 144; *see also* Menton;
Nice; Provence
Freud, Sigmund, 25, 29
Friggitorie (fry shops), 34, 228
Frisèu cö Zebibbo e Pinoli
(Raisin–Pine Nut Fritters),
404
Frisèu di Frutta Secca (Dried
Fruit Fritters), **405**
Frisèu di Mele (Apple
Fritters), **403**
Frisciolata, 144
Frittata, 185, 309, **360,** 433;
Torta di Frittate con Funghi
Porcini, Pesto e Pinoli
(Frittata "Cake" with
Porcini Mushrooms, Pesto,
and Pine Nuts), **185,** 309,
360
Frittelle. See Fritters
Fritters, **177–178, 180–181,**
382, **403–405;** Bean Fritters
(Frittelle di Fagioli), **180;**
Borage Fritters (Friscoë di
Borragine), **181;** Frisèu cö
Zebibbo e Pinoli
(Raisin–Pine Nut Fritters),
404; Frisèu di Frutta Secca
(Dried Fruit Fritters), **405;**
Frisèu di Mele (Apple
Fritters), **403;** Lemon Leaf
Fritters (Frittelle di Foglie
di Limone), **178**
Friuli-Venezia Giulia, 409, 443

Fruit (*frutta*), 9, 10, 14, 33, 35,
39, 40, 55–56, 60, 79, 122,
195, 378, 379–382,
383–386, 389, 392,
396–397, 401, **403–405,**
425; candied fruit (*frutta
candita*), 381–382, 383,
393–394, 396; citrus
(*agrumi*), 381–382, 393;
dried fruit (*frutta secca*), 382,
405; Dried Fruit Fritters,
405; fruit fritters, **403–405;**
lemons, 6, 9, 56, 72, 80, 83,
103, 178–179, 234, 305, 381;
see also listings for individual
fruits
Frying hints, 177
Fugassa all'Euio (Focaccia
all'Olio; Focaccia with
Olive Oil and White
Wine), **123,** 130, 132–134
Fugassa co-a Çiòula (Focaccia
con la Cipolla; Focaccia
with Onions), **130**
Fugassa co-a Murcia
(Ponentine Olive Focaccia),
133, *135*
Fugassa co-a Sarvia (Focaccia
con la Salvia, Sage
Focaccia), **132,** *135*
Fugassa co-e Patatte (Focaccia
con le Patate; Potato
Focaccia), **134**
Fugassa co-e Porpe (Levantine
Olive Focaccia), **133**
Fugassa co-o Romanin
(Focaccia col Rosmarino;
Rosemary Focaccia), **132**
Funghi porcini, 9, 14, 34, 91,
175, 184, 185, 222, 225, 227,
230–231, 245–246, 260–261,
278–279,
280–282, 308–311, 425–427,
428, 448; about *funghi
porcini,* 425–427; Agnello
con Olive e Funghi (Lamb
Stew with Olives and
Mushrooms), **372;**
Bruschetta con Funghi
Porcini (Mushroom Toasts),
175; cleaning *funghi porcini,*
426; Crema di Ceci e
Funghi Porcini (Chickpea
Puree with Porcini
Mushrooms), **278–279;**
cutting *funghi porcini,* 426;
freezing *funghi porcini,*
426–427; Funghi Porcini al
Pesto e Pinoli (Fresh
Porcini Mushrooms with
Pesto and Pine Nuts), **185;**
Funghi Porcini con Pinoli
(Porcini Mushrooms with
Pine Nuts), **308;** Funghi
Porcini e Patate al Forno
(Baked Porcini Mushrooms
and Potatoes), **310;** Salad
with Walnuts and Porcini
Mushrooms (Insalata con
Noci e Funghi Porcini),
184; sautéing *funghi porcini,*
426; Penne con Funghi e
Timo (Penne with

Mushrooms and Thyme),
227; Risotto Valpolcevara,
260–261; Rotolo Maria Pia
(Mushroom–String Bean
Roll), **245–246;** Tagliarini
ai Porcini (Tagliarini with
Porcini Mushrooms),
230–231; Tocco di Funghi
(Mushroom Sauce), **91,**
209, 210, 211, 222, 225;
Torta di Frittate con Funghi
Porcini, Pesto e Pinoli
(Frittata "Cake" with
Porcini Mushrooms, Pesto,
and Pine Nuts), **185,** 309,
360; using *funghi porcini,*
427; Zuppa di Funghi e
Patate (Mushroom and
Potato Soup), 272,
280–281; Zuppa di Porcini
e Lumache (Mushroom and
Snail Soup), **282**

Gallette del marinaio (sailor's
biscuits; sea biscuits), 16,
120, 151, 296, 338, 341–342
Gallina Lessa Ripiena (Boiled
Stuffed Chicken), 283,
361–362
Garda, Lake, 64, 448
Garibaldi, Giuseppe, 20, 22,
152, 166, 318
Garlic (*aglio*), 15, 55–56, 60,
62–64, 66–67, 97–98, 132,
271–273, 427, 433
Garlic Sauce (Aggiada), 17, 90,
97–98, 219, 285, 369, 427
Garlic Soup (Zuppa di Aglio),
132, 271–272, **273,** 427
Garden Sauce (Paté di
Ortaggi), **85**
Gassman, Vittorio, 24
Gauls, 7, 93
Gavi wine, 245, 415
Genoa (Genova), xiii, 5, 6, 8,
12, 15, 18, 19, 20, 21, 22,
24, 26, 28, 30, 32, 35, 40,
44–45, 55–56, 65, 70, 78,
87, 88, 92–93, 107, 112–113,
117–118, 120, 123, 127, 148,
149, 150, 152, 165, 179, 181,
195, 200, 219, 222, 225, 226,
228–229, 233, 245, 247, 252,
260, 262, 266–267, 271–272,
274–275, 276, 288, 290, 314,
315, 316–318, *327,* 328, 344,
347, 350, 361, 364, 369, 378,
382, 386, 387, 389, 393, *395,*
400, 410–411, 422–423, 432,
433, 442, 443, 447, 448, 449,
455, 461; descriptions of, 5,
18, 55–56, 88, 112–113, 148,
165, 195, 228–229, 262,
266–267
Genoa Cake (Pandolce), 382,
393–394, *395*
Genoa, Gulf of, 36
Genoa, Republic of, 7, 12, 15,
22, 35, 77, 120, 142, 165,
222, 225, 318; coins and
their influence on *corzetti*
pasta shapes, 35, 222, *223,*
224, 225; commerce, 15,

318; relationship to Liguria, 18, 19

Genoese Calf's Liver (Fegato alla Genovese), 97, **369**

Genoese Meat Sauce (Tocco), **107–108**

Genoese people, 6, 12, 15, 16, 20, 22, 23, 45, 112–113, 195, 222, 393

Genoese Sauce, **86**, 101

Genoese Spinach with Raisins and Pine Nuts (Spinasci a-a Zeneize), **297**

Genoise (Genoese Sponge Cake), 35, 382, 386, **400**

Germans, in Liguria, 29, 36, 290–291, 316, 337, 382, 416

Germany, 40, 46, 148, 290

Gewürztraminer wines, 245

Gioconda, La (Ponchielli), 25

Gizzoa (Focaccia con la Salsiccia; Sausage Focaccia), **136**

Gnocchi, 215, **216–219;** Cheese and Vegetable Gnocchi (Gnocchi Variegati), **219;** Chestnut Gnocchi (Gnocchi di Castagna), **218**

Goat, 56, 127, 238, 391

Golfo dei Poeti (Gulf of Poets), 29, 300

Gorgonzola, 133, 243; Focaccette (Cheese Puffs with Gorgonzola), **137–138,** *139;* Focaccia with Gorgonzola, **133;** Lasagne with Gorgonzola, **243**

Götterdämmerung (Wagner), 290

Grains, 33, 40, 276–277, 433; Grain and Bean Soup (Mesc-Ciùa), 272, **276–277**

Gramsci, Antonio, 23

Grand Tour, 29

Grapes (*uva*), Ligurian, 10, 28, 42, 195, 354, 409–415

Graves, Charles, 67, 337

Greece and Greeks, 7, 46, 105, 422, 448

Greens (*verdura*), 14, 34, 62, 103, 156, 157, 158, 161, 162, 184, 199, 255, 283, 295, 324, 361–362, 349, 423; Gallina Lessa Ripiena (Boiled Stuffed Chicken), 283, **361–362;** Pansôti (Pasta Filled with Herbs and Greens), 35, 52, 77, 118, 127, 199, 200, 202, 212, 247, **258–259,** 432, 433; Seppie in Zimino (Stewed Cuttlefish with Greens), **351;** *see also* Borage; Chervil; Chicory; Lettuce; Lovage; Savory pies; Sorrel; Torte

Grimaldi family of Monaco, 6

Hake (*nasello*), 285, 329, 424

Ham, 324; *see also* Prosciutto cotto; Prosciutto crudo

Hamburg, 26, 318

Hanbury, Villa, 29, 72, 382

Hawaii, 378

Hawthorne, Nathaniel, 435

Hazelnuts (*nocciole*), 9, 56, 317, 374–375, 428

Hemingway, Ernest, 378

Herbs (*erbe*), in Liguria, 9, 14, 15, 16, 17, 18, 24, 26, 27, 28, 33, 35, 42, 44, 49, 55–56, 62–64, 66–78, 98, 101, 122, 148, 232, 258–259, 283, 288, 324, 393; herb-flavored focaccias, 34, 132; herb sauces, 62–71, 73–75, 86, 98, 101, 150, 199, 232, 367; Pansôti (Pasta Filled with Herbs and Greens), 35, 52, 77, 118, 127, 199, 200, 202, 212, 247, **258–259,** 432, 433; *see also* Basil; Marjoram; Mint; Oregano; Rosemary; Sage; Tarragon; Thyme

Holland, 24

Honey (*miele*), 10, 109–111, 382, 390, 445; Rose Honey, **110;** Violet Honey, 109, **111,** 389

Hyères, 7, 138

Iberia, 166, 284

Ice cream and ices, 112, 118, 381, 382, 386, 392

Iceland, 323, 435

Idler in Italy, The (Blessington), 228–229, 237, 266

Imperia, 18, 19, 24, 28, 45, 52, 120, 142, 182, 200, 238, 317, 324, 334, 410–412, 430, 433, 435, 445, 448–453, 458–460; *see also* Oneglia; Porto Maurizio

Impero River, 24

Innocents Abroad, The (Twain), 112–113

Insalata di Calamaretti e Patate (Salad of Baby Calamari and Potatoes), **191**

Insalata con Noci e Funghi Porcini (Salad with Walnuts and Porcini Mushrooms), **184**

Invernizzina (cheese from Liguria), 126–128, 132, 137; *see also* Crescenza; Stracchino

Involtini con Carciofi (Veal Rolls with Artichokes), **363**

Isabella, Queen of Spain, 12, 13

Islamic and Arab influence in Liguria, 12, 46, 62, 77, 127, 148

Italian Baker, The (Field), 123

Italy for the Gourmet Traveler (Plotkin), 9, 433

Italy Revisited (Graves), 67, 337

Japan and Japanese, 14, 105, 389

Jenkins, Nancy Harmon, 39

Kasha, 276

Kasper, Lynne Rossetto, 39

Keats, John, 29, 422

Kummer, Corby, 39

Lago Maggiore, 290–291

Lamb (*agnello*), 371–372; Agnello con Carciofini (Lamb with Baby Artichokes), **371;** Agnello con Olive e Funghi (Lamb Stew with Olives and Mushrooms), **372**

Land of Italy, The (More), 7, 72

Lasagne, 52, 56, 76, 84, 199, 203, 208, 209, 210, 213, **242–244;** Lasagne al Pesto (Lasagne with Pesto), **242;** Lasagne al Pesto Bianco (Lasagne with White Pesto), **244;** Lasagne Portofino (Lasagne with Pesto and Gorgonzola Cheese), **243**

La Spezia, vi, xiii, 5, 12, 17, 18, 19, 22, 27–29, 40, 42, 45, 93, 99, 104, 105, 136, 138, 174, 218, 236, 240, 244, 264, 276, 284, 288, 290–291, 298, 300, 314, 330, 366, 378, 381, 382, 410–412, 428, 432, 434, 444, 455, 462

La Spezia, Gulf of, vi, 7, 29, 300, 428

Lattughe Ripiene (Stuffed Lettuce Rolls), 283, **298,** 428

Lavagna, 7, 9, 338, 354

Lavender (*lavanda*), 9, 24, 44, 410, 427

Lawrence, D. H., 29, 105, 300

Lawson, William, 295

Lazio, 17, 18, 64, 92, 177, 396, 421–422, 432

Leeks (*porri*), 236; Spaghetti con Pomodoro e Porri (Spaghetti with a Sauce of Tomatoes and Leeks), **236**

Lemons, 6, 9, 56, 72, 80, 83, 103, 178–179, 234, 305, 381, 383, 398; *I Limoni* ("The Lemon Trees") (Montale), 179; Lemon Leaf Fritters (Frittelle di Foglie di Limone), **178**

Le Poittevin, Alfred, 18

Lerici, 300, 428

Lettuce (*lattuga*), 9, 34, 42, 55–56, 62, 103, 283, 298, 428; Stuffed Lettuce Rolls (Lattughe Ripiene), 283, **298,** 428

Levante, Riviera del, 7, 19, 29, 71, 76, 99, 101, 104, 117, 127, 133, 144, 174, 226, 288, 349, 370, 412–415, 449, 455, 461–462

Levanto, 7, 71, 314

Liguri, 6, 12

Liguria: agriculture, 39–45, 120, 225, 295, 327, 381, 409, 412; architecture and art, 46, 88, 92–93, 113, 149, 405, 406; beauty of, 5–6, 8, 9, 14, 18, 24, 28–29, 35, 46, 112–113, 266–267, 300; ceremonies and feasts, 16, 26, 118, 276, 312, 314–319,

343, 412; churches and religion, 30, 31, 39, 44, 67, 87, 119, 148, 165–166, 314–319, 343, 393; civilization, 6, 7, 12, 14, 15, 39–45, 119, 148, 152, 314–319; colors of, xv, 8, 9, 10, 46; commerce, 12, 15, 23, 32, 40, 42, 44, 55–56, 62, 77, 88, 113, 117, 119, 120, 165, 228–229, 247, 271, 276, 284, 316–318, 337, 378, 430; compared with French Riviera, 6, 7, 72; dialect, 18, 45, 107, 117, 144, 247, 276, 302; dialogue between land and sea, 15, 16, 23, 27, 33, 35, 37–45, 59, 90, 130, 151, 165, 247, 260, 288, 314–319, 324, 340; emigration from, 32, 289; *entroterra*, 18–19, 24, 25, 32, 40, 42, 46, 120, 225, 230, 238, 317; fishing, 10, 12, 32, 42, 59, 67, 314–319; flower-growing, 9, 10, 12, 24–25, 44, 72, 92, 110, 111, 382; food (*see* Ligurian cuisine); gambling and gaming, 30, 138; geography, 8, 18, 92–93, 117; history, 18, 22, 117, 119, 314–319, 410 (*see also* Liguria, civilization, *above*, and listings for cities); landscape, 6, 15, 24, 40, 42, 46, 92–93, 117, 138, 266–267; map, 4; markets, 25, 40, 72, 148, 271, 367; medicine, 44, 138, 148, 152, 416–417, 429; origins, 6–8, 119; political figures, 22–23, 28, 165; relationship to Genoa, 18, 19, 45, 117; relationship with England and British people, 17, 92–93, 138; relationship with Russia and Russians, 29–30, 138; social fabric (*tessuto sociale*), 19, 23, 39–45, 55–56, 112–113, 118, 130, 148, **152,** 165, 314–318; sunlight and sunshine in, 8, 10, 11, 16, 19, 27, 39, 46, 312–313; tourism and visitors, 7, 18, 20, 28–30, 32, 42, 138, 148, 354; traditions and wisdom, 36, 39–46, 118, 130, 131, 152, 165–166, 174, 247, 313, 314–318, 334, 338, 340, 354–354, 393, 413, 429; transportation, 17, 42, 92–93, 117, 354–355, 413; vegetation, 5, 9, 10, 36, 42, 44, 72, 148, 179

Ligurian cuisine: Arab influence on, 62, 127, 148, 214, 351, 382; Asian influence on, 77, 90, 351, 382; baking and bakers, 44, 46, 51, 117–122; components of, 16, 25, 28, 33–35, 40, 42, 55–56, 59,

Ligurian cuisine (*continued*)
187, 199–200; equipment
for preparation, 49, *50*,
51–53, *54*, 144, 229, 457;
evolution of, 6, 9, 10, 12,
14–18, 28, 30, 32–33, 35,
40, 55–56, 117–122, 127,
199–200, 220, 247, 338, 410;
fragrance, 33–35, 62, 118,
130, 148, 228–229, 382, 383,
410; home cooks, 32–33,
42, 55–56; how Ligurians
eat, 33–34, 55–56, 59, 118,
122, 130, 148, 151, 190,
228–229, 274–275, 324;
impact of cruise ships and
tourism, 32–33, 318;
ingredients, availability, and
sources, 34–35, 39–44, 59,
117–122, 148, 419–437,
439–462; preservation and
storage, 16, 39, 44, 53,
59–60, 78, 190, 312–313, 338;
relationship with French
Riviera food, 17, 120, 233,
344, 381; sophistication of,
33, 49; structure of meals,
34, 118, 228–229, 324
Ligurians: actors, 24; character,
12, 23, 36, 46, 55–56, 138,
148, 152, 229, 237, 354–355;
children, xv, 44–45, 67, 118,
131, 148, 247, 430; and
clothing, 112–113, 138, 148;
fishermen (*pescatori*), xv, 10,
16, 23, 26, 32, 36, 39–40,
42, 44–46, 59, 118, 119, 130,
153, 314–319, 324, 334, 336,
338, 339, 410, 430; frugality
of, 12, 23–24, 33, 40, 46,
55–56, 59, 74, 171, 174, 220,
274–275, 284; immigrants
in California, 32, 289; and
Italian politics, 22–23; life
expectancy, 14, 40; men,
36, 40, 44, 67, 112–113, 119,
130, 131, 152, 228–229,
314–319, 354–355;
musicians, 24, 25; old
people, xv, 15, 25, 39–45,
152, 167, 247, 312, 314–318,
334, 413; origins, 6, 12;
physical characteristics, 15,
40, 148, 229; political
figures, 22–23, 314;
resourcefulness and
inventiveness of, 6, 10,
39–46, 55–56, 312–313,
314–319; sailors and
mariners, xv, 12, 16, 19, 23,
26, 28, 32, 40, 46, 55, 118,
119, 120, 130, 151, 190,
314–318, *319*, 338, 430;
sports and, 15; tenacity of,
6, 19, 23, 118, 152; witches,
273; women, 15, 19, 23, 26,
28, 40, 44–45, 59, 67,
112–113, 119, 130, 131, 148,
228–229, 273, 312, 314–319,
337, 354–355, 412, 45, 179
Ligurian Fruit Pie (Spungata
Ligure), 396–397

Ligurian Sea (*Mar Ligure*), 10,
189, 314, 316, 434
Ligurian-Style Pasta Sheets
(Pasta Sfoglia alla Ligure),
199, **208**
Liver, 56, 97, 252–253, 369;
Fegato alla Genovese
(Genoese Calf's Liver), 97,
369
Loano, 7
Lombardy (Lombardia), 7, 8,
12, 22, 126, 200, 243, 401,
422, 423, 432
London, 5, 29, 416
Loren, Sophia, 200
Lovage, 9
Luni, 8, 411, 415
Lunigiana, 28, 264, 411, 415

Machetto (Sardine Sauce),
103, 140–141
Machetusa, 103, 141
Maiale alle Olive (Pork Loin
with Black Olives), **370**
Manarola, 192, 312, 413
Manitoba, 425
Mantua, 432
Manuelina restaurant (Recco),
127, 398
Manzo Negretto (Stewed
Beef with Onion Sauce),
366
Marche, 386
Marconi, Guglielmo, 25
Maria Alexandrovna, 30
Marjoram (*maggiorana*), 9, 44,
77, 78, 199, 224, 232, 427,
428; Crema ai Pinoli e
Maggiorana (Pine Nut-
Marjoram Sauce), 56, **78**,
150, 211, 218, 219, 222; La
Pagioada (Marjoram-
Noodle Soup), 271, **284**;
Pasta alla Maggiorana
(Marjoram-Flavored Pasta),
210, 224
Marò (Fava Bean Sauce), **90**,
150, 210, 216, 221, 285
Marrons Glacés (Candied
Chestnuts), 10, **387–389**,
400, 424
Marsala wine, 391, 393, 404
Mastroianni, Marcello, 24
Maupassant, Guy de, 20
Mazzini, Giuseppe, 22
Meat (*carne*), 14, 17, 28, 33, 40,
55–56, 59–60, 65, 77, 83,
97, 199, 252–253, 297, 259,
364–372, *373*, **374–377**, 429,
447; Agnello con Carciofini
(Lamb with Baby
Artichokes), **371**; Agnello
con Olive e Funghi (Lamb
Stew with Olives and
Mushrooms), **372**; Cima
Ripiena (Stuffed Veal
Breast), 359, **367–368**;
Coniglio all'Aggiada
(Rabbit with Garlic Sauce),
376–377; Coniglio alle
Mandorle (Rabbit with
Almonds), **374–375**; Fegato
alla Genovese (Genoese

Calf's Liver), 97, **369**;
Maiale alle Olive (Pork
Loin with Black Olives),
370; Manzo Negretto
(Stewed Beef with Onion
Sauce), **366**; Ravioli di
Carne (Meat-Filled
Ravioli), **252–253**;
Tomaxelle (Little Veal
Rolls), 297, 359, **364–365**
Meat sauces, **107–109**, 209,
211, 216, 225
Mediterranean Diet, 14
Mediterranean Sea, xiii, 5, 8,
10, 20, 28, 46, 88, 92, 138,
194, 237, 267, 284, 290,
297, 300, 329, 335, 344,
416, 422, 428, 433, 448
Mediterranean, The (More), 88
*Mediterranean Winter Resorts, A
Practical Handbook to the
Principal Health and Pleasure
Resorts on the Shores of the
Mediterranean* (Ball),
416–417
Menton(e), 6, 7, 72, 335, 354,
381
*Mentone and the Riviera as a
Winter Climate* (Bennet),
335
Meringue Sponges:
(Sciumette), **398–399**
Mesc-Ciùa (Grain and Bean
Soup), 272, **276–277**
Michelangelo, 8
Milan, 8, 20, 22, 26, 33, 126,
274, 382, 389, 393
Milk, 55–56, 76–80, 126, 127,
391
Miller, William, 354
Millet, 433
Mint (*menta*), 9, 232
Modena, 432
Moldeto, Lorenzo, 118
Moltedo, Titta, 126–127
Monaco, Republic of, 6
Monet, Claude, 405
Monkfish (*pescatrice, rospo*), 285,
332–333; Rospo al
Vermentino (Monkfish in a
Vermentino Wine Sauce),
333; Rospo con Carciofi
(Monkfish with
Artichokes), **332**
Montale, Eugenio, 20, 24, 179
Monte Carlo (Monaco), 7, 30
Monte Faccio, 195
Montemarcello, 27
Montesquieu, Charles–Louis
de, 233
More, Jasper, 7, 72, 88
Mortadella, 28, 192–193, 298
Mortar and pestle, 16, 17, 49,
50, 51, 53, 62–64, 66, 74,
75, 77, 78, 83, 102
Mortola, 72
Moryson, Fynes, 155
Moscardini (baby octopus), 324,
352, 353, 424; Moscardini in
Umido all'Aglio (Steamed
Baby Octopus with Garlic),
352

Mostarda, 16
Mosciame (dried tuna), 338
Mullet (*triglia*), 233, 325, 334,
335, 337, 424
Muscoli Ripieni (Stuffed
Mussels), **192–193**
Mushrooms (*funghi*) 14, 34,
55–56, 91, 209, 210, 211,
222, 225, 230–231, 233,
245–246, 308–311, 425–427,
428, 448; Tocco di Funghi
(Mushroom Sauce), **91**,
209, 210, 211, 222, 225; *see
also Funghi porcini*
Mussels (*cozze, muscoli*), 104,
192–193, 324, 337, 424, 428,
432; Muscoli Ripieni
(Stuffed Mussels), **192–193**;
Sugo di Muscoli (Mussel
Sauce), **104**

Naples, 20, 30, 32, 86, 140,
166, 199, 291, 359, 386, 432
National Pasta Museum
(Rome), 200
Ne, 361
Nervi, 25, 29–30
Newman, Paul, 200
New Mexico, 425
New York, 130, 351
New Zealand, 323
Nice, 6, 17, 22, 30, 120, 142,
144, 344, 381, 382, 410
Nietzsche, Friedrich, 27
Noah, 340
Noli, 25, 237
North America, 33, 49, 60,
110, 111, 126, 203, 247, 271,
274, 281, 323, 354–355,
422–425, 427, 428,
432–434, 447
Norway and Norwegians, 12,
14, 318, 323, 324, 435
Nostromo (Conrad), 318
Novi Ligure, 247
Nuts (*noci*), 9, 10, 14, 17, 33,
40, 42, 49, 62–78, 382, 393,
396, 428
Nut sauces, 12, 17, 77, 428

Octopus (*polpo*), 12, 105–106,
324, 352, 424; Paté di Polpo
(Octopus Sauce), **105–106**
Octopus, baby (*moscardini*),
324, 352, 353, 424;
Moscardini in Umido
all'Aglio (Steamed Baby
Octopus with Garlic), **352**
Octopus of Tellaro, 29, 105,
300
O'Faolain, Sean, xv
Olive oil (*olio d'oliva*), 13–17,
25, 33–35, 40, 44, 56, 60,
62–65, 96, 172, 173, 177,
230–231, 233, 288, 295, 350,
371, 423, 428–431, 448–455;
Pane e Olio (Bread with
Olive Oil), **172**
Olive oil museum (Oneglia),
430
Olive paste (sauce, paté), 85,
94, 133, 251, 285, 429,
449

Olives (*olive*), 13–17, 25, 34–35, 44, 72, 85, 94, 95, 133, 140, 142, 175, 188, 233, 240, 251, 285, 296, 325, 346, 350, 370, 372, 381, 382, 429; Agnello con Olive e Funghi (Lamb Stew with Olives and Mushrooms), **372;** "Caviar" (Sauce), 85, **94,** 133, 251, 285, 429, 449; Focaccia with Olives, **133;** Maiale alle Olive (Pork Loin with Black Olives), **370;** Pasta al Forno con le Olive Nere e Capperi (Baked Pasta with Black Olives and Capers), **240;** Pasta (Paté) di Olive, 85, **94,** 133, 251, 285; Pesce alla Ligure (Fish, Ligurian-Style), 324, **325;** varieties (*see* Taggia; Taggiasca olives)

Olive trees, 7, 9, 10, 25

Oneglia, 24, 52, 142, 144, 182, 200, 430, 448

Onion (*cipolla*), 56, 60, 81, 109, 130, 144, 160, 306–307, 366; Cipolle Ripiene (Stuffed Onions), **306–307;** Focaccia with Onions, **130;** Torta di Cipolle (Onion Savory Pie), **160**

Oranges (*arance*), 72, 381, 383

Orata (Gilthead bream), 325, 329, 424

Oregano (*origano*), 9, 429

Ormeasco wine, 412

Orvieto wine, 333

Ospedaletti, 7, 72

Oxford, 93

Pacciugo (Portofino Ice Cream), 381, **392**

Pacific Ocean, 323

Paganini, Niccolò, 24, 252

Palermo, 20

Pallavicino, Cammillo, 55

Palm trees, 5, 9, 92, 410

Pancetta (unsmoked bacon), 311

Pandolce (Pandöçe; Sweet Genoa Cake), 382, **393–394,** *395*

Pane e Olio (Bread with Olive Oil), **172**

Pane e Pomodoro (Tomato Bread), **174**

Panèra, 382

Paniccia (Chickpea "Bread"), 144, **147**

Panettone, 382, 393

Pansôti (Pasta Filled with Herbs and Greens), 35, 52, 77, 118, 127, 199, 200, 202, 212, 247, **258–259,** 428, 432

Paris, 5, 91, 93

Parma, 22, 28, 284, 432

Parmigiano-Reggiano cheese, 14, 28, 62, 64, 66, 70, 71, 73, 74, 77, 99, 192–193, 200, 202, 274–275, 423, 432, 443

Parragi, 7, 26

Parsifal (Wagner), 291

Parsley, 62, 64, 75, 427

Pasta, 9, 10, 12, 14, 16, 33–35, 49, 52–53, 55–56, 59, 73, 78, 81, 85, 120, 122, 166, **197–265,** 272, 288, 423, 424, 428, 429, 432; Agnolotti, 247; Anolini, 199; Barbagiuai (Fried Pumpkin Ravioli), **257;** borage-flavored pasta, 199, **209;** capelli di angelo, 287; Chestnut Gnocchi, **218;** Chestnut Noodles, **211;** Chestnut *Trofie,* **221;** Conchiglie, 105, 241; cooking, 202; Corzetti del Levante (Stamped Corzetti), 35, 53, 56, 78, 104, 200, 203, 208, 210, **222,** *223,* **224,** 432; Corzetti della Valpolcevara (Figure-Eight Corzetti), 35, 78, 200, **225,** 432; cutting pasta into noodles, 212–213; dried, 199, 432; *fideli,* 55–56; fresh (egg) pasta, 199, **203–207,** 424, 432; Gnocchi, 77, 81, 84, 200, 202, 215, **216–219,** 433; Gnocchi di Castagna (Chestnut Gnocchi), 81, **218;** Gnocchi Variegati, 81, 84, **219;** Lasagne, 52, 56, 76, 84, 199, 203, 208, 209, 210, 213, **242–244;** *maccheroni* (macaroni), 2–3, 237, 238–239, 240, 288, 366; Marjoram-Flavored Pasta, **210;** Mandilli di Sæa (Silk Handerkerchiefs), 52, 208, 213, **214;** Pansôti (Pasta Filled with Herbs and Greens), 35, 52, 77, 118, 127, 199, 200, 202, 212, 247, **258–259,** 432, 433; penne, 74, 81, 84, 227, 232, 238–239, 240, 366; Pumpkin Ravioli, **256, 257;** Ravioli, 25, 35, 52–53, 56, 107, 195, 199, 200, 203, 208, 209, 210, 212, 228, **247–259,** 276, 283, 432, 433; Rotolo Maria Pia, **245–246;** spaghetti, 32, 35, 203, 234–235, 236; Spinach-Flavored Pasta, **209;** tagliarini (taglierini, tagliatelline), 81, 84, 195, 203, 208, 209, 212–213, 230–232; *tagliatelle,* 52, 76, 78, 98, 107, 199, 203, 208, 209, 210, 212, 230; testaroli, 200, 202; tortellini, 199; tortelloni, 77, 199; *trenette,* 35, 74, 104, 200, 202, 226, 432; Trofie (Troffie), 68, 118, 200, 202, **220–221,** 276, 398, 432; Trofie di Castagna (Chestnut *Trofie*), **221**

Pasta ai Pinoli con Ricotta e Rosmarino (Pasta with Pine Nuts, Baked Ricotta, and Fresh Rosemary), **238–239**

Pasta al Forno con le Olive Nere e Capperi (Baked Pasta with Black Olives and Capers), **240**

Pasta alla Maggiorana (Marjoram-Flavored Pasta), **210**

Pasta (Paté) di Olive, 85, **94,** 133, 251, 285, 429, 449

Pasta Sfoglia al Borjagine o Agli Spinaci (Green Pasta Flavored with Borage or Spinach), 199, **209**

Pasta Sfoglia all'Uovo (Fresh Egg Pasta Sheets), 199, **203–207,** 208, 230, 248–259, 287

Pasta Sfoglia alla Ligure (Ligurian-Style Pasta Sheets), 199, **208,** 213, 214, 432

Pasta Shells with Octopus Sauce (Conchiglie al Paté di Polpo), **241**

Paté di Ortaggi (Garden Sauce), **85,** 219, 285, 362

Paté di Polpo (Octopus Sauce), **105–106,** 241

Peaches (*pesche*), 9, 382, 383, 392, 400, 401, 405, 410; Stuffed Peaches (Pesche Ripiene), **383**

Peas (*piselli*), 9, 34, 56, 287, 311, 371; Zimino di Carciofi e Piselli (Casserole of Artichokes and Peas), **311**

Pecorino cheese, 14, 56, 62, 64, 66, 68, 70, 71, 73, 194, 200, 202, 423, 432, 443; Fresh Fava Beans, Salami and Pecorino Cheese (Fave, Salame e Pecorino), **194**

Pegli, 138

Penne, 74, 81, 84, 227, 232, 238–239, 240, 366

Penne con Funghi e Timo (Penne with Mushrooms and Thyme), **227**

Penneise, u (Ligurian cat minders), 165

Peperoncino (hot pepper), 14, 16, 99

Pepper, black, 56

Peppers (*peperoni*), sweet and hot, 14, 16

Pepper, white, 76

Perfume, 12, 381

Pertini, Sandro, 23

Pescatori. *See* Ligurians, fishermen

Pesce alla Ligure (Fish, Ligurian-Style), 324, **325**

Pesce alla Praese (Small Fish as Prepared in Prà), **328**

Pesce al Vapore (Poached Fish), **285–286,** 324, 326

Pesce azzuro, 12, 323, 328

Pesto, 16, 25, 35, 60, **62–71, 73–76,** 79, 90, 107, 118, 166, 185, 200, 211, 212, 214, 216, 218, 219, 222, 225, 226, 242, 243, 251, 254, 255, 256, 257, 272, 274–275, 276, 398, 428, 432, 433, 450–456; Antico, **68;** Bianco (White Pesto), 63, **76,** 209, 219, 222, 244; di Camogli, **69;** Classico, 66, 68–71, 73; Corto (with tomatoes), 63, **74;** Dolce (Sweet Pesto), **73;** di Dolceacqua, **73,** 75; Forte (Sharp Pesto), **74;** al Frullatore (Blender Pesto), 63, **75;** Funghi Porcini al Pesto e Pinoli (Fresh Porcini Mushrooms with Pesto and Pine Nuts), **185;** Gastronomico (for tourists), **75;** Lasagne al Pesto, **242;** Lasagne al Pesto Bianco (Lasagne with White Pesto), **244;** Lasagne Portofino (Lasagne with Pesto and Gorgonzola Cheese), **243;** del Levante, **71;** origins of, 62–63; del Ponente, **71;** di Recco, 25, **69;** storage of, 65; Torta di Frittate con Funghi Porcini, Pesto e Pinoli (Frittata "Cake" with Porcini Mushrooms, Pesto, and Pine Nuts), **185,** 309, 360; Trenette alla Genovese (*Trenette* with Pesto, Potatoes, and String Beans), 65, **226;** della Valpolcevara, **70;** Vegia Zena (Old Genoa), **70**

Philippines, 378

Phoenicians, 12, 410

Picasso, Pablo, 25

Pictures from Italy (Dickens), 195

Piedmont (Piemonte), 7, 8, 12, 22, 32, 44, 63, 96, 183, 200, 243, 247, 290, 386, 391, 409–411, 422, 423, 433, 436, 443, 458

Pieve Ligure, 117

Pigato wine, 89, 103, 124, 144, 147, 208, 214, 222, 245, 336, 409–412, 415, *413,* 436

Pigna, 391

Pikovaya Dama (Tchaikovsky), 30

Pineapple, 378, 405

Pine nuts: *see also Pinoli;* Crostini con Spinasci (Spinach Toasts with Raisins and Pine Nuts), **176;** Friscêu cö Zebibbo e Pinoli (Raisin–Pine Nut Fritters), **404;** Funghi Porcini con Pinoli (Porcini Mushrooms with Pine Nuts), **308;** Pasta ai Pinoli con Ricotta e Rosmarino (Pasta with Pine Nuts, Baked Ricotta, and Fresh Rosemary), **238–239;** Pine Nut–Marjoram Sauce, 56,

Pine nuts (*continued*)
78, 150, 210, 218; Salsa di
Pinoli, Capperi e Acciughe
(Sauce of Pine Nuts,
Capers, and Anchovies),
102; Spinasci a-a Zeneize
(Genoese Spinach with
Raisins and Pine Nuts),
297; Torta di Frittate con
Funghi Porcici, Pesto e
Pinoli (Frittata "Cake" with
Porcini Mushrooms, Pesto,
and Pine Nuts), **185,** 309,
360
Pinoli, 10, 34, 55–56, 60, 62,
64–71, 73, 78, 102, 150,
176, 185, 199, 238–239, 297,
308, 309, 374–375, 428,
432–433; *see also* Pine nuts
Piombo, Sebastiano del, 165
Pirrone, 410
Piscialandrea, 120, **142–143;**
see also Pizzalandrea
Pissaladière, 142
Pizza, 35, 52, 119, 140, 142
Pizzalandrea (also called
piscialandrea, pissadella), 35,
120, **142–143**
Pliny, 415
Poached Fish (Pesce al Vapore),
285–286, 326
Polenta, 147, 200, 228, *263,*
264–265, 433; Polenta
Incatenata ("Enchained"
Polenta), 200, **264–265**
Polpettone (or Polpetta; String
Bean–Potato Tart), 228,
295, **302,** 433
Pomodori secchi (sun–dried
tomatoes), 10, 60, 83,
312–313
Ponchielli, Amilcare, 25
Ponente, Riviera del, 7, 19,
24, 25, 29–30, 71–72,
81, 85, 90, 94, 103, 110, 133,
138, 144, 147, 174, 194, 222,
238, 344, 346, 354–355, 359,
374, 381, 405, 409–412, 415,
434, 435, 450–454, 458–461
Pontedassio, 24, 200, *431*
Porcini mushrooms: See *Funghi
porcini*
Pork (*maiale*), 14, 33, 56, 77,
136, 370; Maiale alle Olive
(Pork Loin with Black
Olives), **370**
Pornassio, 412
Portofino, 7, 19, 26–27, 29, 36,
40, 117, 120, 181, 233, 234,
243, 381, 382, 392
Porto Maurizio, 24, 334, 412,
430
Portovenere, 28, 233
Portugal and Portuguese, 15,
324, 435, 456
Potatoes (*patate*), 9, 14, 60, 65,
134, 191, 200, 215, 226,
228, 264–265, 272,
280–281, 295, 302, 310, 324,
433; Insalata di Calamaretti
e Patate (Salad of Baby
Calamari and Potatoes),
191; Focaccia di Patate, **134;**

Funghi Porcini e Patate al
Forno (Baked Porcini
Mushrooms and Potatoes),
310; Mushroom and Potato
Soup (Zuppa di Funghi e
Patate), 272, **280–281;**
Polenta Incatenata (Polenta
with Potatoes and
Cabbage), **264–265;**
Polpettone (String
Bean–Potato Tart), 228,
295, **302;** Seppie in Umido
con Patate (Stewed
Cuttlefish with Potatoes),
350; Stoccafisso alla Chelbi
(Stockfish with Vegetables),
347–348; Trenette alla
Genovese (*Trenette* with
Pesto, Potatoes, and String
Beans), 65, **226**
Poultry (*pollame*), 14, 33, 44,
55–56, 229, 310, 359,
361–362
Pound, Ezra, 27
Prà, *327,* 328, 422
Prebóggion, 156, 258–259, 427,
433
Prescinseua, 55, 60, 63–64, 68,
71, 77, **79–80,** 126, 162,
219, 423, 433, 436
Primizie, 84
Provence, 6, 17, 18, 24
Prosciutto cotto (boiled ham),
28, 432, 434
Prosciutto crudo (air-cured ham),
28, 192, 432, 434
Puddinda, La, 27
Puglia, 64, 97, 119, 177
Pumpkin (*zucca*), 14, 256, 257;
Barbagiuai (Fried Pumpkin
Ravioli), **257;** Pumpkin
Ravioli, **256**

Quarto dei Mille, 22
Queen of Spades (Tchaikovsky),
30
Quiliano, 412

Rabbit (*coniglio*), 14, 359,
374–377, 411, 434; Coniglio
all'Aggiada (Rabbit with
Garlic Sauce), **376–377;**
Coniglio alle Mandorle
(Rabbit with Almonds),
374–375
Raisins, 161, 176, 297, 382,
383; Crostini con Spinasci
(Spinach Toasts with
Raisins and Pine Nuts),
176; Friscêu cö Zebibbo e
Pinoli (Raisin–Pine Nut
Fritters), **404;** Spinasci a-a
Zeneize (Genoese Spinach
with Raisins and Pine
Nuts), **297;** Savory Pie
with Greens, Pine Nuts,
and Raisins (Torta di
Verdura, Pinoli e Uvetta),
161
Rambles on the Riviera
(Strasburger), 36
Rapallo, 7, 27, 29, 32, 117
Raspberry syrup, 392

Rattatuia (Tomato-Eggplant-
Zucchini Sauce), **84,** 219,
285
Ravioli, 25, 35, 52–53, 56, 107,
195, 199, 200, 203, 208,
209, 210, 212, 228,
247–259, 276, 283, 432,
433; Cheese-Filled Ravioli,
247, **254, 255;** cooking
ravioli, **250;** Fish-Filled
Ravioli, 247, **251,** 285;
Herb-Filled Ravioli, 247,
252–253; Meat-Filled
Ravioli, 247, **255;** Method
1 for making ravioli,
248–249; Method 2 for
making ravioli, **249;**
Method 3 for making
ravioli, **249–250;** Pumpkin-
Filled Ravioli, **256, 257;**
Ravioli di Magro, **254;**
Vegetable-Filled Ravioli,
247, **255**
Recco, 25, 28, 68, 117–118,
126–127, 200, 220, 222,
276, 398, 424
"Redbait" (*rossetti*), 287, 334,
424; Frittata di Rossetti
("Redbait" Omelette), **334;**
Whitebait Soup (Minestra
di Bianchetti), **287**
Reggio Emilia, 432
Rennet, 79, 456
Rheingold, Das (Wagner), 5,
290–291
Rhine River, 291
Rice and risotto, 55–56, 85,
158, 200, 260–261, 366,
433; Risotto Valpolcevara,
260–261; Savory Pie, with
Rice and Greens (Torta di
Riso e Verdura), **158**
Ricotta, 63–64, 69, 71, 76, 77,
79, 81, 210, 219, 222,
238–239, 257, 423, 433–436;
Pasta ai Pinoli con Ricotta
e Rosmarino (Pasta with
Pine Nuts, Baked Ricotta,
and Fresh Rosemary),
238–239; Ricotta con le
Cipolle (Onion-Scented
Ricotta), 60, **81,** 210 222
Rifaldi, Giovanni, 347
Ring des Nibelungen, Der
(Wagner), 5, 290–291
Ripieno (filling for pasta),
248–259
Risorgimento, 22
Risotto Valpolcevara, **260–261**
Riviera dei Fiori, 24
Riviera, French. See French
Riviera
*Riviera: Sketches of the Health
Resorts of the Northern
Mediterranean Coast of France
and Italy from Hyères to
Spezia, The* (Sparks), 36
Rizzo, Rocco, *ix–x,* 119, 120,
133, 151
Romans, 7, 12, 17, 92–93, 415
Rome, 17, 18, 20, 22, 67,
92–93, 165, 200, 291, 386,
421, 432, 433

Rosemary (*rosmarino*), 9, 27,
132, 144–145, 232, 238–239,
273, 410, 427, 434; Focaccia
with Rosemary, **132,** 273;
Pasta ai Pinoli con Ricotta
e Rosmarino (Pasta with
Pine Nuts, Baked Ricotta,
and Fresh Rosemary),
238–239
Roses, 9, 24, 72, 382; Rose
Honey (*Miele alle Rose*), **110**
Rosewater, 110
Rospo al Vermentino
(monkfish in a Vermentino
wine sauce), **333**
Rospo con Carciofi (Monkfish
with Artichokes), **332**
Rossana, Laura: 367–368
Rossese di Dolceacqua wine,
86, 244, 375, 405, 436
Rossetti ("redbait"), 287, 424;
Frittata di Rossetti
("Redbait" Omelette), **334;**
Whitebait Soup (Minestra
di Bianchetti), **287**
Rossini, Gioacchino, 91, 290
Rotolo Maria Pia
(Mushroom–String Bean
Roll), **245–246**
Rue, 62
Ruskin, John, 266
Russian Orthodox churches,
30, *31*
Russians, in Liguria, 29–30,
138, 416
Ruta, 26, 36

Sage (*salvia*), 9, 27, 56, 132,
133, 232, 410, 427;
Gorgonzola Focaccia with
Sage, **133;** Sage Focaccia,
132
Sagra dello Stoccafisso
(Badalucco), 317–318, 324,
435
Sagra del Pesce (Camogli), 26,
316–317, 343
Sailors and mariners, xv, 12,
16, 19, 23, 26, 28, 32, 40,
46, 55, 118, 119, 120, 130,
151, 190, 314–318, *319,* 338,
430
Sailor's biscuits (*gallette del
marinaio*), 16, 120, 151,
296
St. Francis of Assisi, 44
St. John's Day, 44
Saint Petersburg, 29
St. Mark, 165
Saints, 39, 42, 44
St. Tropez, 7
Salads (*insalate*), 103, **296,** 429
Salami (*salame*), 25, 28, 56, 96,
150, 194, 195, 447; Fresh
Fava Beans, Salami and
Pecorino Cheese (Fave,
Salame e Pecorino), **194**
Salsa alla Genovese (Genoese
Sauce), **86,** 101, 285
Salsa di Pinoli, Capperi e
Acciughe (Sauce of Pine
Nuts, Capers, and
Anchovies), **102,** 141, 285

Salsa di Pomodori Secchi
(Sun-Dried Tomato Sauce),
83
Salsa per i Pesci Fritti (Sauce
for Fried Fish), **99–100,**
186, 190
Salsa Verde all'Antica
(Old–Fashioned Herb
Sauce for Fish), 16, **101,**
285, 361, 367
Salt (*sale*), 14, 16, 28, 40, 44,
55–56, 63–64, 66, 177, 202,
432, 435
San Federico, 44
San Fortunato, 316
San Francisco, 32, 289, 318
San Fruttuoso, 26–27, 67
San Giacomo, 314
Sangiovese wine, 412, 415
San Lorenzo, Feast of, 312
San Marzano tomatoes, 82,
140, 236, 347–348
San Remo, 7, 19, 24–25,
29–30, 31, 40, 72, 120,
140–141, 142, 174, 200, 314,
316, 350, 354–355, 367, 382,
396
San Remo Pizza (Sardenaira),
35, 120, **140–141,** 142
San Rocco, 26, 120, 166
Santa Fe, 425
Santa Margherita Ligure, 7,
26–27, 117, 118, 123, 130,
234, 337, 424
Sant'Olcese, 171, 194, 195, 447
Saracens, 7, 127
Sardenaira (San Remo Pizza),
35, 120, **140–141,** 142
Sardines (*sardine*), 12, 40, 56,
103, 140–141, 142, 328, 335,
410; Machetto (Sardine
Sauce), 410
Sardinia, 10, 14, 62, 64, 68,
194, 333, 410, 415, 432, 458
Saronno, 401
Sarzana, 28, 366
Sassello, 44, 401
Sauces, condiments, and
spreads, 16–17, 34, 40, 44,
51, 53, 55–56, **57–111,** 122,
199, 382, 450–456;
Artichoke Sauce, **89,** 251,
422; cheese sauces, 212,
216; *diavolicchio,* 16; for fish
and seafood, **83, 86, 90,**
97–102; made of fish and
seafood, **103–106,** 141;
herb-based sauces, 62–71,
73–75, 86, 98, 101, 150,
199, 232, 367; in jars, 16;
meat-based, **107–109,** 209,
211, 212, 216, 225; *mostarda,*
16; mushroom sauces, **91,**
209, 210, 211, 216, 230–231;
nut–based sauces, **62–71,**
73–78, 109, 141, 150, 199,
209, 210, 212, 216, 218,
258–259, 428; oil-based
sauces, **62–71, 73–78,**
84–85, 86, 89–92, 94, 96,
99–106, 199, 429; pesto, 16,
25, 35, 60, **62–71, 73–76,**
79, 90, 107, 118, 166, 185,
200, 211, 212; Salsa Verde
all'Antica (Old-Fashioned
Herb Sauce for Fish), 16,
101, 285, 361, 367; sun-
dried tomato, **83,** 254, 255,
435; tomato 10, 32, 60, **82,**
212, 216, 234–235, 251, 254,
255; vegetable-based sauces,
81–86, 89–92, 94, 96–98,
109, 209, 210, 211, 216, 254,
255, 361; walnut, 12, 35, **77,**
79, 107, 150 200, 210, 219,
222, 247, 258–259, 428;
Tocco di Funghi
(Mushroom Sauce), **91,**
209, 210, 211, 222, 225; *see*
also Pesto; Ricotta con le
Cipolle; Tocco; Tocco de
Noxe; *and other individual*
listings
Sausage (*salsiccia*), 14, 55–56,
96, 324
Savona, xiii, 12, 18, 19, 25, 28,
30, 44, 71, 89, 158, 237,
257, 282, 287, 314, 318, *319,*
346, 363, 374, 387, 401,
409–412, 435, 443–444,
449, 453–454, 460–461
Savory pies, 33, 35, 52, 103,
115–116, 119, 148, **154–164;**
see also Torte
Sbira, la (tripe soup), 271–272
Scaloppe di Branzino in
Crema di Asparagi (Sea Bass
Fillets in Asparagus Sauce),
330–331
Scandinavia and Scandinavians,
12, 14, 46, 318, 323, 324,
435, 456
Schiaffino, Simone, 318
Schneer, Dr. Joseph, 152
Sciacchetrà wine, 411, 415
Sciumette (Little Meringue
Sponges), **398–399**
Scotto, Renata, 24
Sea biscuits (*gallette del*
marinaio), 16, 120, 151, 296
Seafood. *See* Fish and seafood
Seagull, The (Chekhov), 262
Secolo XIX, Il (Liguria's
newspaper), 19, 463
Second World War, 26, 117,
127, 243, 337
Seppie del Pescatore
(Fisherman's Cuttlefish
Casserole), 349
Seppie in Umido con Patate
(Stewed Cuttlefish with
Potatoes), 350
Seppie in Zimino (Stewed
Cuttlefish with Greens), 351
Sessarego, Rosa, 118
Sestri (di) Levante, 7, 241, 288,
289, 410
Shaw, George Bernard, 421
Shelley, Percy Bysshe, 29, 300
Shrimp, 81
Sibelius, Jean, 27
Sicily, 9, 10, 20, 22, 35, 199,
200, 291, 323, 391, 421, 432
Siegfried (Wagner), 290
Slight Reminiscences of the
Rhine, Switzerland and a

Corner of Italy
(Boddington), 46
Snails (*lumache*), 282;
Mushroom and Snail Soup
(Zuppa di Porcini e
Lumache), **282**
Soave, 124
Socca, 120, 144; *see also*
Farinata
Social fabric (*tessuto sociale*), 19,
23, 39–45, 55–56, 112–113,
118, 130, 148, 152, 165,
314–318
Soprano, Licia and Bruno, 182,
457
Sordi, Alberto, 24
Sorghum, 433
Sori, xiii, 25, 69, 117
Sorrel, 9
Soups (*minestre, zuppe*), 34, 65,
269–289; broth, a note on,
280–281; chicken stock or
broth, Ligurian, 283, 284,
361–362; Chickpea Puree
with Porcini Mushrooms
(Crema di Ceci con Funghi
Porcini), **278–279;** fish
broth, **285–286,** 287; Fish
Soup (Ciuppin), **289;** Garlic
Soup (Zuppa di Aglio), 132,
271–272, **273;** Grain and
Bean Soup (Mesc-Ciùa),
272, **276–277;** Marjoram-
Noodle Soup (La Pagioada),
271, **284;** Minestrone
(Menestron), 65, 271–272,
274–275; Mushroom and
Potato Soup (Zuppa di
Funghi e Patate), 272,
280–281; Mushroom and
Snail Soup (Zuppa di
Porcini e Lumache), **282;**
Stuffed Lettuce Rolls in
Broth, **283, 298;** vegetable
broth, 282, 283; Whitebait
Soup (Minestra di
Bianchetti), **287**
Spaghetti, 32, 35, 203,
234–235, 236; Spaghetti con
Pomodoro e Porri
(Spaghetti with a Sauce of
Tomatoes and Leeks), **236;**
Spaghetti Poveri ("Poor"
Spaghetti), **234–235**
Spain, 12, 25, 40, 85, 284,
323–324, 435, 448, 456
Sparks, Edward I., 138
Spelt (*farro*), 55, 272, 276–277,
444; Grain and Bean Soup
(Mesc-Ciùa), 272, **276–277**
Spezia. *See* La Spezia
Spices (*spezie*), 12, 15, 33, 49,
55–56
Spinach, 56, 148, 176, 209,
219, 258–259, 297, 365;
Crostini con Spinasci
(Spinach Toasts with Raisins
and Pine Nuts), **176;** Pasta
Sfoglia Agli Spinaci
(Spinach-Flavored Pasta),
209; Spinasci a-a Zeneize
(Genoese Spinach with
Raisins and Pine Nuts), **297**

Spinola family, 56
Spungata Ligure (Ligurian
Fruit Pie), **396–397**
Squash, 14, 42, 56
Squid (*calamari*), 12, 191
Stella Maris, 26, 40, 314
Stoccafisso alla Chelbi
(Stockfish with Vegetables),
347–348
Stockfish (*Stoccafisso;* dried
cod), 12, 56, 317–318, 324,
346–348, 433, 435, *437,* 456;
Buridda (Stockfish Stew),
344, **346;** Stoccafisso alla
Chelbi (Stockfish with
Vegetables), **347–348**
Stracchino (cheese from
Liguria), 126–128, 132, 137,
424; *see also* Crescenza;
Invernizzina
Stracchino (cheese from
Lombardy), 126, 132, 424,
443
Strasburger, Eduard, 36
Strauss, Levi, 32, 318
Strawberries, 382, 389, 392
Strawberry festival, 389
Streifzüge an der Riviera
(Strasburger), 36
String beans (*fagiolini*), 65, 226,
228, 245–246, 295, 302;
Polpettone (String Bean–
Potato Tart), 228, 295,
302, 433; Rotolo Maria
Pia (Mushroom–String
Bean Roll), **245–246;**
Trenette alla Genovese
(*Trenette* with Pesto,
Potatoes, and String Beans),
65, **226**
Stuffed Mussels (Muscoli
Ripieni), **192–193**
Stuffed Peaches (Pesche
Ripiene), **383**
Stuffed Veal Breast (Cima
Ripiena), 359, **367–368**
Stuffed Vegetables (Verdura
Ripiena), **305**
Stuffed Zucchini (Zucchine
Ripiene), **304–305**
Suez Canal, 88
Sugar, 55–56
Sugo di Carciofi (Artichoke
Sauce), **89,** 251, 422
Sugo di Muscoli (Mussel
Sauce), **104,** 222
Sugo Negretto (Beef and
Onion Sauce), 109, **366**
Sugo di Pomodoro Fresco
(Fresh Tomato Sauce), **82**
Sun-dried tomatoes, 10, 60,
83, **312–313,** 435
Sun-drying of foods, 10,
312–313
Sun and sunshine, 8, 10, *11,* 16,
19, 27, 39, 46, 312–313
Swiss people in Liguria,
29–30, 416
Switzerland, 12, 30, 46, 88, 416
Sylvaner wine, 245

Taggia, 24, 25, 85, 94, 95, 133,
140, 449

Taggiasca olives, 25, 94, 95, 133, 140, 142, 175, 188, 240, 296, 325, 346, 350, 370, 429, 432, 449

Tagliarini (taglierini, tagliarini, tagliatelline), 81, 84, 195, 203, 208, 209, 212–213, 230–232; Tagliarini ai Porcini (Tagliarini with Porcini Mushrooms), 230–231; Tagliarini alle Erbe Fresche, 98, 232

Taleggio, 126

Tagliatelle Bastarde (Chestnut Noodles), 211

Taranto, 165

Tarragon, 9, 165

Tassone, Lidia, 328

Tchaikovsky, Piotr I., 30

Teas and tisanes, 44, 401

Tebaldi, Renata, 124

Tellaro, 27, 29, 105, 300, 301, 330

Tessuto sociale. See Social fabric

Testana, 220

Thailand, 24, 422

Thus Spake Zarathustra (Nietzsche), 27

Thyme (timo), 9, 27, 86, 144, 232; Penne con Funghi e Timo (Penne with Mushrooms and Thyme), 227

Tocco (Genoese Meat Sauce), 107–108, 222

Tocco de Noxe (Walnut Sauce), 12, 35, 77, 79, 107, 150, 200, 210, 219, 222, 247, 258–259, 428

Tocco di Funghi (Mushroom Sauce), 91, 209, 210, 211, 222, 225

Tokyo, 60

Tomato Bread (Pane e Pomodoro), 174

Tomato-Eggplant-Zucchini Sauce, 84

Tomatoes (pomodori), 10, 14, 35, 42, 56, 60, 74, 82–84, 234–235, 236, 260–261, 312–313, 347–348, 435–436; Risotto Valpolcevara, 260–261; Spaghetti con Pomodoro e Porri, 236; sun-dried (pomodori secchi), 10, 60, 83, 312–313, 435; tomato-leek sauce, 236

Tomato paste (concentrato di pomodoro), 10

Tomato sauces, 10, 32, 82–85, 234–235, 236, 251, 254, 272, 298

Tomaxelle (Little Veal Rolls), 297, 359, 364–365

Toronto, 10

Torta di Frittate con Funghi Porcini, Pesto e Pinoli (Frittata "Cake" with Porcini Mushrooms, Pesto, and Pine Nuts), 185, 309, 360

Torta di Zucchine (Zucchini Tart), 303

Torta Pasqualina, 35, 52, 162–164

Torte (savory pies), 33, 35, 52, 103, 115–116, 119, 148, 154–164, 171, 272; basic torta recipe 1, 154; basic torta recipe 2, 154; Torta di Carciofi e Verdura (Savory Pie Filled with Artichokes and Greens), 157; Torta di Cipolle (Onion Savory Pie), 160; Torta di Riso e Verdura (Savory Pie Filled with Rice and Greens), 158; Torta di Verdura (Savory Pie Filled with Greens), 156; Torta di Verdura, Pinoli e Uvetta (Savory Pie with Greens, Pine Nuts, and Raisins), 161

Travels Through France and Italy (Smollett), 288

Trenette, 35, 74, 104, 200, 202, 226, 432; Trenette alla Genovese (Trenette with Pesto, Potatoes, and String Beans), 65, 226

Trentino, 389

Trieste, 386, 443

Triora, 24, 41, 120, 273, 433

Tripe, 271–272

Tristan und Isolde (Wagner), 291

Trofie (or troffie), 68, 118, 200, 202, 220–221, 276, 398, 432; Trofie di Castagna (Chestnut Trofie), 221

Trombetti, 256

Truffle (tartufo), 134

Truffle Focaccia, 134

Tuna (tonno), 12, 56, 85, 324, 338, 424

Tunisia, 12, 324, 424

Turin (Torino), 20, 22, 290, 389

Turkey (Tacchino), 14

Tuscany (Toscana), 8, 17, 64, 92, 174, 177, 244, 333, 366, 409–415, 436, 444, 448–449, 458

Twain, Mark (Samuel Clemens), 112–113

Umbria, 64, 177, 448

United States of America, 32, 40, 148, 432, 443, 446–447

Uova Sode con Salsa (Hard-Boiled Eggs with Special Sauce), 186

Valéry, Paul, 148

Valle Argentina, 25

Valle d'Aosta, 8

Valle d'Impero, 24, 371, 430

Valle di Nervia, 391, 405

Valpolcevara, 25, 195, 225, 260; see also Corzetti; Risotto

Varigotti, 25

Vatican, 9

Veal, 56, 77, 107, 297, 298, 309, 363–365, 367–368; Beet Green Rolls (Involtini di Bietole), 299; Cima Ripiena (Stuffed Veal Breast), 359, 367–368; Involtini con Carciofi (Veal Rolls with Artichokes), 363; Tomaxelle (Little Veal Rolls), 297, 359, 364–365

Vegetable–red wine sauce, 86

Vegetables (legumi e verdura), 14, 16, 17, 28, 33, 34, 39, 40, 42, 44, 55–56, 59–60, 65, 83, 96, 107, 122, 154, 156–158, 160–164, 177, 199, 211, 256, 274–275, 293–313, 347–348, 367–368, 432, 433, 436, 448–456; broth, 282, 283; from the New World, 14, 194, 216, 256, 303, 433; polpettone, 295; soup (minestrone), 274–275; Stoccafisso alla Chelbi (Stockfish with Vegetables), 347–348; stuffed, 28, 55–56, 78, 107, 171, 283, 295, 298, 304–307, 432; tortes and pies, 33–35, 52, 154–158, 160–164, 228, 272, 295, 423; Vegetable and Cheese Ravioli, 255

Venetians, 7, 12, 15

Veneto, 324, 389, 433, 435

Venice, 20, 30, 88, 165, 291, 369, 433

Ventimiglia, 8, 25, 29, 56, 72, 93, 178, 314, 382, 405, 411–412

Verdura Ripiena (Stuffed Vegetables), 305

Vermentino wine, 103, 124, 187, 188, 208, 222, 245, 333, 336, 374–375, 377, 409–412, 415, 413, 436, 458; Rospo al Vermentino (Monkfish in a Vermentino Wine Sauce), 333

Vernaccia di San Gimignano wine, 100, 124, 333, 336, 415, 436, 458

Vernazza, 436

Verdi, Giuseppe, 22, 25, 290

Via Aurelia, 17, 92–93

Villaggio, Paolo, 24

Vinegar, 55, 187, 238, 369, 436

Violet Honey (Miele alle Viole), 109, 111, 390

Violets, 72, 109, 111, 390; Castagne al Profumo di Viola (Violet-Scented Chestnuts), 390; Crema di Castagne al Profumo di Viola (Violet-Scented Chestnut Puree), 109

Virgil, 62

Visciole cherries, 396

Vittorio Emanuele, 22

Volpedo, 382, 383

Volpini, Lorenza, ix, 137, 139

Volpini, Roberto, ix, 137

Volpini, Simone, ix, 137

Wagner, Richard, 5, 290–291

Walküre, Die (Wagner), 290

Walnuts (noci), 34, 62, 64, 68, 70, 71, 73–77, 184, 428; Salad with Walnuts and Porcini Mushrooms (Insalata con Noci e Funghi Porcini), 184; Walnut Sauce (Tocco di Noxe), 12, 35, 77, 79, 107, 150, 200, 210, 219, 222, 247, 258–259, 428

Tocco di Funghi (Mushroom Sauce), 91, 209, 210, 211, 222, 225

Wheat, 14, 423

Whitebait (bianchetti), 56, 144, 287, 335, 424; Whitebait Soup (Minestra di Bianchetti), 287

Wilde, Oscar, 6

Wine (vino), Ligurian, 10, 14, 34, 40, 42, 55–56, 86, 100, 103, 123–125, 140, 146, 147, 171, 187, 188, 208, 222, 224, 225, 230–231, 233, 244, 245, 333, 336, 350, 354, 359, 374–377, 401, 405, 407–414, 415, 436, 458; Fugassa all'Euio (Focaccia all'Olio); Focaccia with Olive Oil and White Wine), 123; see also Chianti; Ciliegiolo; Cinqueterre; Coronata; Dolcetto; Orvieto; Pigato; Rossese di Dolceacqua; Soave; Vermentino; Vernaccia di San Gimignano

Wintering in the Riviera with Notes of Travel in Italy and France and Practical Hints to Travellers (W. Miller), 354–355

World War One, 337, 430

World War Two, 26, 117, 127, 243, 337

Yeats, William Butler, 27

Yogurt, 79, 424, 433

Zaniboni, Maurizio, 387–388

Zimino di Carciofi e Piselli (Casserole of Artichokes and Peas), 311

Zucchini (zucchine), 14, 42, 84, 287, 303; Torta di Zucchine (Zucchini Tart), 303; Zucchine Ripiene (Stuffed Zucchini), 304–305

Zuppa di Aglio (Suppa d'Agliu; Garlic Soup), 132, 271–272, 273

Zuppa di Funghi e Patate (Mushroom and Potato Soup), 272, 280–281

Zuppa di Porcini e Lumache (Mushroom and Snail Soup), 282

Zurich, 290